LIFE ON WINGS
THE FORGOTTEN LIFE AND THEOLOGY OF
CARRIE JUDD MONTGOMERY (1858-1946)

LIFE ON WINGS

THE FORGOTTEN LIFE AND THEOLOGY OF CARRIE JUDD MONTGOMERY (1858-1946)

JENNIFER A. MISKOV

CPT Press
Cleveland, Tennessee

Life on Wings
The Forgotten Life and Theology of Carrie Judd Montgomery
(1858-1946)

Published by CPT Press
900 Walker ST NE
Cleveland, TN 37311
USA
email: cptpress@pentecostaltheology.org
website: www.cptpress.com

Library of Congress Control Number: 2012931766

ISBN-10: 1935931296
ISBN-13: 9781935931294

Cover photo, Carrie in her Salvation Army uniform. Used with permission of the Salvation Army.

DEDICATION

To my parents who have always been there to support and encourage me in everything that I have followed my heart to do.

Joseph and Deanna Miskov

Thank you for your unconditional love and belief in me.
I love you dearly.

Other Books by Jennifer A. Miskov

Water to Wine: Experiencing God's Abundance in the Canary Islands

Spirit Flood: Rebirth of Spirit Baptism (In light of the Azusa Street Revival and the life of Carrie Judd Montgomery)

Silver to Gold: A Journey of Young Revolutionaries

All available at www.silvertogold.com

CONTENTS

Chapter 6

Analysis of Pentecostal Themes within Carrie's
Pneumatology 228

ACKNOWLEDGEMENTS

This work has taken me on quite a journey through the past four years. It was only after I moved from California to England so that I could study revivals that I came across Carrie Judd Montgomery's story. That she also lived the majority of her life in California makes this study even more meaningful. Throughout my research, I have had the opportunity to intersect with many great people from both continents. Just a few are mentioned below.

England
I am greatly indebted to Allan Anderson for introducing me to Carrie in his *Spreading Fires*. His comments and insights in relation to my work and his friendship have been a great support. I am also grateful to Mark Cartledge whose feedback on my work and care for me as a person is something that I will always appreciate. His wife Joan has been a blessing in connecting me with employment during my time in England and it has been a great privilege to journey along side of Mark's daughter Becky in her pursuit after God.

My colleague Gerald King has provided feedback on my work over the past few years. I want to also thank all my other colleagues and Andrew Davies at the University of Birmingham for their encouragement and helpful comments during the seminars. Others like Lisa and Ngoma let me stay in their home for a few weeks when I needed a place to stay, and their encouragement and excitement for my work has been a blessing. Special thanks to Becky, Craig, and Ben Whitelaw for their friendship and support. Yogi Pardhi, Ania Kolonko, Than Pham, Sara Husseini and other post graduate students with whom I have shared life have enriched me through their friendship.

I want to thank my church family at Birmingham Vineyard Network House (McNeils, Kay, Colin, Jo and many others) and more recently the church plant of Grace Vineyard (Inksters, Bristows, and the others) for all the support, encouragement, friendship, and family away from home I have experienced in you. Special thanks to Bonnie and Margaret for their excitement in relation to my paper for the Society of Pentecostal Studies conference in 2010 which encouraged me to publish *Spirit Flood: Rebirth of Spirit Baptism for the 21st Century in light of the Azusa Street Revival and the life of Carrie Judd Montgomery*.

The Healing on the Streets team, Jackie Tearle, Sandra Eagle, Becky Cartledge, Nick Corbett, and the rest of the gang, it has been such a privilege and honor to bring God's kingdom of love and healing to the people in the heart of the city. You are all beautiful people.

A very special thanks to all those who have been a part of The Silver to Gold Project in one way or another. It was nice to have another outlet besides academics during my time there. Jo Bullock, Affi Luc and Alice, Emma Rushton, Andrew, Joe, and many others are just a few of the many who have been an incredible support to me. Also, Alex and Christy, Shivani, Mal, and Tracy, trips to Starbucks have been a wonderful break and I value each one of you.

California

I cannot thank my family enough for all their support and love throughout my life. I am super blessed to have such supportive and encouraging parents. Thanks mom and dad for everything! My brother is an inspiration who goes into the heart of disaster stricken countries to bring relief and support to those who need it the most. My sister has such a beautiful and pure faith and she has to be one of the best single mothers I have ever seen in my life. Thank you for always rooting for me, Sis. Justin, thanks for going after God, you are a special young man with a heart exploding with compassion for others. My Aunt Adrienne and Uncle Fred have always been very encouraging as has my grandfather Perry Winslow, whose support of this project makes me very grateful. Thanks to my whole extended family for all the support!

Thanks to David and Rachel McNutt, the Pewthers, Bob and Penny Fulton, Ade and Frannie Collie, the Scherers, Jamie Gillentine, Linda Costa, and the many others who have believed in, supported, and prayed for me over the years. Yadira, Ruthie, Cristina, Davina, Laurie, and so many other precious friends who have journeyed with me over the past years, your friendship is like gold to me! To the ladies from my small group at Anaheim Vineyard who are now all grown up and many married, I love that you are following your hearts and living the beautiful purposes God has put in your heart. Keep shining and know that you do make a difference!

A heartfelt thanks to the team at Iris Ministries in Redding, California who let me work on the finalization of this manuscript in their wonderful little office and to Mike and Yvonne Thomas who opened up their hearts and their home to provide for me for a month while in Redding.

Financial help
I am thankful for the financial support in various ways through Perry Winslow, Ade and Frannie Collie, Linda Costa, the McNutts, the Inksters, The Panacea Society, Gilchrist Educational Trust, Ithiel Conrad Clemmons Student Travel Award, The Foundation for Pentecostal Scholarship (www.tffps.org), the Roberts Fund from the University of Birmingham, and the amazing ways that God never ceases to amaze me in how He comes through again and again to take care of me.

Research
I am indebted to Daniel Albrecht who went before to pave the way to help make this study possible. With a much harder job of accessing resources than today, he saw the gold inside of Carrie nearly twenty years ago and laid important foundations. I am thankful for Kimberly Alexander and her work in relation to Carrie as well as her encouragement. Cecil M. Robeck took extra time to invest his thoughts into my completed work to help refine it even more. I greatly value and appreciate his excitement and encouragement for this work. I am grateful for Paul Chappell, David Petts, Jennifer Stock, Gastón Espinosa, Paul King, Joe McIntyre and all of the others who have recognized something significant in Carrie to include her in their narratives. Thanks to David Roebuck for providing me with an opportunity to have *Silver to Gold* and *Spirit Flood* available at the Society of Pentecostal Studies conferences. Those in the women's caucus at SPS have been an encouragement as well as Lee Roy Martin, who believed in me enough to publish my very

first article in the *Journal of Pentecostal Theology*. I am glad to be able to partner with him and John Christopher Thomas at CPT Press to bring Carrie's important story to life.

Special thanks to archivist Daniel DeLandro at the Buffalo State University who allowed me to search tirelessly through microfilm to find 'Miraculous Cures in Connecticut', *The Buffalo Daily Courier*, (Thursday) February 20, 1879 (the actual newspaper article of Mrs Mix's testimony of healing that Carrie's father read to her just before she was healed). Thanks to those at the New York State Library who provided me other valuable newspaper articles as well. At Nyack College, Mike Scales graciously welcomed me and demonstrated that the vision is still strong within A.B. Simpson's original Bible school. Librarian Sunya Notley also was very helpful as was Charles Galbreath, Carol Anne Freeman, Ron Walborn, and the other staff in extending hospitality to me. Jenn Whiteman in Colorado Springs, Colorado at the Christian and Missionary Alliance Archives was available to help me whenever I needed anything and she helped me access a picture of Carrie with A.B. Simpson as well as their archived magazines online.

Thanks to Darrin Rodgers, Glenn Gohr, and all others who have submitted and recovered primary sources that are now available through the Flower Pentecostal Heritage Center. It was there that I was able to access the *Triumphs of Faith* periodical as well as many other important sources.

The Berry family, Loren and Beth Berry, Jim, Don, Bruce provided me with many wonderful primary sources, oral tradition, took me on a tour of the Cazadero Camp meeting, showed me a secret spot in the woods where Carrie used to get away and to pray, gave me a roof over my head, food, and good company during my visit. It is nice to see the church planting heritage and passion for more of the Spirit still alive in the family. It was good to connect with Terry Dunham, Kathleen Dombrowski, and the others in conjunction to the Home of Peace in Oakland, California where they let me go through an abundance of primary sources. 'Tripod' the three-legged cat is unforgettable.

Elena Nipper at my undergraduate school, Vanguard University, was very gracious to me and gave me free photo copies and shared in the excitement with this project. Teresa at www.healingandre

vival.com is doing a tremendous labor of love through her project which I accessed during my studies.

Jan Hornshuh Kent at the Open Bible Heritage Center in Eugene, Oregon was key in helping me to discover Carrie's influence for this network of churches as I looked through *Bible Standard* issues. Susan Mitchem from the Salvation Army National Headquarters in Virginia sent me several articles from *War Cry, The Conqueror*, as well as a few photographs of Carrie and her family in their Salvation Army Uniforms. Judy Vaughn, a Salvation Army historian, was also helpful and supportive in pointing me to sources.

I am thankful to Heidi Baker, not only for her excitement in regard to my studies and for doing an interview in relation to Carrie Judd Montgomery but also for inspiring me in my faith over the years. It has been a great joy to introduce her more fully to a kindred spirit in Carrie.

There are so many more people I want to thank, but that would probably be another book in itself! For all those I have missed, for those who have loved, supported, encouraged, given me a home-cooked meal, participated in The Silver to Gold Project, been my friend, thank you, thank you, thank you! Your investment in my life will never be forgotten. Most of all, I can not believe how amazing God has been in my life and how His destiny for me continues to unfold. Bob Dylan's song, 'Make You Feel My Love', sung so beautifully by Adele, fills me with a deeper understanding of the relentless love that Jesus has for me. His love is too overwhelming to contain and I am filled with an abundance of grace and gratitude. So as my dad would say, for all the work that has been done, 'To God be the glory!'

LIST OF ILLUSTRATIONS

Figures

ABBREVIATIONS

AG	Assemblies of God
AGH	*Assemblies of God Heritage*
BECHS	Buffalo and Erie County Historical Society
CAMW	*The Christian Alliance and Missionary Weekly*
CJM	Carrie Judd Montgomery
CMA	The Christian and Missionary Alliance
FPHC	Flower Pentecostal Heritage Center (Springfield, MO)
HOP	Home of Peace
JPT	*Journal of Pentecostal Theology*
JPTSup	Journal of Pentecostal Theology Supplement Series
LRE	*The Latter Rain Evangel*
NIDPCM	S. Burgess and E. Van Der Maas (eds.), *The New International Dictionary of Pentecostal and Charismatic Movements: Revised and Expanded Version* (Grand Rapids: Zondervan, 2002)
PE	*The Pentecostal Evangel*
Pneuma	*Pneuma: The Journal of the Society for Pentecostal Studies*
TF	*Triumphs of Faith*
SA	Salvation Army

1

INTRODUCTION

1.1 Closing the Gaps

Several historiographers have listed Carrie Judd Montgomery (1858-1946) alongside a handful of men when describing the most influential shapers of the Divine Healing Movement. A few scholars have also noticed to some degree her influence within the Pentecostal Movement. However, on the whole, the extent of her contribution within both movements has been overlooked.[1] Biographies exist on other female healing evangelists like Maria Woodworth-Etter, Aimee Semple McPherson, and Kathryn Kuhlman, but besides Carrie's personal autobiography, there are no such books published on her life and ministry up to this point, only small articles or inserts within larger texts.[2] Besides an unpublished master's thesis completed over twenty years ago, Montgomery generally receives little attention in relation to her contribution to the movements; many times these other works are based on the master's thesis, her auto-

---

[1] S.M. Burgess and G.B. McGee, 'Signs and Wonders', in S. Burgess and E. Van Der Maas (eds.), *NIDPCM* (Grand Rapids: Zondervan, 2002), pp. 1066-67, and Paul G. Chappell in his 'The Divine Healing Movement in America' (PhD diss., Drew University, 1983) mention Carrie in their works.

[2] Edith Blumhofer, *Aimee Semple McPherson: Everybody's Sister* (Grand Rapids: Eerdmans, 1993); Wayne Warner, *Maria Woodworth-Etter: For Such a Time as This* (Gainesville: Bridge-Logos, 2004). Several biographies of Kathryn Kuhlman have been written, including those by Benny Hinn (1999), Wayne E. Warner (1993), and Roberts Liardon (1996). My bibliography shows the majority of known writings up to this point that mention Carrie.

biography, or a very small sample of her periodical.[3] It is because of this deficit within the history of both the Divine Healing and Pentecostal Movements that I initially chose to undertake this research.[4]

My research is focused specifically on articles she wrote between the years 1880-1920 because these were her crucial years within the Divine Healing and Pentecostal Movements.[5] My goal was not to provide a history of the time period or of the movements Carrie was a part of since those have already been described by other scholars. Instead, my goal was to delve as deeply as possible into her personal story and two theological themes that emerged from her life so that scholars can place her into the context of history they have already defined. Overall, this work seeks to discover Montgomery's significance within the history and context of the Divine Healing and Pentecostal Movements. As specific themes emerged in the study, the following questions were explored: What was Carrie's theology of healing? What was the significance of her Pentecostal Spirit baptism and how did it affect her theology of divine healing? How does her story inform the history of early Amer-

---

[3] Daniel E. Albrecht, 'The Life and Ministry of Carrie Judd Montgomery' (Master's thesis, Western Evangelical Seminary, 1984).

[4] I chose to apply some contributions of Feminist Standpoint Epistemology in my area of historical research because this approach seeks to give voice to a forgotten figure as a means of empowering. In this I refer to her as 'Carrie' instead of 'Montgomery' because her first name has a softer and more feminine feel. Mary Margaret Fonow and Judith A. Cook, 'Back to the Future: A Look at the Second Wave of Feminist Epistemology and Methodology', in Mary Margaret Fonow and Judith A. Cook (eds.), *Beyond Methodology: Feminist Scholarship as Lived Research* (Bloomington: Indiana University Press, 1991), p. 1. See also Brian Roberts, *Biographical Research* (ed. Alan Bryman; Philadelphia: Open University Press, 2002), p. 124.

[5] I gave authority and weight according to when the articles were written and how reliable the source was. For example, I placed more weight on her healing accounts published closer to the actual date of her healing than of her reminiscences years later. The overarching method I utilized for this research was Inductive Analysis. This type of analysis along with Naturalistic Inquiry allows patterns and themes to emerge from the research rather than imposed predeterminations directing it. In inductive analysis, there is an absence of 'preexisting expectations'. This type of analysis spends time observing and discovering patterns. This goes against Deductive Analysis which presents its hypothesis and theory before beginning research. One of my initial goals was to gather all possible primary source material on Carrie's life. After this, I surveyed all of her known and accessible writings, focusing my first reading to find historical facts. I then synthesized the analysis to present a historical framework for her life and ministry. Michael Quinn Patton, *Qualitative Evaluation and Research Methods* (London: Sage Publications, 2nd edn, 1990), pp. 40-41, 44, 390.

ican Pentecostalism? What legacy did she leave behind? This is the first time that a historical biography has been laid out that has also included a formulation of Montgomery's theology of healing and her pneumatology. It is to the historical sketch of her life that we now turn.

2

A RADICAL EVANGELICAL AND THE
MOVEMENT SHE HELPED TO SHAPE

This chapter will explore the potential impact Carrie had within the Divine Healing Movement. The first section will trace early influences that shaped her life and ministry in relation to healing and will present Carrie's healing account. The next section will build upon her healing story by thematically exploring different areas of her ministry that grew as a result. The development of Carrie's writing career, healing homes, and teaching ministry will be analyzed here. The final section will place Carrie within the context of some of her friends and influential shapers of the Divine Healing Movement to understand her role in the movement. Within the framework of the formation of the Divine Healing Movement, the following key question will be explored: What role did Carrie's healing account and ministry play in the expansion of the Divine Healing Movement and its themes?

2.1 Formative Years: 1858-1879

2.1.1 Family Background
Carrie's mother, Emily Sweetland Judd (1822-1910), was especially influential in the early formation of her Christian faith. Carrie's mother, however, did not receive religious training as a child because her father was only converted while on his death bed. It was not until Emily came into contact with some Christians during her 'girlhood' that she talked to the local Episcopalian minister about

her faith. Soon after this interaction, she converted to Christianity when she took Jesus 'as her Saviour'.[1] Emily held a firm, strict, fair, yet loving role in managing the household. She also set the religious scene in her home by insisting that the family have morning worship together. Carrie later admitted that she tried to avoid this at times because she did not want to be late for school. However, it was through observing her mother's avid prayer life that Carrie was later led to realize 'that God was a real Being, and that He was listening to her prayers'.[2] Carrie's grandparents on her mother's side, the Sweetlands, were pioneers in western New York where Emily grew up. It may have been while visiting her relatives at their farm that Carrie discovered her love of poetry.[3] She likely inherited this interest from her mother who had published poems in one of their church papers and possibly also from her father who was said to be good at poetry yet less active in it.[4]

Carrie's father, Orvan Kellog Judd (1815-1890), had a very 'amiable disposition' and trusted most of the family discipline to Carrie's mother.[5] Orvan graduated from Union College in New York and then studied law like his brother. However, because he possessed great peacemaking abilities, he initiated quick reconciliation between parties, thus helping clients avoid the courts. Disliking the career of a lawyer, he willingly jumped at the offer of his friend William G. Fargo to become a banker for American Express in the Buffalo of-

---

[1] Carrie Judd Montgomery, *Under His Wings: The Story of My Life* (Los Angeles: Stationers Corporation, 1936), p. 29. She later became a member of her local church.

[2] Montgomery, *Under His Wings*, pp. 13, 15. In her 'Some Secrets of Faith', *TF* 31.4 (April 1911), pp. 74-75, Carrie further noted her mother's influence:

> Although mother and father both lived very Godly lives, they were quite reserved with us in speaking of Spiritual truths. My dear mother had sometimes related wonderful answers to prayer which had come into her life, and I believe it was really through her deep inner life of prayer, that God was striving with me; but she was at that time very timid about giving expression to these things.

[3] Frances E. Willard and Mary A. Livermore (eds.), *A Woman of the Century: Fourteen Hundred-Seventy Biographical Sketches Accompanied by Portraits of Leading American Women in All Walks of Life* (Buffalo, NY: Charles Wells Moulton, 1893), pp. 512-13. It was said that her 'mother taught her to count the meter as she stood a tiny child at her knee'.

[4] Mrs O.K. Judd, 'The Fount Revealed', no date, and *idem*, 'What Shall the Harvest Be?' (R.E. Judd, Printer, 260 Conn. St., Buffalo, NY, no date). See also Montgomery, *Under His Wings*, pp. 17, 19.

[5] Montgomery, *Under His Wings*, p. 10.

fice. He continued in this profession for over thirty years.[6] He was an avid reader and was passionate about learning new things. He was sometimes referred to by his children as a 'Walking Encyclopedia' because of his vast knowledge on a wide range of subjects. While he was raised in the Presbyterian faith, once married, he changed over to the Episcopal Church 'so that there might be no division in the family'.[7] He was also a part of the original formation of St. Mary's-on-the-Hill (Episcopal) and selected as 'warden', a position he held for over ten years.[8] Being a part of forming religious communities was something that would later be passed on to his daughter.

Figure 1
Carrie as a child, sometime in the 1860s

---

[6] 'Leaning on the Lord: Miss Judd's Decline and Rise', *The Daily Constitution* (Atlanta, GA, November 8, 1879). Montgomery, *Under His Wings,* pp. 12-13.

[7] Montgomery, *Under His Wings,* p. 19.

[8] H. Perry Smith (ed.), *History of the City of Buffalo and Erie County*. II. *The Churches* (Syracuse, NY: D. Mason & Co., Publishers, 1884), p. 289. This is demonstrated by the fact that he was present at the meeting held on April 1, 1872 'for the purpose of incorporating a church'.

2.1.2 Growing Up

Carrie Frances Judd was born on April 8, 1858 in Buffalo, New York, and grew up under the umbrella of American Evangelicalism.[9] As a child, she attended Trinity Church (Episcopal) where Edward Ingersoll was the rector.[10] Besides going to Sunday school, she also attended the Buffalo Seminary for her primary school where the Bible was read and where there were morning prayers each day. Carrie, the fourth of eight children, enjoyed school and shared her father's passion for learning. She also grew up with the desire to be a school teacher when she was older. At the age of nine, she studied Latin, with French soon to follow. She excelled in her class and even won the Jesse Ketchum Medal for her scholastic achievements.[11]

Besides some successes, Carrie's childhood was also filled with challenge and loss. At the age of ten, her compassion was already stirred to help the sick and suffering. One of her classmates, Eliza, had a severe injury. Carrie was granted permission to visit and read to her friend. Shortly after this, Carrie's older sister Emma, contracted pulmonary tuberculosis while visiting relatives. When her sister came home, Carrie waited on her. Shortly after, Emma died at the age of twenty. Following this tragedy, Carrie began to ponder eternal things more seriously.[12] Around this same time her family also decided to move.[13] While their new home was being built near-

---

[9] Carrie's hometown of Buffalo was marked during the 1800s by steady growth and also tension over the issue of slavery. The population of Buffalo in 1855 was 72,214. By 1860 it was 81,126, and in 1865 it was 94,210 (Smith, *History of the City of Buffalo and Erie County*, p. 149).

[10] Smith, *History of the City of Buffalo and Erie County*, p. 286. He was rector from 1844-1874, yet continued to remain Rector Emeritus until his death in 1883.

[11] Montgomery, *Under His Wings,* pp. 26, 29. In 1876, she was also selected as an active member for the Lincoln Birthday Association, for which she wrote a song in 'The Lincoln Birthday Association', *Courier and Republic, Evening Republic* (Buffalo, NY, March 30, 1876).

[12] Montgomery, *Under His Wings,* pp. 20-21. Because of the finances that were used to try and help her sister, the Judds could no longer afford to send Carrie and her sisters to the private seminary school and thus she had to go back to a public school.

[13] According to the city directory, Carrie grew up in a home on 4 Cary Street, by 1868 had moved into 18 Cary Street, and somewhere in between 1869-1870 moved to her new home on 260 Connecticut Street. This information was found by looking through *Buffalo City Directory* (E.R. Jewett Publisher) and *Thomas' Buffalo City Directory* (Thomas, Howard and Johnson Publishers) between the years of 1858-1871.

by, Carrie's mother took some of the children to visit relatives in Michigan, Chicago, and Wisconsin. Carrie was invited along on this adventure so that she could help take care of her three younger siblings. While in Chicago, Carrie forgot to look both ways first when crossing the tracks and nearly got sucked into a train. She attributed her protection to God's sending 'His Angel' to watch over her that day.[14] Aside from her near death incident, Carrie was thrilled to have the opportunity to travel and see more of the country.

Shortly after returning to Buffalo, Carrie's younger brother Eddie had a severe fall and was critically injured. Since she 'had been taught to believe in prayer, and had had some marked answers' to her own prayers at various times before then, she decided to go alone to her room and pray for him. She later spoke with confidence to her mother, believing that 'Eddie would get well'. He recovered shortly after. Early signs of faith that challenged her mother were clearly evident in Carrie. In response to Carrie's prayers for her brother, her mother told her afterwards that her faith had encouraged her to 'persevere in prayer for Eddie's recovery'.[15] If Carrie's reflections of this event many years later were accurate, this reveals her belief in praying for healing even at a young age.[16]

Even though Carrie had already prayed for healing, she had still not felt secure in her faith up to this point. After the Judds had settled into their new home, two missionaries to Turkey visited Carrie's mother and took an interest in both Carrie and her sister Jennie. Carrie's interaction with these women caused her to think more deeply about her own faith. The missionaries sent both Carrie and her sister letters inquiring about their salvation. While her sister wrote back, Carrie was silent because she could not comment either way about her salvation at that point. She admitted that at that time she struggled to understand the concept that 'one must be born

---

[14] Montgomery, *Under His Wings,* p. 24.

[15] Montgomery, *Under His Wings,* pp. 25, 48. It was believed that he had erysipelas which the doctors thought would be fatal. Carrie also later prayed for her friend May to be healed, but she did not recover.

[16] There were some limitations on this research that must be admitted. Carrie's autobiography was filled with stories that happened earlier on in her life, which means that her memory could have been unclear. In her role as editor, she often chose to edit out the darker side of life to her readers. Much of the research had to be based on her material and how she wanted to be portrayed to the public eye.

again'. Upon reflection in her autobiography, she realized that 'God was striving with [her] at an early age', especially 'feeling conviction for sin under the preaching of Dr. Edward Ingersoll'.[17]

More assurance of faith came when Carrie was eleven years old and saw her mother lecture her brother Frank about 'sin and its final, awful consequences'. As a result of observing this interaction, Carrie experienced 'deep conviction' for her own sin which caused her to 'repent' to God; after that she claimed she had strength like never before to 'resist temptations'.[18] Throughout Carrie's writings, she did not mention much more about her possible conversion experience and the above recollection was only written towards the end of her life. Daniel Albrecht cites Carrie's statement from her autobiography that her 'deepest conviction of sin came' during this same time.[19] This is the closest he gets to describing anything near a conversion experience. Diana Chapman, who wrote a book on forgotten women in the Pentecostal Revival, also sees this as the time when 'Carrie made a commitment to follow the Lord'.[20] Jeannette Storms believes that 'this incident pricked Carrie's conscience, prompting her to pray and receive God's grace'.[21] However, that Carrie specifically named dates for both her healing and then later her Pentecostal Spirit baptism experience and was not specific about her conversion suggests that she experienced it more as a process than as a crisis experience, with this being the moment of conviction when she became more serious about her faith.

Influenced by religious parents, Carrie grew up in an environment where she was naturally inclined toward Christianity. In 1847, Horace Bushnell wrote *Christian Nurture* which encouraged people, especially mothers, to bring up their children in the Christian faith so that they would not need to be converted later on. Some see that Bushnell shifted the 'mantle of evangelistic responsibility from the

---

[17] Montgomery, *Under His Wings,* pp. 26, 29.

[18] Montgomery, *Under His Wings,* pp. 29-30.

[19] Albrecht, 'The Life and Ministry of Carrie Judd Montgomery', p. 6 and quoting Montgomery in her *Under His Wings,* p. 31.

[20] Diana Chapman, *Searching the Source of the River: Forgotten Women of the Pentecostal Revival in Britain* 1907-1914 (London: Push Publishing, 2007), p. 70.

[21] Jeannette Storms, 'Carrie Judd Montgomery: The Little General', in James R. Goff, Jr. and Grant Wacker (eds.) *Portraits of a Generation: Early Pentecostal Leaders* (Fayetteville: University of Arkansas Press, 2002), p. 273.

professional revivalist and placed it on the shoulders of the Victorian mother'.[22] This thinking appears to be similar to the way in which Carrie was raised as is evidenced in the way her mother strictly implemented morning devotions and instilled other Christian values. The choice that Carrie made to repent where 'God granted to [her] His forgiving grace' possibly catalyzed her already growing and developing faith and made it more serious and intentional.[23] However she interpreted it, she claimed that the conviction she felt that day gave her a deeper understanding of her faith than she had had before. It was also shortly after this instance that she was confirmed by Bishop Arthur Cleveland Coxe.[24] One of the key things that stuck in her mind from the sermon he gave that day was when 'he instructed us to swiftly obey the voice of the Spirit', a theme that would later become significant throughout Carrie's life.[25]

---

[22] Curtis D. Johnson, *Redeeming America: Evangelicals and the Road to Civil War* (Chicago, IL: Ivan R. Dee, 1993), p. 64. David W. Bebbington, *A History of Evangelicalism: People, Movements and Ideas in the English-Speaking World. III. The Dominance of Evangelicalism: The Age of Spurgeon and Moody* (Downers Grove, Illinois: Intervarsity Press, 2005), pp. 34-35. American Evangelicals in the mid 1800s believed different things about conversion. Some people believed it happened as a crisis experience and others believed that it happened in a process over time.

[23] Montgomery, *Under His Wings*, p. 29.

[24] Smith, *History of the City of Buffalo and Erie County*, pp. 286, 289 and Truman C. White (ed.), *Our County and It's People: A Descriptive work on Erie County New York* (Boston, NY: The Boston History Company, 1898), II, pp. 37-39. Carrie also recalled, 'I had been brought up in the Episcopal church and had been confirmed when a girl of fourteen, giving myself to God at that time as best I could' ('Some Secrets of Faith', *TF* 31.4 [April 1911], pp. 74-75). Carrie greatly admired Coxe (1818-1896), who was also a poet himself and was featured in the same *The Poets and Poetry of Buffalo* (1894) that Carrie was. Additionally, he wrote songs, held strong views, and was very active in missions. It was most likely in relation to her move that she left Trinity Church and began attendance to St. Mary's-on-the-Hill (Episcopal) which her dad was a part of forming. It was here that she received her confirmation. Revd C.F.A. Bielby was the rector there during her teenage years and he also provided her with a letter of proof about her healing later on. See also Montgomery, *Under His Wings*, pp. 29-31.

[25] Carrie Judd Montgomery, 'A Talk on Faith', *Confidence* 7.9 (September 1914), p. 174. This was taken from a message she gave at the Cazadero Camp Meeting in California that year. See also many accounts in her *Under His Wings*.

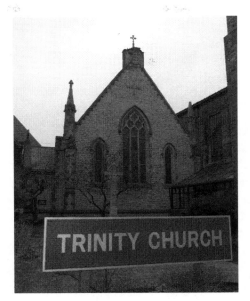

Figure 2
Trinity Church in Buffalo, New York,
where Carrie attended in her early years

Figure 3
Picture of Carrie as a child.

Into her adolescent and teenage years, Carrie continued to develop her poetry and writing skills.[26] When she was only fifteen years old, her mother encouraged her to approach the editor of the *Buffalo Courier* to ask if he would publish her poetry. Carrie was accompanied by her older brother on this successful mission as the editor ended up publishing many of Carrie's poems.[27] When Carrie was still a teenager, her eldest brother Charlie invited her to move to Dansville, New York to work for an editor of a health magazine. He believed that the fresher air there would help improve her health. Carrie decided to leave one thing she loved, her studies, to take the opportunity to go on this new adventure where she gained some valuable experience working for the magazine. However, while there, she became ill and was encouraged to return home.

At first she was disappointed to have to leave until she received a letter stating that she was needed back home. She was to help care for her father who had pneumonia and her sister Jennie who had whooping cough, which later turned into bronchial consumption. Her mother prayed greatly for them both, but in the end, while Carrie's father was spared, Jennie died.[28] Carrie had to deal with the realities of suffering yet again; losing a second sister likely shook her faith at the time. Soon after the loss, Carrie's parents decided that she was too ill to continue her schooling. Around this time, her brother moved to Linden, a small town near Buffalo, and asked her to join him to keep house and cook for him. Since she was no longer in school, she jumped at the chance to try something new and was given permission to go. She made many friends there, one of whom introduced her to the growing Temperance Movement.[29]

---

[26] This reflected the change of the era from Industrialization to Romanticism.

[27] Carrie F. Judd, 'A Ghost', *Courier and Republic, Evening Republic* (Buffalo, NY), 1874, and Montgomery, *Under His Wings,* p. 28. She also asked the editor, David Gray, to be compensated for her work but he could only pay for news articles.

[28] Carrie recalled that her mother was heartbroken for some time after losing her second child. In response to her mother's great mourning over her sister's death, Carrie recalled saying at the time, 'Mother, it seems as though you only cared for Jennie, and do not care for the rest of us now'. Carrie later wrote how that 'remark was used of God to awaken her [mother] to the depth of her grief, so she unselfishly put it away, and lived for the rest of us' (Montgomery, *Under His Wings,* p. 34).

[29] Bebbington, *A History of Evangelicalism,* p. 243. This movement was started in the 1820s and originally sought to limit alcohol consumption until later it grew in intensity to where it tried to prohibit the use of alcohol.

Carrie quickly joined the movement and refused to take any medicine with alcohol mixed in.[30] Temperance reform had begun at
some level in the United States in the early nineteen century.
Frances Willard (1839-1898) was influential in seeking to bring reform in this area through leading the Women's Christian Temperance Union. She was a Methodist who 'promoted innovative strate-
gies for preserving the values of Victorian America', and she also
encouraged women to preach.[31] It was Willard who later edited a
book that included Carrie in the mix of the most influential women
of the century.[32]

During Carrie's time in Linden, she started a Sunday school with
the neighborhood children. This was one of the popular methods
of training young people in the Christian faith in the late nineteenth
century.[33] Her mother came to visit her and also supported her by
sending Sunday school materials. After about a year of living there,
this pioneer returned home and commenced school once again.
With her brother away and after losing two of her older sisters, Carrie became the eldest of the siblings at home at that time and needed to help her mother in organizing the household. Shortly upon
her return, she began to teach a Sunday school class in Buffalo and
'soon became deeply attached to the dear little girls' who had also
become devoted to her.[34] It was during this first year back at home
that Carrie engaged in a spiritual struggle to give up 'all' things to
God. The Holiness Movement with its prevalent theme of absolute
surrender may have contributed to this desire that stirred inside of

---

[30] Montgomery, *Under His Wings,* pp. 28-36. While Carrie was initially involved with the Temperance Movement and even later with her husband when
they prohibited the use or selling of alcohol on their land, it never became one of
her main emphases.

[31] Mark A. Noll, *A History of Christianity in the United States and Canada* (Grand
Rapids: Eerdmans, 1992, 1998), pp. 296-97. This desire to use their moral ideals
to change the laws of the day was fulfilled on January 17, 1920, when the Eighteenth Amendment was passed prohibiting the making, selling, or transporting of
alcohol. The amendment was soon overturned.

[32] Willard and Livermore, 'Montgomery, Mrs. Carrie Frances Judd', pp. 512-
13.

[33] Bebbington, *A History of Evangelicalism,* p. 102.

[34] Montgomery, *Under His Wings,* pp. 37, 40-41, 63. One of her Sunday school
classes became so large that she asked her church leader if they could all meet at
her home on Sundays because there was more room. He agreed and occasionally
came to preach to them there.

Carrie.[35] Wanting to 'surrender all' but at the same time struggling to give up her talent for writing, she remembered that she 'gave all but that one thing, and about that I said, "No, it is good and I do not have to give it up." He pressed it upon me that I had to surrender it to Him.'[36] She finally told God, 'I am going to hold it [her talent for writing] tight in my clasped hands, but if Thou MUST have it, tear my hands apart'. She later realized though that 'when God has a controversy with a soul, trouble is sure to follow'.[37]

Figure 4
Carrie as a teenager

---

[35] See Hannah Whitall Smith, *The Christian's Secret of a Happy Life* (Chicago: F.H. Revell, 1883. Reprint, USA: Kessinger Publishing, no date). While Smith's book was written after Carrie's struggle to surrender, the themes in the Holiness Movement were present during Carrie's time.

[36] Carrie Judd Montgomery, 'The Life on Wings: The Possibilities of Pentecost', an address given at the Stone Church in Chicago in 1910, *TF* 32.8 (Aug 1912), p. 173. '[A]nd finally I told Him I would hold on to it as tightly as I could and He would have to pull it away from me'. See Appendix 5 for the full article.

[37] Montgomery, *Under His Wings*, pp. 46-48.

2.1.3 The Fall: January 6, 1876

Shortly after her spiritual struggle to 'surrender all to God', Carrie's hopes and dreams of writing and becoming a teacher were shattered when she fell hard on the icy ground on her way to school. Her arms were full of books when she slipped and twisted awkwardly before hitting the stone sidewalk that cold day in 1876.[38] No one else was around to help this seventeen year old, so she just sat there stunned. Finally mustering up enough strength in the midst of the pain and the cold, she continued to school, but her condition deteriorated rapidly, a fact which was visible to many who saw her at school that day. She took two days off but shortly after, compelled by a vision of becoming a teacher one day, she headed straight back into the classroom where she remained weak and fragile.[39]

Soon after, Carrie discovered that one of her classmates, whom she had gone out of her way to befriend, was extremely sick. When she went to visit, she saw that her friend May was delirious. Not too long after, Carrie received news that May had died. This was a terrible blow to the already frail Carrie and most likely contributed to her deteriorating health. Since the doctors' help brought no improvement, Carrie had to give up her schooling once again. She was soon confined to bed with a condition of the nerves called 'hyperesthesia of the spine, hips, knees and ankles'.[40] Hyperesthesia is an 'unusual or pathological sensitivity of the skin to sensory stimuli, such as pain, heat, cold, or touch ... A condition involving unusual sensitivity to sound is called auditory hyperesthesia whereas increased sensitivity to touch is called tactile hyperesthesia'.[41] From Carrie's description of her symptoms, it is likely that she had a severe case of all of the above.

Her sickness additionally put a drain on the family's resources. Regardless of the fact that medical practice was not known as a viable profession then, Carrie's father had little other choice and paid about $2,000 for the best doctors in town.[42] No one could do any-

---

[38] 'Leaning on the Lord', *The Daily Constitution,* November 8, 1879, p. 1.

[39] Montgomery, *Under His Wings,* p. 48.

[40] 'Leaning on the Lord', p. 1.

[41] Biology Online, <http://www.biology-online.org/dictionary/Hyperesthesia>.

[42] 'Leaning on the Lord', p. 1.

thing to help Carrie. The lack of medical expertise in the 1800s is not surprising as it is recorded in Buffalo's history that

in most of the counties of our State [New York], with a few honorable exceptions, practitioners were ignorant, degraded and contemptible. It was not uncommon even, especially in the newly-settled northern and western parts of our State, to find men who, never having read a volume of medicine, but armed with the title of 'doctor,' were introduced to an extensive practice, and a reputation of imposing authority.[43]

Medicine in the late 1800s was much different from what it is today with all the advances and professionalism it carries. In Carrie's time there were not many full time professional doctors and there were sharp debates and controversies in regard to the different medical practices. Bleeding out the disease, inducing vomit, putting leeches on one's head, and blistering were some of the ways these nineteenth century 'doctors' tried to help their patients. Nancy Hardesty's section 'No Doctors, No Drugs' in her book *Faith Cure* (2003) goes into more detail and provides a helpful analysis of the medical practice during Carrie's time.[44] While the insufficient medical care was drying up the Judds' resources, Carrie's mother came up with the idea to compile Carrie's poems and sell them.[45] Hesitant at first, Carrie finally approved and many people agreed to buy the book before it was published so that the project could be financed.[46] The supportive response toward the book helped the Judds in their financial situation.

At the time of Carrie's sickness, prayer for healing was not popular and testimonies of healing were rare.[47] In recounting her story years later, Carrie mentioned that during her illness, others did not even know how to pray for healing but only for an alleviation of suffering. They would offer such prayers, and sometimes they

---

[43] Smith, *History of Buffalo and Erie County*, p. 415.

[44] Nancy A. Hardesty, *Faith Cure: Divine Healing in the Holiness and Pentecostal Movements* (Peabody: Hendrickson Publishers, 2003). See also Montgomery, *Under His Wings*, p. 91.

[45] Carrie F. Judd, *Lilies from the Vale of Thought* (Buffalo, NY: H.H. Otis, 1878).

[46] Montgomery, *Under His Wings*, pp. 51-52.

[47] For an overview of this theme in Carrie's time, see Heather D. Curtis, *Faith in the Great Physician: Suffering and Divine Healing in American Culture, 1860-1900* (Baltimore: The John Hopkins University Press, 2007).

would help.[48] Even though it was a grave illness, Carrie still believed that she heard from God with a 'little prophetic hint of things to come' that she had a specific mission to complete. Her mother, not wanting to raise hopes in light of what looked to be the inevitable, responded, 'Your mission may be to lie here and suffer and be an example of patience to others, as you have been'. Carrie responded by telling her that she believed she had an *active mission* to complete.[49] This conversation took place at the beginning of a wave that would continue to build and eventually overturn theories and theologies relating to divine healing in her time. Heather D. Curtis traces this transition in her *Faith in the Great Physician: Suffering and Divine Healing in American Culture, 1860-1900*.[50] Curtis describes the shift from when many Christians believed that God wanted to use suffering to grow patience in people's lives, to the time when many believed that He wanted to heal and restore health. The role that Carrie played in this shift will be explored as the chapter progresses.

On January 6, 1877, Carrie's illness grew worse when she 'was prostrated by a violent attack of the nervous system' and found out she had spinal fever.[51] What 'seemed to be tuberculosis of the spine' developed into 'tuberculosis of the blood' which permanently forced her to give up even the thought of school and her aspirations of becoming a school teacher.[52] Her illness was severe, being 'prostrated with spinal complaint ... the trouble extended to all the large joints' and she 'could not be touched, even by herself without great suffering'.[53] Her days in bed grew into months and then years. She could not bear to see light or to be touched without great discomfort.[54] A small pillow under her head felt 'like a block of

---

[48] Montgomery, *Under His Wings,* p. 50. This, however, contradicts her story of earlier praying for her baby brother and witnessing his healing. Chapter 5 will cover this more.

[49] Montgomery, *Under His Wings,* p. 53.

[50] For a discussion on the transition from when people believed that suffering was a gift from God and a way for a person to demonstrate patience in Him to a time when people believed that sickness was not from God but that He wanted to heal, see Curtis, *Faith in the Great Physician.*

[51] 'Leaning on the Lord', p. 1.

[52] Carrie F. Judd, *The Prayer of Faith* (Chicago, IL: F.H. Revell, 1880; Reprint, New York and London: Garland Publishing, Inc, 1985), p. 9. See also Carrie Judd Montgomery, 'I am the Lord that Healeth Thee', *LRE* 2.4 (January 1910), p. 22.

[53] 'Disease Cured by Prayer', *The Sun* (New York), October 29, 1885, p. 3.

[54] Montgomery, *Under His Wings,* pp. 50-54.

stone'.[55] For over eleven months she could not even sit up on her own. In the spring of 1878, she finally began to start feeling a little better. Soon after though, the warm summer weather caused her to go into a relapse. Adding even more grief, in January of 1879, Carrie lost her grandmother who lived in the same house.[56]

The pain Carrie claimed to experience during these few years was awful. In her own words she said,

> I was emaciated to a shadow, and my largest veins looked like mere thread. Nothing could keep me warm, and the chill of death seemed upon me. A great part of the time I lay grasping for breath, and I suffered excruciatingly. Even the weight of my arms and limbs seemed to be almost unendurable, and this terrible strain was constant. My pulse could scarcely be found, and I was not expected to live from one day to the next.[57]

While language could have easily been colorful beyond reality in Carrie's time, it is doubtful she elaborated greatly in regards to the extreme pain she experienced. A test done in 1919 by Gordon Holmes on a case with this identical illness had the person who experienced Hyperesthesia saying 'It's as if knives heated in Hell's hottest corner were tearing me to pieces'.[58] Additionally, Carrie's body wasted away to only 85 pounds during that time.[59] After having already lost two of her sisters, the outlook for Carrie's health and life looked grim and 'her death was expected daily'.[60] Carrie's mother even allowed a few close friends in to say their final goodbyes to Carrie.[61]

[55] Judd, *The Prayer of Faith*, p. 10.

[56] Judd, *The Prayer of Faith*, p. 50.

[57] Judd, *The Prayer of Faith*, p. 12.

[58] John B. Mullen, M.D., 'Acute Hyperesthesia After Spinal Trauma', *Neurosurgery* (Congress of Neurological Surgeons, 1979), p. 432.

[59] 'Miss Carrie F. Judd's Spine: It Was Out of Order but the Lord Healed It', *Chicago Daily Tribune*, December 6, 1888, p. 3.

[60] 'Disease Cured by Prayer', p. 3.

[61] Albrecht, 'The Life and Ministry of Carrie Judd Montgomery', p. 16.

2.1.4 The Rising: February 26, 1879

'There was no excitement but a feeling of faith and confidence'.[62]

– Carrie F. Judd, 1879

A glimmer of hope came Thursday, February 20, 1879, when Carrie's father read an article in *The Buffalo Daily Courier* about a 'colored woman' who had a great ministry of healing.[63] Sarah Anne Freeman Mix (1832-1884), more often referred to as Mrs Edward Mix from Connecticut, was healed of tuberculosis in 1877 when Ethan Otis Allen (1813-1902) prayed for her.[64] Allen was one of the early pioneers in the Divine Healing Movement who was healed of consumption, now known as tuberculosis, in 1846 when he asked his Methodist class leaders to pray the prayer of faith for his healing. Even though divine healing was integrated into John Wesley's (1703-1791) teachings, the class leaders were reluctant at first to pray for Allen since 'praying for the sick was not a normative part of their ecclesiastical practice or teaching'.[65] Some believe that Allen was the first American to engage in faith healing as his full time ministry as well as to link Christian Perfection with divine healing. Utilizing Mk 16.17 as his key verse, Allen expected healing to be instantaneous whenever he prayed. Paul Chappell says that since Allen had 'the first systematic divine healing ministry in America, A.B. Simpson entitled him the "Father of Divine Healing" in this nation'.[66] Rather than building a large base, Allen served as an itinerant minister who traveled and went to people's homes to pray for their healing as he did in the case of Mix. In the article that Carrie's father read that day, it was reported that Allen believed Mix 'had the power of healing in her'.[67]

---

[62] 'A Modern Miracle', *Buffalo Commercial Advertiser*, October 20, 1879.

[63] 'Miraculous Cures in Connecticut', *The Buffalo Daily Courier* (Thursday) February 20, 1879. This article was originally printed in the *Springfield Republican* and reprinted in *The Buffalo Daily Courier*. See Appendix 2 to read original article.

[64] Mrs Edward Mix, *The Life of Mrs. Edward Mix* (Torrington: Press of Register Printing Co, 1884. Reprint, New York: Syracuse University Press, 2002), p. 210. See also 'Christian Alliance Meeting', *TF* 16.2 (Feb 1896), p. 48 where there is mention that when Allen was in his 80s, he met Carrie on the West Coast.

[65] Chappell, 'The Divine Healing Movement in America', pp. 88-89.

[66] Chappell, 'The Divine Healing Movement in America', pp. 91, 104 referring to William T. McArthur, *Ethan O. Allen* (Philadelphia: Office of the Parlor Evangelist, no date but possibly around 1890), p. 32.

[67] 'Miraculous Cures in Connecticut'.

After Mix was healed, she began to pray for people in her neighborhood who came to her seeking healing. Doctors even sent patients to her for prayer and by 1879 she had already 'treated' over 230 people, 'some of them with wonderful success'. According to one newspaper article, 'the doctors in the vicinity say Mrs. Mix has a wonderful power of some kind, but they claim that she is successful only with functional or chronic diseases, and that most of her cures are effected among the lower and more superstitious classes'.[68] While the Judd family was more in the middle to upper class, the success Mix had with 'functional or chronic' diseases likely caught their attention.

Finally, 'after Mr. Judd managed to make the patient [Carrie] understand' the significance of Mix's healing account, Carrie asked her sister Eva to send a letter requesting prayer.[69] Carrie told her to write that she 'believed [Mix's] great faith might avail' for her recovery.[70] To their surprise, the Judd family received a quick response from Mix on Tuesday, February 25, 1879.[71] Carrie immediately followed the instructions on the letter to get rid of all her medicines and trust 'wholly into the care of the Almighty'.[72] Mix's take on medicine at the time was no doubt influenced by Allen's. Mix also told Carrie to 'begin to pray for faith'.[73] Central to the letter was an encouragement to claim the promise found in the prayer of faith in Jas 5.15 as well as an encouragement to get up and *act in faith* regardless of feelings.[74] A time was also arranged when each side would pray for healing. The night before the planned prayer time, Carrie claimed she slept a little better than before and her digestion im-

---

[68] 'Miraculous Cures in Connecticut'.

[69] 'Leaning on the Lord', p. 1.

[70] 'A Modern Miracle'.

[71] Judd, *The Prayer of Faith*, p. 13. This is a quick turn around. The newspaper article was printed Thursday February 20, 1879 and by Tuesday the 25th they had already received a response to set aside time to pray the very next day. The letter was dated February 24, 1879. See Chapter 4 for the full text of the letter, which can also be found in Mrs Edward Mix, *Faith Cures and Answers to Prayer* (New York: Syracuse University Press, 2002), pp. 38-39. See also 'A Modern Miracle' and 'Leaning on the Lord', p. 1.

[72] 'Leaning on the Lord', p. 1.

[73] 'A Modern Miracle'.

[74] 'And the prayer of faith will save the sick, and the Lord will raise him up. And if he has committed sins, he will be forgiven' (Jas 5.15 KJV). At the time she received the letter, Carrie did not realize the prayer of faith found in Mrs Mix's letter was in the Bible, see Montgomery, 'The Life on Wings', p. 171.

proved some. Even though no one showed up to Mix's regular prayer meeting that day due to poor weather, she and her husband prayed for Carrie nonetheless. Carrie's family also engaged in prayer in a separate room.[75]

When recalling this account several months later, Carrie remembered that during this set apart time of prayer, on Wednesday, February 26, 1879, she entered into a spiritual struggle where she attempted to overcome the doubts that clouded her mind. She recalled that in the midst of her struggle, she 'felt a sudden and remarkable increase of faith, different from anything which [she] had ever experienced. There was no excitement but a feeling of faith and confidence'. About 3.30 pm that day, finally 'feeling victory', Carrie, 'without the least fear or hesitation ... turned over and raised up alone for the first time in over two years'.[76] A reporter recalled that Carrie, 'who after suffering until death was expected to end her agonies at any moment, was suddenly made well enough to get out of the bed to which she had been long confined'.[77] She walked with 'little support' from her nurse, to her chair.[78] She later claimed that when she walked that first day, she felt awful pain for a moment but then felt the Spirit say not to look at the wind and waves but at Jesus.[79] Aside from her brief improvement in the summer before, this was the first time Carrie put this much weight on her feet in two years. She slowly began to improve from that moment on. According to her nurse, over the next few days, her skin color went from a 'yellow, dead look' to one 'pink and full of life'.[80] She also began to regain her speech and her appetite. By April, she was well enough to walk up and down the stairs and go

---

[75] Judd, *The Prayer of Faith*, p. 19.

[76] 'A Modern Miracle'.

[77] 'The Efficiency of Prayer', *The Buffalo Courier*, November 15, 1881.

[78] 'A Modern Miracle'. The majority of accounts mention the nurse 'gave Miss Judd a little assistance and she walked about nine feet to a chair', as in 'Leaning on the Lord', p. 1. However, in 'The Efficiency of Prayer', she states that she walked across the chamber 'without any assistance'. In light of the first two earlier accounts, this was likely an exaggeration.

[79] Carrie Judd Montgomery, 'Some Secrets of Faith', *TF* 31.4 (April 1911), p. 76.

[80] This was recorded in her nurse's diary on February 28, 1879, and referenced in 'Leaning on the Lord', p. 1 and Judd, *The Prayer of Faith*, pp. 16-17.

outside.[81] Less than six months after her healing account, she was back leading her Sunday school class.[82]

While some counted Carrie's case as 'A Modern Miracle', as is reflected in the title of the account in the *Buffalo Commercial Advertiser*, still others were more skeptical or had different interpretations of what the cause of her healing really was. Some thought that it was Mix's letter that stirred up hope and gave Carrie the strength to be made better. One lone reporter claimed that God had told Carrie ahead of time that her sickness was coming.[83] Others believed that her healing came as a result of positive thinking or that it was the 'power of the mind over matter'. They said that with 'great inspired thought in her brain and a determined purpose to put this thought into practice, she made the first step'. Rather than emphasize God as divine healer, some pointed to her healing as a case of the 'divine

---

[81] For Carrie's 1879 healing account from her perspective, see her *The Prayer of Faith*, pp. 9-21; Montgomery, *Under His Wings*, pp. 48-60; 'The Anniversary of My Healing', *TF* 27.2 (Feb 1907) pp. 25-26; 'Songs of Deliverance', *TF* 16.3 (March 1896), pp. 49-51; 'The Life on Wings: The Possibilities of Pentecost', *TF* 32.8 (Aug 1912), pp. 169-77; 'Notes of Praise', *TF* 35.2 (Feb 1915), p. 29; 'God's Covenant of Healing', *TF* 38.3 (March 1918), pp. 49-54; 'Forty Years of Blessing and Ministry', *TF* 39.2 (Feb 1919), pp. 43-44; and 'I am the Lord that Healeth Thee', *LRE* 2.4 (January 1910), p. 22. To see secular printed accounts: 'A Modern Miracle'; 'Leaning on the Lord', p. 1; 'A Supposed Miracle Through Prayer', *Brooklyn Eagle*, February 29, 1880, p. 2; 'The Efficiency of Prayer'; 'Healed by Faith. Miss Carrie Judd, of Buffalo, Tells the Story of Her Cure', *Chicago Daily Tribune*, June 15, 1884, p. 11; 'Disease Cured by Prayer', p. 3; and 'Miss Carrie F. Judd's Spine: It Was Out of Order but the Lord Healed It', p. 3. Carrie also regularly celebrated and remembered her healing account by publishing articles on the anniversary date of her healing.

[82] 'Leaning on the Lord', p. 1.

[83] 'Healed by Faith', p. 11. In this article, a reporter in Chicago who heard Carrie speak a few years after her healing claimed that she heard from God ahead of time that her sickness was coming. In recounting her story, he wrote that she was deeply affected by the last lines of Theodoro Monod's consecration hymn which encouraged 'entire self-surrender to God's will'. This reporter said that Carrie was questioned in a whisper if she would be afraid to have 'a long sickness to prove [her] submission to God's will?' After she said she would submit to whatever God had, the voice again whispered to her saying, 'Spinal disease', although at that moment she did not know what that was. Not long after this encounter he claimed that she had her fall and her two year illness. This unique and interesting perspective—Carrie's illness given to her in a similar way as it was given to Job—does not appear in her writings or other secular accounts. While this account is likely embellished, and it is highly doubtful that Carrie knew the specifics of her disease, the closest potential prophetic insight she had leading up to her illness might be found in a poem she wrote when she was sixteen years old entitled, 'Fettered'. See this in her *Under His Wings*, p. 37.

in humanity'.[84] Others saw it as an act of faith, or an act of God. Regardless of what others believed, Carrie was sure that her recovery was not due to positive thinking; she believed that it was God who had healed her.

Carrie and Mix continued to correspond after her healing.[85] When Mix came to visit her in New York, Carrie recalled that 'one real joy that I had soon after my healing was a visit from Mrs. Mix … I remember how glad I was to see her and how I loved her'. Influenced by Allen's model of discipleship, Mix met Carrie in Buffalo where they partnered in ministry together. In Carrie's words, 'she and I went out together to visit friends in our City who were ill, and to offer prayer for them, and the glory of God certainly came down upon us when we were engaged in prayer'.[86] These two 'spiritual sisters' shared a special friendship built on 'mutual support' and were a source of encouragement in each other's lives for the few years before Mix's death in 1884.[87]

2.2 Seeds Begin to Grow

The few years immediately following Carrie's healing set significant things in motion. It was in those important years that three trends in her life were born that lasted throughout her entire life. First, her writing began to flourish. Besides publishing *The Prayer of Faith* (1880), in January 1881 Carrie commenced her periodical entitled *Triumphs of Faith*, which she would continue editing until her death. Second, in June 1880 she opened up a room in her house called 'Faith Sanctuary'. People came to learn about and pray for healing there; the room set aside for this purpose would later give birth to the healing homes that she would facilitate throughout her lifetime.

---

[84] 'A Supposed Miracle Through Prayer', *Brooklyn Eagle*, February 29, 1880, p. 2.

[85] Mix, *The Life of Mrs. Edward Mix*, p. 126. As a result of her connection with Carrie's healing, Mix's popularity began to spread. Mix not only administered the 'James 5 prayer' to people, but from what she understood it to mean at that time, she also prayed for people to be baptized in the Holy Spirit. E.W. Lynde, who was healed through her prayers, recalled in 1880 that Mix 'anointed me with oil in the name of the Lord, and laid her hands on me, and asked the Lord to baptize me with the Holy Ghost, and it came'.

[86] Montgomery, *Under His Wings*, pp. 54-60.

[87] Rosemary D. Gooden, 'Introduction', in Mix, *Faith Cures, and Answers To Prayer*, p. lviii.

And finally, the Thursday prayer meetings she initiated would be the beginning of her speaking ministry on the subject of divine healing that would later lead her into a lifelong itinerant preaching career.

Before looking at the development of Carrie's ministry, it is important to point out that there were also changes going on within Evangelicalism.[88] Around this same time, people moved beyond seeing God as Judge and began to see Him as Father. The incarnation of Christ also earned more attention while the subject of hell lost most of its power. David Bebbington states that among Evangelicals of the time, broadly speaking, 'it is clear that piety, though definitely Trinitarian, was emphatically Christocentric' with an emphasis on a relationship with Jesus more than with God the Father.[89] Curtis Johnson additionally declares that people began to move from focusing on God, the Father, to highlighting

> a loving Jesus who exhibited feminine virtues of obedience, submission, gentleness, and long-suffering faithfulness. Instead of emphasizing correct doctrine or saving grace, devotionalists sought a closer walk with Jesus, a Savior who not only atoned for the sins of all but who befriended and solved the personal problems of those who loved him.[90]

The Holy Spirit received about the same attention as did God the Father. After 1830, Devotionalism began to gain power in the home and by the 1880s had an even wider influence.[91] These changes provide the context for the emergence of Carrie's ministry within the American Evangelical currents of her time.

---

[88] Bebbington, *A History of Evangelicalism*, pp. 117-19, 130, 137, 148, 182. I use the term 'Evangelical' very broadly and generally. There was a reaction against the Enlightenment, and a corresponding attempt to move the culture towards Romanticism, which provided Evangelicals with a new way of looking at the world by emphasizing 'spirit and emotion' over and above 'reason'.

[89] Bebbington, *A History of Evangelicalism*, pp. 5-6, 85, 183, gives a broad definition of American Evangelicalism preceding the Civil War to include Christians who believed in the 'Second Birth', the Second Coming of Christ, the idea that God wanted to 'redeem America', and '*Sola Scriptura*', the idea that the Bible rather than religious professionals had authority in the believers' life.

[90] Johnson, *Redeeming America*, p. 64.

[91] Johnson, *Redeeming America*, pp. 24-25. In the 1850s, Horace Bushnell adapted a poetic delivery to his sermons and helped to infiltrate Evangelicalism with Romanticism. See also Bebbington, *A History of Evangelicalism*, p. 163.

2.2.1 The Editor: Writer's Block Removed

Word spread fast about Carrie's healing, partly as a result of the report that was printed in her local newspaper, *The Buffalo Commercial Advertiser*, October 20, 1879 under the title 'A Modern Miracle'.[92] From there, the article continued to be reprinted and spread even as far as England.[93] Carrie's popularity grew quickly and as early as 1881, an article in her local newspaper declared 'that many of our citizens are familiar ... with the miraculous cure of Miss Carrie F. Judd of this city'.[94] Carrie claimed that she had received 'hundreds of letters from those who were interested to know if the story of [her] healing was true'.[95] The number of letters increased so much that she decided to write a book about healing which emphasized the 'James 5 prayer'. In 1880, at only 22 years of age, Carrie published *The Prayer of Faith*.[96] She later recalled that 'she had not received any teaching from any human being on the subject of Divine Healing, so all the precious truths that came', were given to her directly from the Holy Spirit.[97] While she admitted earlier that she 'had often heard of faith cures', and portions from W.W. Patton's book *Remarkable Answers to Prayer* had been read to her before her illness, these were accounts of healing rather than teachings on the subject.[98] A.B. Simpson also said that before attending Charles Cullis' faith convention in 1881, he too had not heard much about faith healing or had ever read a book about it.[99]

---

[92] 'A Modern Miracle'.

[93] Carrie's article was copied again and again until it finally reached *The Christian Herald* in England. Elizabeth Baxter, wife of the editor of *The Christian Herald*, was the same person who was instrumental in translating and spreading Carrie's *Prayer of Faith* abroad as well (Montgomery, *Under His Wings*, p. 59).

[94] 'The Efficiency of Prayer'.

[95] Montgomery, *Under His Wings*, p. 65.

[96] Judd, *The Prayer of Faith*.

[97] Montgomery, *Under His Wings*, pp. 65-66. When she first attempted to write this book she struggled and had to surrender it all back up to God. She said, 'I began to realize that, even though we may have great revelations of the things that are "freely given us from God", yet we must have *words* given us by the Holy Spirit, to enable us to tell these things with power'. Cf. her 'Some Secrets of Faith', *TF* 31.4 (April 1911), p. 76, where she wrote, 'We hear much on this [Divine healing] now, but I had never heard one word of such teaching, so the Holy Spirit alone was instructing me'.

[98] Judd, 'Have Faith in God', in Mix, *Faith Cures and Answers to Prayer*, pp. 37-39.

[99] Chappell, 'The Divine Healing Movement in America', p. 257.

Carrie's book was revolutionary at the time because there were not many books on the theology of divine healing up to that point.[100] Carrie later recalled that 'Dr. Cullis had published two small books which contained testimonies of healing, but, so far as I know, there were no books published in this country at that time which contained Bible teaching on the subject'.[101] She was likely referring to the book Cullis' Willard Tract Company published in 1872 entitled *Dorothea Trudel; or, The Prayer of Faith* and also his own *Faith Cures; or Answers to Prayer in the Healing of the Sick*, published in 1879 (a book she received only after her healing account).[102] It appears that the few other early books on divine healing had not made it into Carrie's hands before her healing account. Swiss writer Otto Stockmayer released his book on divine healing, *Sickness and the Gospel*, in 1878.[103] The same year Carrie published her book (1880), William E. Boardman released *The Lord that Healeth Thee,* and he gave Carrie a signed copy in 1881.[104] Ethan O. Allen also published his book *Faith Healing* in 1881. A.B. Simpson published books on healing after this but these did not reach Carrie until later.[105] In light of these, Carrie's *Prayer of Faith* was one of the earlier books published on divine healing. Hardesty notices that Carrie's was 'the first book in the United States to contain a biblical defense of the doctrine of faith healing rather than just testimonies to it'.[106] In 1888, a Buffalo newspaper claimed that up until then, her book 'reached an edition of 22,000 volumes in the United States' besides being 'remarkably successful in England' and had already been translated, through the help of Elizabeth Baxter, into French, Dutch, German, and Swe-

---

[100] More on this in Chapter 4.

[101] Montgomery, *Under His Wings,* p. 65. See also her 'Some Secrets of Faith', p. 74.

[102] While *Dorothea Trudel; or, The Prayer of Faith* had Cullis' name on it, it originally came from an unidentified author and was translated into English from German. See 'The Man Who Believed God', Healing and Revival Press <http://healingandrevival.com/BioCCullis.htm>

[103] Raymond J. Cunningham, 'From Holiness to Healing: The Faith Cure in America 1872-1892', *Church History* 43.4 (December 1974), p. 501.

[104] The inscription of Boardman's book said: 'Carrie F. Judd, With much love from friend in England, October 25th, 1881, 1 Thess V:25'. The signed copy can be viewed at the Home of Peace.

[105] Montgomery, *Under His Wings,* p. 103.

[106] Hardesty, *Faith Cure,* p. 56.

dish.[107] By 1893, the circulation of her book had grown to around 40,000 copies.[108]

Shortly after publishing her first book on divine healing, Carrie received even more letters from sick people who were interested in learning about healing and receiving prayer.[109] She and her brother Charlie both had the same idea that she should publish a monthly magazine on the subject. Her brother gave her $50.00 as a donation to help get it started. After speaking with a well-intentioned Methodist elder who discouraged her from the project, Carrie continued 'to wait on God about this matter'.[110] Finally, she was convinced that this was something God was leading her to do so she decided to put her brother's full donation into 1,000 copies for the first issue.[111] Having no resources for issue number two, if people did not respond favorably and quickly then that would be the end of her endeavors with the periodical. Nevertheless, she avidly distributed the copies of her first issue to everyone interested. Surprisingly, many people who received her periodical began to send in money for subscriptions. Thus, Carrie successfully launched *Triumphs of Faith* in January 1881 and continued writing and editing it throughout her entire life, for over 60 years. In 1885, she changed the *Triumphs of Faith* running banner from 'Devoted to Faith-Healing, and to the Promotion of Christian Holiness' to 'Now thanks be unto God, which always causeth us to triumph in Christ. 2 Cor. 2.14'. By 1886, she already had a circulation of around 2,200 readers.[112] In

---

107 'For and of Women', *The Buffalo Express*, October 28, 1888.

108 Willard and Livermore, *A Woman of the Century*, p. 513.

109 'Alleged Miracle', *Buffalo Courier*, April 23, 1883. One example is Richard Huffman, who was told by physicians that his sickness of a paralyzed nervous system and hardening in his spinal column was incurable. Not too long after that, he got a hold of Carrie's *Prayer of Faith*. 'He was so much struck by its contents that he wrote to her and proposed that she should pray for him at her weekly prayer meetings'. See also 'Faith in Prayer', *The St. Paul Sunday Globe* (MN), February 5, 1882, p. 8.

110 Carrie recalled that Mr W.L. Gregory 'thought it would be too much of a venture for me to make, and he evidently thought that it would not be a success'. Carrie put weight on what the community of Christians around her was saying but at the same time made her own decision according her own interpretation of hearing God's voice. She also made it clear that Gregory was and continued to be a family friend (*Under His Wings*, p. 76).

111 Montgomery, *Under His Wings,* pp. 76-77.

112 Receipt from Great Central Fire Proof Show Printing House in Buffalo, showing that she purchased 2,200 copies of *Triumphs of Faith* for the October 1886 issue.

1899, she wrote that the magazine 'is a monthly journal, purely un-denominational, and devoted to the promotion of Christian Holiness and Divine Healing (from a scriptural standpoint alone)'.[113] Her emphasis on holiness, healing, and living a triumphant life is evident in her headings.

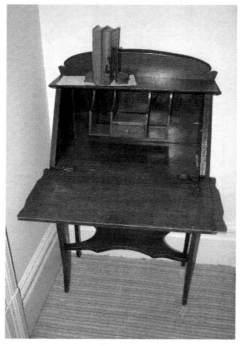

Figure 5
This is believed to be a desk that Carrie used,
currently located at the Home of Peace.

Carrie's talent for writing was reactivated after her healing and began to flourish even beyond what she anticipated as a young girl. Writing in various forms became a tool that she used throughout her life.[114] While Carrie went out and prayed for people, many times

---

[113] Banner on *TF* 19.4 (April 1899), p. 96.

[114] 'Healed by Faith', p. 11. Besides the books and periodical, she also continued to write personal letters throughout the years. One reporter stated in 1884 that she wrote 100 to 150 letters every week. Whether folklore or truth, he also reported that 'on one occasion she had walked a mile through snow-drifts to see a sick child, and as soon as she laid her hands on her the fever abated and the sore throat and swelling began to disappear, convincing the infidel father of the power of God to heal'.

others who were influenced by her literature came to her to learn more about and to experience healing.[115] One of the constant themes that was evident in and which fueled her writings was her passion to bring healing to others. The timing of Carrie's healing encounter was critical for her success because it provided her with a platform to write and speak within the earliest developments of the movement. If Carrie had been healed ten or twenty years later, she might have remained relatively unknown to many people and her crucial pioneering voice through her *Prayer of Faith* may have blended in with other already prominent voices; her story might have just been another testimony of healing among a stack of many. The timing of Carrie's healing played an important part in her literature gaining momentum.

2.2.2 The Visionary: Development of Carrie's Healing Homes

Besides writing, another way that Carrie sought to give away what she had received came through the facilitation of healing homes. A healing home was a place where people could go for an extended time to learn about and pray for healing. But did Carrie act as catalyst for the expansion of healing homes in the late 1800s or was she merely a part of the growing wave of healing homes? This will be addressed, along with an analysis of patterns that were prevalent within her homes over the years. Before giving an account of the development of her healing homes, however, it is important to see what had already been done in this area to situate Carrie into her context. Note that this section will go beyond the normal order of events so that the full development of her healing homes can be traced and analyzed.

2.2.2.1 Brief History of Healing Homes

Faith homes, or healing homes, being funded through answers to prayer alone, had some origins in George Müller (1805-1898). Müller was originally from Prussia but later moved to England. In 1835, he opened an orphanage in Bristol and financed it through prayer alone, based off the principle found in Phil. 4.19. Müller combined the orphanage work of Pietist, August Hermann Francke (1663-1727) of Halle, Germany with the 'emerging "faith work" principles

---

[115] 'The Ministers', *Chicago Daily Tribune*, September 30, 1884, p. 8. Pardington was one of these. When he was 13 he read Carrie's first book and believed in its message. He came out to visit her and receive prayer from her and he was healed.

of Johannes Evangelista Gossner (1773-1858) of Berlin'.[116] This newer way of approaching mission was also advocated by Edward Irving (1792-1834) in 1824 when he preached at the London Missionary Society. There, Irving challenged the old way of mission that had boards of directors and ran like a business. Influenced by Romanticism, he believed that missionaries needed to depend upon God alone for all their financial support.[117] Müller's choice to rely upon God alone for his provision became a pattern that many after him would follow.[118] Carrie was influenced by him in her own ministry and she later published many articles by or about him in her periodical.[119] She also had a great level of respect for him, in one article referring to him as a 'man of mighty faith'.[120] She was said to have encouraged people to 'be like George Müller' because he was a man of the Bible,[121] and she claimed to have had met him at one point in her life.[122]

Another influence towards healing homes was Johan Christoph Blumhardt (1805-1880), a Lutheran who started his ministry of

---

[116] Donald W. Dayton, *Theological Roots of Pentecostalism* (Metuchen: Scarecrow Press, 1987. Reprint, Peabody: Hendrickson Publishers, 2000), pp. 121-22.

[117] Bebbington, *A History of Evangelicalism*, p. 185. Early origins of using the 'James 5 prayer' for healing are also seen in Edward Irving's life. See Vinson Synan, 'A Healer in the House? A Historical Perspective on Healing in the Pentecostal/Charismatic Tradition', *Asian Journal of Pentecostal Studies* 3.2 (2000), p. 190.

[118] Hardesty, *Faith Cure*, p. 17.

[119] Carrie Judd Montgomery mentions him in her 'Chosen Unto Service', *TF* 18.10 (Oct 1898), pp. 217-20. She printed the following articles (and others) by George Müller: 'Word on Faith', *TF* 11.4 (April 1891), pp. 75-78; 'Stewards of the Lord' *TF* 12.1 (Jan 1892), pp. 1-6; 'Believing God' *TF* 20.12 (Dec 1900), pp. 267-68; 'Reading and Meditating on God's Word', *TF* 24.12 (Dec 1904), pp. 278-80; 'Conditions of Prayer', *TF* 25.8 (Aug 1905), pp. 187-88. Unknown authors also mentioned him in *Triumphs of Faith*. In an article entitled 'Mighty Faith', *TF* 16.5 (May 1896), pp. 119-20, an unknown author wrote about Müller's great faith. Another mentioned him in 'How Shall I get Faith?', *TF* 18.11 (Nov 1898), p. 260. An article entitled 'George Müller's Bible' appeared in *TF* 20.4 (April 1900), p. 96. In *TF* 20.5 (May 1900), pp. 119-20, an article taken from *The Gospel Message* entitled 'The Lord's Last Dealings with George Müller', by unknown author, told the story of Müller's financial struggle just before he died, but he fully believed his prayers for provision would be answered. It was nine months after his death that a great amount of money was donated and it could be said that his prayers were answered.

[120] Carrie Judd Montgomery, 'Living by Faith', *TF* 22.3 (March 1902), p. 51. She also quoted him later in this same issue.

[121] 'The Sixth Day', *Los Angeles Times*, June 3, 1896, p. 9.

[122] Carrie Judd Montgomery, 'Confidence in Him', *TF* 31.8 (Aug 1911), p. 169.

healing in 1843 in Möttlingen, Germany. After a doctor could do nothing to help a young woman in the town with 'wild demoniacal possession', the case was brought before Blumhardt.[123] He initially hesitated and feared approaching this complex situation until some from his church challenged him by saying, 'If you do not wish to shake our belief in your preaching you cannot retreat before the evil one'.[124] He agreed with them and called them to unite with him in prayer according to the 'James 5 prayer'. He then prayed for Katarina (or Gottlieben) Dittus and 'eventually the evil spirit departed, declaring "Jesus is the Victor!"'[125] After hearing of this deliverance, many flocked to him, seeking prayer for healing. Chappell notes that the Lutheran Consistory at the time 'ordered Blumhardt strictly to confine himself to advising submission and patience in sickness' rather than administering healing.[126] Because of this opposition, he resigned and opened a church manse as a faith home nearby in Bad Boll, Germany. He demonstrated and taught that healing was available and accessible in his present time.[127] Carrie also included stories of Blumhardt's ministry in her journal over the years.[128]

Dorothea Trudel's (1813-1862) ministry got its start when several of her co-workers at the florist shop became very ill and could not be cured through medicine. She pondered the 'James 5 prayer'

---

[123] 'The Christian Convention: Homes of Divine Healing', *The Word, Work and World* 5.10 (New York, October 1885), p. 253. This healing 'led rapidly to a widely extended ministry in helping the victims of mental and physical suffering, which at length absorbed his whole time … Many, of course, came for spiritual rest and refreshing; but there were wonderful cases of healing and still more marvelous recoveries of the insane'.

[124] Charles Spurgeon, 'Jesus Is Victor', *TF* 34.7 (July 1914), p. 167.

[125] After two years of being frustrated that he could not help her, he said 'Is there no clergyman in this village who can pray? I can do nothing here'. Blumhardt hesitated at first but then prayed for her. That saying later became a mark of his ministry. See Spurgeon, 'Jesus Is Victor', p. 167; *Johann Christoph Blumhardt* by Fredrick Zundel (1880); Hardesty, *Faith Cure,* p. 20; and Chappell, 'The Divine Healing Movement in America', pp. 32-41.

[126] Chappell, 'The Divine Healing Movement in America', p. 35.

[127] He was influential in Karl Barth's thinking. Blumhardt also believed that sickness was the result of sin and that it came from the devil. According to Chappell, Blumhardt was also influential among those who later developed the 'kingdom now' theology. See Chappell, 'The Divine Healing Movement in America', pp. 35-36.

[128] Carrie printed an article by Henry Drummond who visited Blumhardt's ministry entitled, 'Pastor Blumhardt at Home-Wonders of Divine Healing at Bad Boll', *TF* 9.11 (Nov 1889); pp. 247-52. See also Charles Spurgeon's commentary on Blumhardt in his 'Jesus Is Victor', p. 167.

and decided to pray for her fellow employees. Soon after she prayed, they all recovered. Following their healings, the 1851 epidemic hit Switzerland. Trudel was flooded with people who came to her seeking healing. She responded by opening healing homes in Männedorf. She was significantly influenced by the prayer found in James 5 and when she could not find any elders to pray for and anoint the sick, she stepped in to do the praying. This 'James 5 prayer' later played an important role not only in relation to Carrie's personal healing but also in regards to her ministry that followed. Carrie published and mentioned Trudel in her *Triumphs of Faith* as is seen in 'Extracts from the Writings of Dorothea Trudel' in 1909.[129]

Otto Stockmayer (1838-1917), of Berne, Switzerland, was introduced to divine healing on Easter day in 1867 when one of Trudel's successors, Samuel Zeller, laid hands on him to pray for healing. Influenced by this experience and by utilizing the same methodology found at Trudel's center of ministry, several years later, he opened up a faith home in Hauptweil, Thurgau, Switzerland.[130] Stockmeyer became known as a systematic theologian of the Divine Healing Movement. As mentioned before, he wrote some of the earlier literature in relation to the theology of divine healing. He was also involved in the Keswick conventions in Britain. The Keswick Higher Life movement was influenced by the American Holiness Movement but because of some theological differences in relation to sanctification and other issues, developed into its own tradition.[131] Many of Carrie's friends were a part of this stream within the Holiness Movement.

Charles Cullis initiated one of the first known faith homes in America on September 27, 1864, even before he fully believed in or understood divine healing.[132] It was not until the late 1860s that he also integrated the 'James 5 prayer' into his Boston ministry. On May 23, 1882, he dedicated his official Faith Cure House which was

---

[129] Dorothea Trudel, 'Extracts from the Writings of Dorothea Trudel', *TF* 29.1 (Jan 1909), p. 20.

[130] 'The Christian Convention: Homes of Divine Healing', *The Word, Work and World* 5.10 (New York, October 1885), p. 254, and Chappell, 'The Divine Healing Movement in America', pp. 49-50.

[131] See Chapter 6 for more on the Keswick Movement.

[132] Chappell, 'The Divine Healing Movement in America', pp. 107-108.

modeled after Trudel's work in Männedorf.[133] Cullis also adopted Müller's financing option by faith alone for his home for the 'Indigent and Incurable Consumptives'.[134] After already having set an important foundation for Carrie to build upon, the two later became good friends. He became a significant leader for the American Divine Healing Movement and will be mentioned further.

Carrie fits into the picture at about this point. She began her journey towards healing homes in 1880 when she opened up Faith Sanctuary, a room in her own house to pray for the sick. Less than two years later, in April of 1882, she officially opened up a separate home called Faith Rest Cottage in Buffalo, New York, followed by the Home of Peace in Oakland, California in 1893. She was also the first person to bring healing homes to the West Coast of the United States. Carrie adopted Müller's philosophy of looking to God alone for provision. Several other women opened up homes around the same time or just after Carrie, and they adopted a similar structure and philosophy. Mary H. Mossman (1828-1914) opened a healing home in New Jersey in 1881.[135] Charlotte Murray and Elizabeth Baxter were a part of opening up a healing home in conjunction with William E. Boardman's ministry in May of 1882 in London.[136] Carrie's friend and one time assistant editor, Elizabeth Sisson, helped in this home at different times. This was also the place where Andrew Murray experienced his healing.[137]

British-born Elizabeth Baxter (1837-1926), wife of the founder and editor of *The Christian Herald*, was also involved in the Keswick Conventions in England.[138] Baxter experienced her personal conversion in 1858 and from then on began conducting prayer meetings for women in a workhouse. During that time, a lady suffering from epilepsy was brought to her. Baxter expounded the Gospel and the woman was converted to Christianity. After that, Baxter

---

[133] Cunningham, 'From Holiness to Healing', pp. 501-502, and Chappell, 'The Divine Healing Movement in America', p. 140. Although this home was indeed dedicated on that date, it was not ready to house guests until September of that same year.

[134] Chappell, 'The Divine Healing Movement in America', pp. 107-108.

[135] Hardesty, *Faith Cure*, pp. 57-59.

[136] Bebbington, *A History of Evangelicalism*, p. 188 and Chappell, 'The Divine Healing Movement in America', pp. 201-203.

[137] 'The Christian Convention: Homes of Divine Healing', *The Word, Work and World* 5.10 (New York, October 1885), p. 254.

[138] Chappell, 'The Divine Healing Movement in America', p. 205.

saw that if God could save then He could also heal, so she prayed for the woman and she was healed.[139] Through speaking at some of the same conferences with Carrie in the United States, these two became friends and kept in touch throughout the years. Baxter regularly visited Carrie at her Buffalo Faith Rest home in the early days and later visited her in her California home.[140] During Carrie's missionary journey in 1909, she visited Baxter at the Bethshan home.[141] Carrie also had many of Baxter's books in her personal collection. Baxter's articles were published in the periodicals of Cullis and Simpson, and Carrie also published her writings regularly in *Triumphs of Faith*.[142] Baxter was the one who was influential in the translations of Carrie's *Prayer of Faith* into other languages.[143]

Sara M.C. Musgrove (1839-1933) was another woman who facilitated a healing home following her own healing. Musgrove had been an invalid for four years before she was healed in January of 1882, after Ethan O. Allen traveled from Massachusetts to New York to pray for her. Following this account, she actively followed the James 5 prescription of anointing with oil when she prayed for the sick.[144] It was Allen who encouraged her to open her healing

---

[139] Hardesty, *Faith Cure,* p. 21.

[140] See, Carrie F. Judd, 'A Convention for Christian Life, Divine Healing, Evangelistic and Missionary Work', *TF* 5.9 (Oct 1885), p. 240, which reports on the convention that met on Oct. 20-23, 1885 in Philadelphia with A.B. Simpson, Mrs Baxter from London, and Miss Carrie Judd. See also Montgomery, *Under His Wings,* p. 68.

[141] Carrie Judd Montgomery, '1909 Personal Unpublished Journal, Trip Around the World', June 13.

[142] Some of the articles by Baxter that Carrie published in her journal are: 'The Holy Spirit' *TF* 5.11 (Nov 1885), pp. 242-47; 'The Power of the Holy Ghost', *TF* 9.3 (March 1889), pp. 65-68; 'Self-satisfaction or Satisfying God', *TF* 9.7 (July 1889), pp. 145-48; 'Healing in the Wilderness', *TF* 11.5 (May 1891), pp. 97-100; 'In Him', *TF* 21.5 (May 1901), pp. 113-16; 'In the Last Days', *TF* 25.2 (Feb 1905), pp. 27-30; 'Divine Healing – Why was Hezekiah Sick?', *TF* 25.7 (July 1905), pp. 148-51; 'Divine Healing – Nebuchadnezzar', *TF* 25.9 (Sept 1905), pp. 204-208; 'The Ministry of the Spirit', *TF* 28.6 (June 1908), pp. 129-31; 'Casting All Your Care', *TF* 31.8 (Aug 1911), pp. 176-79; 'The Law of Life', *TF* 34.5 (May 1914), pp. 103-105; 'Suffering According to the Will of God', *TF* 37.11 (Nov 1917), pp. 247-50; and 'What is Self?', *TF* 40.10 (Oct 1920), pp. 238-39.

[143] Montgomery, *Under His Wings,* p. 67. She published it in German and French and was instrumental in the translations of the Swedish and Dutch editions as well.

[144] Mrs Dr Howe, 'A Marked Case of Healing in "Experiences of Spiritual and Physical Healing"', *TF* 7.11 (Nov 1887), p. 264.

home in 1883. She ran her Fourfold Gospel Mission in Troy, New York for 41 years.[145]

As has been shown, Carrie was at the beginning of the tide of healing homes springing up in North America. It was only after Carrie's healing home was already initiated that A.B. Simpson decided to open his own home in New York City. His 'Home of Rest' was a precursor to his Berachah Home (House of Blessing), which was officially opened on May 5, 1883.[146] By 1894, John Alexander Dowie (1846-1907), 'a Scot who discovered divine healing in Australia before propagating it in America', opened a healing home in Chicago called Divine Healing Home Number One.[147] A few years later it grew and he named it Zion Divine Healing Home. In Topeka, Kansas in 1898, Charles Parham (1873-1929) opened up his healing home called Bethel Healing Home. John G. Lake's healing rooms only started in Washington and Oregon in 1913, and it was through a man healed in Carrie's healing home in Buffalo that Lake was first inspired to enter into the healing ministry.[148] A more detailed look into the formation and development of Carrie's own healing homes will now be helpful.

2.2.2.2 Faith Sanctuary (1880-1882)

Shortly after Carrie's healing, the Judd family decided to set aside the largest room in the house, not for its social use, but as 'a room devoted to prayer'.[149] They did this in response to an article by Revd Dr Bolles in *The Living Church* that encouraged Christians to have a place exclusively in their homes for prayer. The room they chose for this purpose was just below where Carrie was confined for near-

---

145 'A Long and Useful Life', *The Alliance Weekly* LXIX.3 (Harrisburg, PA, January 20, 1934), pp. 39, 46. Sara Minot Chase Musgrove was connected with the CMA as was A.B. Simpson.

146 'The Past Year at the Berachah Home', *The Word, Work and World* 5.5 (May 1885), p. 158. This article mentions that Carrie was a visitor to the home during this time as well.

147 Bebbington, *A History of Evangelicalism*, p. 188.

148 Letter from John G. Lake to Carrie Judd Montgomery dated April 22, 1911. See also J.R. Zeigler, 'John Graham Lake', in *NIDPCM*, p. 828.

149 Carrie Judd, 'Faith Rest-Cottage', *TF* 2.2 (Feb 1882), pp. 19-20. They also consecrated another room, 'The Prophets Room', for guests briefly visiting their city.

ly two years during her severe illness.[150] The Judd family originally had not intended the room to be much beyond a 'consecrated' place of prayer for themselves. However, because more and more people responded to Carrie's healing account and requested prayer for both physical and spiritual healing, they set up 'weekly faith-meetings' there. One summer evening in 1880, Carrie and her family met with some friends to dedicate their special room.[151] They named it 'Faith Sanctuary' and continued meeting there to pray for the sick and for the requests sent by letter. Carrie later recalled that 'sometimes dear ones wrote from a little distance away begging permission to attend our meeting, and to remain with us over night, or for a longer time. My dear mother felt sympathy with these dear sufferers, and was willing to take one or two at a time into her own home'.[152] The Judd family used the sleeping room over the Faith Sanctuary to let guests stay for this purpose. These rooms were significant and possibly can be considered 'sacred spaces' in Carrie's early life as they served as a door to her first healing home.[153]

2.2.2.3 Faith Rest Cottage (1882-1892)
In response to the pressures imposed by the constant stream of visitors, as well as recognizing a need to accommodate more people, Carrie decided that it was time to expand. While 'in silent prayer beside an invalid friend', she claimed that the idea for a faith home

---

[150] Carrie Judd, 'Faith Sanctuary', *TF* 1.1 (Jan 1881), p. 12. Here Carrie wrote that 'this room, from its location directly below me, shared in the exclusion and silence of the one in which the suffering and helplessness held me a prisoner'.

[151] Judd, 'Faith Sanctuary', p. 13.

[152] Montgomery, *Under His Wings,* p. 83.

[153] Carrie was healed in the room just above where they held these meetings. It was also in 'Faith Sanctuary' where they celebrated her wedding reception. See Anna W. Prosser, 'Wedding Bells', *TF* 10.6 (June 1890), p. 121. Two weeks after her wedding in May of 1890, Carrie's father also died in this same 'Faith Sanctuary' room. See her 'Gone Home', p. 145, and 'The Present Outlook of our Work', *TF* 10.7 (July 1890), p. 147. For more discussion on 'sacred space', see Jennifer A. Miskov, 'Coloring Outside the Lines: Pentecostal Parallels with Expressionism. The Work of the Spirit in Place, Time, and Secular Society?', *JPT* 19 (2010), pp. 94-117; Heather D. Curtis, 'Houses of Healing: Sacred Space, Spiritual Practice and the Transformation of Female Suffering in the Faith Cure Movement, 1870-1890', *Church History* 75.2 (Sept 2006), pp. 598-611; Candy Gunther Brown, 'From Tent Meetings and Store-front Healing Rooms to Walmarts and the Internet: Healing Spaces in the United States, the Americas, and the World, 1906-2006', *Church History* 75.2 (Sept 2006), pp. 631-47; and Michael Gregory Hughes, *Sacred Space and the Sanctification of Time with Reference to Orthodox Christian Communities in Birmingham* (Master's thesis, University of Birmingham, UK, 2003).

came to her.[154] The time had 'fully come' for her to share the vision for Faith Rest Cottage in her February 1882 periodical. At that point, she had already received some money that she had put aside for this possible work. She urged her readers to pray alongside her for this cause and soon after, people began to donate money. She found a home in her neighborhood and rented it from a Christian lady who was sympathetic towards her cause. While Carrie did not initially have enough money beyond the first few months rent, she chose to believe that if God had initiated something, then He would also bring provision to complete the work.[155] Faith Rest Cottage was officially opened on April 3, 1882 and was informally 'consecrated' a few days later.

Carrie made it clear that Faith Rest Cottage was not a permanent home or a hospital. There would be instruction on healing, waiting on God, and praying for healing, and one should only come if they were willing to take the step of faith and truly believe that they could be healed. It was also a place of rest where people from any denominational background were welcome to come. The maximum time that a person could stay was for one week, unless special exceptions had previously been made. It was important that guests followed guidelines to communicate with her before coming so that she could ensure there was sufficient space. The guests had access to the many books that were available in the cottage. Additionally, if Carrie did not have too much to do, she would visit her guests several times a day. She also led a Thursday night prayer meeting from 7.30-9.00 pm and a Tuesday Bible study at 3.00 pm in which her guests were invited to attend.

Influenced by Müller's example, Carrie did not charge her guests to stay at the home but accepted offerings instead. She said that 'all the expenses of the home are met by money sent in answer to prayer', and 'no one is ever asked to give'.[156] She admitted that sometimes this faith work added some worry and stress to her life. One time a guest came having spent all she had on a one-way train ticket

---

[154] Judd, 'Faith Rest-Cottage', p. 20.

[155] Carrie Judd Montgomery, 'The Beginning and the End', *TF* 7.1 (Jan 1887), p. 7. While this thinking came into print a few years after Carrie's home was started, it was likely being formed in her during times like this as is demonstrated through her actions.

[156] 'Disease Cured by Prayer', *The Sun* (New York), October 29, 1885, p. 3.

and then expected Carrie to pay for her return ticket. Another time towards the end of 1882 it was reported that her 'faith cure' home was in danger of being closed because of 'financial difficulty'.[157] While Carrie regularly encountered real financial struggles, she continued to 'surrender' these things in prayer and claimed to receive provision of resources time and time again. As time went on, a bigger house was needed as Faith Rest Cottage began to outgrow itself. A visitor wrote that 'as much as Miss Judd longs to entertain more of God's dear children at this place, her heart is larger than the house she dwells in, and if the many who are expecting to come this summer are to find a resting-place, it must be by prayer for the means to rent or buy enlarged accommodations'.[158] On May 1, 1885, Carrie found that those prayers were answered and she expanded her work to a larger home.[159]

Carrie also had to deal with conflict among the guests occasionally.[160] Mrs Wright, who took her daughter to Carrie's faith home, stirred up trouble because she did not get the results for which she had hoped. A reporter followed the story and wrote that 'despite praying and anointing, [Mrs Wright's] daughter grew worse, and finally the mother and daughter were unceremoniously turned out, after wasting much time and money'. As Carrie never charged anyone to stay in her home, the money Mrs Wright must have been referring to was likely the costs related to transportation from her home in Olsan to Carrie's home in Buffalo. Regardless of this unsatisfied 'customer' at Carrie's faith home, the reporter continued on by writing that 'few believe that Miss Judd misused the Wright's. Many of the best citizens of Buffalo patronized Miss Judd and

---

[157] 'Faith Cure In Buffalo', *City and Vicinity*, November 27, 1882. See also an untitled report in *Buffalo Express*, May 18, 1890, in which the reporter mentions that there was no likelihood that the home would be soon closed as 'considerable money' had been donated to its upkeep and maintenance (Montgomery, *Under His Wings,* p. 85).

[158] 'The Rest', *TF* 3.4 (April 1883), p. 93. This article was written by an unnamed guest from Buffalo who had stayed previously at Carrie's Faith Rest Cottage.

[159] Carrie F. Judd, 'Faith Rest-Cottage', *TF* 5.6 (June 1885), p. 144.

[160] Cunningham, 'From Holiness to Healing', p. 504. These conflicts that Carrie experienced were not uncommon in regards to healing homes during that time. There are cases where people died while staying in a healing home, and sometimes the authorities and the presses got involved.

churches generally endorsed her work'.[161] From this reporter's account, it appears that at that time many people knew of Carrie's reputation and held some level of respect for her.

Carrie was known in the community because of her healing account and her faith home. It was said by one New York reporter that 'Buffalo is one of the strongholds of the believers in faith cures, for it is here that Miss Carrie Judd runs her faith home'.[162] Her home was known as a place 'where many have been relieved of their load of sin and sickness'.[163] A reporter for the *Buffalo Express* even said that Carrie's Faith Rest had 'become as famous as the Shrine of St. Anne de Beau Pre, and the seeming miracles performed there were more wonderful, though less advertised, than any accredited to the holy coat in the Cathedral at Treves'.[164] From the secular press, it appears that Carrie was well known in her state during the late 1800s.

Carrie's example in Buffalo inspired many others, especially other women, to open healing homes. Dora Griffin Dudley learned about healing through a friend who had heard about Carrie and shared *Prayer of Faith* with her. One month after her own healing, Dudley sought to help another who needed healing from a broken arm. She read her friend part of Carrie's *Prayer of Faith* and the next day she was well enough to do her own laundry and even go to a religious meeting.[165] Following this account, Dudley decided to

---

[161] 'Faith Cure In Buffalo'. 'Patronise' in Carrie's time meant to regularly visit or call upon.

[162] 'Disease Cured by Prayer', p. 3.

[163] 'The Work at Home: Notes by the Evangelist and Superintendent: Buffalo, NY, Jan. 26, 1891', *CAMW* 6.9 (Feb 27, 1891), p. 139.

[164] 'Wealthy Warriors: A Rich Salvationist and His Famous Wife … Romance and Religion', *The Illustrated Buffalo Press*, May 8, 1892, p. 4. St. Anne de Beau Pre (whom Catholics believe was the mother of the Virgin Mary) has a shrine/basilica built for her in Québec, Canada which lies just north of Buffalo, New York. Of this place of pilgrimage (especially for Catholics) it was said, '[O]n either side of the main doorway are huge pyramids of crutches, walking-sticks, bandages, and other appliances left behind by the cripples, lame, and sick, who, having prayed to St. Anne at her shrine, have gone home healed' (C. Leclerc, 'Sainte Anne de Beau-pré', Catholic Encyclopedia 1913 found <http://en.wikisource.org/wiki/Catholic_Encyclopedia_(1913)/Sainte_Anne_de_Beaupr%C3%A9). See also http ://www.ssadb. qc.ca > to learn more about St. Anne and the miracles that still take place there even today.

[165] Hardesty, *Faith Cure*, pp. 65-67. See also Paul L King, *Genuine Gold: The Cautiously Charismatic Story of the Early Christian and Missionary Alliance* (Tulsa: Word & Spirit Press, 2006), p. 34. Mrs Shepley was the friend.

open up a healing home of her own. Carrie was the guest speaker who helped dedicate this house in Grand Rapids, Michigan on February 10, 1887. The new home was called 'Beulah', a name which would later become integrated in Carrie's own California faith work.[166] This healing home was just one of many homes that Carrie was influential in inspiring to take root. The significant influence of Carrie's example and the rise of the Divine Healing Movement led to the founding of over thirty known faith homes in North America by 1887.[167]

Shortly after Carrie married George Montgomery and went to visit San Francisco, Mrs Mattie A. Stein temporarily took over running Faith Rest in Carrie's absence. Carrie ventured out to San Francisco for what initially was only intended to be a few months. Up until 1890, Carrie was not sure where God would lead, and she was still trying to raise enough money to purchase a permanent Faith Rest home in Buffalo. After about two years of traveling back and forth between the East and West Coast, the Montgomerys decided to relocate permanently to California. Though her Faith Rest at 323 Fargo Avenue in Buffalo shut down in 1892, the ethos of the home traveled with her and came alive on the other side of the country.[168]

2.2.2.4 Home of Peace (1893-present)

In 1892, Carrie believed that she should set up a faith home in Oakland since 'unforeseen circumstances have removed [her] field of labor to the Pacific coast, where Christian work of all kinds is greatly needed'.[169] At that point, there were no known healing homes in California. Carrie's new home became the first healing home on the West Coast.[170] Its initial purpose was for temporary visits in order

---

[166] "'Beulah,'" A New Faith Home', *TF* 7.3 (March 1887), pp. 60-61. 'Beulah', taken from Isa. 62.4, means married; it was commonly used in Holiness and Divine Healing circles in her day. More on this in Chapter 3.

[167] Richard M. Riss, 'Faith Homes', in *NIDPCM*, pp. 630-32.

[168] Carrie Judd Montgomery, 'Faith Rest Cottage will move to Beulah, California', *TF* 12.5 (May 1892), p. 120.

[169] Carrie Judd Montgomery, 'The Work and the Workers', *TF* 12.2 (Feb 1892), p. 35.

[170] Montgomery, 'Faith Rest Cottage will move', p. 120. Carrie asked permission from the people who donated the money if it could be transferred for the home in California, and all but one allowed her to appropriate the funds in that direction. At that point she had $1,340 and needed $2,500 for the new home in

Figure 6
The Home of Peace, Oakland, California

Figure 7
The Home of Peace, Oakland, California

to seek physical healing and spiritual refreshment. Carrie wrote that 'so many sick ones are harassed by family cares at their own home, that they cannot take the necessary time for Bible study in this di-

Oakland. By February of the following year, architects had already begun drawing up the plans for the new California home.

rection'.[171] Her home answered that need. During the process of preparing for this new faith home, something symbolic happened on April 20, 1893. George Montgomery, who became Carrie's husband in 1890, was walking with the workers who had just marked the foundation line, when they saw the first white dove from their area come from out of nowhere. The dove flew over the spot where the home was to be built then circled around George's head. This 'sign' impressed them both, and at George's suggestion, the name of the home was called the Home of Peace.[172] Moreover, Carrie's husband contributed financially towards this project so that they could build a larger home than originally anticipated. The home was in a prime location for Carrie's growing vision.[173]

The 'few' she mentioned who would gather at the home's dedication on November 7, 1893 turned out to be over 150 people.[174] George offered a prayer; Carrie shared an account of her healing; and a friend closed the dedication with a Bible reading from Isaiah 58.[175] J.P. Ludlow and his wife, former missionaries to Japan, were appointed to live in and manage the Home of Peace in its early stages.[176] It is notable that very quickly after the home was up and running, Carrie already 'gave it away' into someone else's care and allowed them to take on ownership. She invited others to get involved in this work so that she could expand in other areas of ministry.

This continuation of her work in Buffalo shared its same core values. Carrie stated that 'those who are willing to yield soul and body to the Lord, and to trust Him fully as their Great Physician, would be apt to receive any benefit from a stay at this Home'.[177] She

---

[171] Carrie Judd Montgomery, 'The Work and the Workers', *TF* 13.2 (Feb 1893), p. 47. It must be noted that Carrie also welcomed non-Christians. Similar to many others in her time, she would regularly speak to them about salvation and help them to convert to Christianity prior to teaching and praying for healing.

[172] Montgomery, 'The Work and the Workers', *TF* 13.5 (May 1893), p. 118.

[173] Carrie Judd Montgomery, 'Dedication of the Home of Peace', *TF* 13.11 (Nov 1893), p. 265. See also her 'Proposed Faith Home', *TF* 13.3 (March 1893), p. 95.

[174] Copy of original hand written invitation accessed through the Flower Pentecostal Heritage Center.

[175] Carrie Judd Montgomery, 'Home of Peace', *TF* 13.12 (Dec 1893), pp. 296-98.

[176] J.P. Ludlow, 'Home of Peace', *TF* 14.1 (Jan 1894), pp. 5-7.

[177] Montgomery, 'Home of Peace', p. 199.

reiterated that the Home of Peace was not a hospital and that if people were seriously ill, they needed to be accompanied by a nurse or a friend who could take care of them. She also recorded 'unusual waves of glory' falling in the Home of Peace. In its early years, Carrie said that the home was consistently full of people who needed help 'either in soul or body. It has proved to be the very gate of heaven to many weary souls; tired Christian workers have here renewed their strength, sick bodies have been healed and hungry hearts have been filled with the waves of peace for which they were longing'.[178] The home also acted as a church as Carrie would many times give a Sunday message there.

At the end of 1895, Carrie adjusted her focus for the home and decided to concentrate on training. She told her readers that 'after much prayer for many months, we have decided to turn the Home of Peace, at Beulah, into a training school or Bible institute, for the purpose of training young lives for usefulness in the Master's service'.[179] The Home of Peace was transformed into the Shalom Training School which provided missionary training for young women ages 18-30 years old (See Chapter 3, below). One of the other reasons that Carrie decided temporarily not to utilize the Home of Peace for its original purpose was because she realized that people could just as easily receive healing in their own homes. By 1895, she found that 'those visiting the Home have often depended too much upon us personally, and this in itself has been a barrier in the way of their healing. The Home of Peace will not be open longer to the sick as guests'.[180] She followed this with an explanation that they would continue to pray during their Thursday night Christian Alliance Meetings in Oakland for all prayer requests received.

This change in the home did not last long. By the beginning of 1896, the home was once again open to a limited number of guests, but this time there was an additional emphasis on training up Christian workers. H.C. Waddell and his wife were appointed to operate

---

[178] Carrie Judd Montgomery, 'Pentecostal Blessing', *TF* 15.3 (March 1895), p. 60.

[179] Carrie Judd Montgomery, 'Shalom (Peace) Training School for Christian Workers', *TF* 15.10 (Oct 1895), p. 232.

[180] Montgomery, 'Shalom (Peace) Training School for Christian Workers', p. 232.

the home and help teach the guests during this training phase.[181] At that time, Waddell stated, 'The Home of Peace will not be closed against guests during the school session, but in so far as we have room, guests will be received and be given the benefits of the special classes if they so desire'.[182] During this year, Carrie's emphasis shifted from divine healing to equipping and training. Her connection with the Salvation Army may have influenced this shift. By late 1897, the home was fully opened once again with training for missions integrated into the divine healing focus. After Carrie's Pentecostal Spirit baptism experience in 1908, the Home of Peace added Pentecostal themes to its healing themes as well.

Today the Home of Peace is still operating, even 60+ years after the founder's death. The current Home of Peace, which is non-denominational, is used more as a conference center, and it now charges a fee for guests to stay.[183] There are 22 rooms for missionaries needing a short rest as well as several apartments for retired missionaries. Until recently, one of the major functions of the Home of Peace was a packing and shipping service to help send supplies to missionaries. This service began when the Montgomerys found out that two missionaries to China lost all their things because of packing issues. After this, they transported packages for missionaries abroad.[184] Because supplies can easily and cheaply be bought in foreign countries now, the emphasis on shipping has changed. When I visited in 2008 and in 2010, it was serving primarily as a conference center in addition to a home of rest for missionaries. The house has also survived two major San Francisco earthquakes since it was

---

[181] H.C. Waddell, 'The Home of Peace', *TF* 16.2 (Feb 1896), pp. 46-48. He instituted a program in which participants spent three periods of 30 minutes throughout each day in silence and prayer. This program later became the basis of his The Pentecostal Prayer Union.

[182] Waddell, 'The Home of Peace', pp. 232-33. He earlier said,

But in the past the school and home life have not been joined as we desire to now have them, in admitting our guests to the special classes in the school, and so providing for them, if they choose it, daily teaching in the riches of the kingdom. This will fully carry out the original idea of the Home in the mind of Brother and Sister Montgomery, and fulfill the ideal of a complete work of the Holy Spirit.

[183] By at least 1907, guests were charged to stay there with missionaries receiving a discounted rate (Inga Thorgeson, 'The Home of Peace', *TF* 27.12 [Dec 1907], p. 280).

[184] Jennifer Stock, 'Carrie Judd Montgomery and the Home of Peace', *AGH* 9.1 (Spring 1989), p. 5.

built, one in 1906 and the other 1990. Before the first one in 1906, Carrie was suddenly awakened and felt 'led out in prayer' to pro- phetically put 'the blood of Jesus by faith over all the houses in Beulah'.[185] Shortly after she went back to sleep, she was abruptly awakened by the violent earthquake that devastated the city. The Home of Peace recorded no major damages from those incidents.

After her move to California, Carrie's healing home model was duplicated throughout the West Coast. One of the guests who stayed at her Faith Rest in Buffalo opened a home in Washington State. These and others who started similar works embraced the same values that Carrie modeled by 'teaching of a full Gospel and helping those who are seeking the Lord for health, or a deeper spir- itual life'.[186] Miss Clara Miner and Miss Inga Thorgeson, who at one point ran the Home of Peace in Oakland for several years, branched off and started their own healing home in Los Angeles. Carrie regu- larly visited them and held meetings in their home when she trav- eled to Los Angeles.[187] Through her healing home and California base, Carrie played an important part in disseminating Divine Heal- ing themes throughout the West Coast.

2.2.2.5 Patterns

There is a pattern in the types of guests who stayed with Carrie in her New York home versus her California home. The earlier guests who stayed in the Buffalo home went specifically for healing, and then from there, many went out to the mission field or started min- istries following their own healing accounts. Conversely, many of the guests who came to the Home of Peace in Oakland were al- ready missionaries and were seeking a place of rest and refreshing before going back onto their fields. Carrie Bates' story will help to demonstrate the use of the two homes. Bates went to the Buffalo Faith Rest home as a life-long invalid. Soon after that visit, she was healed and eventually went to India as a missionary. Years later, she

---

[185] Carrie Judd Montgomery, 'God's Deliverances', *TF* 26.4 (April 1906), p. 88. She said, 'About two hours before the terrible shock, I was awakened and felt a sense of danger. I was led out in prayer, and in the most definite manner led to put the blood of Jesus by faith over all the houses in Beulah'. See also Wayne Warner, 'Home of Peace Celebrates Centennial', *AGH* 13.3 (Fall 1993), p. 18.

[186] H.F. and S. Tyler, 'Bethel Faith Home', *TF* 15.7 (July 1895), p. 168.

[187] Carrie Judd Montgomery, 'A New Faith Home in Los Angeles', *TF* 31.6 (June 1911), p. 143.

visited Carrie at the Home of Peace for rest and refreshing.[188] While throughout the years Carrie did have a range of guests who did not fit into this mold, this is a general pattern that many times was characteristic in her guests.

The variety of guests who stayed in her California home was diverse. Many of those who filtered into Carrie's Oakland home were made up of friends, people seeking healing, or later on, people seeking the Pentecostal baptism of the Holy Spirit. Ethan O. Allen, who indirectly played a crucial role in Carrie's healing account, paid a visit to the Home of Peace in the late 1890s when he was 83 years old.[189] T.P. and Manie Payne Ferguson and even Finis E. Yoakum (1851-1920) stayed there in 1907. Yoakum was healed in a Christian and Missionary Alliance meeting in Los Angeles in January of 1895 from an injury which occurred to him after he was struck by buggy cart driven by a drunk driver. After his healing, it was recorded that he 'discontinued the practice of medicine and instead treated his patients by prayer'.[190] He founded the Pisgah faith home in Los Angeles in 1906 to help the outcasts and drunkards who wished to reform.[191] Frank Bartleman and his family also stayed in the Home of Peace on April 1, 1908.[192] Miss Mayo from Upper Room Mission in Los Angeles stayed there as well. It was recorded that William J.

---

[188] Carrie B. Bates, *The Christian Alliance* 16.7 (Feb 14, 1896), p. 166 and 'The Lord My Healer and Keeper', *TF* 17.3 (March 1897), pp. 50-55. Bates was healed from dyspepsia one March 25, 1883 while staying with Carrie at Faith Sanctuary.

[189] Carrie Judd Montgomery, 'Christian Alliance Meeting', *TF* 16.2 (Feb 1896), p. 48.

[190] *Los Angeles Times* (Aug 19, 1920). Alexander Boddy also wrote that Yoakum was 'best of all known for his "Faith healing ..." [he was] a Bishop of the Drunkards and the Harlots' (Alexander Boddy, 'The Editor in Southern California: Dr/ Yoakum's Work at Los Angeles', *Confidence* 5.11 [Nov 1912], p. 248).

[191] 'Some Information', *Word and Witness* 9.12 (Malvern, Arkansas, Dec 20, 1913). One reporter noticed that 'he is not considered by the leading Pentecostal people in his own city (Los Angeles), also up and down the coast, as a full fledged Pentecostal Preacher'. The author continued on to say that Yoakum did great things in regards to healing 'but he does not take a real stand for the outpouring of the Spirit according to the book of Acts with the speaking in tongues or the signs following as the Pentecostal people do'. While Yoakum was in Los Angeles near where the Azusa Street Revival took place, he never truly converted to Pentecostalism but did integrate many things from the movement into his work and faith.

[192] Home of Peace Guest Book 1906-1910 original handwritten copy researched at and courtesy of the Home of Peace. Bartleman wrote Isa. 59.16 in the guest book: 'And He saw that there was no man, and wondered that there was no intercession' (emphasis original).

Seymour and his wife stayed at the Home of Peace several times and also attended some of Carrie's meetings. Carrie wrote in her personal journal that 'We had a very blessed time' with the Seymours in their 1909 visit.[193] In their 1912 visit, Sadie Cody, who was running the Home of Peace at that time, wrote that 'we had sweet fellowship with our Brother Seymour of Los Angeles, and Mrs. Edith Hill-Booker, National Evangelist for the W.C.T.U., who were recently our guests for a time. The Lord greatly blessed Brother Seymour's coming among us'.[194] In September of 1912, Alexander A. Boddy, the Vicar of All Saints Vicarage in Sunderland, England, stayed at the home and also spoke in several of the meetings there. He left the following message in the guest book: 'Psalm 121. Shall ever thank God for the friendship and hospitality of our beloved Host and Hostess'.[195] Harold Needham and Elizabeth Baxter also stayed there as did Stanley F. Frodsham.[196] In 1931, Zelma Argue visited the home along with her parents and wrote that 'the refreshment, perfume, and inspiration of this happy visit will accompany me to far fields'.[197]

People came from all across the globe and across denominational barriers to visit Carrie at the Home of Peace. The original guestbook of 1906-1911 records visitors from the surrounding Oakland area, Los Angeles, Santa Barbara, Washington, Boston, Maryland, Hawaii, Japan, China, South Africa, Canada, India, Jerusalem, and Palestine. From 1911-1919, people came from Los Angeles, Buffalo, the Stone Church in Chicago, Kansas City, Texas, Oregon, Germany, England, Sweden, China, Japan, Venezuela, Fiji, and Mukti, India. From 1928-1938 people also came from as far as Johannesburg, South Africa. Some of the guests who stayed in the home were tied to organizations like the Southern California Sunday School Association, Pandita Ramabai's Mukti mission in India,

---

[193] Montgomery, '1909 Personal Unpublished Journal', p. 320. One of the meetings they attended was held on Tuesday November 16, 1909. According to Sadie Cody who wrote 'Home of Peace Letter', *TF* 32.6 (June 1912), pp. 125-26, the Seymours were also there in the summer of 1912.

[194] Sady Cody, 'Home of Peace Letter', *TF* 32.6 (June 1912), p. 126. W.C.T.U. is Women's Christian Temperance Union.

[195] Home of Peace Guest Book 1911-1919.

[196] Carrie Judd Montgomery, 'Pastor A.A. Boddy of England', *TF* 34.3 (March 1914), pp. 51-52.

[197] Home of Peace Guest Book 1928-1938 original handwritten copy researched at and courtesy of the Home of Peace, p. 85.

the Christian and Missionary Alliance, the Salvation Army, the Assemblies of God, and other Pentecostal affiliations.[198]

Decline

One might wonder why the model of healing homes was very popular in the late 1800s but then relatively disappeared until its recent resurgence.[199] Ronald Kydd believes that the decline in healing homes came because Americans wanted immediate satisfaction, which also meant that healing should come instantly.[200] This, however, came more as a result of the doctrine of healing in the atonement gaining momentum than because of American culture. I would agree with Vinson Synan, who argues that one possible factor contributing to the shift was the rise in healing evangelists who took center stage.[201] Large crusades and evangelistic tent meetings began to draw the masses away from the humble environments of the healing home. Being healed through the prayers of a charismatic figure became more attractive to people than getting away to a quiet place where they could learn how to pray the prayer the faith for themselves. In agreement with Kimberly Alexander and Richard Riss, I would propose that the most significant factor that contributed to this decline was that the doctrine of divine healing became more embedded within the churches that arose from the movement. Because many churches finally began to teach and advocate healing, the need to get away somewhere 'safe' to learn about it was no longer necessary.[202]

---

[198] People also came from the Pentecostal Assembly in Pasadena as well as the Pigsah Home in Los Angeles.

[199] Margaret Poloma, 'Old Wine, New Wineskins: The Rise of Healing Rooms in Revival Pentecostalism', *Pneuma* 28.1 (Spring 2006), p. 62. About thirty years ago, John Wimber helped to democratize healing once again, and in the late 1900s Cal Pierce was led to dig up the wells of John G. Lake's ministry of healing rooms. There is a newer revival of healing rooms emerging in various forms today all around the world. This resurgence has a more revivalistic bent, as many, like Pierce, are attempting to tap into 'wells of revival'. Other models have arisen because of a need to take healing outside the walls of the church, as can be seen in the Healing on the Streets model started by Mark Marx at a Vineyard Church in Ireland. See Chapter 5 for a fuller discussion on recent healing paradigms.

[200] Ronald A.N. Kydd, *Healing through the Centuries: Models for Understanding* (Peabody, MA: Hendrickson Publishers, 1998), p. 200, n. 4.

[201] Synan, 'A Healer in the House?', p. 201.

[202] Riss, 'Faith Homes', p. 632, and Alexander, *Pentecostal Healing: Models in Theology and Practice* (JPTSup, 29; Blandford Forum, UK: Deo Publishing, 2006), p. 58. One of the reasons healing homes became so popular in the first place in the

In Summary

Throughout the development and operation of Carrie's healing homes on both coasts, the ethos of divine healing was always there. While other emphases like Pentecostal Spirit baptism were integrated as a result of Carrie's own spiritual journey, at the core of the homes there was always a desire for healing, whether that be spiritual or physical. Carrie's West Coast healing home came nearly twenty years before the famous John G. Lake's healing rooms, which only started some years after his return from Africa in 1913.[203] Chappell rightly notes that 'although [Carrie] was not the first healing evangelist on the West Coast (both Alexander Dowie and Maria B. Woodworth-Etter had ministered there before), she was the first there to establish a permanent healing ministry, including the first faith healing home'. He also writes that Carrie was the 'product of the first generation of faith healing propagators in America and the only West Coast faith healing advocate to be personally familiar with and molded by these pioneers'.[204] With her experience of working alongside the great leaders of the Divine Healing Movement, she continued to spread the divine healing message through her new base on the West Coast. It was through Carrie's pioneering efforts that she became one of the earliest people to initiate healing homes on both sides of the country as well as inspire others to open healing homes. Because of this, she played a crucial role in the increase of healing homes and the advancement of divine healing themes in the late 1800s.

2.2.3 The Preacher: Itinerant Speaking Ministry

Through her passion to see people healed and her advocacy of missions, Carrie connected and made friends with people from all around the world. It was through many of these personal connections with people staying in her healing homes that she got invited to speak at churches and conferences. A second thing that was born in Carrie's life very shortly after her healing account was her itinerant preaching career. Not only was Carrie a preacher, but her mes-

---

late 1800s was because divine healing within many Evangelical churches was initially rejected and the need for teaching and praying for the sick went unmet. Because of this, many flocked to the incubators of healing homes to learn about these things and to receive healing.

203 Zeigler, 'John Graham Lake', p. 828.
204 Chappell, 'The Divine Healing Movement in America', p. 249.

sage was also radical – divine healing had been an uncommon subject in the church for some years. In the early part of Carrie's speaking ministry, she realized that the message of divine healing was 'exceedingly unpopular with most of the ministers and laymen'.[205] One of her friends, Carrie Bates, also admitted that the first time she heard of divine healing, she 'thought, as so many do, that it was fanaticism, and that the day of miracles was past'.[206] Regardless of potential opposition she would face because of the message, Carrie felt the need to share her testimony with any who would listen.

Itinerant Preacher

Not too long after her healing account was publicized, Carrie was invited to speak at a Union Holiness Meeting held at a Methodist Church. Initially, she struggled to accept the invitation because it came from outside her Episcopalian tradition. She eventually decided to speak there despite denominational differences, and the experience prepared her for an ecumenical healing ministry to follow.[207] Between the summer of 1880 and January 1883, Carrie had initiated Thursday evening prayer meetings, Tuesday afternoon Bible studies, and a once a month prayer meeting for foreign missionaries.[208] The meetings provided Carrie with training for her many preaching opportunities to come. Encouragement and additional platforms created by A.B. Simpson also contributed to her development as a preacher.[209]

---

[205] Montgomery, *Under His Wings,* p. 70.

[206] Bates, *The Christian Alliance,* p. 166.

[207] Carrie F. Judd, 'Faith Work', *TF* 4.12 (Dec 1884), p. 267.

[208] 'Meetings-Faith Rest Cottage', *TF* 3.1 (Jan 1883), p. 24, and *TF* 6.4 (April 1886), p. 96. In the summer of 1880, Carrie began a Thursday evening prayer meeting in her Faith Sanctuary. By January of 1883, she also initiated a Tuesday afternoon Bible study. Additionally, on the first Tuesday evenings of each month there was a special meeting devoted to praying specifically for foreign missions.

[209] Judd, 'Convention for Christian Life, Divine Healing, Evangelistic and Missionary Work in 1885'. This convention was for 'all who desire a deeper Spiritual Life, a special baptism of the Holy Spirit for service, a quickening in the truth, life, and work of the Lord, and in the hope of His appearing ... to receive Him as their Healer' (p. 240). She followed this by speaking at a Convention for Christian Life and Work and Divine Healing in a YMCA building in Buffalo, New York on Oct. 27-Oct. 31, 1885. The emphasis of this convention was for all those 'hungering for a fuller manifestation of Christ in their souls and bodies', and their intention was that they would 'meet together to wait upon Him for a special outpouring of His Holy Spirit' (*TF* 5.10 [Oct 1885], p. 240).

As a single woman in her twenties and into her early thirties, Carrie had a busy speaking schedule. She received many invitations from people who had received healing through her ministry. One example of this came when J. Calnon, who had previously been 're-stored to health while waiting on the Lord at the Faith Rest in Buffalo', invited Carrie to speak at his Congregational church in Cleburne, Texas.[210] Through the late 1880s, Carrie spoke at faith homes, conferences, and churches from a variety of denominational backgrounds, sometimes speaking multiple times at the events.[211] When she was not speaking, she met with people at appointed times in her hotel room to pray with them. Carrie spoke to large and small crowds, both in and outside the relative safety of church buildings. In 1891, it was recorded that she once spoke to over five hundred people outside a saloon.[212]

Carrie's style of speaking was gentle, simple, and appeared to have profound and long-term effects. A. Coplin remarked that 'Sister Carrie Judd Montgomery was much aided in her sweet, tender and clear presentation of the word of truth and life'.[213] Carrie's daughter, Faith, remembered her as having a gentle oratory skill, while others claimed that she spoke with 'eloquent power'.[214] Carrie's presence and her messages also acted as a seed, or catalyst, in certain environments. In 1891, Warren Collins wrote of Carrie's impact at his church in Texas saying, 'Since the last visit of our much loved sister, Mrs. Carrie Judd Montgomery, last year, we have been receiving a constant baptism of the Holy Spirit. The seed sown has borne abundant fruit. The city has been blessed with almost a constant revival ever since'.[215] In 1892, after Carrie returned to New York for a brief visit, Simpson remarked that 'our friend has lost none of her former unction and power, but has grown

---

[210] Carrie F. Judd, 'The Work and the Workers', *TF* 10.3 (March 1890), p. 64.

[211] During an Oakland convention in 1890, she gave eight addresses. See her 'The Work and the Workers', *TF* 9.10 (Oct 1889), pp. 233-35.

[212] Carrie Judd Montgomery, 'The Work at Home: A Word from California', *CAMW* 7.14 (Oct 2, 1891), p. 221. This was in conjunction with the Christian Alliance.

[213] A. Coplin, 'Convention at Oakland, Cal.', *CAMW* 5.18 (Nov 7, 1890), p. 284.

[214] 'At Beulah Park: Ministers and Laymen Preach the Word of Life to Great Audiences', *The Morning Call* (San Francisco), July 13, 1892, p. 8.

[215] Warren Colins, 'The Work at Home: The Work of the Lord in Ft. Worth, Texas', *CAMW* 6.16 (April 17, 1891), p. 250.

deeper, mellower and tender in her spirit and address, and is still God's chosen vessel for bringing great blessing to multitudes of hearts'.[216] *The New York Times* in 1893 announced a special meeting where 'the principal address will be made by Mrs. Montgomery, who, as Carrie Judd, spoke here [First Methodist Episcopal Church on Broadway Street in Los Angeles] several years ago with great success, and is well remembered'.[217] Her presence and her messages had a profound effect in certain environments.

Women in Ministry

Besides her controversial message of healing, Carrie also filled a controversial ministry role as a woman preacher. One of the sharpest tensions in relation to Evangelical women in the late 1800s had to do with the issue of women in the pulpit.[218] For Quakers and in some strands of Methodism, it was permitted that women could preach, but for most other churches in the Evangelical movement, there was controversy over the subject.[219] Women were allowed to fundraise and even lead Sunday school, but to be able to preach from the pulpit was another thing altogether.[220] Charles G. Finney worked not only toward revival and social reform in America, but also for 'unpopular' causes like women's equal rights.[221] Women

---

[216] A.B. Simpson, 'Editorial: Mr. and Mrs. Montgomery', *CAMW* 8.17 (April 22, 1892).

[217] 'Thanksgiving Services', *The Los Angeles Times*, November 29, 1893, p. 4.

[218] Throughout his narrative, Wayne Warner discusses Woodworth-Etter's struggle to be a woman and a preacher (*Maria Woodworth-Etter: For Such a Time as This* [Gainesville: Bridge-Logos, 2004]). See also Nigel Scotland, *Apostles of the Spirit and Fire: American Revivalists and Victorian Britain* (Milton Keynes, UK: Paternoster, 2009), and Laceye C. Warner, *Saving Women: Retrieving Evangelistic Theology and Practice* (Waco: Baylor University Press, 2007), for integrated discussions in relation to other women in ministry during this time and before.

[219] George M. Marsden, *Religion and American Culture* (New York: Harcourt Brace Jovanovich, Publishers, 1990), pp. 22-23. Quakers were revolutionary in inviting and allowing women to preach. Anne Hutchinson (1591-1643) preceded this as she was an early woman who challenged the clergy's authority by preaching in her own home and in 1637 was exiled from Puritan Massachusetts 'for claiming to hear a direct voice from God's spirit, a doctrine that challenged Puritan reliance on the Bible alone'. She was exiled and in 1643 died 'at the hands of Indians'.

[220] Bebbington, *A History of Evangelicalism*, p. 224.

[221] Marsden says that Finney 'and other evangelists with whom he worked closely were leaders in the often unpopular causes of the abolition of slavery and greater equality for women. Oberlin College in Ohio, Finney's base after 1835,

preaching and intermixing with men did not come easily or without controversy in many environments in the late 1800s.

David Bebbington identifies that in Carrie's time Evangelicals were 'the group most responsible for the Victorian ideal of separate spheres', where men would be free to roam in public life but where women were confined to their limited and 'private sphere of home'.[222] A study of the letters and diaries of American women from 35 different families between the 1760s and 1880s reveals this separation of spheres.[223] The research demonstrates how natural it was for women to mix with other women and how unnatural it was to have a woman address an audience of men. Phoebe Palmer's 1859 book, *The Promise of the Father*, encouraged women to preach as long as they did not undermine or take authority over men. Catherine Booth's call to give equal freedom to the female officers in the Salvation Army was also helpful in advancing the cause. But while these and many social causes like the Temperance Movement empowered women to speak up and be heard, women preachers were not the norm in the American Christian culture that Carrie was exposed to at that time. Bebbington notes that even with these causes, 'female preaching nevertheless remained unusual' and that in the later 1800s within Evangelicalism, 'the prevailing opinion in most denominations was definitely against female ministry'.[224] Carrie experienced this in her ministry firsthand in 1889 when some churches shut their doors to her first because she was a woman preacher and second because she preached to 'negros'.[225] Nevertheless, she did not consider her gender an obstacle to sharing her testimony or teaching on divine healing. While her Bible studies were consistently comprised of women, many other times when she spoke at conventions, churches, or at her healing home, the audience was mixed. This was a bold statement for a woman of her time.

---

was the Americas' first coeducational college' (Marsden, *Religion and American Culture*, pp. 62-63).

[222] Bebbington, *A History of Evangelicalism*, p. 216.

[223] Carroll Smith-Rosenberg, 'The Female World of Love and Ritual: Relations between Women in Nineteenth-Century America', in Linda K. Kerber and Jane Sherron De Hart (eds.), *Women's America* (New York: Oxford University Press, 3rd edn, 1991), pp. 189-90.

[224] Bebbington, *A History of Evangelicalism*, p. 225. He recalls a story of how in 1891, at a Methodist church in Victoria, a crowd was drawn together because of the 'novelty' of a female preacher.

[225] Carrie F. Judd, 'The Work and the Workers', *TF* 9.5 (May 1889), p. 118.

Carrie's near neglect of entering the debate regarding whether or not women could preach, and her faith in following through with the things she felt God had called her to regardless of her gender, inspired many women towards ministry. The potential controversy of women in ministry was never a big issue for Carrie. My research up to 1920 revealed that she did not directly write in defense of her ministry but rather continued on in the work to which she believed God had called her.[226] Not only did she go against the grain and teach the unpopular message of divine healing, but she operated as a woman preacher. This is a truly remarkable endeavor to take on for a young woman living in Victorian times. Through Carrie's determination to share what God had done for her, she also became one of the first female healing evangelists to itinerate across North America.[227] In doing so, she was also one of the first to spread divine healing themes to the West Coast.

It was in the few years following her healing account that Carrie took three risks that became seeds that later grew and developed throughout her entire life. First, her writing became a major vehicle in spreading divine healing themes worldwide. Second, she initiated one of the earliest healing homes in the country as well as the first one on the West Coast which inspired many, especially women, to initiate their own healing homes. Third, she shared her testimony at a church outside of her denomination which would later lead to her expansive ecumenical ministry. As her writing, healing homes, and teaching became hallmarks of her life and ministry, a look at the soil in the American Divine Healing Movement in which these things grew will help to reveal her impact there.

2.3 'Pioneers in the Revival of this Great Truth'

It is impossible to talk about Carrie and the Divine Healing Movement separately because of the intricate role she played in helping to shape and form the movement. The movement in North America was birthed out of the Holiness Movement in the late 1800s with

---

[226] Mr Judd, 'Should Women Prophesy?', *TF* 6.12 (Dec 1886), pp. 270-73. See also Katherine Bushnell, 'Women Preachers; Why Obscure the True Reading?', taken from *Peniel Herald* in *TF* 24.11 (Nov 1904), pp. 259-61, where she uses Ps. 68.11-12 to demonstrate that God wants women to preach.

[227] Chapman, *Searching the Source of the River*, p. 66.

the majority of early advocates coming from the East Coast. Many of the Holiness people who influenced Carrie were also part of the Keswick Movement. Just as the Divine Healing Movement cannot be divorced from Carrie's life, the same applies for its key players; they too cannot be absent when retelling her story. As Sarah Mix and Elizabeth Baxter have already been mentioned, a necessary look into the lives of a few of Carrie's other contemporaries will be presented. William E. Boardman, Andrew Murray, A.J. Gordon, and A.B. Simpson will be highlighted because of the significant role they played in the movement. However, when exploring the Divine Healing Movement and its key players, one must first begin with Charles Cullis.

2.3.1 Charles Cullis

Charles Cullis (1833-1892) was known as 'a major leader of the broader Holiness Movement in the wake of the revival of 1857-58' even before laying significant foundations for the Divine Healing Movement.[228] An Episcopalian physician from Boston, he was one of the earliest people to help spread the doctrine of divine healing in America. In 1897, R.K. Carter stated that Cullis had done 'more than any other man to bring healing by faith to the attention of the church in the last century'.[229] At a time when divine healing was relatively unheard of in the popular and active sense, Cullis began to pray for the sick to be healed.

Ever since April 20, 1862, Cullis desired to help the terminally ill. That was the day he was confronted by a sick person who was turned away from the hospital because of his incurable illness. Cullis was impacted so much that two years later he opened a healing home for those who were too sick to be admitted into the hospital and had to await death on their own.[230] Initially, Cullis wanted to help alleviate his guests' suffering until they died by helping them become spiritually whole and able to end their days with dignity. However, in the late 1860s, the prayer of faith in Jas 5.14-15 captured his attention.[231] This prayer made him look at his approach to

---

[228] Dayton, *Theological Roots of Pentecostalism*, pp. 122-23. See also Chappell, 'The Divine Healing Movement in America', p. 104.

[229] R. Kelso Carter, *'Faith Healing' Reviewed* (Boston and Chicago: Christian Witness, 1897), p. 109; quoted in Dayton, *Theological Roots of Pentecostalism*, p. 122.

[230] Chappell, The Divine Healing Movement in America, pp. 107, 110-13.

[231] Cunningham, 'From Holiness to Healing', p. 501.

sickness differently. Several years following his new discovery, he put the prayer of faith to the test. In 1870, after praying the prayer of faith and anointing Lucy Drake with oil, she was healed of a brain tumor.[232] This was a turning point in his life toward taking the Bible literally and embracing the possibilities of divine healing. Since the early 1870s, Cullis had recorded many healings of people who adopted this prayer of faith. While he associated divine healing with salvation and saw that it was provided for in the atonement, he also continued to administer medicine, a practice that made his views controversial.[233]

Cullis attended Phoebe Palmer's Holiness meetings when on a trip to New York City in 1862.[234] Influenced by Palmer, he too started a Tuesday meeting to help people experience a greater depth of holiness.[235] As Palmer's meetings emphasized entire sanctification and were open to people from all different types of denominations, including Baptists, Quakers, Congregationalists, Episcopalians, Mennonites, and more, Cullis' Tuesday consecration meetings, lasting 23 years, followed a similar pattern.[236]

Towards the late 1800s, Cullis initiated rescue missions, several homes for cancer patients, a church, an orphanage, a college for African Americans, and a publishing company called the Willard Street Tract Repository. He also befriended W.E. Boardman and reprinted his book, *The Higher Christian Life*. During a trip with Boardman in 1873, Cullis and his wife visited George Müller's orphanage in Bristol, England, Johan Christoph Blumhardt's healing center in Bad Boll, Germany, and some of Dorothea Trudel's faith cure homes in Mannedorf, Switzerland.[237] The trip was significant for him because it was upon his return that he began to proclaim

---

[232] Chappell, 'The Divine Healing Movement in America', p. 129.

[233] Dayton, *Theological Roots of Pentecostalism*, p. 122. More discussion on this in Chapter 4.

[234] Chappell, 'The Divine Healing Movement in America', p. 110.

[235] Alexander, *Pentecostal Healing*, pp. 9, 12, 17.

[236] C.E. Jones, 'Holiness Movement', in *NIDPCM*, p. 727. Dayton, *Theological Roots of Pentecostalism*, pp. 67-68. See also Jennifer A. Miskov, 'Missing Links: Phoebe Palmer, Carrie Judd Montgomery, and Holiness Roots within Pentecostalism', *PentecoStudies: An Interdisciplinary Journal for Research on the Pentecostal and Charismatic Movements* 10.1 (2011), pp. 8-28 for more on the development of Palmer's theology.

[237] Chappell, The Divine Healing Movement in America', p. 200.

publicly the new healing doctrine in ways he had not done before.[238] Cullis was also later among the people who continued to pray for Carrie's complete recovery and who corresponded with her after her healing.[239] At one point, Carrie contemplated joining his two year training course at the Deaconess' House but ended up deciding against it because of the growing number of people seeking her out at that time.[240] In 1890, when Carrie was speaking at a Christian Alliance meeting in Boston, she had the opportunity to visit Dr Cullis' work there in Grove Hill. She had a personal meeting and prayer time with him and was also invited to visit his home.[241] Years after Cullis died, Carrie wrote, 'we remember how many times he has knelt with us in prayer, claiming with the most child-like faith, and in the most simple language, some blessing we needed from the Lord'.[242] His encouragement to her and the foundations he laid for the emergence of the Divine Healing Movement helped pave the way for her and others to build upon.

2.3.2 The Divine Healing Movement

The Divine Healing Movement 'as a self-aware movement, with an ideology and agenda' roughly spans from 1870 to the early twentieth century. Faith Cure, Faith Healing, and Divine Healing were all used to refer to the same American movement of which Carrie was a part. Cullis originally named the movement 'faith-cure' but then A.B. Simpson and Andrew Murray later referred to it as the 'Divine Healing movement' because they wanted the emphasis to be more on God who does the healing rather than on the people who have faith.[243] One of the most in-depth resources in relation to this healing movement is a PhD dissertation called 'The Divine Healing Movement in America' by Paul Gale Chappell, completed in 1983. His work traces key players and shows how Phoebe Palmer and the Holiness Movement helped pave the way for this 'faith cure' movement to emerge, which also later became integrated within

---

[238] Cunningham, 'From Holiness to Healing', p. 501, Chappell, 'The Divine Healing Movement in America', p. 132, and Hardesty, *Faith Cure*, p. 16.

[239] Judd, *The Prayer of Faith*, pp. 19, 28.

[240] Carrie Judd, 'Faith-Work', *TF* 4.12 (Dec 1884), p. 265.

[241] Carrie Judd Montgomery, 'The Work and the Workers', *TF* 10.7 (July 1890), p. 166.

[242] Carrie Judd Montgomery, 'Death of Dr. Cullis', *TF* 12.8 (Aug 1892), p. 191.

[243] Alexander, *Pentecostal Healing*, pp. 9-10.

Pentecostal and Charismatic movements.[244] The belief in healing in the atonement, which will be examined in Chapters 4 and 5, was a foundational belief for many in the movement along with the prayer of faith found in James 5. The movement was also anchored in premillennial eschatology.[245]

The Divine Healing Movement's newer perspective of healing was revolutionary and controversial at the same time, even within denominations. Throughout 1883-1884, two different Presbyterians, Robert L. Stanton and Marvin R. Vincent opened up a debate on this issue in the *Presbyterian Review*.[246] Carrie was on the side of Stanton as were many of the other healing pioneers. One of the reasons why people opposed divine healing was because they thought miracles were a part of history rather than a potential present reality to be realized.[247] Another reason was because people associated healing with Christian Science which Carrie opposed time and time again.[248] Still, others struggled with accepting that healing could be in the atonement.[249] The press also directly opposed Carrie because of her association with the Divine Healing Movement. In 1895, one newspaper article had the heading, 'A Newly Arrived Minister Says It [Faith Healing] Is the Work of the Devil. Opposes Mrs. Montgomery'.[250] Carrie was unafraid to answer back and did so less than week later in an article entitled 'Letters From the People: Healing

---

[244] Chappell, 'The Divine Healing Movement in America', pp. ii, v, vi.

[245] Alexander, *Pentecostal Healing*, pp. 8-9.

[246] Cunningham, 'From Holiness to Healing', pp. 505-506.

[247] Bates, *The Christian Alliance*, p. 166.

[248] 'Wealthy Warriors: A Rich Salvationist and His Famous Wife', p. 4. In 1892, Carrie, while with her husband George, said, 'We don't believe that Christian Science is Scriptural at all'. George initially hesitated to be open to the divine healing movement because he confused it with Christian Science before his own healing. See George S. Montgomery, 'What Hath God Wrought!', *TF* 12.12 (Dec 1892), pp. 265-67. Carrie along with others in the Divine Healing Movement adamantly wrote articles explaining the difference between divine healing and Christian Science. One secular example is Bernard Shaw, Dr Kent, and Attorney D. Donohoe Jr. and Mrs Carrie Judd Montgomery, 'Was Christian Science Responsible for Harold Fredric's Death?, *The San Francisco Call*, November 20, 1898, pp. 21, 26. Carrie also printed a defense for this by Anna W. Prosser, 'So-called "Christian Science"', *TF* 10.3 (March 1890), pp. 49-52; and W.T. Hogg '"Christian Science" Unmasked', *TF* 10.10 (Oct 1890), pp. 224-27.

[249] Cunningham, 'From Holiness to Healing', pp. 509-12.

[250] 'Testing Faith Healing, Newly Arrived Minister Says It Is the Work of the Devil, Opposes Mrs. Montgomery', *The San Francisco Call*, November 4, 1895, p. 9. Revd A.P. Truesdell also opposed her from the platform of his pulpit.

By Faith: Mrs. Carrie Judd Montgomery Gives an Explanation of Her Belief'.[251] In her biography many years after these accounts, Carrie reflected,

> I have spoken of the great opposition to Divine Healing which we, who were pioneers in the revival of this great truth, often encountered, but it is a joy to remember some of the precious people who were a comfort to us in those early days and who stood with us in faith for the revival of the Lord's gracious work of holiness and healing among His people.[252]

Some of these 'precious people' who stood together with her for the cause of divine healing will now be highlighted.

2.3.3 Fellow Pioneers

In describing the spread of the Divine Healing Movement, Chappell writes in some depth about the following five key people: Boardman, Murray, Gordon, Montgomery, and Simpson. When Burgess and McGee write about the same movement, Carrie is listed alongside Cullis, Simpson, Gordon, and Dowie as a 'radical evangelical' who 'inspired the evangelical faith-healing movement in America'.[253] In Curtis' description of the four most prominent shapers of the 'devotional ethics of divine healing', she mentions Carrie alongside Cullis, Gordon, and Simpson.[254] In all these lists, Carrie is the only woman mentioned.[255]

William E. Boardman (1810-1886), a Presbyterian originally from Smithfield, New York who was influenced by Cullis, helped develop transatlantic connections within the Divine Healing Movement. He authored the influential book, *The Higher Christian Life* (1858), which was important in spreading holiness themes to those outside of

---

[251] 'Letters From the People: Healing By Faith: Mrs. Carrie Judd Montgomery Gives an Explanation of Her Belief', *The San Francisco Call*, November 13, 1895, p. 6.

[252] Montgomery, *Under His Wings*, p. 72.

[253] S.M. Burgess and G.B. McGee, 'Signs and Wonders', in *NIDPCM*, pp. 1066-67.

[254] Curtis, *Faith in the Great Physician*, p. 20. She writes, 'Upper-middle-class Protestants such as Charles Cullis, A.J. Gordon, Carrie Judd, and A.B. Simpson, I contend, were primarily responsible for the shaping of the devotional ethics of divine healing'.

[255] It must also be noted however that Mix, Sisson, and even later, Maria Woodworth-Etter were also influential within this movement.

Methodism.[256] He also wrote *Faith Work under Dr. Cullis* (1874).[257] Boardman regularly attended Palmer's Tuesday meetings and was a part of the Keswick conventions.[258] His 1880 book, *The Lord that Healeth Thee,* contributed to his becoming an influential speaker within the movement as it was one of the early books on the theology of divine healing. By 1885, the Boardmans had moved permanently from the United States to England to continue their work there. Because of his success, many came to London seeking to learn about healing. He personally invited Carrie to his healing conference in 1885 and said that her 'presence with us will be thoroughly appreciated'.[259] She also printed many of his articles in her periodical throughout the years.[260]

In 1882, Andrew Murray (1828-1917), a Dutch Reformed pastor from South Africa, went to Baxter's healing home in association with Boardman's ministry to seek healing. Murray had a throat disorder that hindered and could possibly have destroyed his preaching career.[261] After three weeks at the Bethshan home in London and sitting under Boardman's teaching, he received complete healing. Before returning home, Murray also visited Trudel's homes in Swit-

---

[256] William E. Boardman, *The Higher Christian Life* (1858); repr. (USA: Kessinger Publishing, 2007). Melvin E. Dieter claims that the book 'opened the doors of non-Methodist churches to the revival's [revival of 1858] teachings more widely than any volume which had preceded it' (*The Holiness Revival of the Nineteenth Century* [Metuchen, NJ, and London: The Scarecrow Press, Inc, 1980], p. 56). Chappell also records that there were over 100,000 copies of this book sold throughout America and England and the message in the book caused him to have an even greater influence in the Holiness Movement as well ('The Divine Healing Movement in America', pp. 195-96).

[257] William E. Boardman, *Faith Work under Dr. Cullis in Boston* (Boston: Willard Tract Repository, 1873).

[258] Hardesty, *Faith Cure*, pp. 17, 32, Dieter, *The Holiness Revival of the Nineteenth Century*, p. 120, and Chappell, 'The Divine Healing Movement in America', pp. 198-203.

[259] W.E. Boardman, Personal letter to Carrie, Dec. 19, 1884. In the end, Carrie never made it over to England for the conference.

[260] W.E. Boardman articles include 'Let Jesus In', *TF* 4.8 (Aug 1884), pp. 179-80; 'He Careth for You', *TF* 8.10 (Oct 1888), pp. 236-37; 'How is a Suffering One to know if it be God's Will to Heal Without Means?', *TF* 26.10 (Oct 1906), pp. 206-208; 'Receiving', *TF* 32.5 (May 1912), pp. 160-61; 'The Father's Rod', *TF* 33.4 (April 1913), pp. 95-95; 'The Lord that Healeth Thee', *TF* 40.1 (Jan 1920), pp. 19-22; and 'The Great Need of Our Own Time', *TF* 62.1 (Jan 1943), pp. 4-6.

[261] It is interesting to note that his 1879 throat disorder caused him to have two 'silent years' of suffering before he surrendered everything to God and was eventually healed. Carrie's two year illness had a similar element of surrender.

zerland which were then being run by Samuel Zeller. Murray later went on to become influential in both the Holiness and Divine Healing Movements. In 1895, he was invited to be the keynote speaker at the Keswick Convention in England and at the North-field Convention in the United States.[262] He also wrote a book called *Divine Healing* (1884) that spelled out the Scriptural reasons why one should expect healing in that day. Additionally, he conducted meetings with Cullis and Simpson. Carrie and others published many of his articles in their periodicals throughout the years.[263]

Adoniram Judson Gordon (1836-1895) grew up a Baptist and was friends with and worked alongside Dwight L. Moody at times. Gordon seriously began to contemplate divine healing after witnessing an instantaneous healing at one of Moody's conferences in Boston in 1877. While in Boston, he became a supporter of Cullis' ministry which he promoted in several of his writings. He was known for the periodical that he started in 1878 called *The Watchword*. This paper had the goal of presenting Christian doctrines 'biblically rather than theologically, experimentally rather than controversially', in order to grow the believer's faith.[264] He was a featured author not only in Carrie's *Triumphs of Faith*, but also in Cullis' *Times of Refreshing*, William Piper's *Latter Rain Evangel*, Baxter's *Christian Herald*, and Simpson's *Word, Work, and World*. Carrie also had the opportunity to meet him during a visit with Cullis.[265] By 1882, he had become

---

[262] Chappell, 'The Divine Healing Movement in America', pp. 214-16 and Hardesty, *Faith Cure,* p. 64.

[263] E.g. Carried printed the following articles by Andrew Murray: 'Rivers of Living Water', *TF* 19:10 (Oct 1899), pp. 233-35; 'Boldness in the Blood of Jesus', *TF* 19.11 (Nov 1899), pp. 245-47; 'God's Prescription for the Sick', *TF* 21.3 (March 1901), pp. 58-60; 'Prayer According to God's Will', *TF* 21.6 (June 1901), pp. 141-42; 'The Certainty of the Answer to Prayer', *TF* 22.3 (March 1902), pp. 62-64; 'The Lord that Healeth Thee', *TF* 22.7 (July 1902), pp. 145-47; 'The Life of Love', TF 22.12 (Dec 1902), pp. 265-69; 'Sickness and Death', *TF* 23.2 (Feb 1903), pp. 43-45; 'Fervent and Effectual Prayer' and 'Pray Through', *TF* 24.2 (Feb 1904), pp. 41-43; 'Jesus Bore Our Sickness', *TF* 32.8 (Aug 1912), pp. 183-85; and 'The Will of God', *TF* 34.1 (Jan 1914), pp. 21-22.

[264] Earnest B. Gordon, *Adoniram Judson Gordon. A Biography with Letters and Illustrative Extracts Drawn from Unpublished or Uncollected Sermons and Addresses* (Revell: New York, 1896), p. 154. Quote taken from a personal letter that Ernest B. Gordon quoted in the above work, cited in Chappell, 'The Divine Healing Movement in America', p. 223.

[265] Montgomery, *Under His Wings,* p. 123.

'one of the leading advocates and apologists for the faith healing movement' and published his influential *The Ministry of Healing*. While Cullis did not go so far as to create a theology and doctrine on faith healing, Gordon picked up the pieces and formulated a theology which helped to validate and make the movement more legitimate in America. Among other causes, he also became an advocate for the women's rights movement, prohibition, helping the unemployed, and protecting Chinese immigrants.[266] Additionally, in 1889, he founded the Boston Missionary Training School, later known as Gordon College, with its focus 'to prepare laypeople, especially women, for missionary service'.[267]

These are just a few of the primary people who helped shape the Divine Healing Movement with whom Carrie connected in one way or another. A deeper look at those involved in the Divine Healing Movement may lead to the lives of Otto Stockmayer, Ethan O. Allen, Elizabeth Sisson, and later figures like John Alexander Dowie and Charles F. Parham, to name a few. One person who must not be forgotten or overlooked in regards to the Divine Healing Movement is A.B. Simpson. As will be demonstrated, he was not only a significant leader within the Divine Healing Movement, but he also played a key role in Carrie's life throughout the years.

2.3.4 A.B. Simpson: Kindred Spirits[268]

Canadian Albert Benjamin Simpson (1843-1919) was incredibly influential in the theology of the Healing Movement. He built important foundations for many within Pentecostalism and also founded the Christian and Missionary Alliance. He began as a pastor of a Presbyterian church in Ontario before moving to Kentucky in 1873 to pastor a church there. In 1874 and shortly after reading Boardman's *The Higher Christian Life*, he claimed to receive what he understood at the time as his Spirit baptism experience.[269] By 1879, he moved to New York City to pastor a Presbyterian church. Becoming ill and needing rest, in the summer of 1881, he brought his

---

[266] Chappell, 'The Divine Healing Movement in America', pp. 220-28.

[267] Noll, *A History of Christianity in the United States and Canada*, p. 291, and Alexander, *Pentecostal Healing*, p. 19.

[268] See Jennifer A. Miskov, 'Kindred Spirits', *Alliance Life* (March 2011). Assessable <http://www.alliancelife.org/article.php?id=580>

[269] C. Nienkirchen, 'Albert Benjamin Simpson', in *NIDPCM*, p. 1069.

family to a camp meeting led by Cullis in Old Orchard, Maine.[270] While there, one Friday afternoon he went by himself into the woods and engaged in a struggle to receive the 'truth' of divine healing. He made three specific pledges to God in relation to that issue at that time.[271] As a result, he fully embraced divine healing for his own life. Shortly after this, his daughter was ill and he prayed for her healing. Through her recovery, Simpson's wife was also convinced of divine healing. When he returned to New York City after the camp meeting, he resigned so that he could start his own outreach to those outside the church. Evangelizing the masses had been something he had wanted to do for years yet he continually faced opposition from higher church officials when branching out to do this kind of work. With his independent work, no institution could get in the way as it had before. Through his evangelistic passion to reach the marginalized, the rich *and* the poor, and to build a 'truly classless church', he took a big risk financially and gave up his previous salary, having no initial support for this ministry.[272] His work soon multiplied and he became very successful in his endeavors.

Like Cullis, Simpson actively sought to live his faith. He opened six rescue missions, an orphanage, churches that embraced all social classes, and even a home to help prostitutes get off the streets. In October 1883, he founded a Missionary Training College which later developed and is continuing today under the name of Nyack College. That same year he opened his home for the purpose of making it a healing home. In 1887, while at Old Orchard, he formed the

---

[270] Chappell, The Divine Healing Movement in America, pp. 255-58.

[271] A.B Simpson, *The Gospel of Healing* (New York: Christian Alliance Publishing Co., 4th ed., 1890), pp. 53-54, 58-59. These pledges were

1. As I shall meet Thee in that day, I solemnly accept *this truth* as part of thy Word, and of the Gospel of Christ and, God helping me, I shall never question it until I meet Thee there. 2. As I shall meet Thee in that day I take the Lord Jesus as my physical life, for all the needs of my body until all my life-work is done; and God helping me, I shall never doubt that He does so become my life and strength from this moment, and will keep me under all circumstance until His blessed coming, and until all His will for me is perfectly fulfilled. 3. As I shall meet Thee in that day I solemnly agree to *use* this blessing for the glory of God, and the good of others and to speak of it or minister in connection with it in any way in which God may call me or others may need me in the future.

[272] Chappell, 'The Divine Healing Movement in America', pp. 255-59.

Christian Alliance and the Missionary Society. In 1897, he merged these two into one organization called the Christian and Missionary Alliance that is still active today.[273] For 38 years, Simpson held meetings where he often encouraged people to receive salvation and sanctification before praying for healing. Simpson also earnestly sought to diffuse any possible over-attention on himself whenever teaching. Much of the time he let others pray the prayer of faith and anoint for healing so that people would not assume that healing came through him, but rather through God.[274] In 1888, a reporter for *The New York Times* said that the belief in divine healing

> was so largely misunderstood and misrepresented that [Simpson] felt called upon in view of these facts to say that they do not pretend to work miracles, but that they are simple Christians and believers in God's word, and that all can have the same privilege of being healed if they will.[275]

Besides defending the cause of divine healing, Simpson also advocated the movement by organizing many conventions and writing about divine healing. In addition to authoring over seventy books, he also started a periodical in 1881 called *The Word, Work and World*, which came after Carrie's *Triumphs of Faith* was initiated. Simpson's Fourfold Gospel of Jesus as Savior, Sanctifier, Healer, and Coming King, was adopted by Carrie and many in the Divine Healing Movement and was even later woven into Pentecostal theologies like that of Aimee Semple McPherson.[276] Simpson attempted to remain balanced on these four views and treated them like 'wheels' so as not to overemphasize one at the expense of the other.[277]

---

[273] Alexander, *Pentecostal Healing*, p. 21.

[274] Hardesty, *Faith Cure*, pp. 41-44.

[275] 'The Christian Alliance', *The New York Times*, October 12, 1888. Like Carrie and then later John Wimber, Simpson contributed to the democratization of healing.

[276] Carrie Judd, 'Old Orchard Convention', *TF* 7.9 (Sept 1887), pp. 203-204; *idem*, 'Report of Christian Convention', *TF* 8.1 (Jan 1888), p. 4; and *idem*, *TF* 8.7 (July 1888), p. 167. Simpson set out his Fourfold Gospel with Jesus Christ as 'set forth, crucified and risen, as the Saviour, Sanctifier, Healer, and coming Lord'. Carrie supported these truths and even offered the opportunities to get a fourfold badge through her journal as well as spoke regularly and published articles on the truths found in the Fourfold Gospel.

[277] Chappell, 'The Divine Healing Movement in America', p. 272. Simpson took a stand against John Alexander Dowie at one time because he felt that he

It was when Simpson was being awakened to the possibilities of divine healing himself that he came across Carrie's testimony. When he read her first article in *Triumphs of Faith* entitled 'Faith Reckonings', it struck a familiar chord inside him. He was impressed with her story so much that he reprinted it in his own journal even before meeting her.[278] When they met for the first time in 1883, Simpson showed Carrie his magazine with her article printed in it; this meeting was the spark of a lifelong friendship and recognition of kindred spirits between the two of them.[279] Even before Carrie realized that Simpson had heard of her, she was encouraged by a friend to meet the 'most Christlike man her friend had ever seen. [Carrie] found he knew her work and writings, and they were one'.[280] Simpson immediately made room for her to expand her ministry and acted as an encourager, a spiritual father, and a 'beloved friend'.

Simpson encouraged and created space for Carrie to speak over the years. She claimed that he 'was greatly used of God to thrust me out more fully into public service, that is, especially the platform work, although God had already made real use of my pen'.[281] In 1909, Carrie visited Simpson at one of his conferences. She recalled,

[W]e did not expect to remain East long enough to attend this Convention, but Mr. Simpson kindly urged us to be present, saying that in spite of a full program, previously arranged, he would be glad to make openings for us to give testimony and Bible teaching. This he did, by arranging an extra meeting in the Tabernacle every evening ... These meetings were well attended and the Lord gave us great liberty in Bible teaching about the Holy

---

only emphasized one truth (healing) of the Fourfold Gospel rather than a balanced view.

[278] The first article she published was 'Faith Reckonings', *TF* 1.1 (Jan 1881), pp. 1-4 which told about her healing encounter and emphasized that one simply needs to *act* on the promises God has already given. See also Montgomery, *Under His Wings,* p. 98.

[279] By this time he had also reprinted another article of Carrie's entitled 'Our Position in Christ' from her *TF* 2.1 (Jan 1882), pp. 1-3, in his *Word, Work, and World* 1.6 (July 1882), pp. 251-52.

[280] 'Christian Alliance', *Los Angeles Times,* June 2, 1896, p. 14.

[281] Montgomery, *Under His Wings,* p. 99.

Spirit's Fullness, Receiving Him by Faith, and kindred sub-jects.[282]

After the convention closed, Simpson said that 'in some respects this has been the most wonderful Camp Meeting we have ever held at Old Orchard'.[283]

Carrie also considered Simpson a spiritual father and invited him to play that role, referring to him at one point as the 'kind of friend whom we always think of as our pastor'.[284] This was not a positional relationship like the one that would have resulted had Carrie been a member of his New York City church. She was from Buffalo and unable to be a part of his congregation; nonetheless she still gave him a place of spiritual authority in her life and participated in ministry alongside him throughout the years. Simpson baptized Carrie in water and later, interestingly enough, it was at one of his conventions in 1889 where Carrie was introduced to the man who later became her husband.[285] In addition to being invited to help perform Carrie's wedding ceremony, Simpson was also later called upon to baptize their daughter Faith in 1892.[286] Carrie was additionally a part of the formation of what is now known as the Christian and Missionary Alliance, being listed as the first recording secretary.[287] Christian and Missionary Alliance historian Paul King writes that after Carrie became secretary of the Christian Alliance, she 'would become one of the most significant "charismatic" leaders in the

---

[282] Carrie Judd Montgomery, 'Old Orchard Convention', *TF* 29.8 (Aug 1909), p. 178.

[283] Montgomery, 'Old Orchard Convention', p. 179.

[284] Montgomery, 'The Work and the Workers', *TF* 10.7, p. 167.

[285] Carrie Judd Montgomery, 'Miraculously Healed by the Lord Thirty Years Ago', *LRE* 2.1 (Oct. 1909), p. 9. See also Carrie F. Judd, 'The Work and the Workers', *TF* 9.7 (July 1889), p. 118; 'All For the Poor: Rich Salvationists to Work in the Slums of New York: Romantic Story of a Couple', *Middletown Daily Press*, April 12, 1892, p. 1; and Hardesty, *Faith Cure*, p. 45.

[286] Anna W. Prosser, 'Wedding Bells', *TF* 10.6 (June 1890), p. 122, and Carrie Judd Montgomery, 'The Work and the Workers', *TF* 12.5 (May 1892), pp. 118-20. Simpson was a part of leading Carrie's wedding ceremony, and later on after his toast, he continued to create space for Carrie to speak publicly by calling for her to give a speech at her own wedding, which she gladly did.

[287] Carrie Judd, 'Old Orchard Convention', *TF* 7.9 (Sept 1887), pp. 203-204; *idem*, 'Report of Christian Convention', *TF* 8.1 (Jan 1888), p. 4, and *idem*, *TF* 8.7 (July 1888), p. 167. In 1887, Carrie also listed herself as recording secretary for Simpson's Convention for Christian Life and Work and Divine Healing. Unity between the denominations and a desire to see Jesus only were also markers of this convention.

C&MA for more than twenty years'.[288] And because their early leaders believed that 'loyalty in the Christian Alliance does not mean loyalty to the Christian Alliance, but to Him who is the author of the Alliance, and to the Christian Alliance only as it breathes the very spirit of Christianity', her affiliation with them did not later inhibit her from becoming a part of other organizations like the Salvation Army.[289]

At one point Simpson even wanted Carrie to join his ministry in New York City. She might have said yes, but at that point in her life she already had her own growing healing ministry. Nevertheless, she continued to hold Christian Alliance meetings and stayed connected to Simpson even after her move to the West Coast. She also initiated and led the Buffalo Branch of the Christian Alliance and later established an Oakland Branch after her move.[290] She regularly invited Simpson to come out to California to speak at conferences, even seeking to 'detain him as long as possible for meetings on this Coast'.[291] Their friendship continued to endure the test of time, distance, and different denominational affiliations after her move.

While Simpson's theology of divine healing influenced Carrie, she also inspired and encouraged this influential leader in many ways as well. It was only after her healing home was established (April 1882) that Simpson also established his healing home (May 1883). Her writings also influenced him so much that he shared her articles with his readers. This demonstrates the impact she had on him personally as well as the level of respect he held for her and her theology. Simpson referred to Carrie as 'our beloved friend' in his magazine and consistently spoke kindly about her.[292] He even wrote a poem for her on her wedding day.[293] At a convention in Buffalo in

---

[288] King, *Genuine Gold*, p. 24.

[289] 'Christian Alliance', *Los Angeles Times*, June 2, 1896, p. 14.

[290] Carrie F. Judd, 'Report of the Christian Convention in Buffalo, NY', *TF* 5.11 (Nov 1885), pp. 241-42, and 'The Work and Workers', *TF* 11.10 (Oct. 1891), pp. 238-39; 'The Work at Home and Abroad. Christian Alliance Notes. List of Auxiliaries and Branches', *CAMW* 4.21 (May 23, 1890), p. 330; and 'The Work at Home: A Word from California', *CAMW* 7.14 (Oct 2, 1891), p. 221.

[291] Montgomery, 'The Work and the Workers', *TF* 13.2, p. 47.

[292] 'The Work in California', *CAMW* 5.9 (Sept 5, 1890), p. 130. Though not stated, this article was likely written by A.B. Simpson himself.

[293] Anna W. Prosser, 'Wedding Bells', *TF* 10.6 (June 1890), p. 122, and Montgomery, 'The Work and the Workers', *TF* 12.5 (May 1892), pp. 118-20. The po-

October 1885, he remarked that 'the work of Miss Carrie Judd had prepared the way for much blessing'. He further mentioned that the amount of prayer requests that came from all different places 'showed how far-reaching were the influences and the ramifications of this precious work'.[294]

Figure 8
Carrie with A.B. Simpson and some of the other founders or participants of the CMA (back row: Compton, A.B. Simpson, E.J. Richards, A.E. Funk, Christopherson. Front row, H. Dyke, Carrie Judd Montgomery, ?, Wm. N Ruhl)

While it is probable that Carrie still would have made an impact in the Divine Healing Movement without this connection, one must wonder how that impact was magnified by having people in her life like Simpson, who opened doors, created space, and encouraged her to take steps of faith. Their long friendship proved to be an important source of encouragement for both of them in their ministries and personal lives. The mutual respect and giving to one another of platforms, inspirations of healing homes, theologies of healing, and prayer times together helped to increase their influence in shaping the movement even further. Because Carrie played such

---

em he wrote on the train the night before her wedding was entitled 'To My Dear Friend Carrie Judd'.
[294] *The Word, Work and World* 5.11 (Nov 1885), p. 321.

an important role in Simpson's life, this also magnified her impact within the Divine Healing Movement as a whole.

2.4 A Tipping Point?

Carrie's early years proved to be formative and set a foundation for the rest of her life and ministry. Close to death, she chose to believe the promise found in James 5 and act in faith. Her 1879 healing account ignited a lifelong healing ministry. There were very few publicized healings and books on the theology of divine healing when Carrie had her 'miracle'. This made her story stand out and contributed to others also believing in the possibility that they and their loved ones could be healed. The timing of Carrie's healing and even the way in which it was accomplished was significant to her growing success in the Divine Healing Movement. Her testimony of healing and early literature opened up dialogue in relation to divine healing themes throughout North America and even into England. Her early healing homes also inspired many around the country to initiate similar homes.

In his *Tipping Point: How Little Things Can Make a Big Difference* (2000), Malcom Gladwell demonstrates that in movements or markets or cities, one experience or factor can cause a huge shift. He tells the story of how in Micronesia, the suicide rate in the 1960s was relatively nil. All of a sudden, the rate began to increase rapidly so much so that by the 1980s there were more suicides per capita on the island than anywhere else on the globe. Gladwell looks into what changed this rate so dramatically. He located Rubinstein's research which found that there was a 17 year old boy named Sima who got into a minor argument with his father and therefore decided to end his life through hanging. Ever since then, merely because teenage boys liked to experiment with things extreme, many heard of Sima's example and followed it. Thus, the suicide rate skyrocketed on the island.[295]

---

[295] Malcom Gladwell, *The Tipping Point: How Little Things Can Make a Big Difference* (New York, Boston, London: Back Bay Books/ Little Brown and Company, 2000, 2002), pp. 216-20. The story of Sima comes from anthropologist Donald H. Rubinstein in several of his papers: 'Love and Suffering: Adolescent Socialization and Suicide in Micronesia', *Contemporary Pacific* 7.1 (Spring 1995), pp. 21-53, and 'Epidemic Suicide Among Micronesian Adolescents', *Social Science and Medicine* 17 (1983), p. 664.

Carrie's experience had a similar effect to Sima's, except that instead of advocating death through hanging, she advocated life through healing. People saw that if she could act in faith and be healed, then they could too. She acted as a model that gave people permission to believe in healing and to act in faith. Gladwell's book also records a study done in by sociologist David Phillips, who looked at the effects that front page suicide stories from *Los Angeles Times* and the *San Francisco Chronicle* had on suicide rates in the area. He found that in the ten days following these newspaper headlines, the suicide rates rose anywhere from 3.1 percent to 8.1 percent in the towns studied.[296] The fact that Carrie's healing story was spread in newspapers gave rise to healing becoming more prominent, more accepted, more sought after than it had been before. The key thing to look at here is that shortly after Carrie's healing encounter, there was a sharp increase in healing literature, healing homes, healing outbreaks, and healing perspectives within Evangelical Christianity. Carrie's healing account and the way in which her healing was publicized acted as a catalyst, or a 'tipping point', for divine healing and its movement to go from relatively unknown and emerging, to widespread and controversial.

Carrie advanced her healing ministry without regard to the gender, social, or religious norms of the day. Knowingly or unknowingly, she also contributed to paving the way for future female healing evangelists to come after her. Not only was the timing of Carrie's healing crucial for her own success in becoming a prominent writer, healing evangelist, and opening up healing homes, but her healing account and ministry also functioned as a 'tipping point' for the expansion of the Divine Healing Movement. Her early literature also helped to shift theologies and spread healing themes globally. Further, Carrie was not just a 'Radical Evangelical' who spread an unpopular message, but she also acted as prophetic pioneer to the leaders within the Divine Healing Movement. Because of her unique and timely contributions, Carrie was one of the most influential people involved in the North American Divine Healing Movement.

---

[296] Gladwell, *The Tipping Point*, pp. 222-23, based on David Phillip's paper, 'The Influence of Suggestion on Suicide: Substantive and Theoretical Implications of the Werther Effect', *American Sociological Review* 39 (1974), pp. 340-54.

3

TRANSITIONING INTO A PENTECOSTAL AMBASSADOR

Carrie's early healing experience set a foundation for her life and ministry within the Divine Healing Movement, but how did it position her for early Pentecostalism? While the previous chapter emphasized Carrie's influence within the Divine Healing Movement, this chapter will examine her life preceding and then intersecting the Pentecostal Movement. New York was where she proved to be a catalyst in the Divine Healing Movement, but the winds started to change in 1890 when they blew her to California. This specific year in her life will be highlighted because of the significant transitions she experienced which impacted her life and ministry from that time on. Following this, a look at the expansion of her West Coast ministries will be developed. The second half of the chapter will begin within the context of the Azusa Street Revival and from there explore Carrie's process in approaching the Pentecostal Spirit baptism. An analysis of her 1909 missionary journey will also be presented. A few more famous women healing evangelists will provide the framework in tracing the second half of Carrie's life, beginning with the year 1890 when she was 32 years old, and will mainly focus on her life up to 1920. The key questions that will be asked are: What role did Carrie's earlier ministry endeavors play in building a platform within the Pentecostal Movement? And what impact did her 1908 experience have for the early Pentecostal Movement?

3.1 Year of Transitions: 1890

Several significant things happened in Carrie's life during 1890, making it a crucial time for widening her ministry. In the midst of speaking nationally on the subject of divine healing, Carrie's heart began to sing a new song; in the summer of 1889, she met businessman George Montgomery for the very first time.[1] He invited her to speak at a conference in San Francisco, California and while she was there, she came across Maria Woodworth's ministry. Upon her return to Buffalo in the spring of 1890, Carrie and George were married. During the months that followed, Carrie found herself permanently relocated to the West Coast and was also introduced to the Salvation Army for the first time. We will now take a closer look at these transitions.

3.1.1 Intersections with Elizabeth Sisson and Maria Woodworth-Etter

Leading up to her connection with Maria Woodworth, Carrie had already been a strong advocate for women in ministry through her actions. She encouraged women to open healing homes, provided space for them to have a voice in her periodical, and also partnered with them in ministry. Carrie influenced Elizabeth Sisson (1843-1934) in this way. While originally from Connecticut, Sisson received her sanctification experience under Boardman's ministry and then served in India as a Congregational missionary. When she was on the mission field, she became ill and consequently sought out Boardman's ministry in London again, this time in search of physical healing. While at the Bethshan healing home, she was healed of an 'incurable disease'.[2] It appears that Carrie met Elizabeth after already being acquainted with her younger sister, Charlotte (Lottie) W. Sisson, who was healed while at Carrie's Faith Rest in Buffalo in 1883.[3] It was likely through the connection with Lottie that Carrie

---

[1] Judd, 'The Work and the Workers', *TF* 9.7 (July 1889), pp. 163-65, and Hardesty, *Faith Cure*, p. 45.

[2] Hardesty, *Faith Cure,* pp. 22, 63.

[3] Charlotte (Lottie) Sisson (1849-1934) was healed of an illness she contracted while doing missions work in India. Later, Lottie joined the CMA (she is listed as one of the Vice Presidents in *CAMW* 4.11 [April 4, 1890]), and she was also one of Dr Cullis' missionaries. Carrie was at Lottie's sending service at Dr Cullis' church in Boston and also at her boat dock singing and farewell (Judd, 'Faith-Work', *TF* 3.2 [Feb 1883], pp. 32-34, and Carrie Judd, 'Faith Missionaries', *TF* 4.2

began printing some of Elizabeth Sisson's articles beginning in May 1884.[4] In 1887, Sisson moved from England to Chicago and began spreading the divine healing message. By 1888, she became Carrie's assistant editor and accompanied her to several conferences.[5]

It was during their three month trip to the West Coast from late 1889 until February 1890 that they encountered Woodworth's ministry for the first time. Maria Woodworth-Etter (1844-1924) was a healing evangelist who started her ministry in Ohio in 1880. After she married Philo Harris Woodworth, she experienced great tragedy when six of her seven children died at different times. She reluctantly began to pray for the sick in 1885 after she claimed that she heard God call her to the healing ministry. She preached to crowds of over 25,000 and was even dubbed the 'Trance Evangelist' because of the powerful manifestations people experienced under her ministry.[6] Some scholars believe that she was a precursor, forerunner, or even grandmother to the Pentecostal Movement.[7]

When Carrie and Sisson arrived in the San Francisco area, they were immediately told about the revival under Woodworth's ministry. Carrie was so impressed by these large meetings (consisting of around 2,000-3,000 people) that she even canceled some of her own speaking engagements in order to attend. She reported:

> Although we have ourselves begun work in a Methodist Church in San Francisco, holding afternoon meetings each day, we have felt so impressed with the Holy Ghost power in these Oakland meetings, and have so realized blessing to our own souls through them, that the present leading of the Lord for us is to attend

---

[Feb 1884], p. 35). An endearing picture of Carrie leaning on Lottie is available at <http://ifphc.org>. Carrie also printed some of their articles in *Triumphs of Faith*, more of Elizabeth's than Lottie's. They also traveled at different times with Carrie. One of Lottie's articles entitled 'Importunity or Progressive Prayer' appeared in *TF* 21.12 (Dec 1901), pp. 273-75.

4 Elizabeth Sisson, 'Notes on Acts IV:32', *TF* 4.5 (May 1884), pp. 111-12.

5 'Report of Recent Meetings; New York convention, etc', *TF* 8.11 (Nov 1888), pp. 257-58; Elizabeth Sisson, 'The Holy Ghost and Fire', *LRE* 1.8 (May 1909), pp. 6-10, reprint. One would give a talk in the morning and the other in the evening service. See also, Carrie F. Judd, 'The Work and the Workers', *TF* 10.1 (Jan 1890), pp. 19-23.

6 Wayne Warner, 'Maria B. Woodworth-Etter and the Early Pentecostal Movement', *AGH* 6.4 (Winter 1986-87), pp. 11-14.

7 Wayne E. Warner, 'Maria Beulah Woodworth-Etter', in *NIDPCM*, pp. 1211-13.

Mrs. Woodworth's meetings, and to listen to the fervent Gospel messages poured through her by the Holy Ghost.[8]

Woodworth recognized Carrie in the meetings and used Carrie's reputation to help endorse her ministry against critics. Wayne Warner notes that 'in defending the practice of falling under the power, Woodworth told an *Examiner* reporter that "Sister Judd, the great divine healer, who came out here from New York, has been under the power several times since these meetings began"'.[9] By using Carrie's experience to defend her own ministry, Woodworth demonstrated the level of influence that Carrie had during that time with other female healing evangelists.

In the February 1890 edition of her periodical, Carrie wrote that Woodworth's meetings had expanded so much that they had a tent that could hold up to 8,000 people. She said that there was much opposition to Woodworth's work and that it was to be 'expected where the apostolic spirit and the apostolic power are being revived'.[10] In the early days of the meetings, Carrie appeared to be open to whatever was going on 'in the Spirit' regardless of the controversy surrounding Woodworth's ministry. Carrie's silence over Woodworth's ministry in her March 1890 periodical may have been a result of her trying to process the controversies and rumors in relation to the prophecy given by Erickson, who was affiliated with Woodworth's ministry. Erickson believed and publicly proclaimed that San Francisco and Oakland would experience destruction in the form of an earthquake and tidal wave on April 14, 1890.[11] This did not come to pass on that date.[12] Carrie's public silence on the subject bought her more time to process Woodworth's ministry. During this time, her transitioning outlook went from a supportive and positive stance of Woodworth's ministry to a cautious and questioning one.

---

[8] Judd, 'The Work and the Workers', *TF* 10.1, pp. 21-22.

[9] Maria Woodworth, San Francisco *Examiner* (Jan. 9, 1890); quoted in Warner, *Maria Woodworth-Etter: For Such a Time as This*, pp. 111-12.

[10] Carrie F. Judd, 'The Work and the Workers', *TF* 10.2 (Feb 1890), p. 44.

[11] Carrie F. Judd, 'The Work and the Workers', *TF* 10.4 (April 1890), p. 91. The prophecy caused up to 1,000 people to evacuate and move to higher ground. See Warner, 'Maria Beulah Woodworth-Etter', pp. 1211-13. There is no first name recorded for Erickson.

[12] Woodworth-Etter and others later tied the San Francisco earthquake of 1906 to Erickson's prophecy.

In her April 1890 periodical, Carrie suggested that the trouble surrounding Erickson's prophecy was the 'enemy's' opposition against the work that Woodworth was doing in the city. Carrie distinguished and separated Woodworth from Erickson when she wrote that 'we understand that Mrs. Woodworth is not responsible for these prophecies'.[13] Shortly thereafter, Carrie started to disassociate herself from Woodworth's ministry because she concluded that the meetings were tainted by 'Satan'. As she pulled back, her associate editor, Elizabeth Sisson, stepped forward to join Woodworth's ministry.

By the May 1890 edition of *Triumphs of Faith*, Sisson was no longer Carrie's associate editor, possibly leaving because of some disagreement with Carrie over Erickson's San Francisco earthquake prophecy. Carrie announced this to her readers:

> By mutual consent on the part of the Editor and the Associate Editor the latter now withdraws from her editorial position on this Journal, but we hope to publish occasional articles from her pen. Great trial has come to our dear sister, Miss Sisson, through her connection with those later Oakland meetings, from which issued the false prophecies made by Erickson and others in regard to the destruction of Oakland and San Francisco on April 14th. We are sure that God will overrule all to His glory, and to the good of His faithful child, and that He would not have suffered this great trial of Satan's deception to come to her, without purposes of great love and mercy in His heart toward her.[14]

Sisson even admitted that there may have been a 'lying spirit intermixed' with the work of God in that place. In this same public statement printed in *Triumphs of Faith*, Sisson confessed that she felt like she was left on the 'battlefield', beaten down, and waiting for the 'smoke of battle' to clear in relation to Woodworth's ministry so that she could discern what was from God and what was not.[15] Both Carrie and Sisson referred to the 'later' Oakland meetings in a more negative sense.

Several months after this trying incident, in her September 1890 issue, Carrie reflected negatively in regards to Woodworth's meet-

---

[13] Judd, 'The Work and the Workers', *TF* 10.4, p. 91.
[14] Judd, 'The Work and the Workers', *TF* 10.5, p. 116.
[15] Judd, 'The Work and the Workers', *TF* 10.5, p. 116.

ings. At this point in time, after seeing the results of the havoc caused by Erickson's prophecy, Carrie was decidedly against Woodworth's work. Carrie interpreted that Woodworth was more focused on 'power' than on Jesus and explained,

> [W]e are obliged to alter our opinions somewhat to believe that there must have been something radically wrong with Mrs. Woodworth's teachings and methods of work ... our present convictions are that the great mistake in her work lies in the exaltation of 'the power' above *Jesus Himself.* Her teachings create a tendency on the part of the people to seek to obtain 'power' as an abstract thing, instead of seeking Jesus Himself as the power for service.[16]

While Carrie was initially positive about Woodworth's ministry, controversies caused her to change her opinion a few months later. One of the reasons for this drastic change may have been linked to the realities that during this time Carrie was in heightened emotional states. During these same months of attempting to discern Woodworth's ministry, Carrie got married and then shortly after, her father passed away. In addition to emotional extremes she experienced in her personal life at that time, Carrie also had to deal with the loss of her assistant editor in the midst of all this.

The disagreement over Woodworth's ministry brought tension and strain to her friendship with Sisson. Following the June 1890 edition of her periodical where Carrie printed an article by Sisson, there was a long period of public silence between the two of them. Ten years later, in March of 1900, Carrie went to one of Sisson's meetings in San Jose, California and the public silence was broken.[17] In October 1901, Carrie began to publish Sisson's articles again.[18] Sisson later participated in Carrie's 1914 camp meeting. Sisson continued to travel and hold meetings throughout North America and

---

[16] Montgomery, 'The Work and the Workers', *TF* 10.9 (Sept 1890), p. 213.

[17] Carrie Judd Montgomery, *Date Book for 1900: Handwritten Diary*, March 9, October 7-8. In October of the same year, she hosted Sisson during one of her speaking engagements on the West Coast.

[18] Her debut article after the break was entitled 'A Story about Teeth', by Elizabeth Sisson *TF* 21.10 (Oct 1901), pp. 238-39. When Carrie was on her trip to New England in 1909, she wrote in her personal journal that she 'came to New London ... to see Miss Sisson and Lottie ... It seemed so good to see Lizzie [Elizabeth] and Lottie again ... We had a precious season of prayer together' (Carrie Judd Montgomery, *Date Book for 1909: Handwritten Diary,* July 29).

even throughout Britain, many times accompanied by her sister Charlotte W. Sisson. She toured Texas with F.F. Bosworth and was a friend to Aimee Semple McPherson.[19] She later joined the Pentecostal Movement and was even one of the keynote speakers at the fifth General Council of the Assemblies of God in 1917.[20] Years after the Woodworth controversy had passed, Carrie and Sisson continued to travel in similar circles and share platforms throughout their Pentecostal years.[21]

It is also important to note that nearly twenty years after her initial opposition to Woodworth-Etter's ministry, Carrie later reconciled with Woodworth-Etter and her methods.[22] By 1909, Carrie had become a supporter of Woodworth-Etter's ministry again and even a personal friend. In 1912, Carrie attended several of her meetings in Dallas, Texas. By that point, Carrie's confidence in Woodworth-Etter's ministry was restored and she thought very highly of her command of faith. She wrote that 'we have never seen anyone else rebuke demons and disease with such Heaven-sent authority and power'. She saw that the power of God was present in Woodworth-Etter's meetings 'convicting and converting sinners, healing sick bodies and baptizing saints with the Holy Ghost'. Carrie also noticed that 'When they come to [Woodworth-Etter] with more desire for physical healing than for spiritual healing she refuses to pray for the healing of their bodies until their souls come into right relations with God'. This pattern was also in line with many of the leaders in the Divine Healing Movement like Simpson, who had the tendency to teach about spiritual wholeness and call people to conversion before teaching about physical healing. Likely a new approach in prayer for Carrie, Woodworth-Etter also ordered demons to depart. Carrie recognized 'that Mrs. Etter teaches healing in the Atonement (in the same way that we were taught by the Holy Spirit Himself many years ago)' and also that she encouraged people to press on for more power to do miracles and to 'come under the

---

[19] Mrs E.M. Whittemore, 'Healed and Filled With the Spirit', *TF* 39.1 (Jan 1919), pp. 7-9. In this article, Whittemore mentions attending Aimee S. McPherson's Philadelphia convention after receiving a letter from Lizzie (Elizabeth) Sisson urging her to go. Sisson and McPherson prayed for her and she was healed.

[20] Hardesty, *Faith Cure*, p. 109.

[21] Carrie Judd Montgomery, 'An Eastern Trip in the Lord's Work', *TF* 39.1 (Jan 1919), pp. 12-17.

[22] Woodworth got married in the early 1900s to Samuel Etter.

power'. Carrie observed at one of the meetings that 'the power of God often prostrates them, and even little children are seen "under the power," apparently unconscious to all but God, and with their little faces shining like angels'.[23]

By 1913, Carrie began to share the stage with Woodworth-Etter at camp meetings and other services.[24] Woodworth-Etter even came out to Oakland to work with Carrie before going to minister in San Jose.[25] As Carrie continued to observe her friend's ministry, she was struck by how easily Woodworth-Etter could captivate her audience by speaking for an hour at a time. Carrie noticed that in addition to many who were converted and received their 'Pentecostal baptism', Woodworth-Etter even 'commanded the deaf demons to come out of [a girl's] ears in the Name of Jesus'.[26] Carrie retracted her earlier belief about Woodworth-Etter pointing to herself rather than to Jesus. With a change in heart, Carrie grew in support of Woodworth-Etter's ministry by announcing her camp meetings along with printing several of her articles in *Triumphs of Faith*.[27] In 1917, Carrie even referred to Woodworth-Etter as having the 'gift of healing' which was the first out of only a few times she ever mentioned healing in this way and the only time she connected it to a person.[28]

---

[23] Carrie Judd Montgomery, 'The Mighty Power of God at Dallas, Texas', *TF* 32.12 (Dec 1912), pp. 268-69.

[24] 'World-Wide Camp Meeting in Connecticut', *TF* 33.2 (Feb 1913), p. 48. See also announcement for Apostolic Camp meeting in Connecticut June 1913 in 'Pentecostal Items', *Confidence* 3.6 (March 1913), p. 61.

[25] 'Mrs. Woodworth-Etter's Meetings, and Her Book', *Confidence* 6.4 (April 1913), pp. 72-73, 76-77.

[26] Carrie Judd Montgomery, 'Mrs. Etter's Meetings in Oakland', *TF* 33.3 (March 1913), p. 60.

[27] 'Divine Healing and Signs and Wonders to Lead the People to Christ: Extract of a Sermon by Mrs. Woodworth-Etter. (From Her New Book, Acts of the Holy Ghost.)', *TF* 33.3 (March 1913), pp. 62-64; and also '"Notice. Dedication of Woodworth Etter Tabernacle" in Indianapolis, Indiana' in *TF* 38.5 (May 1918), p. 118.

[28] Carrie Judd Montgomery, 'Precious Revival Meeting in San Francisco', *TF* 37.1 (Jan 1917), p. 20. Following a story of a woman who was healed of swelling in her feet at one of the Etter's meetings but who was surprised when the day after she was actually healed, Carrie wrote, 'showing that her own faith had not been perfect, and yet she had been receptive, and yielded to God, and so had been able to receive healing through the "gift of healing", which it is quite evident God has given Mrs. Etter'. Several years earlier in an announcement by an unknown author, 'Apostolic Faith World-Wide Camp Meeting' (in Los Angeles), *TF* 33.2 (Feb 1913), p. 46, Woodworth-Etter was also referred to as having this gift. The only other time Carrie specifically wrote about the gift of healing was in 'Di-

Despite a rough start, these three healing evangelists eventually came together in mutual support of one another. Part of the initial separation that Carrie experienced with both Woodworth-Etter and Sisson may have been in relation to their being more prepared for Pentecostalism to burst upon the scene while Carrie was still hesitant. While Carrie reconciled with Sisson earlier on, her change of heart in regard to Woodworth-Etter came only after her 1908 tongues experience. Carrie's friendship with Woodworth-Etter continued to grow over the years. When George was ill in 1914, Woodworth-Etter sent Carrie a letter saying that she received the witness from God that he would live. She committed to pray for him and in turn, she also requested prayer for herself and those in her ministry that 'we may with all boldness and authority command all devils to depart in the Name of Jesus'.[29] These three women represent the old guard of living in the midst of the Holiness and Divine Healing Movements and crossing over and taking some of those similar themes into Pentecostal circles. Carrie's place in this will be explored later.

3.1.2 Businessman George Montgomery

George Simpson Montgomery (1851-1930) was born on January 14, 1851 in Northern Ireland to Scottish Presbyterian parents. By 1890, he was said 'to be worth considerably over a million [dollars]'.[30] Like Carrie, he came from a family of eight children. George moved to California when he was in his mid teens. When he grew older, he prospered in mining in Mexico before he returned to San Francisco and became a successful broker.[31] It was on one of his trips to Mexico that he contracted fevers that led to diabetes. In 1888, George went to Japan to have a good time as well as to improve his declining health. His life at that time had been all about 'worldly business

vine Healing in the Book of Proverbs', *TF* 61.9 (Sept 1941), p. 194. More in relation to the gift of healing will be discussed in 4.4.3.

[29] M.B. Woodworth-Etter, 'Letter's from God's Saints', *TF* 34.6 (June 1914), p. 137.

[30] *Express*, May 18, 1890. His parent's were Hugh Montgomery and Jane Moneypenny (her maiden name) (taken from *Montgomery Family* tree, used with permission and courtesy of the Berry family).

[31] 'Home of Peace of Oakland History', <http://homeofpeace.com/history.asp/> accessed January 26, 2009. He also lost his fortune at one point before his conversion and considered suicide by putting a gun to his head. See also Stock, 'George S. Montgomery: Businessman for the Gospel', pp. 4-5, 17-18; and *TF* 9.2 (Summer, 1989), pp. 12-14, 20.

and pleasure' rather than following God.[32] During his trip, he visited several Buddhist and Shinto temples and even bought some
charms from a Buddhist priest to protect him from being shipwrecked.[33] During this voyage, he was alone in his room one night

Figure 9
George Montgomery

and felt the Spirit of God nudge him yet again, and this time he
claimed he heard God say it was the last time He would call him.
He responded by kneeling down and confessing his need for Jesus.
After that night his aim changed from pursuing worldly pleasures,

---

[32] George S. Montgomery, 'What God Hath Wrought!', *TF* 12.12 (Dec 1892),
p. 265.

[33] George S. Montgomery, *Personal Pocketbook Journal* (Sept-Dec 1888), Nov. 3,
1888, used with permission and courtesy from the Berry family. He wrote that he
bought 'charms which the priest a Buddha [a Buddhist priest] said would always
protect me while I carried it at sea from storms or being shipwrecked'.

'to live in the glory of God, and to win precious souls for Him'.[34] Soon after this event and while still on his journey, he went to an American church and noted that the pastor 'spoke very well'. George recalled that he was pleased to meet 'Christians once more who worship the true God – and who lift up the name of Jesus as the only way of salvation'.[35] So while he went to Japan seeking physical health, he received 'spiritual help' instead.

Upon his return home, George continued to struggle with declining health. He consulted physicians but found no relief and only grew worse. He was weakened to the point that the doctors told him he was going to die soon. He later reflected,

> I was quite resigned to die, because I was resting in the finished work of Christ [at this point only for his salvation, not for his healing]. I did not know anything about Divine Healing until one of my physicians in San Francisco came to me and related some marvelous cures which had taken place among his patients, in answer to prayer.[36]

The Christian doctor told him that he believed it to be the hand of God doing divine healings. George still had doubts though and remembered, 'I did not believe, very much, for I thought that the days of miracles were past'.[37] His physician friend however, was persistent and returned another time to convince him of these truths, this time bringing Bible verses to back it up.

Initially, George was concerned that the physician was influenced by Spiritualism or Christian Science, but as George became convinced that the Holy Spirit had become his 'Teacher' and taught him what some specific texts meant, he said, 'I saw that I had no more foundation in God's Word for the salvation of my soul, than I

---

[34] Montgomery, 'What God Hath Wrought!', p. 266.

[35] G. Montgomery, *Personal Pocketbook Journal*, Nov. 4, 1888. There is a possibility that he had his conversion experience the night of November 3, 1888 in between the time he bought Buddhist charms and when he went to a Christian church, which was likely a United Church as he noticed a very mixed crowd of Episcopal, Presbyterians, and Methodists. By November 25 he went to another church and also a prayer meeting and 'was glad to hear the gospel proclaimed as it was'. The pastor spoke out of Matthew 6.6.

[36] Montgomery, 'What God Hath Wrought!', p. 266.

[37] Montgomery, 'What God Hath Wrought!', p. 266. The doctor's name was George Smith.

had for the healing of my body'.[38] His physician convinced him to attend some meetings held in Oakland by John Alexander Dowie in 1888. Dowie personally prayed for him there and George remembered having

> no special manifestation at the time, but ... The next morning I realized the new life which had been imparted, and felt as though I could run like a boy, although before this I had been scarcely able to walk up the stairs ... Health and strength returned, and I was not only healed of Diabetes, but also of chronic rheumatism, which had troubled me for many years and had greatly crippled me at times.[39]

Because of his healing, he chose to honor his earlier commitment to win souls and to live for 'God's glory'. Not long after this, he came across Carrie's ministry. In June of 1889, while Carrie was speaking in Chicago at one of Simpson's meetings, George noticed her.[40] Shortly after their first introduction, he organized a conference on the West Coast for Carrie to come and spread the news of divine healing there. After Carrie's visit, which was the same one where she encountered Woodworth-Etter's ministry for the first time, George went out to Buffalo to meet the Judd family on Carrie's birthday, April 8, 1890.[41]

The paths of these two healed ones aligned and merged a month later on May 14, 1890 in Buffalo. Carrie's local pastor Reverend C.F. Wrigley of St. Mary's Episcopal Church, along with the assistance of Simpson, officiated their wedding ceremony. It was reported that they entered the ceremony standing directly under a 'white dove suspended in mid air'.[42] This symbol of peace later became a

---

[38] Montgomery, 'What God Hath Wrought!', pp. 266-67. The specific texts he looked at were Exod. 15.26, 23.25; Deut. 7.15; Jas 5.14-15; and Mk 11.24.

[39] Montgomery, 'What God Hath Wrought!', p. 267.

[40] Judd, 'The Work and the Workers', *TF* 9.7, p. 118; 'All For the Poor: Rich Salvationists to Work in the Slums of New York: Romantic Story of a Couple', *Middletown Daily Press*, April 12, 1892, p. 1; and Hardesty, *Faith Cure*, p. 45. Western Springs was a suburb of Chicago. Montgomery had a 6'1" stature.

[41] Montgomery, *Under His Wings: The Story of My Life*, p. 132. George was affirmed to Carrie by her father because of his gentleness. Years later, Carrie realized that 'gentleness' was one of his most beautiful traits while at the same time she said 'he had a corresponding strength of character which made him very firm when necessary'.

[42] *Buffalo Express*, May 18, 1890.

significant sign in the naming of their Home of Peace.[43] Even though Carrie's father was weak, he was carried into the wedding room and placed in a chair near the front so he could take part in the ceremony. Shortly after the Montgomerys set out on their honeymoon trip, however, they received some sad news. On May 24, 1890, Carrie's father (at 70 years old) had died.[44] The Montgomerys quickly came home to be with the family during that time. After several weeks, the newly married Montgomerys eventually ventured towards the west once again, ministering to people along the way. Carrie's continuing ministry was a relief to some of her friends who initially feared that her marrying might compromise her ministry. John Salmon, who was influential in the Christian and Missionary Alliance and a friend of Carrie's, wrote,

> Some of us feared that when Sister Carrie got married that she would practically be shelved, as so many ladies are; but I was glad to see that by her marriage her work had been more widely extended; her dear husband having entered heartily into the work of the Lord with his beloved wife.[45]

The surprise of having George in her life would indeed be a key factor 'widely extending' her ministry.[46]

3.1.3 Temperature Change: California

Shortly after her wedding and her father's death, Carrie ventured out to San Francisco for what initially was intended to be a few months.[47] The Montgomerys' trip to the west became a mixture of

---

[43] Anna W. Prosser, 'Wedding Bells', *TF* 10.6 (June 1890), p. 121. Wearing a simple white wedding dress, Carrie, 32 years old, walked down the aisle with a bouquet of her favorite flowers, lilies of the valley. The verse they chose to have printed on their wedding invitations was Jn 2.2, 'And both Jesus was called and His disciples to the marriage'. Their wedding was also in Carrie's Buffalo home and their reception in the very same room where Carrie experienced her healing.

[44] Carrie Judd Montgomery, 'Gone Home', *TF* 10.7 (July 1890), records that he 'died at his residence, 260 Connecticut st., Buffalo, NY, Saturday, May 24, 1890, Orvan K. Judd, aged seventy years, three months, and six days' (p. 145). He was married a total of 42 years at that point. He died in the same room where Carrie was healed. Carrie later remembered that those who came to comfort her mother went away more comforted themselves.

[45] John Salmon, 'Alliance Work in the Home Field', *The Christian and Missionary Alliance* 24.22 (June 10, 1905), p. 365.

[46] *TF* 12.12 (Dec 1892), includes a picture of George.

[47] At that time she was still trying to save money to get a permanent Faith Rest home in Buffalo. Carrie Judd Montgomery, 'Present Outlook of Our Work',

honeymoon, exploration, and ministry opportunities along the way where they connected with people from the Divine Healing Movement throughout their journey. One of the main highlights of Carrie's honeymoon trip had to do with the conversion of a young girl at one of her meetings. Writing of this account, Carrie celebrated, 'I have always praised God for this soul which he gave me on my wedding trip, rejoicing that in the midst of my great happiness God kept me true to Him, and had enabled me to make the interests of His Kingdom first'.[48] Even on her honeymoon, Carrie's focus was in helping those around her be converted to Christianity and receive healing.

Carrie continued to speak and minister with a very busy schedule in various conventions and churches along the way as they journeyed west.[49] Exploring 'God's creation', the Montgomerys also visited Yellowstone National Park. They attempted to have a Bible reading with some of the people there, but Carrie wrote that they 'waited with open Bible for the audience that did not come ... At two of the other hotels in the park, however, we held meetings with

---

TF 10.7 (July 1890), pp. 147-48. Miss Mattie A. Stein was left in charge of the home while Carrie was away.

[48] Montgomery, *Under His Wings,* p. 135. She later printed Katie Murray's (the young girl's) thank you letter in Montgomery, 'The Work and the Workers', *TF* 10.7, pp. 167-68.

[49] Here is an example of Carrie's busy speaking schedule. They arrived in the Chicago area June 21, 1890, where the Convocation of Christian workers was taking place. From there they went to St. Paul in Minnesota at someone's urgent request, where she held a two day conference at someone's home on July 3-4. That Sunday she gave a Bible reading at the People's Church in Minneapolis, which was an 'undenominational Faith Mission'. This church had lost support because it did not want to comply with banning the teaching on 'full Sanctification or Divine Healing' (Carrie Judd Montgomery, 'The Work and the Workers', *TF* 10.8 [Aug 1890], p. 188). From there they then went to the Central Park Methodist Church in St. Paul on Sunday afternoon and gave testimonies of the Lord's healing followed by a consecration meeting. Carrie spoke at the Christian Alliance Convention at Round Lake, NY on July 13-20, 1890. After sharing her testimony of healing there, she was invited to speak at a Methodist Episcopal Church nearby where a Presbyterian church also joined in. During the convention, the New York State Branch of the Alliance was organized. George Montgomery was listed as one of the executive committee members and Carrie one of the vice presidents of the state alliance (Carrie Judd Montgomery, 'Convention at Round Lake, NY', *TF* 10.9 [Sept 1890], p. 216). There were 22 total vice presidents. The Buffalo branch was already formed three years earlier as is recorded in Anna W. Prosser, 'The Work the Christian Alliance in Buffalo, NY', *TF* 10.10 (Oct 1890), pp. 227-28.

the waiters, a number of them giving their hearts to Jesus'.[50] They also connected with a young Roman Catholic woman and were excited to share the gospel with her. After a somewhat eventful and ministry filled honeymoon journey, they finally arrived in California.

There, Carrie quickly became involved in ministry by speaking to several hundred prisoners at San Quentin prison near San Francisco. In the city, even though she still had her Buffalo work, Carrie also had begun weekly parlor meetings that were beginning to grow. These 'consecration meetings' took place every Thursday at 3:00 pm and were 'undenominational' and open to everyone.[51] She eventually outgrew the location and had to move the meetings to a Baptist church nearby. By November of 1890, Carrie ended the meetings because she felt like their purpose had been fulfilled and that the people would go back to their home churches and spread the good news of the 'full Gospel'.[52] Carrie opened up a children's Bible class Saturday afternoons at her house in San Francisco and also continued to receive more and more invitations to speak at nearby churches.[53] She spoke on divine healing and other truths of the Fourfold Gospel while at the Christian Convention in Oakland that same year. Additionally, Carrie established a Sunday school for neglected children at the People's Mission. She admitted that it was tough reaching the kids there at first because they would threaten her with 'stones and blows' to intimidate her.[54] She persisted and the meetings continued on throughout the year.

For much of 1890, Carrie was still possibly looking at returning to Buffalo to continue her work there. Towards the end of the year, however, the Montgomerys decided to relocate permanently to

---

[50] Montgomery, 'The Work and the Workers', *TF* 10.8, p. 190.

[51] Montgomery, 'The Work and the Workers', *TF* 10.11 (Nov 1890), pp. 256-58.

[52] In reference to Simpson's Fourfold Gospel (Montgomery, 'The Work and the Workers', *TF* 10.12 [Dec 1890], pp. 280-81).

[53] Brother A. Coplin, editor of a Holiness paper called *The Christian Evangelist*, invited Carrie and George to speak at his church. On September 14, 1890, Carrie was also invited to speak at First Methodist Episcopalian Church. See also her 'The Work and the Workers', *TF* 10.10 (Oct 1890), p. 232.

[54] Montgomery, 'The Work and the Workers', *TF* 10.11, p. 257. She was likely partnering with people in the CMA and other volunteers at the mission in her initial street work there.

Oakland and set up their ministry there.[55] Their first and only child, Faith, was born on May 25, 1891, and their West Coast healing home was finished in 1893.[56] Through this pioneering move to settle in California, Carrie was among the earliest to spread the doctrine of the Divine Healing Movement to the West Coast. It was also around this time that Carrie intersected with the Salvation Army.

3.1.4 The Salvation Army

Before George got connected to the Salvation Army, he admitted that at first he was uncomfortable with their methods for reaching people for Christ. Their founder, William Booth (1829-1912), started this ministry as a Methodist minister in 1852 when he sought to reach the poor, hungry, and homeless in London. He also went on evangelistic tours to spread the Gospel even further. By 1865, his outreach work continued to expand under the name the Christian Mission, which eventually was changed to the Salvation Army (in 1878).[57] His wife, Catherine Booth (1829-1890), was influential for women in ministry and even wrote a pamphlet called *Female Ministry, or Women's Right to Preach the Gospel* (1859).

It was when George was traveling on a boat and speaking with a member of the Salvation Army that his earlier perception of them changed. While the two were talking, a 'poor, miserable-looking man' approached George's acquaintance and asked if there was any help for someone like him. The Army officer then proceeded to direct him to Christ. As their boat approached the dock, George recalled,

---

[55] Initially, all of Carrie's correspondence continued to be sent to Buffalo. In her periodical, Carrie even continued to write about her Faith Rest Home and the need for money to get a permanent home there. By her October 1890 issue of *Triumphs of Faith*, however, the periodical address was changed from her previous Buffalo residence to her temporary San Francisco address. This demonstrates that at this point she had relocated more permanently than she had originally thought. The Montgomerys later relocated from 1201 Bush Street, San Francisco to Oakland and settled on a large piece of land there, also building a home nearby at 3835 Buell Street (then Orchard Street) for Carrie's mother, 'Grandma Judd'.

[56] For the most part, they continued living there until 1910 when Carrie's mother died. Following this event, they moved back into her mother's old home. This information is taken from an undated typed document with a picture of both George and Carrie, 'Caroline (Carrie) Frances Judd Montgomery' accessed and used with permission of the Home of Peace.

[57] 'The Salvation Army: History', <http://www.salvationarmyusa.org> accessed January 8, 2011.

[I]n the midst of that crowd ['the poor, miserable-looking man'] dropped on his knees and prayed, weeping like a child. All of a sudden light came into his face like a burst of sunshine, and he rose and gave to the hundreds who had gathered around him a testimony that touched many of them visibly.[58]

They later found out that the man had previously been considering suicide. George was struck that day by the influence the Salvation Army officer had just by wearing his uniform in public.

Carrie was introduced to the Salvation Army through her husband.[59] Her first major interaction with their ministry came during the early part of her honeymoon trip while in Boston. The Montgomerys attended the Tenth Annual Gathering of the Salvation Army where they met Ballington Booth, the Commander of the Salvation Army forces in America at that time and one of the founder's sons. Carrie was impressed with all the good work for the proclamation the Gospel that these workers had 'surrendered' their lives to do.[60] She also identified an 'apostolic spirit manifested by the dear Salvationists'.[61] The only other time that Carrie referred to an 'apostolic spirit' and connected it to a person or a ministry was in relation to the early days of Woodworth-Etter's ministry.[62]

The Montgomerys and the Salvation Army shared a similar desire to reach the marginalized and outcast of society; this made it easy for them to partner in ministry together.[63] After the abrupt and

---

[58] 'Wealthy Warriors: A Rich Salvationist and His Famous Wife', p. 4.

[59] 'The Salvation Army: History', <http://www.salvationarmyusa.org>

[60] Montgomery, 'The Work and the Workers', *TF* 10.7, p. 166. She shared with her readers that 'it has been estimated that through the efforts of the Salvation Army alone, 93,000 people are listening to the Gospel every Lord's Day'.

[61] Carrie Judd Montgomery, 'The Work and the Workers', *TF* 11.12 (Dec 1891), p. 275

[62] Montgomery, 'The Work and the Workers', *TF* 10.2 (Oct 1890), p. 232. The term 'apostolic' was used many times within *Triumphs of Faith* by other authors, usually referring to an apostolic age, times, or blessing. See Wm. C. Stevens, 'Divine Healing in Practice', *TF* 11.1 (April 1891), pp. 81-84; W.B. Godbey, 'The Gifts of the Spirit: Workings of Miracles', *TF* 23.3 (March 1903), pp. 67-70; and extract from the English Booklet, 'Scripture on Sickness and Healing', *TF* 27.4 (April 1907), pp. 88-90.

[63] Carrie Judd Montgomery, 'The Work and the Workers', *TF* 11.9 (Sept 1891), pp. 215-16. She believed that officers in the very capable Salvation Army were well suited to continue the ministry. This all came about because her director, 'Brother Kirk', who was running the home, died abruptly and she needed someone to take over.

unexpected death of her director of the People's Mission in San Francisco, Carrie needed someone to take charge of the ministry, so she passed it over to the Army. Similar to the Army's work, the Montgomerys also established a mission in the slums for 'fallen

Figure 10
Carrie in her Salvation Army uniform (1890s)

women in San Francisco', or prostitutes, which lasted for about a year.[64] Because of these connections and after careful consideration, the Montgomerys decided to become affiliated with the Salvation Army. Ballington Booth appointed them as '"National Specials" of the Army' on Thanksgiving Day in 1891. This identification was helpful because

---

[64] 'Will "Slumming" Go: Rich Californians Join the Salvation Army', *Boston Daily Globe*, April 12, 1892, p. 11. 'Fallen women' refers to prostitutes.

if they were regular officers of the army they would have to go wherever ordered. If they were privates they would have no authority to wield the influence of earnestness and wealth which is at their command. Under the new order, they have power, by virtue of an impressive-looking diploma, with a big seal on it, to hold meetings wherever they think best, and are given more liberty than could be had in any other office of the Army.[65]

This special arrangement also enabled them to retain ties with other ministries in which they were involved. Simpson stated that because 'they have not become officers of the Salvation Army, but are simply private members ... therefore their relation to our work is not in any way affected'. Following this, he told his readers how great a blessing the Montgomerys would be to the 'Army as well as the Alliance'.[66] Additionally, because the Christian Alliance was still just a ministry at that time rather than a church organization, Carrie was not bound to choose one or the other. In 1891, she started an Oakland Branch of the Alliance, and possibly through her new interest in the Army, her initial focus was to 'concentrate all our forces in carrying out the glad tidings of salvation to others'.[67] Because of their private membership with the Army, the Montgomerys were free to move in and out of both Army and Alliance circles without any conflicts.

Carrie boldly announced her official affiliation with the Army to her readers in early 1892.[68] Although others may have thought the Army was too 'fanatical', she believed their methods produced many positive results. While people like Simpson supported the

---

[65] 'Wealthy Warriors: A Rich Salvationist and His Famous Wife', p. 4. Also, A.B. Simpson, 'Editorial: Mr. and Mrs. Montgomery', *CAMW* 8.17 (April 22, 1892); and Storms, 'Carrie Judd Montgomery: The Little General', p. 279. Another reason they were made honorary officers was so that George would also be able to keep his business without any trouble. In Montgomery, *Under His Wings,* pp. 144-45, she wrote that 'We joined only as soldiers, but dear old General Booth, who became very fond of my husband after meeting him on this Coast, made us Honorary Officers'.

[66] Simpson, 'Editorial: Mr. and Mrs. Montgomery'.

[67] Carrie Judd Montgomery, 'The Work and the Workers', *TF* 11.10 (Oct 1891), p. 238. Carrie was president and George was treasurer of the branch.

[68] Carrie Judd Montgomery, 'The Work and the Workers', *TF* 12.1 (Jan 1892), p. 17. 'For in the providence of God and by His clear and unmistakable guidance, both my husband and myself have felt it our duty and privilege to identify ourselves with the Salvation Army'.

Montgomerys, there were others who thought they had made a mistake by joining the Army and shared their concerns and disapproval. Carrie received opposition to the teaching of 'the unpopular subject of sanctification' as well as of the Holiness meetings held by the 'despised 'Salvationists'.[69] One of the ways that she defended her new affiliation with the Army was by printing articles by the Booths or other Salvation Army workers. Additionally, she printed articles

Figure 11
George, Faith, and Carrie in their Salvation Army uniforms (1892).
George wrote, 'Yours fighting beneath the Army flag',
and Carrie wrote, 'Yours fighting and trusting'.

in support of the Army written by prominent people such as Francis Willard.[70] In 1892, she also ran an article by Christian Alliance leader, Henry Wilson, entitled 'What the Salvation Army Has Done for Me', and in 1894, she printed 'The Salvation Army in America', where the following statement was made in support of the Army:

---

[69] Carrie Judd Montgomery, 'The Work and the Workers', *TF* 13.3 (March 1893), p. 94.

[70] Francis E. Willard, 'Believes in the Army', *TF* 13.1 (Jan 1893), p. 24. Carrie included a brief letter that Francis E. Willard wrote to the NY *War Cry* (The Salvation Army's own magazine) about her belief in the Salvation Army. Willard, president of NWCTU (National Women's Christian Temperance Union), liked that the Salvation Army went out to the people and that it finally brought the church into a more healthy balance, which included a role for women.

'those who believe that the world is never to be converted to one denomination or another, but to Christ, will bless the Salvation Army for the grand work it has done'.[71] Unashamed of her new involvement, she included a picture of herself wearing the Salvationist's uniform in her January 1893 journal.[72] She also publicly recounted the story of when she wore her Salvation Army bonnet in the train while in New York which caused a lady to approach her. Carrie later had the chance to pray with her and the lady 'had given her heart to God'.[73] Stories like this, in addition to supportive literature in her periodical, contributed to educating her readers about the Army and strengthening her association with them.

The Montgomerys also shared a personal friendship with the founders of the Salvation Army. Carrie heard William Booth speak in December of 1894 and shared,

> [W]e have recently had the great pleasure of a visit from General Booth of the Salvation Army. We cannot express with what feelings of love and reverence we gazed into the face of this great and good man who has been so wonderfully used, in the providence of God, to raise up the largest and most active body of organized Christian workers which exists in the world.[74]

The founder's daughter, Emma Booth Tucker, sent the Montgomerys a letter mentioning that the General 'does not forget you' followed by his extension of sympathy for them in their 'recent trials'.[75] Further, Booth Tucker wrote, 'I know that we shall be friends forever and that no change of any character shall ever come between us'.[76] Beyond friendship with the Booth family, the Montgomerys embraced the whole Army family so much that they decid-

---

[71] *Christian at Work*, 'The Salvation Army in America', *TF* 14.4 (April 1894), p. 86. 'It is to the glory of the Salvation Army that while others have been talking, it has gone down into the highways and by the hedges, yes, in the most foulsome slums, to carry on the work of rescue.'

[72] *TF* 13.1 (Jan 1893).

[73] 'Wealthy Warriors: A Rich Salvationist and His Famous Wife', p. 4.

[74] Carrie Judd Montgomery, 'General Booth', *TF* 15.1 (Jan 1895), pp. 23-24.

[75] Emma Booth Tucker, 'Personal Letter to Mrs. Adjutant Montgomery' (written from The Salvation Army in New York: May 5, 1899), used with permission and courtesy of the Berry family. Additionally, Emma mentioned that the General also enclosed a personal letter to the Montgomerys which should comfort their 'hearts to realize that he does not forget you'.

[76] Booth Tucker, Personal Letter to Mrs. Adjutant Montgomery.

ed to establish what some people referred to as a 'Salvation Army town' in Oakland, which they called 'Beulah'.[77] In addition to what the Montgomerys had already donated to the Army, they further gave them land to establish a refuge home for 'fallen women', a home for the 'Aged and Colored People', and an orphanage.[78] The Montgomerys also helped to establish a home for 'worn-out "soldiers of the cross,"' or tired Salvation Army workers.[79]

After this new commitment to the Army, Carrie emphasized soteriological themes in her periodical with more frequency.[80] On August 5, 1892, she announced that there would be an all night prayer meeting at the Salvation Army headquarters in San Francisco with the focus to pray that a 'wave of salvation would shake the city'.[81] Besides reemphasizing salvation in her periodical and conducting services and prayer meetings for several years in conjunction with the Army, she also actively participated in some of the Army outreaches, the 'slum sister's' ministry being one of the most impactful.[82] George periodically wore his Army uniform as well as shared

---

[77] 'All For the Poor: Rich Salvationists to Work in the Slums of New York: Romantic Story of a Couple', *Middletown Daily Press* (NY), April 12, 1892, p. 1. 'Beulah', taken from Isa. 62.4, means married; it was commonly used in Holiness and Divine Healing circles in her day. Isa. 62.4, 'You shall no longer be termed Forsaken, Nor shall your land anymore be termed Desolate; But you shall be called Hephzibah [My delight is in her], and your land Beulah [Married]' (NKJV). The term 'Beulah' was also known through Paul Bunyan's *Pilgrim's Progress* (1678), and it was integrated in Holiness songs, literature, healing homes, and testimonies. See Dieter, *The Holiness Revival of the Nineteenth Century*, pp. 4, 12. Dora G. Griffin's healing home in Michigan that Carrie assisted in dedicating was called Beulah in '"Beulah", A New Faith Home', *TF* 7.3 (March 1887), pp. 60-61. Carrie's friend, Jennie Smith, the railroad evangelist, wrote *From Baca to Beulah*. The Montgomerys' 'Beulah' land was to be a consecrated place where it was prohibited to drink or sell alcohol. See Carrie's 'The Work and the Workers', *TF* 12.12 (Dec 1892), pp. 285-88.

[78] 'The Salvation Army', *Daily Bulletin* (Auburn, NY), 1891. 'Home for Little Ones: Opening of the Salvation Army Orphanage at Beulah To-Day', *The San Francisco Call*, September 5, 1895, p. 11; and *TF* 17.8 (Aug 1897), p. 181.

[79] 'Will "Slumming" Go: Rich Californians Join the Salvation Army', p. 11.

[80] Montgomery, 'The Work and the Workers', *TF* 10.7, p. 167.

[81] Montgomery, 'The Work and the Workers', *TF* 12.9, p. 211.

[82] See Jennifer A. Miskov, 'Carrie's involvement with the Slum Sisters', at <www.CarrieJuddMontgomery.com> to learn more about Carrie's experiences with this small group of women who became known as the 'Slum Sisters'. Carrie went out with them ministering in saloons and bars until 2.00 am while her husband prayed for her on his own at home. Carrie Judd Montgomery, 'Salvation Army Work in the New York Slums', *TF* 12.5 (May 1892), p. 108; and *idem*, 'Through the Darkest San Francisco', *TF* 12.10 (Oct 1892), p. 220.

his testimony in some of their services. Carrie's daughter participated in the Salvation Army at a young age, and her involvement was highlighted in a local newspaper.[83] At only five years old and dressed in her Army uniform, the article claimed that 'Little Faith' gave talks to the children who lived in the orphanages near her home.[84] The Montgomerys worked with the Salvation Army throughout the years but as Carrie's own ministry began to develop,

Figure 12
George, Faith, and Carrie in uniform

she did not have as much time to give to their work. Towards the end of her life, Carrie reflected that despite her own expanding ministry, 'we never left the ranks of the Army, and I greatly value the friendship and fellowship of my dear officers and soldiers, who are giving their lives to God in this noble and self-sacrificing work'.[85]

---

[83] 'Richest Salvation Junior in the Country', *The San Francisco Call*, August 8, 1897, p. 15.

[84] See Carrie Judd Montgomery, 'Asleep in Jesus', *The Christian and Missionary Alliance* 34.19 (Aug 6, 1910), p. 308, where there is a later picture of Faith with Carrie's mother in remembrance of her death on April 7, 1910.

[85] Montgomery, *Under His Wings*, p. 145.

3.2 The Work Continues and Diversifies: West Coast (1891-1905)

Carrie continued to increase and expand her ministry endeavors in her early years in California. Besides her new connection with the Salvation Army, she also started Cazadero Camp Meetings and

Figure 13
At one of Carrie's Cazadero Camp meetings in the 1890s. George and Carrie are seated in the second row to the right of center.

opened up both the Home of Peace and a missionary training school. Further endeavors went beyond simply meeting people's spiritual needs alone. One reporter described Carrie as an 'eminent Christian worker and philanthropist from Beulah Home' who also sought to help meet more practical needs by opening up orphanages, a school, and a home for the 'Aged and Infirm Colored People'.[86] Many times when Carrie had a vision for something, she prayed, initiated it, and then quickly gave it away to other capable people so that she could initiate further projects. This section will emphasize ministries that Carrie began leading up to the early Pen-

---

[86] See 'Church Record: Life's Mission', *Los Angeles Times*, June 1, 1896, p. 8, where Carrie was referred to as 'the eminent Christian worker and philanthropist from Beulah Home'.

tecostal revivals of the twentieth century. Carrie's second illness and her personal need for healing will also be addressed here.

3.2.1 Cazadero Camp Meetings

When Carrie visited her husband's property in Cazadero for the first time toward the end of 1892, she noticed that 'the scattered community in this locality have no church privileges'.[87] Because of this deficit, she called together a meeting at the hotel there and saw four conversions. This favorable response led her to organize an 'Under the Redwoods; Camp-Meeting at Cazadero' the following year. Her initial plans for the camp meeting included broad enough teaching for everyone of 'Evangelical faith to unite with us'.[88] The first camp meeting took place on July 20-31, 1893, just a few months before she dedicated the Home of Peace.[89] These meetings were filled with people from the Christian and Missionary Alliance, the Salvation Army, and various other denominations.[90] Teaching at the first Cazadero Camp meeting was mainly conducted by people from Holiness backgrounds, the Christian and Missionary Alliance and the Salvation Army being the most prominent.[91] By 1895, Carrie integrated her Army ties so much that 'all the dear people who were attending our Camp Meetings seemed to enjoy the Army Meetings and declared that although they did not wear the uniform they were Salvationists at heart'.[92]

The development of these integrated camp meetings changed throughout the years. Carrie's focus in the early stages was for 'the salvation of sinners and full consecration of believers' as well as holiness and divine healing themes.[93] Her first camp meeting consisted of talks highlighting the coming of the Lord, divine healing, and

---

[87] Carrie Judd Montgomery, 'The Work and the Workers', *TF* 12.11 (Nov 1892), p. 258. Cazadero is Spanish for 'Hunting Ground'. See also her 'Under the Redwoods; Camp-Meeting at Cazadero', *TF* 13.5 (May 1893), p. 126.

[88] Montgomery, 'Under the Redwoods; Camp-Meeting at Cazadero', p. 126.

[89] The Home of Peace was dedicated on November 7, 1893.

[90] Carrie Judd Montgomery, 'Elim Grove, Cazadero', *TF* 15.8 (Aug 1895), pp. 188-89.

[91] Montgomery, *Under His Wings,* p. 154. Some of the early workers were: Charles N. Crittenton, Mr and Mrs M.P. Ferguson, Revd J.S. and Mrs Hervey, Miss Mindora Berry (later known as Mrs Goodwin), and Mr T. Sasao (from Japan).

[92] Montgomery, 'Elim Grove, Cazadero', pp. 188-89, and Melanie Payne Ferguson, 'The Cazadero Camp-Meeting', *TF* 13.8 (Aug 1893), pp. 169-71.

[93] Montgomery, 'Under the Redwoods; Camp-Meeting at Cazadero', p. 126.

foreign missions.[94] Throughout the years, Carrie began to emphasize the Spirit even more. At the 1895 camp meeting, she gave a
message about 'the work of the Spirit'.[95] In 1896, Carrie recorded
that people received the 'baptism of the Spirit to go forth in His

Figure 14
Carrie with banjo (1890s), Ann Jones-Calhoun sitting next to her. Two other
Salvationist women are standing on a railroad track that would bring
people to the camp in Cazadero. The railroad tracks no longer
run through the camp but those two trees are still there.

service with renewed power'. She also later referred to 'droppings
of Pentecostal showers' during that same meeting.[96] How Carrie
understood Spirit baptism at this point will be explored more in
Chapter 6. Carrie continued to organize and be a part of these camp
meetings as they happened sporadically through the years. There
were several gaps when the meetings ceased to take place for vari-

---

[94] Ferguson, 'The Cazadero Camp-Meeting', *TF* 13.8 (Aug 1893), pp. 169-71.
[95] Carrie Judd Montgomery, 'The Work of the Spirit', *TF* 15.9 (Sept 1895), pp.
193-99, was an address she gave at the camp meeting. A few months earlier however, she also wrote 'Pentecostal Blessing', which emphasized similar themes.
[96] Carrie Judd Montgomery, 'Cazadero Camp Meeting', *TF* 16.9 (Sept 1896),
p. 216. The year preceding this meeting, Carrie anticipated, 'We believe that great
baptisms of God's love and power will be poured upon us this year also' ('Under
the Redwoods: An Undenominational Union Camp Meeting [July 18-28, 1895]',
TF 15.6 [June 1895], p. 138). More in Chapter 6.

ous reasons: once because Carrie was too ill to organize it and at
other times because she claimed there was no specific leading from
God at that time.[97] After several years with no meetings, in 1914,
Carrie initiated a significant Pentecostal Camp meeting which will
be probed further.

Figure 15
At a Cazadero Camp meeting in mid 1890s. Carrie is sat in the middle with
Faith, and George is standing in the back on the right.

3.2.2 Missionary Training School

It was during Carrie's first Cazadero camp meeting that several participants were stirred to pray about the possibility of a Missionary
Training School. Just over two years after that initial stirring, on
October 5, 1895, Carrie opened up Shalom Training School which
was housed in the Home of Peace. This was initially a missionary
training base for young women. Most likely influenced by her new
friendship with the Salvation Army, early emphasis was placed on
conversion themes in addition to healing themes.[98] Revd H.C. and
Mrs Waddell were appointed to lead the training school and both
George and Carrie regularly spoke there. They initially wanted to

---

[97] Montgomery, *Under His Wings*, p. 154, and *TF* 18.7 (July 1898), p. 161. Carrie conducted these camp meetings from 1893-1897, 1900-1902, 1906, 1914 (Pentecostal Camp Meeting), 1919.

[98] Carrie Judd Montgomery, 'Missionary Training School', *TF* 14.4 (April
1894)), pp. 86-88.

build an 'undenominational' school and make it 'a real center of spiritual power, from which we may send out many efficient workers for God'.[99] Since they were not concerned to compete with other establishments, they did not look to get accreditation. Waddell wrote that their 'one thought and prayer will be to have students full of faith and the Holy Ghost, and will esteem this far more than any degree of learning without it. The prayer of all related to the school is that it will be made a school in which the Holy Spirit will have supreme control'.[100] Its emphasis on missions was likely modeled after similar schools in New York.[101]

After the first year of operating the training school, they decided to open up attendance to include men as well.[102] Moving into its second year, Waddell said,

> [T]he aim of the school will not be so much to give theological education as to impart in word and spirit essential Christianity, and give such practical preparation to those devoted to Christ as to fit them for living service in the fullness of the Gospel, in the shortest possible time.[103]

During this time, the school re-merged with the Home of Peace and integrated its guests into classes.[104] In 1897, Waddell noted that since the school started, there had been 34 students who went through the school (not including the guests and visitors who also attended the classes). The students were in attendance anywhere from a few months to the whole eight months. Nationalities were mixed between Canadian, Japanese, Austrian, Swedish, and others.[105] Upon completion of the school, one student went to China, two stayed in San Francisco to work among the seamen at a water-

---

[99] 'Shalom (Peace) Training School for Christian Workers', *TF* 15:10 (Oct 1895), p. 232.

[100] H.C. Waddell, 'Shalom Training School', *TF* 17.6 (June 1897), p. 128.

[101] Carrie most likely modeled her school after Simpson's training school in Nyack, New York during that time.

[102] The semester began with an equal number of male and female students.

[103] H.C. Waddell, 'The Shalom Training School for Christian Workers', *TF* 16.8 (Aug 1896), p. 188. The increasing awareness of and talk about the Second Coming of Christ and the need to evangelize the world most likely contributed to adjustment in the school.

[104] See 2.2.2.4.

[105] Waddell, 'Shalom Training School', pp. 127-28. A variety of vocations were represented in the school: 'There have been the sailor, the soldier, the housemaid, the college student, the preacher, the mechanic, farmer, clerk'.

front mission, one went to work with Italians and Mexicans, some headed towards Mexico, one stayed to help at Beulah orphanage, and most were involved in some sort of evangelistic work. The school did not have a long life as they felt it had served its purpose. They soon dissolved the school and let the Home of Peace transform back into its original state. Even without the specific missions school, Carrie continued to support and hold prayer meetings for missionaries through out the years. Her desire for the global spread of Christianity fit well alongside the cultural currents of the day.[106]

Another reason Carrie may have been drawn to missions so much during that time was because it provided a greater opportunity for women.[107] Since many denominations struggled to give women 'full recognition as missionaries', many responded by either founding or joining other missionary societies that were led and organized by women.[108] Many women had to look outside of their denominations for opportunities to exercise authority, preach, or operate in other leadership capacities. Carrie greatly supported the spreading of the Gospel to other nations and readily empowered women in this way.

---

[106] Moody initiated a Bible training school in Chicago (later called the Moody Bible Institute) and through one of his conferences, the Student Volunteer Movement was birthed in 1876 with its main goal to evangelize the world. Presbyterian A.T. Pierson (1837-1911), who later founded the Africa Inland Mission in 1895, also advanced the missions' cause as did A.B. Simpson through his organizations. John R. Mott (1865-1955) published *The Evangelization of the World in This Generation* in 1900 to help further the cause of the Student Volunteer Movement. Robert Elliot Speer (1867-1947), an influential player in the Presbyterian Church, was heavily involved in the Volunteer Movement as well. He wrote *Christianity and the Nations* in 1910, where he admitted faults of missionaries but insisted nonetheless on their need in reaching the world. A.J. Gordon (1843-1919), established his missionary school (Boston Missionary Training Institute) in 1889 to prepare 'common people', especially women, for missions. Global expansion was even pervading American society. A Senator (Albert J. Beveridge) of Indiana boldly proclaimed in 1900 that God set apart the American people to lead in the 'regeneration of the world'. The time from the Civil War to 1920 saw a great amount of change as America was led by Christian leaders for some time who tried to integrate their beliefs into the system (Mark A. Noll, *A History of Christianity in the United States and Canada* [Grand Rapids: Eerdmans, 1992], pp. 290-93).

[107] George M. Marsden, *Religion and American Culture* (New York: Harcourt Brace Jovanovich, Publishers, 1990), p. 115.

[108] Noll, *A History of Christianity in the United States and Canada*, p. 293. In 1902, Abbie Child established the World's Missionary Committee of Christian Women. At the turn of the century, on the mission field itself, roughly sixty percent was made up of single women or wives of male missionaries.

Figure 16
Just outside Beulah Chapel, likely a graduation ceremony for
students in the training school.

3.2.3 Orphanages and Social Action

Into the 1890s, Carrie began to move into more social action initia-
tives, putting most of her time into orphanages to meet the growing
needs around her.[109] Her Beulah Orphanage, which would be the
first of several, was dedicated on September 6, 1895. The primary
purpose of the orphanages was 'that all the children who should
come under its roof should be saved, and find sweet rest in Jesus'
arms'.[110] To help facilitate this, Carrie occasionally held 'little Army
meetings' for the children there in which they shared their testimonies and prayed 'their own simple prayers, with the greatest free-

---

[109] Bebbington, *A History of Evangelicalism*, p. 253. Because many immigrants
flocked to the United States from 1850-1900, the population rapidly expanded in
North America. Many of these new settlers struggled to make a living for themselves and their children, which was one of the causes of the many orphans
around Oakland. In the USA, there were roughly 23 million people in 1850, and
by 1900, the population had grown to 76 million.

[110] Miss E. Stroud-Smith, 'Dedication of Beulah Orphanage', *TF* 15.10 (Oct
1895), pp. 229-31. See also Carrie Judd Montgomery, 'Proposed Children's
Home', *TF* 14.5 (May 1894), p. 119. By January of 1896, Carrie also received boys
into her orphanages.

dom'.[111] Many of the children committed whole chapters of Scripture to memory and prayed fervently for their friends to be converted, for the Montgomerys, and for those on the mission fields.[112] The children regularly attended Sunday school, which was held in the Home of Peace, and sang children's praise songs that Carrie had written.[113] Carrie also facilitated various activities to help the children develop practical skills as well so that they could be 'useful'.[114] She eventually expanded her orphanage by opening a home for younger children called the 'Bird's Nest', the 'Rosebud Home' which was specifically for babies, and the 'Sunshine Home' which was for older girls.[115]

Carrie additionally collaborated with other societies in the area who helped orphans. She was on the board of directors for the Children's Home-Finding Society that regularly sent children to her orphanage.[116] One time after the Society had applied to all the possible homes and found none to help in a situation with a mother of three, Carrie was notified about the family's need. She invited the children to stay with her and provided the mother with work so that she could be near her children.[117] This act of kindness was even more significant when tied to public opposition made against Carrie by the probable father of these children less than a year before.

---

[111] Carrie Judd Montgomery, 'Beulah Orphanage', *TF* 15.11 (Nov 1895), p. 250.

[112] Miss A.J. Freeman, 'The Beulah Orphanage', *TF* 19.1 (Jan 1899), pp. 16-17. Miss A.J. Freeman was the Matron of the Sunshine home.

[113] See Appendix 7 to see one of these songs. Carrie Judd Montgomery, 'More About Beulah Orphanage', *TF* 16.2 (Feb 1896), p. 40, and her 'Beulah Orphanage', *TF* 16.10 (Oct 1896), pp. 233-34.

[114] Carrie Judd Montgomery, 'Beulah Orphanage', *TF* 15.11 (Nov 1895), p. 251. Carrie also consistently tried to devote one afternoon a week to help the children either make scrap books, write poems or stories, teach some how to sew, or do some other 'special treat' with them.

[115] 'Home for Little Ones: Opening of the Salvation Army Orphanage at Beulah To-Day', *The San Francisco Call*, September 5, 1895, p. 11. There is a sketch of the orphanage in this article. Also, 'Dedication of A Bird's Nest', *The San Francisco Call*, November 19, 1897, p. 9, and Carrie Judd Montgomery, 'Beulah Orphanage', *TF* 16.7 (July 1896), p. 165.

[116] 'To Rescue Little Waifs', *The San Francisco Call*, October 2, 1895, p. 10. This society sought to help provide homes for children who were unfit for orphanages because of their 'slum life' history.

[117] 'Deserted Three Beautiful Babes', *The San Francisco Call*, October 3, 1896, p. 11. Under a sketch of the three children, it says, 'The Deserted Little Truesdells, Aged 1, 3 and 5 Years, Who Were Saved From Separation From Their Mother by Mrs. Montgomery, the Beulah Salvationist'.

Revd A.P. Truesdell publicly attacked Carrie's ministry when he said that her faith healing was 'the work of the devil'.[118] Grouping Carrie into the mix of faith-healers and Christian scientists, he believed that the 'faith-healers are all trusting in the devil, and that it is his mission to expose them'.[119] He announced that 'the very idea of teaching people that a broken bone can be healed by faith is enough to show the power that Satan has in this work'.[120] Less than a year after he made these accusations, he abandoned his wife and children and 'left them all to starve' because he 'feared being arrested for cruelty'.[121] When Carrie took in this specific family, it was more than simply helping a stranger in need; it was lending her hand to the family of one who had publicly attempted to destroy and discredit her ministry.

Regardless of how dire their situation, Carrie attempted to welcome the abandoned, the fatherless, and the orphaned into her home whenever she had the space and capacity to receive them.[122] Throughout the years, she continued to stay true to the original vision of the orphanage to receive children 'regardless of color, creed,

---

[118] He declared from his pulpit ('he leased the Asbury M.E. Church at certain times to promulgate his doctrines') that Carrie was 'all wrong' as well as ridiculed her 'long-distance theory' in reference to how she prayed for healing at set apart times far away from the one desiring prayer ('Testing Faith Healing, Newly Arrived Minister Says It Is the Work of the Devil, Opposes Mrs. Montgomery', p. 9). He also opposed her in 'A Girl's Life the Stake, The New Church of Christ Enters the Faith-Healing War', *The San Francisco Call*, November 9, 1895, p. 13.

[119] 'Deserted Three Beautiful Babes', *The San Francisco Call*, October 3, 1896, p. 11. These were common accusations, and similar ones are thrown at those in the Faith Movements even today. See Chapter 5 for more on this.

[120] 'Testing Faith Healing, Newly Arrived Minister Says It Is the Work of the Devil, Opposes Mrs. Montgomery', p. 9.

[121] 'Deserted Three Beautiful Babes', p. 11.

[122] Carrie Judd Montgomery, Handwritten Orphanage Records (various dates: 1895-1897, 1899, 1901-08) accessed and used with permission of the Home of Peace. Some of the designations in these records were as follows: 'father has been out of work', 'mother has other children and struggling', 'father dead' or 'mother dead', 'mother has deserted child', 'father's whereabouts unknown, mother is dead', 'father a criminal', abandoned by drunken mother, 'father missing – supposed to be dead', 'both parents dead', 'lost in S.F. earthquake', 'brought to America by missionaries', parents 'too old for State aid', or found child roaming the streets of San Francisco. See also 'Little Orth Raises a Row: Some Prominent People Called to Court', *The San Francisco Call*, July 26, 1898, p. 9, and 'Old Friends as Enemies: Mrs. Stocker Testifies for Mrs. Prescott', *The San Francisco Call*, August 2, 1898, p. 9.

or nationality'.[123] Carrie also attempted to reintegrate the children whenever possible, whether that meant into new homes where families could adopt them or back with friends and family who were in a better place than before. Throughout the years, Carrie involved her readers in supporting the orphans by giving financially, donating beds, or giving Christmas presents to the children.[124]

Carrie continued with her orphanage work until her hands 'were too full of work for Him'. Towards the end of 1908 and just after her Pentecostal Spirit baptism experience, she felt that God wanted to use her more in the 'exposition of the word of God, as formerly'.[125] The Salvation Army eventually opened up a large children's home which made the need for Carrie's orphanage less necessary.[126] Throughout the 13 years that her orphanages existed, over 800 children had come through.[127] She kept in touch with many of the children, several who went off to be missionaries or some who were later 'saved and baptized by the Holy Spirit' whom she prayed for often that 'the good seed planted in their hearts while yet with us shall remain, and bring forth fruit for God's glory'.[128]

In addition to the development of orphanages on her property, because there was no district school in the area, Carrie initiated a kindergarten and a day school there. The Montgomerys also dedicated land to the Salvation Army to help 'destitute girls who are or-

---

[123] 'Home for Little Ones: Opening of the Salvation Army Orphanage at Beulah To-Day', *The San Francisco Call*, September 5, 1895, p. 11.

[124] Carrie Judd Montgomery, 'Beulah Orphanage', *TF* 18.1 (Jan 1898), pp. 22-23, and *idem*, 'Remember the Orphans', *TF* 19.11 (Nov 1899), p. 258, are just a couple examples of this. Also, in her 'A Personal Word', *TF* 19.2 (Feb 1899), p. 48, she writes about her present financial trials and asks her subscribers to pay for their subscriptions.

[125] Montgomery, *Under His Wings*, p. 163.

[126] After some prayer, she was able to find suitable homes for the children she had left in her home.

[127] Carrie Judd Montgomery, 'Some Important Changes', *TF* 28.12 (Dec 1908), p. 267. Because more and more orphanages had popped up since the earthquake and fire of 1906, Carrie only had 35 of the 80 children still living there which helped her in her transition to close it down a few years later. See also her 'More About Beulah Orphanage', *TF* 16.2 (Feb 1896), p. 40, and 'Beulah Orphanage', *TF* 17.10 (Oct 1897), p. 221. Up until late 1897, 128 children had passed through her orphanages, and of those, she recounted that 'fifteen have been placed in good homes; sixteen have been sent to other institutions; thirty-nine have been returned to friends ... one child has died, and we still have with us fifty-six children'.

[128] Montgomery, *Under His Wings*, p. 163.

phans, half-orphans, or abandoned children'.[129] By 1897, their temperance land at Beulah was filled with various ministries and services for the people in the community. Whenever they donated any

Figure 17
Carrie's orphanage (1890s).
Carrie is third from the bottom on the far right.

---

[129] 'Home for Little Ones: Opening of the Salvation Army Orphanage at Beulah To-Day', *The San Francisco Call*, September 5, 1895, p. 11 (includes a picture of the orphanage). See also Carrie Judd Montgomery, 'Beulah Orphanage', *TF* 15.5 (May 1895), p. 117; *idem*, 'Beulah Orphanage', *TF* 15.11 (Nov 1895), p. 251; 'Helping the Fallen', *The San Francisco Call*, January 7, 1896, p. 8; and Carrie Judd Montgomery, 'More About Beulah Orphanage', p. 31. Carrie also lent the school district room in the orphanage to use until a school could be built ('Beulah Orphanage', pp. 250-52) and 'donated a building lot to the City and persuaded the proper authorities that a school was greatly needed in this locality' (*Under His Wings*, p. 158).

land, the others had to agree that 'no intoxicating liquor shall ever be sold upon said premises'.[130] Some of the various ministries they were a part of were

> the Home of Peace [1893], a training home for foreign missionaries [1894], the Home of Rest for sick Salvation Army Officers [1892], the Colored Folks' Home [one to the Salvation Army in 1895 and another to a California corporation in 1897], the King's Daughters' Home for Incurables, the Children's Orphanage [1895], the Bird's Nest [1897], the Rescue Home [1891 to Salvation Army] and the home of the Montgomerys, besides a few smaller buildings. Most of these homes, perhaps all of them, have been built on land donated by the Montgomerys, who are also interested in the financial support of many of them.[131]

They also opened up Beulah Chapel where Carrie conducted Sunday services; this was a small church across from Home of Peace and is still there today.[132] Their land was proof that they cared not only about people's spiritual needs but also physical ones too, believing that if those needs were met, they would have an even greater opportunity to share their faith with those who stayed with them. Carrie believed that both soul and body were connected and thus she saw it necessary and important to meet the needs of both.[133] The development of the children's homes and other social endeavors demonstrates Carrie's drive to take swift action to help the less fortunate. Carrie spent a lot of time responding to the physical needs around her, even when she had concerns of her own that needed to be addressed.

---

130 'Protected Aged and Infirm: New Home at Beulah Will Be Dedicated Next Sunday', *The San Francisco Call*, August 21, 1897, p. 11.

131 'Dedication of A Bird's Nest', *The San Francisco Call*, November 19, 1897, p. 9. More specifically, George and Carrie transferred some lots on their Beulah land to the 'Home for Aged and Infirm Colored People' in 1897. See 'Protected Aged and Infirm: New Home at Beulah Will Be Dedicated Next Sunday', *The San Francisco Call*, August 21, 1897, p. 11.

132 This later became associated with the Assemblies of God and is currently used in conjunction with the Home of Peace which is running as a Christian conference center. Both are currently non-denominational as of 2011.

133 Carrie Judd, 'The Temple of the Body', *TF* 4.2 (Feb 1884), pp. 25-27. This is one of the many articles where Carrie wrote that healing and redemption was not just for souls but for bodies as well.

3.2.4 Carrie Healed Again

In the midst of her social endeavors, towards the end of 1897, Carrie became severely ill. After much prayer, she improved some but then suddenly got worse with extreme back pain. One of her medical friends thought her 'severe attack of inflammation of the stomach and bowels' was a case of 'grippe'.[134] *The Los Angeles Times* reported that Carrie was 'at death's door, with cerebrospinal meningitis', stating that the physicians believed that 'there is no hope of her recovery'.[135] Still other physicians claimed that she had tuberculosis of the spine, inflammation of the spinal chord, or spinal meningitis. Her spine began to get worse and throb in pain.[136] One of her doctor friends noticed the severity of her illness and advised that she should have 'absolute rest and quiet, and on no account to use [her] brain in any way'.[137] Carrie did not consider that advice necessary and continued her orphanage work, held meetings, and even in the midst of her own frailty and weakness, continued to pray for the sick. She did this until at one point she physically could not continue. She remembered that her

> whole condition became extremely hyper aesthetic, so that I could not bear noise nor jars, and even the singing of the birds seemed unendurable at one time. All the sympathetic nerve centers were greatly disturbed, and in evidence of this my tongue was covered with hard red points. I had such sensitiveness of the nerves that I could listen to nothing in the slightest degree pathetic or startling. Even vibrations in a human voice became distressing to me, and my own voice often jarred me painfully.[138]

It is interesting to notice that Carrie displayed many of the same symptoms from her illness twenty years earlier. Possible connections with her original illness will be explored in Chapter 5.

---

[134] Carrie Judd Montgomery, 'A Miracle of Healing', *TF* 18.7 (July 1898), p. 141.

[135] 'Sparks from the Wires', *Los Angeles Times*, June 10, 1898, p. 5. The end of the article also stated that both the Montgomerys believe in 'faith healing'.

[136] 'Speaks of it as a Miracle: Mrs. Montgomery Tells of Her Healing', *The San Francisco Call*, June 26, 1898, p. 15. Much of this article is recorded in Carrie's own words.

[137] Montgomery, 'A Miracle of Healing', p. 142.

[138] Montgomery, 'A Miracle of Healing', p. 142.

Carrie believed that it must have been for some deeper reason at that time that 'prayer for relief was answered but not for healing'.[139] Her sickness prevented her from writing articles in her periodical for several months and caused her to cancel the Cazadero Camp meeting in 1898 because she was too weak to organize it.[140] Her illness got so bad that she could not even handle much time with George. She commented,

> And then, hardest of all, was the fact that I could enjoy but little of my dear husband's society, for even the vibrations of his tender voice jarred my suffering nerves, so that the most he could do to comfort and help me was to retire to his own room and pour his soul out in prayer for me ... Again and again, when I seemed almost at the point of death, he would lay his hands on me in Jesus' Name, resisting the enemy with steadfast faith, and relief would soon follow.[141]

During this time Carrie was confused and readily struggled to process information. She was so ill that they had to tie a rope around the front steps of her house to keep people out because the tiniest sound caused her trauma. Throughout this time, Carrie continued to refuse medicine.[142]

The Christian Alliance in San Francisco and in Oakland had a day of prayer and fasting on account of Carrie, and the Salvation Army chapters also had prayer meetings for her healing.[143] About the same time of the fast, on June 11, 1898, Carrie's health began to improve. Then between 2.00-4.00 am on the following morning, she

> felt a mighty but very gentle power begin to work in my back, and it seemed as though iron bands were being removed from my spine ... the healing power seemed to penetrate through every nerve and muscle of my back, and removing all distress. There was no excitement, but I felt as quiet as a babe in its mother's

---

[139] Montgomery, *Under His Wings,* p. 159.

[140] Montgomery, 'A Miracle of Healing', p. 147.

[141] Montgomery, 'A Miracle of Healing', p. 145.

[142] Montgomery, 'A Miracle of Healing', p. 143. A further look into her view of medicine will be explored in 4.1.2.2.

[143] 'A Third Healing Claimed: Experience of Mrs. Montgomery', *The San Francisco Call,* June 13, 1898, p. 8.

arms … At the same time there came a mighty conviction of the Holy Ghost, like a deep, tender voice, pervading all my spirit, that the work of healing was accomplished.[144]

The following Wednesday, she rode six miles to a Christian Alliance convention in Oakland. She arrived late to a service that A.B. Simpson was conducting. He noticed her and stopped his preaching to lead the whole congregation in a praise song. He then invited her up to the stage to give her testimony of healing.[145] She later wrote to her subscribers how she was originally going to ask them for prayer but was grateful that instead she could celebrate with them because she had been healed.[146]

Following this healing, Carrie became even more interested in missions than she had in the past. She began to print more literature about missionaries and specifically raised money for those on the mission fields. Toward the late 1890s, Carrie specifically focused on raising money for Pandita Ramabai in India.[147] Then starting in 1900, she transitioned to raising financial support for missions in Mexico since her husband was active in missions whenever he went there for business.[148] Carrie additionally began her first Spanish lesson in 1900. In this same year she went on her Eastern trip to Chicago, Cleveland, and New York and reconnected with old friends who were a part of the Divine Healing Movement.

One might wonder if there were any connections with her second healing encounter and her growing outlook toward missions. Because Carrie had already opened up her missionary training school in 1895, two years before her second major healing, this shows that she already had an interest in missions. Participating with Simpson and the Christian and Missionary Alliance had already broadened her missionary outlook. That her mother invited missionaries over to visit when Carrie was younger also lends to the

---

[144] Montgomery, 'A Miracle of Healing', pp. 146, 144.

[145] Montgomery, *Under His Wings*, p. 160.

[146] Montgomery, 'A Miracle of Healing', pp. 141-47.

[147] Carrie Judd Montgomery, 'Who Will Help?', Pandita Ramabai, 'Famine Experience', *TF* 17.5 (May 1897), pp. 112-16, and Carrie Judd Montgomery, 'The Famine in India', *TF* 19.12 (Dec 1999), pp. 285-87.

[148] Carrie Judd Montgomery, 'Christian Work in Mexico', *TF* 20.7 (July 1900), p. 155. She wrote about how her husband went to Mexico mainly on business but had many chances to hand out copies of his small tract that were also printed in Spanish.

fact that an interest in missions was a part of her life before this event. One of the factors that may have contributed to her growing interest in missions might also have been the shift of many Evangelicals moving from a postmillennial view to a premillennial view of Christ's return.[149] This change in thinking brought a sense of urgency in working towards converting 'sinners' sooner rather than later which likely added to Carrie's emphasis on missions. Nearly dying may have also put this into a more focused perspective.

The last decade of the nineteenth century brought some major transitions in Carrie's life. Marrying and moving to the West Coast was a big factor in expanding Carrie's healing ministry. This forerunner became one of the first to open up a healing home on the West Coast as well as one of the earliest people to spread the doctrine of divine healing there. Later, she was healed again after 'thousands' had prayed for her, and upon her recovery, she continued her ministry with an even stronger emphasis for foreign missions.[150] The major physical transitions and all of her social endeavors expanded her influence in relation to healing and also prepared a larger platform for her for the things to come. As she moved into the twentieth century, Carrie was on the verge of a great spiritual transition. It is towards the spiritual temperature being readjusted that we now turn.

---

[149] The postmillennial view holds that Jesus will return after the millennial reign of Christ. The shift towards premillennialism was influenced in one way in 1827 when Edward Irving published a translation written by a Chilean Jesuit entitled *The Coming of Messiah in Glory and Majesty*, which said that Christ would come before the end of the millennium. This newer premillennial thinking contributed to a more pessimistic outlook on society. Things were becoming worse and not better; people in foreign lands needed to be reached with the Gospel as soon as possible. See Marsden, *Religion and American Culture*, p. 60; Bebbington, *The Dominance of Evangelicalism*, pp. 191-93; and William Faupel, *The Everlasting Gospel: The Significance of Eschatology in the Development of Pentecostal Thought* (JPTSup, 10; Sheffield: Sheffield Academic Press, 1996).

[150] 'Speaks of it as a Miracle: Mrs. Montgomery Tells of Her Healing', *The San Francisco Call*, June 26, 1898, p. 15. Part of the expanded title of this article reads: 'When The Call Announced Her Sickness She Says Thousands Commenced to Pray for Her Recovery'.

3.3 The Pentecostal Stamp: A New Experience: 1906-1908

3.3.1 The Azusa Street Revival (1906)[151]

A few years before Carrie's fiftieth birthday, reports of Holy Spirit stirrings in Los Angeles were bustling. The City of Angels was receiving special attention as it was experiencing a revival that would later contribute significantly to the birthing of American Pentecostalism.[152] William Joseph Seymour, an African American whose parents had been slaves, was a key leader in this movement. In January of 1906, Seymour attended Charles Fox Parham's Bible school in Texas where he learned about a new kind of Spirit baptism.[153] He soon left there for an opportunity to take over a church in Los Angeles and arrived there on February 22, 1906. He began to teach about the baptism of the Holy Spirit but shortly after was kicked out of the church because of the controversy surrounding the issue. Consequently, he was invited into a home on North Bonnie Brae Street to continue his meetings. On April 9, 1906, there was a great

---

[151] This section on the history of Azusa Street depends heavily upon Miskov, 'Coloring Outside the Lines', pp. 94–117. For a good overview of the revival see Cecil M. Robeck, Jr., *The Azusa Street Mission and Revival: The Birthplace of the Pentecostal Movement* (Nashville, TN: Thomas Nelson, Inc., 2006).

[152] While the specific origins of Pentecostalism are still highly controversial, most scholars can at least admit that the Azusa Street Revival holds great significance in the movement. See Allan Anderson, *Spreading Fires: The Missionary Nature of Early Pentecostalism* (London: SCM Press, 2007), p. 48, and Faupel, *The Everlasting Gospel*, p. 18.

[153] 'The Old-Time Pentecost', *The Apostolic Faith* 1.1 (Sept 1906), p. 1. Giving a pre-history to the workings at Azusa Street, this unknown author (possibly Seymour himself) wrote about Parham's work that it

> began about five years ago last January, when a company of people under the leadership of Chas. Parham, who were studying God's word tarried for Pentecost, in Topeka, Kansas. After searching through the country everywhere, they had been unable to find any Christians that had the true Pentecostal power. So they laid aside all commentaries and notes and waited on the Lord, studying His word, and what they did not understand they got down before the bench and asked God to have wrought out in their hearts by the Holy Ghost. They had a prayer tower in which prayers were ascending night and day to God. After three months, a sister who had been teaching sanctification for the baptism with the Holy Ghost, one who had a sweet, loving experience and all the carnality taken out of her heart, felt the Lord lead her to have hands laid on her to receive the Pentecost. So when they prayed, the Holy Ghost came in great power and she commenced speaking in an unknown tongue.

move of the Holy Spirit there in which people responded by speaking and singing in tongues.[154]

As more and more people were drawn to the meetings, the home proved incapable of holding everyone. Seymour along with some others found and leased an old vacant building on Azusa Street which they named the Apostolic Faith Mission (also referred to as the Azusa Street Mission). One of the biggest breakthroughs at Azusa Street was that the walls of race and gender were broken. Frank Bartleman recorded the revival first hand and observed that 'the "color line" was washed away in the blood'.[155] Also, because many involved in the revival believed that Jesus was returning soon, missions occurred at a rapid rate. Early Pentecostals also wanted to see 'apostolic power' and 'the gifts restored back to the church'.[156] In response to the dying religion in their day, they sought to 'restore an ineffective or compromised church to its former state'.[157] There was also much experimentation in regards to the manifestations of the Holy Spirit. Spirit baptism with the 'initial evidence' of speaking in tongues to follow became a cornerstone and key element that drew people to the mission.[158] Over the next few years, the Azusa

---

[154] Robeck, *The Azusa Street Mission and Revival,* pp. 6-7.

[155] This is in reference to the 'blood' of Jesus. Frank Bartleman, *Azusa Street: The Roots of Modern-day Pentecost* (April 1925, Los Angeles; Reprint, S. Plainfield, NJ: Bridge Publishing, Inc., 1980), p. 54.

[156] Florence Crawford, *The Apostolic Faith* 1.9 (June to Sept 1907), p. 2. See also Harvey Cox, *Fire from Heaven: The Rise of Pentecostal Spirituality and the Reshaping of Religion in the Twenty-first Century* (London: Cassell, 1996), p. 102.

[157] Robeck, *The Azusa Street Mission and Revival,* p. 121. See also *The Apostolic Faith* 1.2 (Oct 1906), p. 1. In an article, possibly written by Seymour himself, entitled 'The Pentecost Baptism Restored', there is much language centering on the idea of restoration. 'All along the ages men have been preaching a partial Gospel. A part of the Gospel remained when the world went into the Dark Ages. God has from time to time raised up men to bring back the truth to the church'. He noted how Luther, Wesley, and Cullis restored certain aspects of the Christian faith and then added that 'now he [God] is bringing back the Pentecostal Baptism to the church'. See also Steven L. Ware, 'Restorationism in Classical Pentecostalism' in *NIDPCM*, p. 1019 who maintains that in Restorationism 'something went very wrong very early in the history of the Christian church, so that the simple and biblical teaching and practice of the apostles was gradually corrupted'. Latter Rain thinking also stems from this.

[158] 'The Old-Time Pentecost', p. 1. Speaking in tongues played a major part in the Azusa Street Revival even from the very beginning. Robert Mapes Anderson also comments on this in his *Vision of the Disinherited: The Making of American Pentecostalism* (New York and Oxford: Oxford University Press, 1979), p. 4. The devel-

Street Revival was visited by people from all over the world who were either curious about this 'new' manifestation of the Spirit or others who desired to experience it for themselves. Once participants had their Pentecostal Spirit baptism experience, they would readily testify and share about their empowering experience.[159]

3.3.2 Carrie's Caution (1907)

In 1906, Carrie's husband went to investigate the Azusa Street Revival and returned with a positive report. Even though he was optimistic about what he saw there, Carrie was so busy running her various ministries that she did not have the time or energy to consider the new signs at Azusa Street then.[160] She had also heard of accounts from India and abroad of similar things happening separately from Azusa Street. However, even with these reports, she continued to remain cautious about the new manifestations. This hesitation may have resulted from the disillusionment that came from her earlier affiliation with Woodworth-Etter's ministry when Erickson's prophecy never came to pass.

In January of 1907, Carrie recalled her recent trip to Los Angeles and noticed that some Christians were apt to miss the real thing because of their fears of fanaticism. While Carrie cautiously approached the growing phenomena that included speaking in tongues, she did not recognize the significance of the Azusa Street Revival at that time when she said,

> Many of the missions seem powerless and lifeless. There is no real revival as a whole in Los Angeles, but only here and there a little company who are trusting God fully and receiving a rich experience of His grace. Some of the white people who first re-

---

opment of the initial evidence doctrine changed and was modified over the years within various Pentecostal groups.

[159] Robeck, *The Azusa Street Mission and Revival,* p. 154. From a different perspective, James Dunn notices Spirit baptism as the 'most distinctive aspect of Pentecostal theology' (*Baptism in the Holy Spirit: A Re-examination of the New Testament Teaching on the Gift of the Spirit in relation to Pentecostalism today* [London: SCM Press, 1970], introduction page).

[160] George's Pentecostal Spirit baptism and manifestation of tongues happened not long after Carrie's in 1908. See her 'Recent Trip to Mexico', *TF* 33.12 (Dec 1913), p. 271. She shared an account of a 'Chinaman' that she led to the Lord in Spanish and then mentioned that 'Mr. Montgomery began praying in the power of the Spirit a language which sounded like Chinese', which consequently the man could understand.

ceived special blessing among the colored people in the Azusa street meetings, have organized little gatherings in different parts of the city, and continue to receive gracious manifestations of God's presence. Much that seemed excitable and abnormal about the work has died down, but a real work of grace and power remain in many hearts.[161]

As a Pentecostal presence arose in Oakland near her home however, Carrie was finally able to attend a meeting. She was impacted when she saw a young Spirit-baptized girl 'shining' in God's 'glory' and urging her friend to be converted. Struck by this, Carrie later reflected on this account saying, 'I had myself received marvelous anointings of the Holy Spirit in the past, but I felt if there were more for me I surely wanted it, as I could not afford to miss any blessing that the Lord was pouring out in these last days'.[162]

The revival hit even closer to home when in her July 1907 periodical, Carrie mentioned that 'one of our dear workers there has received a mighty baptism of the Holy Ghost and speaks and sings in a foreign tongue. She has never been so deeply satisfied and so rejoicing in the Lord before, almost sweetly consecrated to His service'.[163] During this same time there was a revival occurring with the children in the Home of Peace as well. When Carrie saw these things first hand, it caused her to do some deep soul searching.[164] She began to hunger for something she had not previously realized existed at a personal level. Even though she had already experienced the Holy Spirit's presence and healing, she still felt that there was something more.[165] As a result of these stirrings, she began to petition others for prayer. She 'wrote to a dear brother who was won-

---

[161] Carrie Judd Montgomery, 'The Work in Los Angeles', *TF* 27.1 (Jan 1907), p. 14. She went to a meeting in Pasadena led my Mr Post, where she saw sweet unity present 'and the quiet but powerful manifestations of the Spirit of God in the speaking with tongues, and interpretations of the messages'. While still cautious, this account reveals that Carrie was drawn to the Pentecostal experience and was positive about it while still searching these things out for herself at the same time as not to 'miss' anything of the 'fulness of blessing'.

[162] Montgomery, *Under His Wings*, p. 164. The girl was around 9 years old.

[163] Carrie Judd Montgomery, 'Beulah Notes', *TF* 27.7 (July 1907), p. 168.

[164] Much of this section in relation to Carrie's Pentecostal Spirit baptism is heavily dependent upon Jennifer A. Miskov, *Spirit Flood: Rebirth of Spirit Baptism for the 21ˢᵗ Century* (Birmingham, UK: Silver to Gold, 2010), pp. 31-32.

[165] For Daniel E. Albrecht's account, see 'The Life and Ministry of Carrie Judd Montgomery', pp. 129-34.

derfully filled and blessed to pray for me that I might be filled with the Spirit. He prayed, and I only seemed to get more hungry'.[166] Carrie was finally so 'hungry' to experience the Spirit in a similar way that she took a break from her daily tasks to specifically search out these things.

3.3.3 Another Divine Encounter (1908): Carrie's Pentecostal Spirit Baptism Experience

In 1908, Carrie decided to take a trip back east to clear her head and take some focused time to think and pray about things in relation to the Pentecostal revival. She met up with some of her longtime friends in Cleveland who had received their Pentecostal experience, and she urged them to pray with her. She later reflected on this prayer time saying,

> As these dear ones prayed for me, the Spirit said, 'Take.' I waited and was afraid to do this, lest I should go back in this position of faith. The Spirit said again, and yet again, 'Take,' and finally I received the Spirit, by faith, to take complete possession of spirit, soul and body, and testified thus to the dear ones praying for me. I kept on tarrying at His feet for the manifestation of His gracious presence ... That same evening, in a measure, I began to experience His power, but He held me steadily to my position of faith, not letting me get my eyes on manifestations.[167]

Similar to the way that Carrie approached healing, she also approached the Pentecostal Spirit baptism. She chose to believe that by faith, she had already received her experience even if the manifestations had not yet come. Her application of 'taking' things by faith, whether that be healing, God's provision, or even Pentecostal Spirit baptism is prevalent here. Even in this, Carrie still continued to pray for the manifestations to come.

After the prayer meeting with her friends in Cleveland where Carrie did not speak in tongues, she returned to Chicago and reunited with longtime friend Lucy E. Simmons. According to Carrie, Simmons was one of her first personal friends who had received the 'fulness of the Spirit, with the sign of speaking in tongues. She was

---

[166] Carrie Judd Montgomery, 'Miraculously Healed by the Lord Thirty Years Ago', *LRE* 2.1 (Oct. 1909), p. 8.

[167] Carrie Judd Montgomery, '"The Promise of the Father": A Personal Testimony', *TF* 28.7 (July 1908), p. 147. See Appendix 4 for full article.

a consecrated child before this, but now the glory of God rested upon her'.[168] Carrie admitted that she was at first somewhat skeptical of the 'Pentecostal fullness', but after seeing the effects that it had on Simmons, she was more open.[169] Carrie and Simmons spent some time 'tarrying' in the Lord's presence during her visit. She also said that 'the cry was still in my heart, although I was standing by faith. On Monday, June 29th [1908], less than a week from the time I took my stand by faith, the mighty outpouring came upon me'.[170] When that happened, Carrie began to sing out to God and some of the words stuck in her throat so that she could not speak well. Simmons believed that God was taking away her English language to give her a new tongue. Carrie agreed and 'took' by faith the promise in Mk 16.17 of speaking in new tongues. She related the following:

In a few moments I uttered a few scattered words in an unknown tongue and then burst into a language and came pouring out in great fluency and clearness. The brain seemed entirely passive, the words not coming from that source at all, but from an irresistible volume of power within, which seemed to possess my whole being, spirit, soul and body. For nearly two hours I spoke and sang in unknown tongues (there seemed three or four distinct languages). Some of the tunes were beautiful, and most Oriental. I tried sometimes to say something in English, but the effort caused such distress in my throat and head, I had to stop after a few words and go back to the unknown tongues. I was filled with joy and praise to God with an inward depth of satisfaction in Him which cannot be described ... The rivers of living water flowed through me and divine ecstasy filled my soul ... Passages from the Word of God came to me with precious new meanings.[171]

---

[168] Montgomery, *Under His Wings*, p. 165.

[169] *Confidence* No. 8 (Nov. 15, 1908), p. 5.

[170] Montgomery, '"The Promise of the Father"', p. 148.

[171] Montgomery, '"The Promise of the Father"', p. 148. See also her 'Miraculously Healed by the Lord Thirty Years Ago', *LRE* 2.1 (Oct. 1909), p. 9, where she wrote,

I remember when Mr. Simpson literally baptized me in the Atlantic Ocean, I dreaded the water and was afraid of those big waves, but I was bound it would be a thorough work, I said, 'If my head begins to pop up, be sure to

This manifestation of speaking in tongues came just under a week after she had claimed her Spirit baptism experience which she had already begun to understand in Pentecostal terms.

In 1909, Carrie reflected that the results of her Pentecostal Spirit baptism experience brought her nothing but increase and satisfaction in ways she had yet to experience fully. She observed that there was a great multiplication of joy, holy stillness, love, power to witness, 'teachableness', hunger for the Word of God, and a spirit of praise.[172] She also claimed to have received 'greater power for service, and increased fellowship in prayer and praise'.[173] She saw that her 'fuller baptism' helped bring her 'freedom of the mind from all care', which had not been settled up to that point.[174] Additionally, Carrie noted that the experience also had a physical effect; she described her life as one where she mounted up with wings and gained physical strength in her body. She also said that she had more of the 'constant indwelling of the Healer'.[175]

It must be noted that Carrie was already a profound and influential writer and healing evangelist in her day before her Pentecostal Spirit baptism experience. Roughly thirty years after her divine healing encounter and at the age fifty, while after initial hesitation, Carrie embraced this newer experience of the Holy Spirit with the man-

stick it under,' and that was the way I felt about the Spirit's baptism. I wanted God to put my head under, and He did.

[172] Carrie Judd Montgomery, 'A Year with the Comforter', *TF* 29.7 (July 1909), pp. 145-49, and *Under His Wings,* p. 170. See also her '"The Glory of His Grace"', *TF* 29.1 (Jan 1909), pp. 2-3 where she said,

> The marvelous revelation of Himself through the Spirit of God to my spirit, soul and body since my Pentecostal baptism, is absolutely beyond expression. The precious reality of His grace, the perfection of His love in my spirit, the absolute rest and quietness of my mind (having the mind of Christ) and the indescribable quickening of my mortal body by His life-giving Spirit (Rom. viii:11), seem infinitely beyond any experience I have had in the past, freighted as the past has been with His blessing (more on this in Chapter 6).

[173] Montgomery, *Under His Wings,* p. 170.
[174] Montgomery, 'The Life on Wings', pp. 171-74. See Appendix 5 for full article.
[175] Carrie Judd Montgomery, 'Christ's Quickening Life for the Mortal Body', *TF* 28.8 (Aug 1908), p. 170. After her Pentecostal Spirit baptism she claimed to receive a 'quickening' in her physical body as well. See her 'Christ's Quickening Life for the Mortal Body', *TF* 28.8 (Aug 1908), p. 169. Daniel E. Albrecht also realizes that 'a sense of the immediate presence of God had been "increased" in her life since her Pentecostal baptism' ('The Life and Ministry of Carrie Judd Montgomery', pp. 119, 143).

ifestation of tongues. Regardless of her previous success, she saw that there was something more for her in the Spirit, so she pursued it. As a result of her 1908 experience, besides her spirituality being deepened, there were also several more immediate changes that followed. By December 1908, Carrie believed that God led her to give up her orphanage work so that she could give more time to the ministry of the Bible.[176] Following her 1908 experience, in her periodical she also began to share her testimony and encourage others to receive the Pentecostal Spirit baptism while at the same time making sure to emphasize love as its best result.[177] Another change that came was that, in addition to supporting overseas missionaries, Carrie felt led to go overseas herself. She had regularly ministered at a local and even national level, but after her 'Pentecostal fullness', she was empowered to minister at an international level as well.

3.4 Pentecostal Ambassador: 1908-1946

3.4.1 Missionary Zeal Expanded (Jan. 23-Sept. 16, 1909)

Less than six months after she received the manifestation of tongues, Carrie and her family went on a missionary journey around the world.[178] On her voyage, she shared her Pentecostal experience with missionaries in China, gave an Easter sermon at Pandita Ramabai's ministry in India, and spoke at Alexander Boddy's Sunderland Convention in England.[179] After roughly five months overseas, Carrie continued to spend a few more months traveling on a national level and speaking at some of Simpson's Alliance conventions before returning home. A couple of questions that will be explored in relation to her missionary trip are the following: Did Carrie originally set off on her trip with the intent to 'convert' Christians to receive their 'Pentecostal fullness'? And how did the mis-

---

[176] Montgomery, 'Some Important Changes', p. 267. Because more and more orphanages had popped up since the earthquake and fire of 1906, Carrie only had 35 of the 80 children still living there, which helped her in her transition to close it down a few years later.

[177] Carrie Judd Montgomery, 'Together in Love', *TF* 28.9 (Sept 1908), pp. 193-95, '"By this all Men Shall know"', *TF* 28.11 (Nov 1908), pp. 241-43.

[178] Montgomery, *Under His Wings*, p. 171. Many of the details of this trip are also taken from Carrie's *Date Book for 1909: Handwritten Diary*.

[179] Many of the missions she visited were either CMA or newly Pentecostal.

sionaries respond to Carrie when she shared a controversial message which many of them had previously rejected?

International Tour

Before Carrie's 1908 tongues experience, she primarily ministered in person at a local and national level. Even at home, however, she received many international children into her orphanage and multicultural students into her training school. She also regularly supported foreign missionaries and printed their letters in her periodical. It was only after Carrie had her 1908 tongues experience that she decided to minister at an international level beyond Mexico.[180] Her 1908 experience proved to be a significant spark that moved her beyond merely supporting those on the mission field, motivating her to go to the field herself. On January 23, 1909, Carrie, George, and Faith, along with friend Bessie Woods, sailed from San Francisco headed towards China.[181]

Carrie had been drawn to China for some years and had already supported its missionaries since at least 1894.[182] Although the Chinese people had been on her heart for some years, after her Pentecostal Spirit baptism, she wrote that she was filled with an even more 'remarkable love' and 'intercession for them'. Additionally, when she spoke in tongues for the first time, others claimed that she spoke in Chinese and Mandarin.[183] On their way to China, they passed through Hawaii, and Carrie noticed a hunger in some of the Christians there to receive the Pentecostal baptism. At this point in time, most references that Carrie made in relation to Spirit baptism or similar terms had to do with 'enduement of power' for service

---

[180] George Montgomery, 'Extracts from Mr. Montgomery's Letters', *TF* 25.3 (March 1905), p. 71. George had been involved in evangelistic work in Mexico before this trip as well as all throughout 1905 and on and off throughout the years.

[181] S.R. Break, 'Outward Bound', *TF* 29.2 (Feb 1909), p. 27. Bessie Woods was from Canada and the boat was called 'Manchuria'.

[182] Judd, 'The Word and Workers', *TF* 10.2. A few years later, 'Letter from Hong Kong', *TF* 15.5 (May 1895), p. 110, was an account from a missionary to China to whom Carrie had previously donated funds that were raised at her Cazadero Camp meetings.

[183] Carrie Judd Montgomery, 'Speaking in Tongues (A Personal Testimony)', *TF* 30.11 (Nov 1910), p. 253. Beyond this, however, she did begin taking Chinese language lessons in preparation for her journey. Conversely, many early Pentecostals expected to show up to a foreign land and be able to communicate by means of their new tongues.

and much of the time also meant that the experience was followed by the sign of tongues.[184] Carrie recognized that there were a few there who had already received the Pentecostal baptism, but she commented on the great need for someone wise in the Bible to go and teach the people more about it.[185]

Passing through Japan, they made it to China in mid February 1909. As Carrie toured Hong Kong, Shanghai, and other areas of China, she saw one of the purposes of her trip begin to unfold. It was there that she came across many disillusioned and confused missionaries in regards to the forming Pentecostal Movement. After sharing with her readers about encountering a great 'prejudice against the Pentecostal Movement' in China because of all the fanaticism and 'wildfire' connected to it, she saw that God had used her 'to remove prejudice from honest and hungry souls'.[186] She went on to explain,

> Dear ones who were even tempted to feel that the movement was of the devil, or who were greatly perplexed over the sad havoc wrought by lack of wisdom, are now seeing that there is another side to the matter, and that while the enemy is surely working in these last days, and that they must not miss the real blessing because of the counterfeit. We have had an abundant reason to see why the Lord sent us to China. Some dear Pentecostal people themselves have also felt that they greatly needed the Bible teaching which the Lord has enabled us to give them.[187]

Carrie additionally mentioned that she encountered a 'very prominent missionary' in China who was previously greatly opposed to the Pentecostal Movement before meeting her.[188] After hearing the Montgomerys' testimony and teaching on the subject, Carrie claimed that this missionary became much more open to the movement as a whole.

---

[184] The development of her understanding of Spirit baptism both before and after 1908 will be examined in Chapter 6. See also B.H. Irwin, 'My Pentecostal Baptism, A Christmas Gift', *TF* 27.5 (May 1907), pp. 114-17, and John Salmon, 'My Enduement', *TF* 27.12 (Dec 1907), pp. 269-71.

[185] Carrie Judd Montgomery, 'Letter from Mrs. Montgomery', *TF* 29.3 (March 1909), p. 50. The letter was dated February 1, 1909.

[186] Carrie Judd Montgomery, 'Letter from Mrs. Montgomery', *TF* 29.5 (May 1909), p. 115.

[187] Montgomery, 'Letter from Mrs. Montgomery', *TF* 29.5, p. 115.

[188] Montgomery, 'Letter from Mrs. Montgomery', *TF* 29.5, p. 116.

India

After China, instead of returning home as planned, Carrie believed God was leading her to India and then to return home via England.[189] She passed through Singapore before arriving in India in early April, 1909. There she visited Albert Norton's orphanage in Dhond. She had supported him over the years and printed updates of his orphanage work in her periodical. From there she went to Kedgaon and spent a few days with Pandita Ramabai (1858-1922) at her orphanage in Mukti. Ramabai started the home in 1895 to rescue young women who were left destitute as a result of child marriages or widowhood. By 1900, she had taken in up to 2,000 people because of a famine that hit the land. She especially helped Hindu women realize that they could have new life in Christ. In early 1905, Ramabai was 'convicted' to begin praying for revival and enlisted many others to do the same.[190]

It was on June 29, 1905 at 3:00 am that the Holy Spirit fell on one of Ramabai's volunteers. Minnie Abrams recorded the story saying,

> The young woman sleeping next to her awoke when this occurred, and seeing the fire enveloping her, ran across the dormitory, brought a pail of water and was about to dash it upon her, when she discovered that she was not on fire. In less than an hour nearly all of the young women in the compound gathered around, weeping, praying, and confessing their sins to God. The newly Spirit baptized girl sat in the midst of them, telling what God had done for her and exhorting them to repentance.[191]

The very next day, Ramabai was teaching from John 8 in her 'usual quiet way' when Abrams claimed that the Holy Spirit stirred up intense intercession among the girls so much that Ramabai had to stop talking. The room was filled with the 'presence of God' and

---

[189] Montgomery, *Under His Wings*, p. 171.

[190] Anderson, *Spreading Fires*, pp. 77-89. She shared her hunger for revival with others and enlisted seventy people to join her in her efforts. Shortly after this, there were 550 people who met two times a day to pray. Six months later, she urged the students in her Bible school to give up their 'secular' studies so that they could preach the gospel in the neighboring villages. Thirty women responded to this call and began to pray daily with each other for 'more of Jesus'.

[191] Minnie F. Abrams, *The Baptism of the Holy Ghost and Fire* (Kedgaon: Pandita Ramabai Mukti Mission, 1906), p. 1.

many were weeping and praying, hungering after God. Immediately following this, prayer meetings took over the center so much that even school classes were suspended. Abrams recalled that many experienced a deep burning of the fire of the Holy Spirit, causing them to realize at a deep level the price Jesus paid for them. This was followed by a great joy of their salvation that followed.[192] Ramabai is an important figure in Pentecostal history because later within this revival, speaking in tongues broke out even before reports from Azusa Street Revival had made it there.[193] Because of this, the Mukti mission is seen as one of the early centers in relation to global Pentecostalism.

Carrie first introduced Ramabai to her readers in 1897.[194] She also later became an avid supporter of Ramabai's ministry.[195] At the time Carrie visited the mission, there were about 1,500 people at the orphanage, the majority being women.[196] Ramabai asked the Montgomerys to lead a Pentecostal prayer meeting for the girls there. When they did, they were greatly impressed with the time of intense intercession in unknown tongues in which these Spirit-baptized girls engaged. Carrie was also asked to give a message for the Easter service.[197] During her visit there, Carrie heard more about Minnie Abrams (1859-1912). Abrams, who was in the States on furlough at that time, authored the influential *Baptism of the Holy Ghost and Fire* published by Ramabai in 1906.[198] Abrams saw that the effects of Spirit baptism would be greater mission, and her booklet came out at a time when there was very little literature on the subject. Allan Anderson notes that Abrams was one of the first to give a 'detailed exposition of Spirit baptism (within a Holiness framework) linking

---

[192] Abrams, *The Baptism of the Holy Ghost and Fire*, pp. 2-3.

[193] Anderson, *Spreading Fires,* p. 83. Pandita Ramabai, 'Showers of Blessing', *TF* 27.12 (Dec 1907), pp. 267-69, reprinted from *Mukti Prayer Bell*, pp. 267-69, which is her account of seeing girls in her orphanage praying in tongues.

[194] Pandita Ramabai, 'Famine Experience', *TF* 17.5 (May 1897), pp. 112-16, reprinted from the *Guardian*. Ramabai was also involved in Keswick conventions.

[195] 'Help Needed for Ramabai', *TF* 23.9 (Sept 1903), pp. 206-207.

[196] There were only about a hundred men there at that time.

[197] Montgomery, *Under His Wings,* p. 181, and also her 'Letter from Mrs. Montgomery', *TF* 29.6 (June 1909), pp. 123-29.

[198] Abrams, *The Baptism of the Holy Ghost and Fire* and Minnie Abrams, 'India: A Message from Mutki (Ramabai's Work)', *TF* 28.9 (Sept 1908), pp. 260-61. Abrams wrote 'The Scriptural Evidence of Pentecost' in *Confidence* magazine which Carrie introduced saying that 'her words are full of love and wisdom'.

spiritual gifts with mission'.[199] This book was influential in stirring Simmons to seek her Pentecostal Spirit baptism who in turn prayed with Carrie.[200] It was through Carrie's connection with Ramabai that she sought to become acquainted with Abrams when she returned home. When she finally did make it back home, Carrie and Abrams instantly bonded and even went to Los Angeles to do ministry together.[201] Abrams became a significant connection of Pentecostal revivals in various countries. From India, Carrie stopped by the Peniel Mission School in Egypt before journeying towards England.

England

By May of 1909, Carrie traveled to Europe and the United Kingdom. She passed through France and then spent about a month in England. She met up with Elizabeth Baxter, Cecil Polhill, and T.B. Barratt in London. She later remembered the joy she had when seeing Baxter, 'who had been like a mother' to her in previous years when she came to visit her in Buffalo.[202] Thomas Ball Barratt (1862-1940), who was born in England, moved to Norway and became one of its key Pentecostal leaders. He was also influential in spreading Pentecostal themes in Europe and he started the Pentecostal Missionary Union (PMU) and the International Pentecostal Conferences.[203] Cecil Polhill (1860-1938) who belonged to the CIM (China Inland Mission) was one of the founders along with Boddy in the organization of the PMU for Great Britain and Ireland.[204] Polhill asked Carrie to preach several times while she was in England.[205] Some of these meetings took place at the Bethshan healing home. She also intersected old Salvation Army ties and had lunch with Ar-

---

[199] Anderson, *Spreading Fires*, p. 66.

[200] Lucy E. Simmons, 'An Experience of Pentecostal Baptism', *TF* 28.7 (July 1908), pp. 153-54. Influenced by Abrams' book *The Baptism of the Holy Ghost and Fire*, Simmons was stirred to seek a deeper experience in God. She attended a Christian Alliance convention in August of 1907 where she saw several people who had already received their Pentecostal Spirit baptism, speaking and singing in tongues.

[201] Montgomery, *Under His Wings*, p. 190.

[202] Montgomery, *Under His Wings*, p. 185.

[203] P.D. Hocken, 'Cecil H. Polhill', in *NIDPCM*, pp. 991-92.

[204] D.D. Bundy, 'Thomas Ball Barratt', in *NIDPCM*, p. 365.

[205] Montgomery, *Date Book for 1909: Handwritten Diary*, June 1, p. 136. On May 16 (Sun), Carrie heard Pastor Barratt preach and then she said that 'Mr. Polhill asked me to speak in the first of the meet'g, which I did. In the evening at 7 we spoke at the Bethshan Hall'.

thur Booth-Clibborn while in London, although by that time he had already left the Army. During her time at the Pentecostal Conference, Carrie was approached by many who had been healed in years past after reading her *Prayer of Faith*.[206]

By early June 1909, Carrie made it to Alexander A. Boddy's (1854-1930) convention in Sunderland. Boddy was the editor of *Confidence* and was committed to the Church of England without compromising his growing spiritual hunger to be a part of the Pentecostal revivals.[207] This Anglican vicar was very influential in inviting Pentecostal themes into the Church of England and is noted by some scholars as 'the first leader of Pentecostalism in Britain'.[208] While at his conference, Carrie was invited to give a message there. Carrie appreciated that the Sunderland meetings were 'quiet and precious – no fanaticism in any way'.[209] This is also where she met Smith Wigglesworth for the first time.[210] After her time at the convention, she ventured into Scotland for a quick trip. Towards the end of June 1909, she sailed from England back to the United States.

National Tour

In early July of 1909, Carrie arrived in New York and stayed at the Alliance house. She quickly reconnected with A.B. Simpson who invited her to participate in the Christian Alliance Convention held at his training school in Nyack and also at his Berachah healing home. In one of her talks there, she shared a testimony of her Pentecostal Spirit baptism experience even though she was unsure of how her other Alliance friends might respond. After she had finished, she felt confident that Simpson was supportive of the poten-

---

[206] Montgomery, *Under His Wings*, p. 184. Some of these people were healed 24-28 years previously.

[207] Robeck, *The Azusa Street Mission and Revival*, p. 247, notes that Boddy,

who had recently been baptized in the Spirit but would always remain in Anglican orders, openly identified with what was taking place at the Azusa Street Mission. Instead of bowing to early expectations that he would leave the Anglicans, he helped the burgeoning global Apostolic Faith Movement by fostering comprehensive theological discussions.

[208] Anderson, *Spreading Fires*, pp. 28, 38. Boddy also visited the Welsh Revival and even shared a pulpit with Evan Roberts at one time. He later visited Dowie's Zion City in 1912 and preached at a church there as well.

[209] Montgomery, *Date Book for 1909: Handwritten Diary*, June 1, p. 152.

[210] Montgomery, *Under His Wings*, p. 184.

tially controversial Pentecostal teaching but was not sure how the others took it. She wrote, 'Our own testimony as to the glorious infilling of the Holy Ghost, which we personally experienced a year ago last June, with the gift of tongues, was accepted by Mr. Simpson and (we think) by all the other workers present'.[211] Possibly because of the favor she had with Simpson and also because the Pentecostal experience was still relatively new, there was no Alliance resistance to her teaching on the subject during this time. After a quick trip to New London (Connecticut) to see sisters, Elizabeth and Lottie Sisson, Carrie went on to Boston. By early August she found herself at the Old Orchard Convention in Maine where Simpson continued to create opportunities for her to speak despite an already full schedule. He rearranged the meetings so that there was an extra one each night for her to speak. Simpson claimed that it was one of the most 'wonderful' conventions ever held there where there was great unity in love.[212]

As Carrie journeyed towards her home in California, she continued with her speaking engagements at two more Christian and Missionary Alliance conventions, one in Cleveland, Ohio and one in Chicago, Illinois. During these conventions, she taught on the 'fullness of the Spirit and Divine Healing'.[213] It is interesting to note the order in which she mentioned these two themes. It appears that during this period in her life, themes in relation to her Pentecostal experience were emphasized more when she spoke. Her Pentecostal interest continued when she was a speaker at the Beulah Park convention in Cleveland in mid August 1909. There she prayed for many 'who were hungry for the baptism of the Holy Spirit'.[214] Besides her 1908 experience being at the forefront of her mind, another likely reason why she emphasized the Pentecostal experience more than healing was because most of the churches she visited there had already heard her healing testimony in the past. Carrie

---

[211] Carrie Judd Montgomery, 'Letter from Mrs. Montgomery', *TF* 29.8 (Aug 1909), p. 176. Her words in parenthesis.

[212] Carrie Judd Montgomery, 'Old Orchard Convention', *TF* 29.8 (Aug 1909), p. 179. Teachings there were on Sanctification, Spirit baptism, Divine Healing, and the Coming of the Lord. At some point towards the end of this national leg of her journey, George returned home for business.

[213] Carrie Judd Montgomery, 'Letter from Mrs. Montgomery', *TF* 29.9 (Sept 1909), p. 207.

[214] Montgomery, *Under His Wings,* p. 187.

recognized a new need to help the people understand the Pentecostal Spirit baptism in the midst of the confusion surrounding the issue.

Carrie also saw many of her former friends at these conventions and celebrated the fact that some of them had their Pentecostal Spirit baptism. Canadian Pastor Salmon was one of these Alliance members who received 'a remarkable enduement of the Spirit with utterance in tongues'.[215] Carrie also went to the Chicago Alliance convention in early September where the people welcomed her testimony of Pentecostal baptism and invited her and George to take a service each day. While there, she received an urgent request to speak at a William H. Piper's church. She noted that many at the Stone Church, even Piper's ten year old daughter, had 'received the "latter rain" fullness and speak in tongues'.[216] This church later developed into an early Pentecostal center in Chicago.[217] The Stone Church would be visited by Carrie again in the following year and is the same place she gave her famous address on her Pentecostal experience entitled 'The Life on Wings: The Possibilities of Pentecost'.[218] Throughout her journey, she enjoyed a special harmonious fellowship with the Pentecostal missionaries who had also received their baptism of the Holy Spirit.[219] She also visited Simmons before going through Michigan on her way home. After being gone for about eight months on this international and national excursion, on September 16, 1909, this 51 year old adventurer finally arrived safely back to her Oakland home.

Bridge Builder

While Carrie originally set out on her journey to explore and widen her vision for missions, gradually the need of the missionaries became evident and she responded by bringing clarity over the issues surrounding the Pentecostal experience. While overseas, Carrie encountered some opposition and prejudice against the Pentecostal

---

[215] Montgomery, *Under His Wings,* p. 187.

[216] Carrie Judd Montgomery, 'Letter from Mrs. Montgomery', *TF* 29.9 (Sept 1909), p. 209.

[217] Edith Blumhofer, *The Assemblies of God: A Popular History* (Springfield: Radiant Books, 1985), p. 32.

[218] See Appendix 5. Montgomery, 'The Life on Wings'.

[219] Montgomery, *Date Book for 1909: Handwritten Diary,* Aug. 1, p. 213. Carrie consistently mentioned if there were people present who had their 'Pentecostal fulness' and others who have 'rec'd the baptism of the Holy Spirit'.

Movement because the missionaries were highly suspicious of the 'fanaticism' associated with it. Conversely, Carrie encountered minimal opposition to her Pentecostal message while in the national part of her trip. This was probably because she was sheltered under Simpson's favor, especially on the East Coast, and because she already had strong reputation there. Many of the people had already been exposed to her teaching on healing in the past and were likely more open to hear what she had to say on other issues.

Throughout her entire trip, Carrie brought understanding between Evangelical missionaries and the newly forming Pentecostal Movement. During her missionary journey, she spent time with people in Pentecostal, Apostolic Faith Mission, Christian and Missionary Alliance, Salvation Army, and even Temperance circles. Daniel Albrecht's work rightly emphasizes how Carrie acted as a bridge builder.[220] While Carrie supported the Pentecostal Movement, she did not cut her ties with other religious organizations. Her Episcopalian background, healing ministry, passion for unity in the church, and moderate convictions regarding the manifestations of Spirit baptism built her an extensive reputation. This approachability contributed to her effectiveness in influencing a wide variety of people towards the 'Pentecostal fullness' without alienating them.[221] By addressing the missionaries with Biblical foundations to support her experience, many were encouraged to receive the new experience. Zelma Argue's father, Andrew H. Argue (1868-1959), who was influential in the Canadian Pentecostal Movement, recognized Carrie's influence and reputation when he wrote,

> In 1908, Rev. G.S. Paul said to me: 'when you see a woman like Mrs. Carrie Judd Montgomery receive this wonderful baptism of the Holy Spirit,' meaning in Pentecostal fullness with signs following, 'believe it's of God,' that was the first time I had heard of Sister Montgomery. Her life at that time had a powerful influence for God ... We praise God for sister Montgomery. She has been a real pillar of strength to many, her life has touched thou-

---

[220] This whole theme of Carrie being a bridge builder was the framework that Albrecht built his thesis around in his 'The Life and Ministry of Carrie Judd Montgomery'.

[221] Carrie Judd Montgomery, 'Letter from Mrs. Montgomery', *TF* 29.5, pp. 115-16.

sands, her labours of love and influence have encircled the globe.[222]

Carrie contributed to making the Pentecostal experience more accessible across denominational barriers. Some of her 'old' friends with whom she kept in touch were influenced towards Pentecostalism after hearing her testimony about the experience. She also met many new Pentecostal friends on her trip whom she later encouraged to participate in her 1914 Cazadero Camp meeting several years later. That important camp meeting was to be flavored with Pentecostal themes and included teaching by Smith Wigglesworth.

3.4.2 Cazadero 'World-wide Pentecostal Camp Meeting' (1914)

In 1914 and after a break from her Cazadero Camp meetings, Carrie felt the urge to reunite under the Redwoods, this time with an added emphasis on Pentecostal themes. In anticipation of this meeting, she reflected that the earlier 'Holiness gatherings [were] for the deepening of spiritual life among the saints, and for the saving of the lost' and that these resulted in many being sent into foreign mission fields with great blessing. She continued,

> [B]ut now in these marvelous days of privilege, when God is pouring out the Latter Rain of His Spirit as on the Day of Pentecost, we feel that God is leading us to call a World-wide Pentecostal Camp Meeting, and as His people come together in love and faith, we trust Him for a great down pouring of His Spirit; and that 'Signs and wonders may be done in the Name of His holy Child Jesus.'[223]

Ahead of time, Carrie clearly spelled out that the purpose of the meeting would be 'to see sinners saved, believers baptized with the Holy Spirit in Pentecostal fullness (Acts 2:4), the sick healed according to Mark 16:18 and James 5:14, and to bring about greater unity of the Body of Christ (Eph. 4:13)'.[224] Notice how she ordered these things with 'Pentecostal fullness' placed before healing.

---

[222] Bro. A.H. Argue from Winnipeg, Canada, wrote this on July 8, 1931, which was found in the Home of Peace Guest Book Aug. 14, 1928-1938, original handwritten copy, researched at and courtesy of the Home of Peace, p. 87.

[223] Carrie Judd Montgomery, 'Cazadero World-Wide Camp Meeting', *TF* 34.1 (Sept 1914), p. 23.

[224] Carrie Judd Montgomery, 'World-Wide Camp Meeting', *TF* 34.6 (June 1914), p. 144.

Throughout July, many prominent people connected in one way or another to the Pentecostal Movement came to the camp meeting.[225] Missionaries and leaders from around the world attended as well. Alexander Boddy was there for a short time but left early because of the distressing news of the war.[226] Carrie claimed that British lay healing evangelist and former plumber Smith Wigglesworth (1859-1947) 'felt a clear leading' to participate in the Camp Meeting after receiving her invitation.[227] Carrie quickly created space for him to minister during the meetings. He spoke several times during the camp and led many into their Pentecostal Spirit baptism experience.[228] Carrie later remembered that 'God used him as a channel of blessing to many who sought and received healing, and the baptism of the Holy Spirit'.[229] Wigglesworth became good friends with the Montgomerys and stayed in contact with and visited them in Oakland over the years.[230]

During the meetings, some of the participants were baptized in water in the Austin Creek, and many more were baptized in the Holy Spirit.[231] Carrie remembered that there were often more than eight Pentecostal Spirit baptisms in one day but that they all had lost count because 'the workers had been so fixed upon the Lord' and in helping others 'receive' that they forgot to count.[232] Methodist minister J.N. Gortner was one of these who received his Pentecostal baptism at the camp meeting and later went on to become a

---

[225] July 30, 1914 was the 21st anniversary of the dedication of the Cazadero camp (July 30, 1893 was first Camp meeting there).

[226] Elizabeth Sisson, 'Incidents from Elim Grove Camp Meeting', *TF* 34.8 (Aug 1914), p. 179.

[227] Montgomery, *Under His Wings,* p. 215. See also W.E. Warner, 'Smith Wigglesworth', in *NIDPCM*, p. 1195 and Carrie Judd Montgomery, 'Cazadero Camp Meeting', *TF* 34.8 (Aug 1914), p. 171.

[228] A few of the messages delivered at Cazadero by Smith Wigglesworth and recorded in *TF* are as followed: 'The Confidence that We Have in Him', *TF* 34.8 (Aug 1914), pp. 175-77; '"The Spirit of the Lord is Upon Me"'; *TF* 34.9 (Sept 1914), pp. 204-206; and 'Sons and Joint Heirs', *TF* 35.2 (Feb 1915), pp. 34-38.

[229] Montgomery, *Under His Wings,* p. 215.

[230] Smith Wigglesworth, 'Tributes to Mr. Montgomery's Memory', *TF* 50.10 (Oct 1930), p. 235. In a condolence letter just after George died, Wigglesworth said that he 'was looking forward to seeing him again. I shall miss him much, and his very good and inspiring letters. It was one of the great joys of Oakland to see him there'.

[231] Carrie Judd Montgomery, 'Cazadero Camp Meeting', *TF* 34.8 (Aug 1914), pp. 160-71.

[232] Montgomery, *Under His Wings,* p. 215.

Pentecostal minister, even planting the First Pentecostal Church in Oakland.[233] Many of the meetings took place in a large natural outdoor auditorium encircled with Redwoods. There were also smaller meetings taking place in the prayer tent, sometimes even at the same time as the main services. Besides the people who sought healing in the prayer tent, many also went there seeking their Pentecostal Spirit baptism experience.[234] Elizabeth Sisson described the scene in the tent saying that the whole floor was 'covered with the slain in the Lord, and many constantly "Coming through" in the Baptism with tongues'.[235] Sisson continued to describe that people experienced the 'power of God' even outside of the tent. She also mentioned that on the morning of July 28, 1914, there was a quiet gathering in the Montgomery cottage where 'ten lay on the floor under the power of God. Several came through with tongues, one speaking clearly a number of languages'. Sisson recalled that the biggest mark of the entire camp meeting was unity in love that was characterized in 'proportionately ever-increasing direct power from Heaven' descending on each meeting. Participants also prayed over handkerchiefs and sent them to sufferers with some good results of them being healed.[236]

Some of the messages of the meetings were coated in Pentecostal themes while others were on more general themes. George B. Studd spoke about how the gift of tongues did not come from Azusa Street but from God.[237] George Montgomery gave a message entitled 'In the Time of the Latter Rain' which contributed to the belief that they were experiencing the latter rain at that time.[238] Not

---

[233] Montgomery, *Under His Wings,* pp. 217, 218. He became a minister for the Assemblies of God, but it was noted that he later resigned and became a teacher in San Francisco for Mr Craig's Bible School.

[234] The timing of this camp meeting just before the outbreak of the war may have heightened the intensity of people seeking deep spiritual experiences.

[235] Elizabeth Sisson, 'Incidents from Elim Grove Camp Meeting', *TF* 34.8 (Aug 1914), p. 178. As far as I can determine, Carrie did not use the term 'slain' as Sisson does here. Sisson's usage may stem from her close association with Woodworth-Etter at one time in her life, and being 'slain in the Spirit' was terminology she used in her ministry.

[236] Elizabeth Sisson, 'Incidents from Elim Grove Camp Meeting', *TF* 34.8 (Aug 1914), pp. 179-81.

[237] George B. Studd, '"And There Was A Voice"', *TF* 34.8 (Aug 1914), pp. 182-86.

[238] George Montgomery, 'In the Time of the Latter Rain', *TF* 34.8 (Aug 1914), p. 189.

all the messages directly emphasized Pentecostal themes though. M.M. Pinson spoke on redemption through the blood of Christ; Margaret Gordon talked about the power of prayer; Elizabeth Sisson gave a message entitled 'The Spirit of the Learner'; and Smith Wigglesworth spoke about being sons and heirs of Christ.[239]

This Camp meeting was not only 'memorable' for Carrie, it was also significant for the developing Pentecostal Movement. Many Christian leaders who had been waiting and seeking their Pentecostal Spirit baptism finally received it during the meetings. Many like Gortner left their denominational backgrounds to join this newer Pentecostal Movement as a result. During the meetings, the participants called on the things from the past, the healing and sanctification themes, and built upon them with the new expression of Spirit baptism with the speaking of tongues. At the end of the camp though, what many celebrated the most was the unity and love experienced there. Because of this, they re-named the camp, 'The LOVE Camp Meeting'.[240] This is only a snapshot of how Carrie reached across denominational borders to introduce the 'Pentecostal fullness' to audiences with different denominational backgrounds while maintaining unity in love.[241]

3.4.3 Fully Committed: Official Affiliation with the Pentecostal Movement

It was also in 1914 that Carrie officially united herself with the newly forming Assemblies of God. A certificate of ordination with the Assemblies of God reveals that she was ordained with them as an 'Evangelist and Missionary'.[242] While it took several years after this for the Assemblies of God to become an official denomination, Carrie associated herself with the movement in its earliest stages of

---

[239] These sermons can be found in *TF* 34.8 (Aug 1914) through *TF* 34.10 (Oct 1914), and *TF* 35.2 (Feb 1915).

[240] Elizabeth Sisson, 'Incidents from Elim Grove Camp Meeting', *TF* 34.8 (Aug 1914), p. 180.

[241] Carrie Judd Montgomery, 'Cazadero World-Wide Camp Meeting', *TF* 34.6 (June 1914), p. 144.

[242] 'Certificates of Ordination', Personal Papers of Carrie Judd Montgomery, 1914. These were dated January 11, 1914 before the Assemblies of God was officially formed several months later. Carrie was also listed as 'Editor and Evangelist' in *Combined Minutes of the General Council of the Assemblies of God in the United States of America, Canada and Foreign Lands- 1914-1920*, p. 34 Accessed <http://ifphc.org/DigitalPublications/USA/Assemblies%20of%20God%20USA/Minutes%20General%20Council/Unregistered/1920/FPHC/1914-1920.pdf>

development. Ironically, many of the prominent leaders who later went on to play an important role in this Pentecostal denomination were also nurtured under the leadership of Simpson and came out from under the Christian and Missionary Alliance.[243] Records of communication between Carrie and the leaders in the General Council of the Assembly of God show her involvement in the movement. These reveal that her Beulah Chapel in Oakland acted more as an 'independent assembly but working in cooperation with the General Council'.[244] It is also important to note that Carrie was more concerned with people having their Pentecostal Spirit baptism experience than she was in swaying them to join the Pentecostal Movement. Furthermore, even while Carrie remained affiliated with the Assemblies of God until her death, she never broke off ties or association with the Christian and Missionary Alliance, the Salvation Army, or her other connections. Simpson also continued to invite her to speak at his meetings up until the end of his life regardless of her new affiliation. Interestingly enough, it was around the same time of Simpson's death that Carrie became friends with the prominent Pentecostal healing evangelist, Aimee Semple McPherson.

3.4.4 Intersections with Aimee Semple McPherson (1919)

The first time Carrie mentioned McPherson was in 1918 when she reprinted her article about waiting on God for the baptism of the Holy Spirit.[245] Aimee Semple McPherson (October 9, 1890-September 27, 1944), a Canadian who eventually moved to Los Angeles, was an influential healing evangelist who also founded the International Church of the Foursquare Gospel.[246] Besides Pentecostal influences, McPherson, like Carrie, also incorporated much of Simpson's Fourfold Gospel into her theology and was influenced by the Salvation Army. In January of 1919, Carrie wrote that she had recently ministered with Woodworth-Etter and had also heard McPherson speak for the first time. She said of 'Sister Aimee',

---

[243] Blumhofer, *The Assemblies of God: A Popular History*, p. 33. Paul L. King has a comprehensive list in his *Genuine Gold: The Cautiously Charismatic Story of the Early Christian and Missionary Alliance* (Tulsa: Word & Spirit Press, 2006), pp. 317-30.

[244] 'Annual Questionnaire for Ordained Preachers', Personal Papers of Carrie Judd Montgomery, 1943. The church and the healing home are both currently non-denominational.

[245] Aimee S. McPherson, 'The Gift of the Holy Spirit', *TF* 38.11 (Nov 1918), pp. 258-61, reprinted from *Word and Work*.

[246] C.M. Robeck Jr., 'Aimee Semple McPherson', in *NIDPCM*, pp. 856-59.

We praise God for this sister, who has such a wonderful experience of the Pentecostal baptism, and also of healing, and we are thankful for the way in which He is using her. Since coming home we hear that her meetings are being greatly blessed by God. We hope that we shall have her here in Northern California later on.[247]

By Carrie's March 1919 edition of *Triumphs of Faith*, she wrote an article entitled 'Special Revival Meetings in San Francisco' where she praised the 28 year old evangelist for the work she was doing. She said that 'the Lord wonderfully uses dear Sister McPherson to expound the Word of God in the power of the Spirit, and as one listens to her sermons, one can but realize that they do not proceed from herself but from the Holy Ghost with whom she is so filled'. Carrie then shared with her readers that she hoped 'our dear sister' would hold some meetings in Oakland before returning to Los Angeles. This came to pass when McPherson came as a guest speaker for Carrie's Monday meeting on March 17, 1919, speaking to a larger than normal audience.[248]

By 1920, Carrie actively began to support McPherson's ministry even more. Carrie shared that she saw her speak in Los Angeles and in the same article also encouraged her readers to pray for McPherson's ministry.[249] In 1922, Carrie also saw McPherson speak in

---

[247] Carrie Judd Montgomery, 'An Eastern Trip in the Lord's Work', *TF* 39.1 (Jan 1919), p. 17. Carrie also saw Jennie Smith, the railroad evangelist, on that same trip. In that same issue, Carrie also published an extract of a letter by Mrs E.M. Whittemore which also spoke of McPherson in a supporting way ('Healed and Filled with the Spirit', *TF* 39.1 [Jan 1919], p. 9). Whittemore recalled that E. Sisson urged her to attend McPherson's Philadelphia convention which was where she received prayer from the both of them and was healed. Whittemore was in awe of the way that she could 'feel the actual presence of God through [McPherson's] words of adoration and praise to Him'.

[248] Carrie Judd Montgomery, 'Special Revival Meetings in San Francisco', *TF* 39.3 (March 1919), p. 72. In July, Carrie also reprinted an article by Aimee Semple McPherson called 'The Last Days', *TF* 39.7 (July 1919), pp. 149-50, taken from *Word and Work*.

[249] Carrie Judd Montgomery, 'Letter from the Editor', *TF* 40.2 (Feb 1920), pp. 38-40. She saw her at Victoria Hall. She also published an announcement for McPherson's 'Pentecostal Revival Campaign' to take place in Winnipeg, Canada. Another article by McPherson was printed in July 1920, followed by an announcement a few months later that she would be holding meetings in Oakland in February of the next year. See Aimee Semple McPherson, 'Tarry Until', *TF* 40.7 (July 1920), pp. 150-53, and Carrie Judd Montgomery, 'Aimee Semple McPherson Coming to Oakland', *TF* 40.11 (Nov 1920), p. 263.

Fresno, and into the early 1920s she continued to announce McPherson's campaigns as well as print some of her articles.[250] Following McPherson's controversial disappearance and reappearance in 1926 however, Carrie mentioned the younger evangelist much less in her periodical. For the most part after that event, their 'public' friendship became more 'private' from Carrie's side. Steering away from potential controversy, Carrie took the cautious view once again while still maintaining a friendship.

McPherson, however, continued to quote and reference Carrie's writings all the way up to 1936.[251] In McPherson's *Foursquare Crusader* that year, an article by Carrie was printed with the following reference below her name: 'Carrie Judd Montgomery, greatly loved poet, editor of a religious magazine, and pioneer of the Pentecostal Faith, spoke at Angelus Temple recently. We quote excerpts'.[252] From this information, it appears that even years after Carrie's public silence about McPherson, Carrie continued to maintain ties and even preached at Angelus Temple. Earl Dorrance, who was a part of the Oakland Revival meetings, reported that when McPherson

---

[250] Carrie Judd Montgomery, 'The Prayer of Faith', *TF* 42.2 (Feb 1922), p. 263.

[251] 'Reports of the San Francisco Meetings', *Bridal Call* (April 1919), p. 15. This article mentions that both Carrie and George and also some from their assembly attended some of McPherson's meetings in San Francisco. In 'Oakland, Cal.' *Bridal Call* (July 1919), p. 13, it is reported that 'Two [of McPherson's] meetings were held under the auspices of Sister Carrie Judd Montgomery'. In Kenneth McKenzie, Jr., 'The Prayer of Faith in Sickness,' *Bridal Call* (June 1922), pp. 13-16, he says,

> Is it any marvel that proving the reality of His Word in the ordinary experiences of life, the hungering children of God should ask of Him to fulfill His promises concerning their bodies? Led by this inspired yearning for a greater experience of His love and a fuller obedience to His will, Dr Bushnell, Dorothea Trudel, Otto Stockmayer, Pastor Blumhardt, Karl Andreas, Dr Cullis, Carrie Judd, Dr Gordon, and many others prominent for fidelity and devotion to the Master, have demonstrated beyond doubt that God heals today in answer to the cry of His children as readily and as really as He did in Judea, Samaria and Galile [sic].

McPherson also printed several of Carrie's writings or poems in her periodical. E.g. Carrie Judd Montgomery, 'Shine On', *Foursquare Crusader* (June 5, 1929), p. 16; 'Sweet Love of Christ', *Foursquare Crusader* (October 2, 1929), p. 16; and *Foursquare Crusader* (March 12, 1930), p. 6, where this same poem is reprinted. See also Carrie Judd Montgomery, 'Through the Lattice', *Foursquare Crusader* (March 21, 1934), p. 2 (Excerpt from Heart Melody).

[252] Carrie Judd Montgomery, 'Why So Many Are Sick', *Foursquare Crusader* (June 10, 1936), p. 2.

was in Oakland in 1944 for her final evangelistic campaign, she made sure to send out a red rose to 'Mother Carrie Judd Montgomery who helped Sister in her Oakland Meetings many years before'.[253] Shortly after McPherson's significant message on 'The Foursquare Gospel' in Oakland, she died in her hotel room due to causes which are still controversial.[254]

Carrie's grandson Loren Berry mentioned the respect that Carrie's family had for McPherson and also that his grandparents on the other side of the family, the Berrys, also supported McPherson at times when she needed to get away. [255] From oral tradition and from McPherson's periodicals, it appears that the two healing evangelists continued to stay connected at some level, even if that was somewhat behind the public scene. Why Carrie chose not to promote her friendship with McPherson in the later years is up for question. One reason for Carrie's public silence may have been because of her affiliation with the Assemblies of God while McPherson broke off her association to start her own denomination. McPherson's disagreements with Francisco Olazábal, a spiritual son to the Montgomerys, may have also weakened public ties. That Carrie's references to McPherson tapered off after the 'kidnapping' event in 1926 may have been because Carrie felt the need to publically stay far away from all the controversies relating to McPherson, especially after she already had to deal with the controversies regarding Woodworth-Etter in previous years.[256] Regardless of limited public promotion, it appears that these two maintained a strong lev-

---

[253] Dr Earl W. Dorrance, 'The Oakland Revival: The Final Evangelistic Campaign in the Ministry of the Founder of the INTERNATIONAL CHURCH of THE FOURSQUARE GOSPEL – AIMEE SEMPLE MCPHERSON', *Foursquare Magazine* (Nov 1944), p. 4. In recounting her final service, Dorrance said that 'Later at the close of the altar call, Sister personally gave her favorite red roses to eager members of the audience. She thoughtfully sent one lovely red rosebud to dear 70 year old Mother Carrie Judd Montgomery who helped Sister in her Oakland Meetings many years before, but was now confined by illness'.

[254] See Blumhofer, *Aimee Semple McPherson*, pp. 375, 379, and Matthew Avery Sutton*, Aimee Semple McPherson and the Resurrection of Christian America* (Cambridge, MA: Harvard University Press, 2007), p. 268.

[255] Loren Berry. Interview by Jennifer Miskov March 30-31, 2008. Recording, Cazadero family home, CA. He said that McPherson stayed with the Berrys on their farm to get away from the crowds.

[256] The last mention of Aimee Semple McPherson in *Triumphs of Faith* was in Eva E. Morton's article, 'What's Out Ahead!', *TF* 48.1 (Jan 1928), p. 15, in reference to listening to McPherson on the radio.

el of love, respect, and honor for each other all the way up to McPherson's last days.

While both McPherson and Carrie emphasized healing in their ministries, their approaches differed greatly. Carrie, the older healing evangelist who thrived in the Divine Healing Movement, was in her early sixties when she met the younger healing evangelist who was in her late twenties at the time. Carrie was cut from a Victorian cloth, while McPherson was a woman way before her time in an era when Hollywood was beginning to explode.[257] A generation apart in age and worlds apart in upbringings, these two healing evangelists both effectively brought healing to their generations, one mainly through literature and healing homes, and the other, ahead of her time, through multimedia and the creative arts. Why one has been greatly remembered within popular Christian culture and the other has been nearly forgotten will be discussed in Chapter 7.

3.4.5 Francisco Olazábal and the Expansion of Latino Pentecostalism

Carrie's intersections with Mexican Francisco Olazábal (1886-1937) throughout the years demonstrate some of her impact on the Pentecostal Movement. When Olazábal was a teenager, his mother took him along with her to evangelize in the villages.[258] He eventually rebelled from this religious life and escaped to San Francisco where George Montgomery ran into him, gave him a religious tract, and then 'took him to their home where he was saved'.[259] Later on, he went to Moody Bible Institute in Chicago, and after only six months, R.A. Torrey took him to Los Angeles to help establish a Spanish Mission and a Bible School.[260] Olazábal 'later ran into conflict with Torrey's teaching that the baptism of the Holy Spirit was a

---

[257] McPherson also emerged in a time when Pentecostal people were disillusioned over all the divisions at Azusa Street.

[258] His mother was a full blooded Indian descending from the Aztecs, while his father was Basque from Spain. She was Roman Catholic until she was 'saved' through the influence of Methodists.

[259] Homer A. Tomlinson, *Miracles of Healing in the Ministry of Rev. Francisco Olazábal* (Queens Village, NY: Homer A. Tomlinson, 1939), p. 6. See also Gastón Espinosa, 'El Azteca: Francisco Olazábal and Latino Pentecostal Charisma, Power, and Faith Healing in the Borderlands', *Journal of the American Academy of Religion* 67.3 (1999), pp. 599-600.

[260] When he graduated, he was ordained and sent to pastor a Methodist church in El Paso, Texas. In 1911, at 25 years old, he quit the pastorate so he could attend Moody Bible Institute in Chicago.

definite experience'.[261] It was over this issue that Olazábal left Torrey's ministry. Following this departure, he joined a Methodist
Episcopal church in California and was ordained in 1914.[262]

A few years later, he moved to central California, and it was
around that time that he reunited with the Montgomerys.[263] Gastón
Espinosa notes that to Olazábal's surprise, the Montgomerys 'had
become Pentecostals, a group that he criticized from the pulpit'.[264]
Homer A. Tomlinson also wrote that during this time,

> [Olazábal] visited again the ones who he always felt were his fa-
> ther and mother in the Gospel, George and Carrie Judd Mont-
> gomery, in Oakland, California. They had brought him to Christ
> and into the knowledge and experience of the sanctified life, and
> water baptism. They now had the joy of telling him of the great
> outpouring of the Holy Ghost, with the evidence of 'Speaking
> with other tongues as the Spirit gives utterance.' It was there that
> he was baptized with the Holy Ghost. And at the same time his
> wife was miraculously cured of 'milk leg.' It was a turning point
> in his ministry, in the surging and movings of the Holy Ghost
> within him, and he saw the glory of God in the healing of the
> sick.[265]

It was only after this experience with the Montgomerys that his
'gift of healing was triggered' and that he later went on to preach
alongside Aimee Semple McPherson, who once referred to him as
the 'Mexican Billy Sunday'.[266] He eventually branched out on his

---

[261] Espinosa, 'El Azteca', p. 600. Note that this was even before the sign of
tongues was readily associated with it.

[262] Tomlinson, *Miracles of Healing in the Ministry of Rev. Francisco Olazábal*, p. 6.

[263] He moved so that he could pastor two different churches in Sacramento
and San Francisco.

[264] Espinosa, 'El Azteca', pp. 600-601. Espinosa writes, 'After initially reject-
ing the Montgomerys' newfound message, he became persuaded that the baptism
with the Holy Spirit was a second definite experience and a necessary part of the
Christian life'.

[265] Tomlinson, *Miracles of Healing in the Ministry of Rev. Francisco Olazábal*, p. 7.
This is recorded to have happened in 1917. 'Milk leg' is an inflammation of the
'femoral vein', the main vein of the thigh, because of a clot that blocks the flow.
The leg swells up, becomes pale and is very painful. Ulcers can also develop and
even the pulmonary artery can be affected. The person is usually kept in bed with
leg elevated. Accessed on <http://www.britannica.com> February 24, 2011.

[266] Espinosa, 'El Azteca', pp. 606, 612-13. McPherson was friends with
Olazábal until he refused to join her organization; following this, she was at odds
with him.

own and established the Latin American Council for Christian Churches which he later united with the Church of God in agreement with A.J. Tomlinson.[267] Olazábal died June 9, 1937 but in his last days encouraged his followers to continue on in the work of the Holy Spirit.[268] He was said to have preached to over 250,000 people, and there were 150 churches and around 50,000 members in his denomination by the time he died. Espinosa claims that 'no single Latino religious leader of the early twentieth century has shaped the history and development of the Latino Pentecostal Movement in North America and the Latin Caribbean like Francisco Olazábal'.[269] Throughout his life, he planted and helped form over ten denominations (both Protestant and Pentecostal).[270]

If Olazábal was a significant figure in the Latino Pentecostal Movement, then those who were key catalysts in his life were also a part of his success. The reason I give a more lengthy account of his story is because the Montgomerys' influence in his life is significant on three different levels. On one level, they turned him towards conversion; at another level, they transformed him from a skeptic into a Pentecostal pioneer when no one else before was able to do that. It was through the relationship and history he had with the Montgomerys that he was open to receive his Pentecostal Spirit baptism. Lastly, his wife's healing proved to be a catalyst for his

---

[267] Tomlinson, *Miracles of Healing in the Ministry of Rev. Francisco Olazábal,* pp. 7, 16. In 1923, he went to Texas with a few others and established the Latin American Council for Christian Churches. In Houston, he prayed for and saw a deaf and dumb twelve year old healed. Later on, A.J. Tomlinson convinced Olazábal to unite the 'Latin American Church Council into the fellowship of the Church of God'. The author also stated that 'From this new beginning his faith for healing and the salvation of souls seemed to take on new proportions'.

[268] Espinosa, 'El Azteca', p. 610. Olazábal encouraged people 'to keep the "fire and guidance" of the Holy Spirit at the center of their ministry'.

[269] Espinosa, 'El Azteca', pp. 610-12.

[270] Espinosa, 'El Azteca', p. 598. He was said to have attracted 'over 250,000 Mexicans, Puerto Ricans, Anglo-Americans, Italians, and blacks to his evangelistic services throughout North America and the Latin Caribbean'. Tomlinson in his *Miracles of Healing in the Ministry of Rev. Francisco Olazábal,* p. 7, also claimed that Olazábal 'far outstripped the work among Latin Americans of all Protestant churches put together, and he was largely instrumental in bringing together a company in Mexico City with more than four thousand when he was there, larger than any Catholic Church in Mexico'. He was also said to have influenced a great move of God resulting in bringing over tens of thousands of people into the Pentecostal Movement throughout not only the United States but also Mexico and Puerto Rico.

healing ministry. The impact Carrie had in Olazábal's life over the years demonstrates the direct part she played in the expansion of Latino Pentecostalism.

3.4.6 Finishing Strong: 1920-1946

Throughout the later years of her life, Carrie continued to conduct her meetings, preach, and minister healing to those around her. She also carried on in her many writing endeavors. In 1921, she published *Secrets of Victory,* which was an assortment of her works put together by her assistant Sadie Cody.[271] Before A.B. Simpson died, he also published a compilation of her editorials in a book called *The Life of Praise.*[272] By 1922, Carrie put together some of her poems and published them under the title *Heart Melody,* and in 1936, when she was 78 years old, she published her life story entitled *Under His Wings: The Story of My Life.*

Carrie's husband passed away a few years before this in 1930. Even with him gone, Carrie still continued to run her prayer meetings and the Home of Peace into her old age. She also carried on writing and publishing articles in her periodical right up until her death in 1946 (at 88 years old). Up until 1964, *Triumphs of Faith* continued to remain in circulation to 43 States and 49 foreign countries. Carrie's daughter and son-in-law ran the publication all the way up to the mid-1970s.[273] Carrie outlived her immediate family as well as many other healing evangelists in her era including Elizabeth Sisson, Maria Woodworth-Etter, and Aimee Semple McPherson. According to the sources at hand, Carrie remained faithful to her husband and to the ministry of healing and fullness of the Spirit until the end of her life.

In conclusion, the networks Carrie built through her social endeavors on the West Coast enlarged her platform, strengthened her reputation, and prepared her to have an even greater impact within Pentecostalism. Carrie acted as a pioneer by being one of the first to spread divine healing themes and open a healing home on the West

---

[271] Carrie Judd Montgomery, *Secrets of Victory,* compiled by Sadie A. Cody (Oakland, CA: Office of Triumphs of Faith, 1921).

[272] Simpson originally rolled out the book through the Alliance Colportage Library, but then later, because of the growing demand, Carrie also ended up publishing several editions.

[273] Barbara Cavaness, 'Spiritual Chain Reactions: Women used by God', The Network for Women in Ministry, General Council of the Assemblies of God (Springfield, MO: Enrichment Journal Office, 2011).

Coast. But regardless of her previous ministry success, even at age fifty, Carrie still was 'hungry' to 'take hold of' all that God had for her in her generation. Because of this, she embraced the Pentecostal Spirit baptism experience which in turn inspired many others to do the same.[274] From that point on, Carrie acted as a Pentecostal ambassador, taking Pentecostal Spirit baptism themes even to the nations. Besides her missionary journey, she also integrated Pentecostal themes into her periodical, camp meetings, healing home, weekly meetings, and speaking engagements. Her strong reputation and her many ecumenical connections provided her a platform to influence many to pursue the same experience. It was through her varied and expansive network that Carrie introduced a large number of people to the Pentecostal Movement. As with Olazábal, many of these later became influential leaders within Pentecostalism.[275] Building on her already established platform, Carrie's 1908 tongues experience proved to have profound effects for the expansion of early Pentecostalism.

---

[274] Miskov, *Spirit Flood,* p. 33.
[275] Montgomery, 'Cazadero World-wide Camp Meeting', p. 23. More on this in Chapter 7.

Figure 18
Carrie Judd Montgomery

4

The Prayer of Faith and Healing in the Atonement: An Analysis of Divine Healing Themes in Carrie's Writings (1880-1920)

Building on the history of Carrie's life and ministry from the previous chapters, a look at the formation of her theology of healing will now be explored. Through the research of Carrie's literature from roughly 1880-1920, two major divine healing themes emerged: the prayer of faith and healing in the atonement. How these two themes informed Carrie's understanding of sickness and of healing will be demonstrated. Her view of the origin of sickness, her paradigm for interpreting suffering, and what she believed to be the purpose of healing will be addressed. Additionally, how she viewed the 'gift of healing' will be discovered. This chapter will lay out her healing theology, while Chapter 5 will show how she actualized it and will also engage with present day scholarship and movements in relation to her theology. The crucial question that will be explored here is: To what extent did Carrie influence the formation and early advancement of the doctrine of healing in the atonement?

4.1 *The Prayer of Faith*: **Influences and Perspectives that Shaped Carrie's Theology of Healing**

4.1.1 Carrie's View of Healing before 1879

Did Carrie's faith for healing grow from her experience of it or did it develop another way? While it might appear that the first is the case, there were elements at work shaping Carrie's theology of healing long before her own healing experience in 1879. When she was a child, she prayed in a separate room for her brother Eddie to be healed.[1] This foreshadowed a type of long distance prayer that not only occurred in her healing account but also became a regular part of her ministry. In light of her brother's healing, some significant questions arise: Was Carrie led by the Holy Spirit prophetically at a young age to believe that God was at work healing her brother and acted on that? Or, did her understanding of the Bible at that point cause her to believe that God wanted to heal her brother? In light of her prayer for the healing of her brother, Carrie likely had also prayed previously for her older sister to be healed but without a positive result. The fact that Carrie chose to exclude this in her biography either means that she did not pray for her sister, or more likely, that she chose not to include it in her narrative because there was a negative result. The latter would fit in well with the triumphalism prevalent in her day where miracles were celebrated loudly, but unanswered prayers and the darker and more real sides of suffering and spirituality were mentioned infrequently, if at all.[2] If the latter is truly the case, Carrie would have had to overcome this discouragement to have enough faith to pray again for her brother. Additionally, she may have struggled with why God let her sister die but spared her brother. Regardless of the loss of her sister and the likely discouragement that came with that, Carrie was influenced by her mother's faith and decided to pray, believing that God could heal her brother. This demonstrates that even before her 1879 heal-

---

[1] Montgomery, *Under His Wings*, pp. 24-25. See Chapter 2.

[2] See R. Marie Griffith, "'Joy Unspeakable and Full of Glory': The Vocabulary of Pious Emotion in the Narratives of American Pentecostal Women, 1910-1945', in Peter N. Stearns and Jan Lewis (eds.), *An Emotional History of the United States* (New York: NYU Press, 1998), pp. 218-40. It must be noted that Carrie did include in her autobiography that she prayed for her friend May to be spared who later died. Carrie acknowledged that she was not close enough to God at that time to pray the prayer of faith (*Under His Wings*, p. 48).

ing account, Carrie's faith and theology of healing was already forming.

Into her teenage years, Carrie faced further challenges in her forming faith. Her sister and father were both ill at the same time, and while her father was spared, her sister died.[3] This was the second sister she lost and, at the same time, the second instance she saw healing in her family. She had to deal with both the tragedies of suffering and death as well as the triumphs of healing which occurred in her household all before her own healing experience took place. Carrie likely struggled with some of the following questions during this time: Why did God heal one but not the other? Was the sickness a result of some sin? Or was it a result of lack of faith on the part of one or the other? These questions will be important to keep in mind as the chapter progresses.

Contradictions

In attempting to discern how much Carrie knew about divine healing before her 1879 account, we must take note of the apparent contradictions in her records. In 1920, she remembered during her sickness that 'then mother and I would pray, and God would let a measure of relief come, but we did not know how to look to the Lord for healing'.[4] Reflecting back in her biography published in 1936, she wrote that at the time of her sickness, she and her family 'did not know how to ask the Lord for healing, but we did ask for relief when the suffering was very great, and at times this prayer was wonderfully answered'.[5] This does not make sense in light of the healing of her brother and father. In fact, she did know how to ask God for healing before her own account, as is evident in the outcome of both her brother's and her father's illness.

Carrie also recalled that during her sickness, her mother said to her, "'Your mission may be to lie here and suffer and be an example of patience to others, as you have been." (This was many years ago when Divine Healing had scarcely been heard of.)'[6] Here, Carrie left

---

[3] Montgomery, *Under His Wings,* p. 34.

[4] Carrie Judd Montgomery, "'Who Redeemeth Thy Life From Destruction'", *TF* 40.3 (March 1920), p. 50.

[5] Montgomery, *Under His Wings,* p. 50.

[6] Montgomery, *Under His Wings,* p. 53. See also her 'The Anniversary of My Healing', *TF* 27.2 (Feb 1907), pp. 25-26. Here, Carrie remembered a conversation she had with her mother during her illness:

out some of the context, as does Heather D. Curtis in her presentation of this interchange.[7] Carrie's mother *had* previously prayed for
the healing of her husband and children before this. It is highly likely that Emily Judd had expressed faith for Carrie's healing initially,
but then as the months and years wore on and Carrie's condition
continued to deteriorate, she lost hope and gave up too early. In
Carrie's household, the gap between mother and daughter was not
as wide as Curtis suggests. Even though towards the end of Carrie's
sickness her mother told her that she needed to be like a 'suffering
servant', this may only have been because by that time, Carrie's
term of sickness carried on beyond 'hope'. So while teaching on
divine healing may have been 'scarcely heard of' and not a popular
or widely held belief through the Church in the late 1800s, it had
been practiced in the Judd household in Carrie's formative years
and shaped her theology whether she realized it or not.[8] There was
some element of faith to pray for healing evident in Carrie's mother
that proved, at least in the Judd family, that prayer for healing was
practiced earlier on in Carrie's life than she acknowledged.

Closer to the actual date of her healing, in 1880, Carrie wrote
that before her illness, she 'had often heard of faith cures', and portions of W.W. Patton's book 'Remarkable Answers to Prayer' had
been read to her.[9] This contradicts her later claims of not hearing

---

Among other things I said to her, 'I believe I have a mission yet.' Mother
looked at the worn, emaciated frame and said with a suppressed sigh, 'Your
mission may be to lie here and suffer, and be an example of patience to others, as you have been.' Summoning my little remaining strength, I replied, 'I
mean an active mission, Mother'.

Carrie went on to write a bit later, '"An active mission" was the prophecy I
had uttered in those moments of extreme weakness, and I have often been re-
minded of those words, as He has strengthened me all these wonderful years to
go about in His service'.

[7] Heather D. Curtis, *Faith in the Great Physician: Suffering and Divine Healing in
American Culture, 1860-1900* (Baltimore: The John Hopkins University Press,
2007), pp. 3, 84. Following this interaction between mother and child, Curtis says
that 'this exchange between mother and daughter reveals that the image of the
suffering servant as the epitome of Christian sainthood was less compelling for
young persons of Carrie Judd's generation than it had been for their parents'.
Curtis shows the shift of an overwhelming number Evangelicals from the belief
that passive endurance of suffering was pious to a belief that God's will was that
people be healthy, which could come by taking an active stance on His promises,
especially those found in Jas 5.15.

[8] Montgomery, *Under His Wings,* p. 53.

[9] Judd, 'Have Faith in God', pp. 37-39.

much about divine healing before her account. Possible reasons for this might be that her memory faded or that her later claims distinguished between testimonies and teachings. However, while there may not have been language to describe divine healing at that time, she had already heard testimonies of it. While literature was limited in relation to the theology of divine healing, through the actions of praying for her brother and father as well as having come across Patton's work, Carrie had been exposed to some elements of divine healing earlier on. These instances of suffering and healing demonstrate that Carrie's theology and even her ministry of healing was not a direct result of her 1879 account since there were glimpses of it before then. And while it was her experience that heightened her growing theology and even catapulted her into a full-blown and expansive ministry, her theology of healing was already present, active, and forming even before 1879.

4.1.2 Experience as a Catalyst: Implications of Mix's Letter

While Carrie witnessed both suffering unto death and prayer unto healing in her early life, she also experienced both of these extremes herself when she suffered for nearly two years and then was healed. The *way* in which Carrie experienced her initial healing significantly shaped her ministry that followed.[10] This section will demonstrate how Mix's catalytic letter contributed to and became deeply embedded into the foundations of Carrie's healing theology:

> Wolcottville, Conn., February 24, 1879.
> Miss Carrie Judd:
>
> I received a line from your sister Eva, stating your case, your disease and your faith. I can encourage you, by the Word of God that, 'according to your faith,' so be it unto you; and besides you have this promise, 'The prayer of faith shall save the sick, and the Lord shall raise him up.' Whether the person is present or absent, if it is a 'prayer of faith,' it is all the same, and God has promised to raise up sick ones, and if they have committed sins to forgive them. Now this promise is to you, as if you were the only person living. Now if you can claim that promise, I have

---

[10] 'Long Range Cures: Mrs. Montgomery Rivals Schlatter', *The Sunday Herald* (Syracuse, NY), December 1, 1895, p. 14, and 'Healing at Long Range: Mrs. Montgomery Performs Faith Cures by Correspondence', *The Brookfield Courier* (NY), January 15, 1896.

not the least doubt but what you will be healed. You will first have to lay aside all medicine of every description. Use no remedies of any kind for anything. Lay aside trusting in the 'arm of the flesh,' and lean wholly upon God and His promises. When you receive this letter I want you to begin to pray for faith, and Wednesday afternoon the female prayer-meeting is at our house. We will make you a subject of prayer, between the hours or three and four. I want you to pray for yourself, and pray believing, and then *act faith*. It makes no difference how you feel, but get right out of bed and begin to walk by faith. Strength will come, disease will depart and you will be made whole. We read in the Gospel, 'Thy faith hath made thee whole.' Write soon.

Yours in faith, Mrs. Edward Mix.[11]

4.1.2.1 *The Prayer of Faith* (1880)

One of the major implications of Mix's letter in Carrie's life was the significance of the 'James 5 prayer' which says 'And the prayer of faith will save the sick, and the Lord will raise him up. And if he has committed sins, he will be forgiven' (Jas 5.15 KJV). In 1910, Carrie admitted that at the time she received Mix's letter, she had not realized that the encouragement to pray the prayer of faith came from a verse in the Bible.[12] Regardless of her lack of awareness at the time, Carrie acted on the prescript found in James 5. This 'prayer of faith' later became a focal point and basis for her book *The Prayer of Faith* (1880) where Carrie demonstrated her strong link with the James prayer and tied it to healing.[13] Mix's encouragement to act in faith connected with some of the thinking that came from the Holiness Movement. In light of Phoebe Palmer's theology, if one could act *now* for their sanctification experience, Mix, Carrie, and others wondered why they could not also act *now* in relation to claiming their healing.[14] Both Mix and Carrie simply translated the immediacy

---

[11] Mix, *Faith Cures and Answers to Prayer*, pp. 38-39 and Judd, *The Prayer of Faith*, pp. 13-15.

[12] Montgomery, 'The Life on Wings: The Possibilities of Pentecost', *TF* 32.8 (Aug 1912), pp. 171-74. This was taken from a 1910 sermon. See Appendix 5.

[13] Right in the middle of the title page for the book, the cornerstone for her work, Jas 5.14-15, is written out. She also later claimed that it was the Holy Spirit who wrote *The Prayer of Faith* through her. See her *Prayer of Faith*, p. 24.

[14] Phoebe Palmer, *The Way of Holiness, with Notes by the Way; being a Narrative Religious Experience Resulting from a Determination to be a Bible Christian* (New York:

Palmer gave for sanctification and also applied it to healing.[15] The James 5 instructions became a major foundation for Carrie and others in the Divine Healing Movement. While other literature played a bigger role in Carrie's pneumatology as will be shown in Chapter 6, for the most part it was James 5 and many of the 'cause and effect' Scriptures in the Old Testament that grounded Carrie's theology of healing.[16]

4.1.2.2 Medicine and the Great Physician

Influenced by her first exchange with Mix, Carrie also encouraged people to throw out all medicine so that they could act in faith and rely on the Great Physician alone for their healing. Like Mix, Carrie attempted to shift people's reliance, trust, and faith from medicine to the 'Saviour as the "Great Physician" of your soul and body'.[17] This was a common view among many, though not all, in the early American Divine Healing Movement, especially since the advancement of medicine during that time was poor and many times caused more damage than good.[18] In her *Prayer of Faith,* Carrie wrote that medicine was 'inadequate to meet the needs of suffering bodies, as the moral law has been insufficient to heal and cleanse our souls. Medicine is a most imperfect institution, as all remedial influences

---

200 Mulberry Street, Printed for the author, 1854), pp. 17-18, 105. Here is one example of when Palmer asked someone when he was going to give this sacrifice:

'By the help of the Lord, I will do it *now,*' he replied. A pause of intense interest ensued, when the sister [Palmer], perceiving that another step must be taken ere he had entered, said, 'But, brother, do you *do it* NOW?' A moment of hesitation, and he exclaimed, 'YES, glory be to God, I do! I DO!' and with the most joyful lips he began to rejoice in Christ as his full Savior.

[15] Curtis, *Faith in the Great Physician,* p. 105. Curtis touches on how this movement was more geared towards women in light of the cultural norms of the day. She says that 'Acting faith might restore a man to health, but it would emasculate him in the process', meaning that it might take away his manhood or feminize him in the process.

[16] Carrie also later introduced Mk 16.17 as a key verse, not only for healing but for Spirit baptism as well. The emergence of this verse in her literature may have been influenced by early Pentecostalism. See her 'Strengthened with All Might', *TF* 27.9 (Sept 1907), pp. 193-96.

[17] Judd, *The Prayer of Faith,* p. 37.

[18] *The Christian Alliance* 16.7 (Feb 14, 1896). See also Chappell, 'The Divine Healing Movement in America', pp. 100-101. Ethan Otis Allen was an early advocate who encouraged people to get rid of all medicines. Conversely, Cullis continued to give medicine to his clients and also suffered from a heart problem. See also Dayton, *Theological Roots of Pentecostalism,* p. 131; Chapter 2 in Hardesty, *Faith Cure*; and Judd, *The Prayer of Faith*, pp. 43-44.

outside of Christ are, of necessity, imperfect, because belonging to a sin-stricken world'.[19] Carrie's early stance on the use of medicine was also influenced from her view and desire to live 'wholly' for the Lord without any hindrances; this theme of 'total surrender' was already prevalent within most streams in the Holiness Movement.[20]

While Carrie did not see using medicine as a sin *per se*, she saw that it was not the fullness God had for someone. In *Prayer of Faith*, she wrote,

> But as little as medicine had been able to benefit us, it is strange how some of us cling to it, unwilling to give it up even after the 'prayer of faith' has been offered for us. While it may not be a sin of itself to use medicine when we are looking to the Lord for healing, it often encourages the sin of unbelief, and is, in most cases, a decided hindrance to the complete cure which our Physician would perform, were we willing to trust Him fully. Holding on to the medicine certainly implies a lack of faith, and by a careful and truthful examination of the motives which lead anyone to use it, after prayer has been offered, we shall see that most of them proceed from the sin of unbelief.[21]

At that time in her life, Carrie saw that clinging onto medicine implied 'a lack of faith'. She continued on to refer to King Asa in 2 Chron. 16.12 where he looked to the physicians for help before going to God. She wrote that 'there is danger in putting too much confidence in our fellow-beings, for by doing so we look away from God, and forget to rely on Him'. Many people were obsessed and addicted to medicine during Carrie's time and she wanted to try and free them. Continuing to highlight the prayer found in James, she

---

[19] Judd, *The Prayer of Faith*, p. 81.

[20] Especially with Phoebe Palmer throughout her *The Way of Holiness* (1854), and Hannah Whitall Smith within her *The Christian's Secret of a Happy Life* (Chicago: F.H. Revell, 1883. Reprint, USA: Kessinger Publishing, reprint no date). See also Montgomery, 'The Work and the Workers', *TF* 10.10, pp. 231-33. The Holiness Movement's terminology was filled with words such as 'total', 'full', 'entire', 'wholly', 'all', and 'surrender' that widely influenced leaders later in the Divine Healing Movement as well as saturated Carrie's articles in *Triumphs of Faith*. Additionally, some of the roots of these terms may be found in the religious idealism of Pietism. William Faupel says that the 'Expressions such as 'whole', 'perfect', and 'entire' characterize its quest. Pietism constantly feels the tension between the actual and the ideal' (*The Everlasting Gospel,* p. 55).

[21] Judd, *The Prayer of Faith*, p. 83.

wrote, 'If we have not thought it wrong to seek for medicines to deliver us from the bondage of sickness, why should we fear to be cured by the "prayer of faith," that more perfect healing institution be made by Christ's atonement?'[22] Her early belief in healing and the atonement is shown here; this is important and will be explored further.

Carrie also instructed those who wanted to receive prayer for healing first to throw out all medicines. One example of this is when an ill woman in Albany, New York who had tried all medicines but was not getting better, heard about Carrie's healing account. Because of this, she 'was filled with faith that she could be rescued from near living death'. This woman sought the young 23 year old Carrie to pray with her. Carrie responded and went to her bedside for three days. At Carrie's request, 'all medicines were cast out of the window'.[23] She spent much time in prayer for her along with the woman's family. While it was noted that this woman did not experience the manifestations of her healing immediately, she gradually and slowly began to improve to the point of full health by the time that the newspaper article of her account was published.

The issue of medicine also personally affected Carrie towards the end of 1897 when she became sick again. Carrie proudly proclaimed that she took no medicine but was happy to have physicians diagnose her so that God would get even greater 'glory' for her healing. She continued by saying

> I want to say here that I have no controversy with physicians. Many of them are among my most cherished and honored friends, and I praise God for all they are able to do for suffering humanity. If people have not faith to trust God for healing I always advise them to seek the best medical aid, but when God has called one to trust alone in Him as their Jehovah Rophi ('I am the Lord that healeth thee.' – Ex. xv:26) medicines will not help; they will only hinder.[24]

This example demonstrates that at this point in 1898, Carrie was not totally against the use of medicine if that was where a person

---

22 Judd, *The Prayer of Faith*, pp. 80-88.
23 'The Efficiency of Prayer'.
24 Montgomery, 'A Miracle of Healing', p. 143. See also 'Miss Carrie F. Judd's Spine: It Was Out of Order but the Lord Healed It', p. 3.

was at in regards to his or her faith at that time. Rather, she wanted God alone to be *her* physician and she encouraged others to want the same. If there was one 'weak' in the faith who had not yet fully grasped or been willing to partake in all of God's healing power, she said that that person could take his or her own path. However, it was by no means the best path according to Carrie, as she wanted people to act in faith and experience God alone as their Great Physician.

Carrie wanted to be 'so close' to and reliant upon God for her healing because she believed that trusting God was better than relying on the world's system of medicine. She recalled in 1898,

> When quite young, soon after my first healing, a Christian physician said to me, 'Do you make a vow that you will never take medicine again?' I answered with more wisdom than I then realized, 'Oh, no, I would never dare say that. If I set up my will about it, or if I thought I were better than someone else who did not take medicine, God might have to break my will by compelling me to take it again. But,' I added, 'I pray that I may be kept so close to Him that I always have the joy of feeling His direct touch of healing without any use of medicine.'[25]

At that point in her life, she taught that medicine was something that could be used if people struggled in their faith with this issue. However, she desired to live in faith, trusting in God completely in this area. And while Carrie did wear glasses for her eyesight, she did not consider this medicinal in any way. In response to criticism for doing the same thing, G.F. Taylor in relation to the popular stance against using medicine said that

> [T]he extracting of teeth and the wearing of glasses for the loss of sight in old age may be considered different from the taking of drugs as a remedy for disease. Men grow old and their eye sight fails, even though they may not be diseased. I can see no harm in looking through a microscope to see tiny objects; and perhaps the wearing of glasses to assist the eye sight would be parallel with these cases.[26]

---

[25] Montgomery, 'A Miracle of Healing', p. 143.

[26] G.F. Taylor, *The Pentecostal Holiness Advocate* 3.33 (Dec 11, 1919), p. 10, cited by Alexander, *Pentecostal Healing*, p. 146. Additionally, it was not until 1920 in the

While not specifically stated, Carrie's actions demonstrate that she shared a similar stance.

As a result of Mix's influence, the prayer of faith and seeing God as the Great Physician became embedded into Carrie's theology of healing. While Carrie tied her earlier view of medicine to the sin of unbelief, she later softened her view to emphasize different measures of faith required to rely on the Great Physician alone. This paradigm of measures will become even more important in relation to her pneumatology (see Chapter 6). Even after 1908, Carrie continued to maintain her practice of going to God alone for healing and of abstaining from medicine.[27] Her instructions to throw out medicine and step out in faith resulted in many accounts of miracles credited to the power of the Holy Spirit at work in 'answer to the prayer of faith'.[28] Many of these testimonies fill the pages of her *Triumphs of Faith*.[29] No cases of a negative response to her prescription are mentioned in her periodical. Additionally, while medicine many times caused more harm than good in her day, one might wonder if Carrie would have adapted her view of abstaining from medicine if she had noticed the positive results and advances that exist now. Because of her view of healing in the atonement and her desire to live wholly surrendered unto God, however, it is unlikely that she would have modified her position of seeing God as the Great Physician to include also seeing Him as the Creator

---

Georgia Conference of the Pentecostal Holiness Church, that the debate over the use of medicine caused a severe split. Watson Sorrow and Hugh Bowling believed that it was not a sin to use medicine. This controversy eventually escalated into a personality clash and power struggle where Sorrow and Bowling ended up getting ejected from the movement and started the Congregational Holiness Church on Jan. 29, 1921. See Vinson Synan's *The Holiness-Pentecostal Movement in the United States* (Grand Rapids: Eerdmans, 1971), pp. 191-93,

[27] Montgomery, '"Who Redeemeth Thy Life From Destruction"', p. 50, where she said that '[God] is opening the eyes of many to see how helpless earthly physicians are, no matter how good and conscientious some of them may be. Many of the most noted physicians have stated publicly that their remedies cannot be applied with any exact science, and some have said that all medicine is actually harmful'.

[28] Judd, *The Prayer of Faith*, p. 27. In reference to Acts 2.39, Carrie wrote that 'Peter is speaking of the gift of the Holy Ghost, and none who have felt the wonderful power, which, in answer to the "prayer of faith," gives healing to the soul and body, can doubt that it is the power of the Holy Spirit, promised to all ages and generations'.

[29] Towards the end in many *Triumphs of Faith* issues are accounts of these under the heading, 'Experiences of Spiritual and Physical Healing'.

through whom medicine could have been created for healing purposes as well. And while her experience and the way in which she received her initial healing played a crucial role in the development of her theology and practice of healing, the way that she approached and heavily relied upon the Bible both before and after that event demonstrates even deeper foundations in her theology of healing.

4.1.3 The Bible and Interpretation

While Carrie's experience was significant in catapulting her into her healing ministry, it is important to understand that the Bible was her 'starting point' time and time again. She encouraged people to 'Take God's word as a starting point, as a *fact* which exists before all other seeming facts'.[30] One of the reasons she put so much weight on the Bible was because she viewed it as her 'infallible guide'.[31] She also saw that 'God's word stands for many things not seen, and things that are seen often contradict God's Word'.[32] Carrie saw the Bible as absolute truth that needed to be taken literally and integrated into everyday life. In 1880 and in relation to the 'James 5 prayer', she said, 'Let us look at the literal command which the inspired apostle gives concerning the sick'.[33] She then encouraged her readers to embrace and act upon the prayer of faith. In the context of writing about how rich and abundant God's promises are in His word, Carrie said,

> We are not apt to accept the Bible as literally as we ought. We get into a dangerous habit of considering its exhortations as in a great degree figurative or sacredly poetic, or as relating to past generations and not to our own … If we would accept every command contained in the Bible, as a direct command to us from our Lord, and obey them all as literally as they are intended to be obeyed, we should find inestimable blessings attending such course.[34]

---

[30] Carrie Judd Montgomery, 'Yielding to Doubt', *TF* 22.5 (May 1902), p. 98.
[31] Carrie Judd Montgomery, '"I Will Deliver Thee"', *TF* 28.3 (March 1908), p. 49.
[32] Carrie Judd Montgomery, 'Evidence of Things Not Seen', *TF* 27.3 (March 1907), p. 49.
[33] Judd, *The Prayer of Faith*, p. 24.
[34] Judd, *The Prayer of Faith*, p. 23.

In relation to the above text, Petts notices that 'Bible verses are seen as "promises" which are to be "claimed" by faith'.[35] Carrie did believe that promises found in the Bible could be acted upon and appropriated in her present day. Her understanding of a literal approach to Scripture fit in with the common view of many in the Divine Healing Movement.[36]

Carrie also saw that even the act of reading the Bible was a sacred event. According to Kimberly Alexander, Carrie's Anglican background caused her to see the Bible as more than a road map; she also saw it as the 'presence of God'.[37] Carrie's Holiness roots may have additionally contributed to this perspective. In 1902, Carrie wrote, 'let us also pray, "Lord, make Thy Bible a living Book by Thy Holy Spirit's power that I may ever hear Thy voice through its pages"'.[38] Reading the Bible became of a way of experiencing God and hearing Him speak; there was a spiritual interaction taking place in the process.[39]

By looking at similar literature of the times, Alexander believes that the hermeneutic that came out of the Divine Healing Movement was characterized by reflection upon the Spirit's work in someone's life (their experience), taken together with the Bible to support and confirm that work.[40] While this happened initially in Carrie's life, the majority of other times this was reversed. In most cases after Carrie's healing, Scripture informed and provided the basis for her experience, not the other way around. Like Palmer, Carrie believed that after people acted upon Scripture, their experi-

---

[35] David Petts, 'Healing and the Atonement' (PhD thesis, University of Nottingham, 1993), p. 19.

[36] When referring to the Bible, Carrie often used the terms 'Scripture', 'Word of God', and 'God's Word'.

[37] Alexander, *Pentecostal Healing*, p. 29, points out the significance of theological presuppositions and Anglican roots for both Cullis and Montgomery, so that the 'sacramental nature of their faith comes to bear on how they read the Bible … It is more than just a guidebook, it is Word of God, the presence of God'.

[38] Montgomery, 'Living By Faith', p. 51, writes, '… and thus faith shall spring up spontaneously within my heart and I shall have the joy of pleasing Thee by this living faith. Amen'.

[39] Alexander argues that this type of reading fits within the healing movement, for which the Bible was 'not a commemorative event only; it is sacramental in that the presence of God is manifested there and then in the life of the readers' (Alexander, *Pentecostal Healing*, p. 35).

[40] Alexander, *Pentecostal Healing*, p. 36.

ence and its manifestations would eventually follow.[41] In her articles and teachings, Carrie regularly began with a Scripture verse included in the title or in the introductory text, and then spent the whole article expounding on that one verse or passage. Intermixed into many of her articles were also supporting Scriptures as well as her testimonies or experiences.[42] Using Trinitarian language, in 1902, Carrie wrote about the interplay between the work of the Spirit and the Bible: 'To sum it up briefly, faith is the gift of God through Jesus Christ, ministered by the Holy Spirit, through the medium of God's Word'.[43] Carrie saw that the Bible played a foundational role in one's faith.

It was not until after Carrie's 1908 tongues experience that she ventured into a new way of approaching her sermon preparation. Rather than 'asking God to help' and bless her sermon preparation, she was challenged by her friend, Anna Prosser, to rely completely upon God to give His word 'at the moment'.[44] Carrie struggled with this at first but then felt that she received a Scripture from God directing her to 'open wide' her mouth and then He would fill it. She tried this as she spoke at a mission and then later integrated it into her preparation from time to time. One thing that remained a constant both before and after Carrie's Pentecostal Spirit baptism was her foundation of Scripture and the weight she placed upon it. While she admitted that after her 1908 experience, the Scriptures were opened up to her in even greater ways, Albrecht rightly states that she continued to see the Bible as 'the ultimate authority for faith and holy living' just as she had before.[45]

Both experience and Scripture played an important part in shaping Carrie's theology of healing. While it was Carrie's experience that catapulted her into a public healing ministry, this came as a result of applying a specific Bible passage into her life whether she

---

[41] Carrie Judd Montgomery, 'Healing in the Atonement', *TF* 22.6 (June 1902), pp. 121-22.

[42] Just a few examples of this are: Carrie F. Judd, 'Jesus Crowned', *TF* 8.6 (June 1888), pp. 121-22; '"A Door of Hope"', *TF* 8.7 (July 1888), pp. 145-47; and '"Steadfast Until the End"', *TF* 49.5 (May 1929), pp. 97-101. The list would be quite extensive as the majority of her articles were laid out in this fashion.

[43] Montgomery, 'Living by Faith', p. 51.

[44] Carrie Judd Montgomery, 'Diligent Harkening', *TF* 37.2 (Feb 1917), p. 27.

[45] Albrecht, 'The Life and Ministry of Carrie Judd Montgomery', p. 141. See also Montgomery, 'Some Important Changes', p. 169.

knew it or not at that moment. Experience and Scripture were integrated throughout her ministry and are thus not meant to be mutually exclusive. And while Carrie's healing experience was a catalyst that initiated her growing healing ministry, Scripture was the base upon which her ministry was built. It has been demonstrated that the 'James 5 prayer' became one of the major theological foundations upon which she built her theology of healing. Let us now turn to the other major belief that grounded her healing theology.

4.2 Healing in the Atonement

4.2.1 The Developing Doctrine
While influenced by the Holiness Movement and even earlier, the doctrine of healing in the atonement first became popularized within the Divine Healing Movement. David Petts in his PhD thesis, 'Healing and the Atonement', defines the early doctrine as 'the view that Christians may claim healing from sickness on the grounds that Christ has already carried that sickness from them just as he has carried their sins'.[46] He says that through this doctrine, people believe that they do not need to be sick because 'Christ has already carried [the sickness] for them substitutionally. Once this is understood faith will appropriate the healing which has already been accomplished at Calvary'.[47] The leaders in the Divine Healing Movement saw a connection between sin and illness. Because of this, the atonement could pay the penalty for sin, which also included sickness that resulted from sin in the world.[48]

---

[46] Petts, 'Healing and the Atonement', p. 2. Petts, whose background is one of British Pentecostalism in which he has served in various degrees, examines the doctrine that healing is provided for in the atonement by looking at theological and literary origins, developments and modifications of this, especially in the context of Classical Pentecostals. His study is limited mainly to using New Testament examples of key Scriptures used in the formation of this doctrine; Mt. 8.17, 1 Pet. 2.24, Gal. 3.13, 1 Cor. 11.29-30, Jas 5.14-15, and Mk 16.15-18. A second section of his thesis looks at the relationship between healing and salvation, healing and the gospel, and then breaks down a deeper look at sickness' relationship with sin, Satan, and suffering. Through Alexander's Wesleyan-Holiness Pentecostal paradigm, she sees him as a Pentecostal scholar in the Finished Work stream and concludes that in his thesis 'healing is not provided in the atonement, but is "ultimately" and "indirectly in the atonement"' (*Pentecostal Healing*, p. 235). He comes from a stream more closely related to Carrie than does Alexander.

[47] Petts, 'Healing and the Atonement', p. 1.

[48] Alexander, *Pentecostal Healing*, pp. 42, 44.

Healing in the atonement appropriated through the prayer of faith was an emerging belief embraced by many in the Divine Healing Movement.[49] Some key texts that were used in defense of the doctrine of healing in the atonement were Isa. 53.4-6, Mt. 8.16-17 (which rephrases Isa. 53.4), and 1 Pet. 2.24, with common themes being that by the stripes, or wounds of Jesus, people are healed. Additionally, many Old Testament Scriptures were also popular during this time in relation to healing: Exod. 15.26, Deut. 7.15, Ps. 103.2-3, and Isa. 40.28-31.[50] Carrie similarly used many of these same texts to support her understanding of healing in the atonement.[51]

Origins and influences for the formation of the doctrine of healing in the atonement can be seen even before the Holiness Movement. Johann Cristoph Blumhardt believed that sin was a cause of sickness and that there was a direct correlation between forgiveness and healing; this enabled people to see sickness through a newer perspective.[52] However, because he referred people to doctors and was content to pray for people over a longer period of time for their healing, some see that he did not fully believe in healing in the atonement.[53] Some also recognize that Dorothy Trudel was one of

---

[49] Alexander, *Pentecostal Healing*, pp. 8-9.

[50] In Exod. 15.26, Moses prophesied that the Lord would put none of these diseases on the people if they would listen and do what He commands. Deut. 7.15 says that the Lord will take away all the sicknesses. In 2 Kgs 20.5 Isaiah said to Hezekiah that the Lord will heal him (this was in response to his prayers). In Ps. 30.2 David cried out to the Lord and He healed him. Ps. 103.2-3 says, 'Bless the Lord ... who forgives ... iniquities and heals ... diseases'. Isa. 40.28-31, says, '... He gives strength to the weary ... even the youths will faint ... but those who wait on the Lord ... will mount up with wings as eagles'. Isaiah 53.4-5 talks about how He bore our griefs, was wounded for our transgressions and by His stripes we are healed. Jeremiah 30.17 says, 'For I will restore health to you, says the Lord', and Mal. 4.2 says, 'The Sun of righteousness will arise with healing in his wings" (NKJV). See also Hardesty, *Faith Cure*, pp. 88-89.

[51] See Carrie F. Judd, 'The Lord Our Healer', *TF* 5.12 (Dec 1885), pp. 269-73; Carrie Judd Montgomery, '"Lord, I Believe"', *TF* 21.11 (Nov 1901), pp. 241-42; *idem*, 'Healing in the Atonement', pp. 121-22; and *idem*, 'Redeemed from the Curse', *TF* 22.8 (Aug 1902), pp. 169-71, for a few of these.

[52] Petts, 'Healing and the Atonement', pp. 8-10. Boardman later took a similar stance when he presented a parallelism in relating forgiveness and healing together. Alexander believes the doctrine came about 'as a part of Wesleyan soteriology, as interpreted by the Holiness Movement in the nineteenth century' (*Pentecostal Healing*, p. 8).

[53] Kydd, *Healing through the Centuries*, pp. 43-44. It must be noted that even though Blumhardt did not look for instantaneous healing, it would often happen

the early people to believe in healing in the atonement, but because she put no time pressures on people to receive their healing instantly, this is also debatable.[54] Petts rightly believes that while many others were drawn to 'the prayer of faith' and the belief in divine healing earlier on, 'it was among the followers of Cullis that the doctrine that healing is in the atonement may be clearly seen to have emerged'.[55] Cullis played an important role in convincing people from the Holiness Movement that both healing and salvation were available in the atonement.[56] But because Cullis continued to give medicine to his clients and also suffered from a heart problem, Dayton claims that he never fully adopted the whole doctrine of healing in the atonement.[57] Regardless of Cullis' stance on medicine, his view of associating sin with sickness as well as praying for healing influenced many towards the doctrine. Additionally, Otto Stockmayer's *Sickness and the Gospel* (1878) was one of the early references to healing in the atonement.[58]

Phoebe Palmer's teachings of sanctification as immediately available in the atonement of Christ also played a role in the emergence of the doctrine. Palmer saw that one simply needed to act on what Christ had already accomplished through the cross to be sanctified and 'fully saved'.[59] Ethan O. Allen, Mrs Mix, Carrie, and others in the Divine Healing Movement took Palmer's theology of sanctification one step further to include healing as something freely accessi-

---

in services while he was speaking. More on this in Chapter 5, and also see Jennifer A. Miskov, 'Carrie Judd Montgomery and Contemporary Models of Healing', at <www.Carriejuddmontgomery.com>.

[54] Chappell, 'The Divine Healing Movement in America', pp. 41-49. Trudel's book, *Dorothea Trudel; or the Prayer of Faith. An Account of the Institution for Faith Cure at Mannedorf, Switzerland, and a Life of its Founder* was published in 1874 in Boston by the Willard Tract Repository with Charles Cullis as the editor. See also Kydd, *Healing through the Centuries,* p. 153.

[55] Petts, 'Healing and the Atonement', p. 12.

[56] Alexander, *Pentecostal Healing,* p. 17. See also Hardesty, *Faith Cure,* p. 87.

[57] Dayton, *Theological Roots of Pentecostalism,* p. 131.

[58] Vinson Synan, 'A Healer in the House? A Historical Perspective on Healing in the Pentecostal/Charismatic Tradition', *Asian Journal of Pentecostal Studies* 3.2 (2000), p. 191.

[59] Phoebe Palmer also mentioned the atonement but in terms towards sanctification rather than healing in her *The Way of Holiness* (1854), pp. 56, 239. She said, 'I know "without holiness no man shall see the Lord," and it seems to me as if I should then, with a desperate venture, throw myself upon the infinite merit of the atonement; and I *know I should be fully saved.* I often ask myself, why I cannot do it *now?*'

ble in the atonement.[60] Alexander recognizes that Carrie's application of Palmer's view of sanctification in relation to healing themes
contributed towards 'a more positional understanding of the
atonement'.[61] This means that because of one's position in Christ,
one could take hold of what was already theirs by rights of inheritance which now not only included sanctification but also healing.
Alexander is accurate in her suggestion – Carrie saw God's word as
fact and the basis to stand on in relation to these and other themes.

Another early influence towards healing in the atonement was
Ethan O. Allen, who prayed for Mix's healing. He expected healing
to be instantaneous whenever he prayed and utilized Mk 16.17 as
his key verse. Chappell saw him as

> a radical in the divine healing movement in that he never advo-
> cated the use of medicine or endorsed the service of physicians,
> for he insisted that both demonstrated a lack of total faith and
> trust in God ... this radical position is understandable when it is
> realized that Allen viewed sickness not simply as an encounter
> with a phenomenon of nature, but rather as a confrontation with
> satan and his demonic forces.[62]

Allen believed that Satan and sin were the cause of all sickness.
He also did not limit prayer for healing to the church clergy but rather encouraged all to see their authority in the spiritual battle over
sickness and to pray for others. He believed there were instances
where God did not heal, and that was because God was disciplining
the individual. Besides these already mentioned and Carrie's book
(*The Prayer of Faith,* 1880), many others also contributed to the early
formation of the doctrine in the 1880s, including A.J. Gordon (*The
Ministry of Healing,* 1882), A.B. Simpson (*The Gospel of Healing,* 1885),
and Robert Kelso Carter (*The Atonement for Sin and Sickness; or, A
Full Salvation for Soul and Body,* 1884). Simpson was also one of the
initial people to expound on this theme as well as use terminology
of the four-fold gospel.[63]

---

[60] Judd, 'Jesus Crowned', p. 122, *idem,* 'Redeemed from the Curse', pp. 170-71.
[61] Alexander, *Pentecostal Healing,* pp. 8-9.
[62] Chappell, 'The Divine Healing Movement in America', pp. 91, 100-101.
[63] Simpson, A.B. *The Gospel of Healing* (New York: Christian Alliance Publishing Co., 4th edn, 1890).

Carrie provided space for the early development of this doctrine in her periodical. In 1883, she printed a number of consecutive articles by R.L. Stanton that were later grouped into a book called *Gospel Parallelism: Illustrated in the Healing of Body and Soul* (1883). Stemming from a growing parallelism between sin and sickness, Stanton believed that if the atonement paid the price for sin, it must also have included some of the results of sin which consisted of sickness.[64] In an introductory statement, he wrote that 'it is my aim, in a series of papers, to endeavor to show that the atonement of Christ lays a foundation equally for deliverance from sin and for deliverance from disease; that complete provision has been made for both'.[65] Carrie provided an important platform for his early teachings on healing in the atonement.[66]

Another important figure in relation to early developments on the doctrine was Simpson's associate R. Kelso Carter. He originally agreed with healing in the atonement so much that he wrote a defense for it in his book, *The Atonement for Sin and Sickness: or, A Full Salvation for Soul and Body* (1884). However, after a personal illness where he succumbed to taking medicine and then was restored, he later disagreed with his initial conclusions.[67] In 1897, he wrote a counter argument to his previous book and entitled it *'Faith Healing' Reviewed After Twenty Years*. Over ten years after he had taken his initial stand, he rebutted his own argument point by point. He decided that healing did and could happen in the atonement but that if it did not occur, it did not mean that sin was the reason for a continued illness.[68] He realized that there was a 'now and not yet' element in relation to healing when he wrote that 'we may err, and have erred, in endeavoring to appropriate at the present time some of the final fruits of that sacrifice'.[69] In Dayton's analysis, Carter took out the element of the person being able to claim the direct healing in the atonement and instead 'taught healing as a "special favor," some-

---

[64] Alexander, *Pentecostal Healing*, p. 42.

[65] R.L. Stanton, 'Gospel Parallelism: Illustrated in the Healing of Body and Soul', *TF* 3.4 (April 1883), p. 73.

[66] Storms, 'Carrie Judd Montgomery: The Little General', p. 275.

[67] Judd, *The Prayer of Faith*, p. 80.

[68] Kydd, *Healing through the Centuries*, p. 209. R.K. Carter in the end came to see 'healing not as a right that could be demanded but as a special favor from God'.

[69] R.K. Carter, '"Faith Healing" Reviewed After Twenty Years', *Christian Witness*, 1897, p. 167, cited in Petts, 'Healing and the Atonement', p. 1.

times bestowed, sometimes withheld, according to "the supreme will of our Lord"'. Dayton rightly believes that the extreme doctrine in Carter's earlier book was modified by the 'providence of God' for healing in his later writings.[70] One of the reasons Carter likely modified his earlier view was because he needed a paradigm to deal with the realities of suffering which his earlier view did not adequately provide. This would later become an issue for others as well. Interestingly, after 1895 there was not much mention of Carter in Carrie's *Triumphs of Faith*.[71] This may have been because his newer stance went against Carrie's idea that God wanted to heal all of the time through the finished work of the cross and not through medicine. As some early formations and influences of the doctrine have been described, how Carrie fit in with the shaping and spreading of the doctrine will now be explored.

4.2.2 In Carrie's Theology

Healing in the atonement became a foundational part of Carrie's theology of healing early on. Jeannette Storms writes that while Carrie's 'writings on healings in the 1880s centered on actualizing faith, she did not personally write about healing in the atonement' then. Storms later goes on to say that it was not until April of 1892 that Carrie first began to write about it and that 'in the 1880s she had relied on others to write about healing in the atonement'.[72] Storms is mistaken, however, because Carrie had written about healing in the atonement as early as 1880 in her *Prayer of Faith* when she said, 'If we have not thought it wrong to seek for medicines to deliver us from the bondage of sickness, why should we fear to be cured by the "prayer of faith," that more perfect healing institution made

---

[70] Dayton, *Theological Roots of Pentecostalism*, pp. 130-31.

[71] Carrie Judd Montgomery, 'The Work and the Workers', *TF* 10.4 (April 1890), pp. 90-91; *idem,* 'The Work and the Workers', *TF* 12.7 (July 1892), pp. 164-70; *idem,* 'The Work and the Workers', *TF* 12.10 (Oct 1892), pp. 237-38; and Captain R. Kelso Carter, 'The Guidance of the Spirit', *TF* 12.11 (Nov 1892), pp. 241-46; *idem,* 'The Burning Bush', *TF* 13.11 (Nov 1893), pp. 266-70; *idem,* 'Some New Thing', *TF* 14.1 (Jan 1894), pp. 10-14; and *idem,* 'Entire Consecration', *TF* 14.2 (Feb 1894), pp. 32-35. Montgomery, 'The Work and the Workers', *TF* 10.4 (April 1890), pp. 90-91.

[72] Storms, 'Carrie Judd Montgomery: The Little General', pp. 277, 281. Alexander echoes the view of Storms, saying that 'as early as January of 1882', Carrie 'had written about the benefits of the finished work of Christ on the cross' (*Pentecostal Healing*, p. 151).

ours by Christ's atonement?'[73] Petts correctly realizes that Carrie's book came out a year before Boardman's work on healing and 'contains some of the earliest expressions of the doctrine that healing is in the atonement'.[74] Additionally, in Carrie's very first article for *Triumphs of Faith*, called 'Faith Reckonings' (1881), she wrote about how Christ bore both sickness and sins.[75] This was written before she came into contact with Simpson, which shows that her thinking was independent of his influence.

This theme of healing in the atonement continued to become integrated into her teachings as she expanded her ministry.[76] In 1882, Carrie encouraged her readers to stand on the 'finished work of Atoning sacrifice'.[77] In 1884, she arranged Bible readings on the subject of sickness and she made the following statement, 'Our Righteousness and Healing Complete in Christ's Atonement'.[78] In 1885, Carrie published one of her own addresses entitled 'The Lord Our Healer' where she said,

> You have heard before to-day how Jesus Christ gave Himself as a ransom, as 'an atonement' to bear your sicknesses, and by faith you may claim freedom from them now. Christ has borne them fully away, and you are free in the glorious liberty of the children of God, free from sin and free from sickness ... God's Spirit comes as a messenger, an interpreter, to reveal unto us God's uprightness, and then we may be delivered through the atonement of Jesus Christ. 'By His stripes we are healed.'[79]

As her works demonstrate, Carrie was active in sharing her understanding of healing in the atonement very early on.

---

[73] Judd, *The Prayer of Faith*, p. 80.

[74] Petts, 'Healing and the Atonement', p. 13.

[75] Carrie F. Judd, 'Faith Reckonings', *TF* 1.1 (Jan 1881), pp. 1-4.

[76] Her articles include 'The Lord Our Healer', *TF* 5.12 (Dec 1885), pp. 269-73; '"Lord, I Believe"', *TF* 21.11 (Nov 1901), pp. 241-43; 'Healing in the Atonement', *TF* 22.6 (June 1902), pp. 121-22; 'Redeemed from the Curse', *TF* 22.8 (Aug 1902), pp. 169-71; 'Cast Not Away Your Confidence', *TF* 23.2 (Feb 1903), p. 25, 'Continue in My Word', *TF* 24.4 (April 1904), pp. 73-75; 'Saved by His Life', *TF* 25.3 (March 1905), pp. 49-50; 'All Things Reconciled to Christ', *TF* 25.12 (Dec 1905), pp. 265-67; 'God's Temple-The Body', *TF* 27.4 (April 1907), pp. 73-74; 'Grace Yet Again', *TF* 27.8 (Aug 1907), pp. 169-72; and 'The Sin of Unbelief', *TF* 28.6 (June 1908), pp. 122-23.

[77] Carrie F. Judd, 'Our Position in Christ', *TF* 2.1 (Jan 1882), pp. 1-3.

[78] Carrie F. Judd, 'Bible Reading on Sickness', *TF* 4.5 (May 1884), p. 114.

[79] Judd, 'The Lord Our Healer', pp. 270-71.

In 1902, she wrote several significant articles in relation to healing in the atonement which give a snapshot of her theology at that time. In 'Redeemed from the Curse', she filled her article with references for healing in the atonement and claimed that Christians 'are not only redeemed from sin, but also from sickness'.[80] In one of her most significant articles on the subject entitled 'Healing in the Atonement', she began not with experience, but with a Scripture from Mt. 8.17 (He 'Himself took our infirmities and bare our sicknesses').[81] Here she wrote,

> What marvelous ground-work for claiming Divine Healing from our blessed Lord and Saviour. It is almost too wonderful for us to realize that our dear Saviour has actually borne our sickness and carried our pains, and that therefore we are freed from them, and may claim freedom in His name, but it is gloriously true. When pain or sickness comes upon us, we may say, 'Jesus, Thou hast borne this very sickness, this very pain with which I am now suffering. Thou hast carried away the disease from which the pain proceeds, therefore I resist it through the blood of Thy cross.'[82]

Christ's atonement was the 'ground-work' and basis of divine healing for Carrie. She saw that healing was available because of the blood that was shed on the cross. All that needed to happen was for one to *realize* that truth and claim their healing by activating the prayer of faith.

---

[80] Montgomery, 'Redeemed from the Curse', pp. 170-71. In reference to Isa. 35.8-9, she wrote that 'not only has Jesus borne our sins, but He has also borne our "old man" of sin, and by faith we may claim our freedom and reckon ourselves "dead indeed unto sin, but alive unto God through Jesus Christ our Lord"'. In reference to Gal. 3.13, she continued on by writing that the 'blessed One Who was "made a curse for us" has thereby redeemed us from all the curse of a broken law. (Gal. iii:13). Therefore we are not only redeemed from sin, but also from sickness, for there are many kinds of sickness enumerated among the curses pronounced in Deut.xxviii.' In light of sickness being seen as a curse rather than a blessing, she quoted Pss. 103.3-4 and then continued on that 'the enemy would hurt and destroy our lives. Jesus, our great Redeemer, has taken our infirmities and borne our sicknesses (Matt. viii:16,17), and therefore He lays His healing hand upon us, renews our strength and pours out His own life into our wasted frames.' She also referenced Ps. 107.2 and Rom. 6.2.

[81] Montgomery, 'Healing in the Atonement', p. 121.

[82] Montgomery, 'Healing in the Atonement', p. 121.

Because healing was freely available, Carrie recognized that it was futile to bear a burden that was already borne. On this she said,

> Because Jesus has borne our sin and our transgressions we are commanded to reckon ourselves to be 'dead indeed unto sin,' and in the same manner we may reckon ourselves dead to sickness through the finished work of Christ. Since He has borne each sickness and pain for us, how He feels for us, how blessedly He sympathizes with us, and how greatly He desires to free us from that which we need no longer bear. How it must grieve His loving heart if we continue to bear what He has already borne for us.[83]

The connection between sin and sickness is evident here. In this same article, Carrie also recalled one woman's story who applied this to her life and exclaimed, 'I am healed. I was healed more than eighteen hundred years ago, and I have only just found it out'. When Carrie heard this she observed that 'her face was shining with holy joy at this wonderful discovery. Yes, Jesus had healed her on His cross, where He bore her sickness, and as soon as she saw this, her faith took hold of His finished work, and she was free'.[84] According to Carrie, this woman was healed the moment she chose to 'take hold' of the healing found in the atonement. Healing could be 'obtained' in Christ's name because of what He had done on the cross. The doctrine of healing in the atonement was additionally integrated into many of her articles after her 1908 tongues experience and throughout her life.[85] This reveals that her Pentecostal

---

[83] Montgomery, 'Healing in the Atonement', pp. 121-22.

[84] Montgomery, 'Healing in the Atonement', p. 122. Carrie referred to Job 33.14-24 where Elihu approached Job. She said that 'because God provided in Christ a ransom or atonement for sickness as well as for sin, therefore healing may be obtained in His name and His life surging through our bodies will make our flesh fresher than a child's'. This was in connection with Matthew 8.

[85] From my study of *Triumphs of Faith* up to 1920, I would argue that Carrie retained the theology of healing in the atonement after her Pentecostal baptism. See Carrie Judd Montgomery, 'The Work of the Holy Spirit', *TF* 32.11 (Nov 1912), pp. 241-44, where she used Mt. 8.17 to describe that 'He took our infirmities and bare our sicknesses'. Cf. her 'Overcoming Faith', *TF* 36.6 (June 1916), pp. 121-24; 'Full Redemption for Spirit, Soul and Body', *TF* 39.3 (March 1919), pp. 49-53; and 'Such As I Have Give I Thee', *TF* 40.8 (Aug 1920), pp. 169-71, as well as other articles she printed her in periodical by other authors like Wm. Franklin (India), 'Healing in the Atonement', *TF* 30.3 (March 1910), pp. 56-8;

Spirit baptism experience did not shake her belief in this doctrine.[86]

4.2.3 Early Advocate

While others were also involved in the early formation of the doctrine of healing in the atonement within the Divine Healing Movement, Carrie's early literature (1880) demonstrates that she was among the earliest contributors. Petts also recognized this and chose to research Carrie and Simpson specifically since they 'were among the earliest major proponents of the doctrine'. Additionally, and of even greater importance to his thesis, Petts admits it is 'the life and work of Carrie Judd Montgomery, where the doctrine that healing in the atonement can not only be clearly seen but can be seen to have transferred from the Holiness Movement into the proto-Pentecostalism of her day'.[87] And it did not stop there, as Carrie continued to take this doctrine into Pentecostalism itself. Alexander is also on the right track when she recognizes that 'Finished Work Pentecostal theology was not original with William Durham. Carrie Judd Montgomery clearly had discussed Finished Work as early as 1882, probably being informed by Phoebe Palmer'.[88] And as has already been shown, Carrie taught on this theme even earlier in 1880, predating Durham's teaching by at least four years.

While Carrie was not the exclusive person to originate the doctrine, it has been demonstrated that she was one of the early advocates to teach, popularize, and spread it globally through her networks.[89] And if it is true that Carrie was influential in the development of the doctrine itself, it must also be true that she has been a

---

Word and Work reprint '"By Whose Stripes Ye Were Healed"', *TF* 32.3 (March 1912), pp. 61-62; Max I. Reich, 'The Atonement and Divine Healing', *TF* 38.2 (Feb 1918), pp. 28-30; and unknown author, 'Divine Healing in the Atonement', *TF* 39.1 (Jan 1919), p. 24. See also E. May Law, 'A Testimony to Heal and to Keep', *TF* 37.4 (March 1917), pp. 54-57.

[86] Carrie Judd Montgomery, 'Full Redemption for Spirit, Soul and Body', *TF* 39.3 (March 1919), pp. 49-53, and M.J.W., 'Experiences of Spiritual and Physical Healing', *TF* 10.1 (Jan 1890), pp. 23-24. Through the years, Carrie extended and expanded terminology in relation to healing in the atonement to also include 'Full Redemption for Spirit, Soul and Body' rather than just soul and body.

[87] Petts, 'Healing and the Atonement', pp. 18, 13.

[88] Alexander, *Pentecostal Healing*, pp. 227, 69. Carrie's periodical was also the first publication in that stream as well.

[89] Diana Chapman recognizes Carrie's impact for British Pentecostalism and notes that 'her main contribution was to provide a theology of divine healing for the emerging movement' ('The Rise and Demise of Women's Ministry in the Origins and Early Years of Pentecostalism in Britain', *JPT* 2.2 [2004], p. 220).

source of influence for Pentecostalism and other streams who have adopted the theology and/or practice of the doctrine.[90] A.J. Tomlinson was directly influenced by Carrie in this way when he was first introduced to the doctrine through her literature.[91] People like Smith Wigglesworth, Aimee Semple McPherson, Oral Roberts, John Wimber, Bill Johnson, and many others have integrated or adapted a form of healing in the atonement into their healing practice.[92] While more discussion in relation to present day intersections will come in the next chapter, in 1993 Petts discovered that some like the Church of God (USA) and the Assemblies of God[93] (USA, Great Britain, and Ireland) have also adopted healing in the atonement and that

> the doctrine has been retained not only in the wording of formal doctrinal statements but that it has been and continues to be promulgated, at least by some within the groups in question, in much the same form as it was originally propounded by A.B. Simpson and Carrie Judd Montgomery.[94]

Carrie's influence can be seen within present day Charismatic and Pentecostal streams that hold to the earliest form of the doctrine or a variation of it.[95]

---

[90] See Petts, 'Healing and the Atonement', pp. 24, 33, 58, and Donald Gee, *Trophimus I Left Sick* (London: Elim, 1952), p. 5. Other significant people who have come from this Finished Work stream which Carrie heavily influenced are healing evangelists/itinerant preachers Aimee Semple McPherson and Mattie Crawford. Maria Woodworth-Etter contributed to shaping this stream as well.

[91] Gardiner H. Shattuck, 'Ambrose Jessup Tomlinson (1865-1943)', in Edward L. Queen, Stephen R. Prothero, and Gardiner H. Shattuck (eds.) *Encyclopaedia of American Religious History* (New York, NY: Facts on File, Inc., 3rd edn, 2009), p. 991.

[92] See Miskov, 'Carrie Judd Montgomery and Contemporary Models of Healing' at <www.Carriejuddmontgomery.com> for a more in depth study on this.

[93] 'Statement of Fundamental Truths', in *The General Council of the Assemblies of God*, p. 6. Accessed May 23, 2011, <http://agchurches.org/Sitefiles/Default/RSS/AG.org% 20TOP/Beliefs/SFT_2011.pdf>. Article 12 on Divine Healing says, 'Divine healing is an integral part of the gospel. Deliverance from sickness is provided for in the Atonement, and is the privilege of all believers (Isaiah 53:4, 5; Matthew 8:16, 17; James 5:14-16)'.

[94] Petts, 'Healing and the Atonement', pp. 33, 58. See also Alexander, *Pentecostal Healing*, pp. 69, 228, where she writes that 'a rather surprising finding emerges from a reading of early Finished Work Pentecostal literature, where the prevalence of what has more recently been understood as the Word of Faith or Health and Wealth Movement is widespread'.

[95] This will be discussed further in Chapter 5.

4.3 Origins of Sickness and Suffering: God, Satan, or Sin?

Carrie's belief in healing in the atonement informed and provided the basis for many other areas of her theology. This was the framework for the way she interpreted sickness. We will now begin to explore what Carrie saw were the root causes of sickness. Did she believe that sickness came from God, Satan, or as a result of sin? Understanding what Carrie saw as the source of sickness will help bring to light the way in which she formed her theology of healing and ordered it in a specific way. Additionally, how she viewed suffering in light of her view of healing in the atonement will also be identified.

4.3.1 Sickness: A Result of Sin for the Purpose of Discipline

Less than a year after her healing, Carrie connected sickness with Adam's fall. She said that 'Sin, sickness and corruption are upon all humanity because of the first Adam's sin; but we may be delivered from sin, sickness and corruption because of the atonement of Christ, "the last Adam"'.[96] While she believed sickness could be connected to original sin, as her view developed, she regularly connected sickness to personal sin as she did in her own situation. Carrie believed that her own sickness came as a result of her unwillingness to surrender all to God.[97] She associated the cause of her own illness as suffering that God allowed because she had sinned. Her interpretation of her own sickness demonstrates that she believed that at times, God allowed sickness to come as a means of disciplining his children. It also reveals that she saw that sickness could come as a result of sin. This idea of cause and effect in relation to sin and sickness became a prominent theme for Carrie, especially in her earlier years.

Following her healing, Carrie taught that God allowed sickness to come in response to sin or for some greater purpose. In a 1884 Bible reading she arranged around the theme of sickness, the majority of passages demonstrate that God was the one who allowed sickness to come when people disobeyed His commands, when

---

[96] From there she referenced 1 Cor. 15.22 (Judd, *The Prayer of Faith*, p. 61).

[97] Montgomery, 'The Life on Wings', p. 173, wrote, 'and finally I told Him I would hold on to it [her talent for writing] as tightly as I could and He would have to pull it away from me'. See Appendix 5 for full article. See also her *Under His Wings,* pp. 46-47.

they broke His covenant (Lev. 26.14-16), when they lived in sin (Mic. 6.13 and Pss. 107.17-19), or when they took communion in an unworthy manner (1 Cor. 11.27, 30-31).[98] In 1885, Carrie wrote that sickness was not God's fault but rather that 'all your troubles have come from your own "infirmity," even your lack of faith'.[99] In regards to Job, she suggested that his sickness came because he did not immediately 'hearken' to God and he needed to be refined. She wrote,

> If you have not hearkened diligently to the voice of the blessed Saviour, or if you have been going in your own way instead of His, God may have had to let the enemy lay his hand upon you with sickness. It has been God's voice to you, speaking through the sickness, but the sickness itself has come through the enemy's, for when Satan said to God; 'Put *Thine* hand upon Job,' God answered, 'Behold, he is in *thine* hand.' Satan wanted to do what many try to do today, attribute Job's disease to God's hand, but *God's* hand is a hand from which healing ever flows.[100]

Carrie described that it was Job's fault that sickness came upon him, but she was also careful to explain that it came through Satan's hand, not God's. She saw sickness as a 'voice' that God sometimes spoke through, although that was only when a person did not listen the first time. Carrie's view of Job was informed by her foundational belief of healing in the atonement which inferred that sickness was connected to sin.

In 1910 and after her Pentecostal Spirit baptism, Carrie continued along this same trajectory when she wrote, 'As we study God's blessed Word cover to cover we find that while sickness and sin

---

[98] Carrie F. Judd, 'Bible Reading on Sickness', *TF* 4.5 (May 1884), pp. 112-13. See her 'Chastened Before God', *TF* 23.10 (Oct 1903), pp. 217-18. Years later in '"For This Cause,"' *TF* 30.12 (Dec 1910), pp. 265-68, Carrie also suggested that if one took the Lord's Supper in a wrong manner, sickness and death could result. Cf. her 'Full Redemption for Spirit, Soul and Body', *TF* 39.3 (March 1919), pp. 49-53. This was in relation to Isa. 43.1 and Deuteronomy 28, where she wrote that curses which included sickness are the result of disobedience. In 'Glorifying God', *TF* 40.7 (July 1920), using Mal. 2.2, she wrote that if people do not listen to his commands he will bring a curse. More on this in Chapter 5.

[99] Carrie F. Judd, 'Our "Infirmity"', *TF* 6.3 (March 1886), p. 57. Many of her early writings are filled with instances that have a 'cause and effect' nature.

[100] Judd, 'The Lord Our Healer', pp. 269-70. See also A.B. Simpson, 'Divine Healing in the Book of Job', *TF* 19.3 (March 1899), pp. 67-69, and 'God's voice in sickness', *TF* 22.7 (July 1902), pp. 162-65, which looks at Job 33.

have a most intimate connection, either directly or indirectly, yet repentance and healing have also the same intimate connection'.[101] In 1916, she believed that a 'judging spirit is the foundation of much evil, and sorrow, and trouble, and sickness of the body'.[102] Even into 1920, Carrie continued to teach that sin caused sickness when she used the example of when Miriam got leprosy as a result of the negative things she believed about Moses. Carrie used this story to demonstrate how people's words directly related to their health.[103] Carrie was not alone in that many in the Divine Healing Movement also believed this.[104] Petts says that for the early proponents of healing in the atonement,

> the doctrine meant that there is a strong correlation between sickness and sin; that it cannot be God's will for Christians to be sick; that Christians do not need to be sick; that if a Christian is sick it is a result of either sin or of a lack of faith; that the use of medicine is not necessary and that to resort to it is an indication of lack of faith. The view also carries with it the implication that divine healing should not be understood to have ceased with the apostolic era.[105]

Carrie's views greatly resonate with and contributed to the above description. For Carrie, there was a definite connection between sin and sickness, a view which continued to show up in her writings both before and after her 1908 tongues experience. Overall, sickness came from Satan, but God allowed it at times as a form of discipline or punishment for disobedience or some other sin. Additionally, if sickness was a result of sin, then it could also be reversed by walking in obedience and acting in faith.

4.3.1.1 Divine Health

If Carrie believed that sin was connected with sickness, one might wonder if holiness, being right before God, or one's spirituality was

---

[101] Carrie Judd Montgomery, '"Touch Not Mine Anointed"', *TF* 30.3 (March 1910), pp. 51-52. Anna W. Prosser said a similar thing in her 'The Connection of Satan with Disease', *TF* 21.3 (March 1901), pp. 53-58.

[102] Carrie Judd Montgomery, '"Judge Not"', *TF* 36.11 (Nov. 1916), p. 244.

[103] Carrie Judd Montgomery, 'Words of Warning', *TF* 40.6 (June 1920), pp. 121-24. She also cited 1 Pet. 3.8-10 here.

[104] Alexander, *Pentecostal Healing*, p. 41.

[105] Petts, 'Healing and the Atonement', p. 24.

connected with health. In reference to 2 Cor. 4.10-11, 16, Carrie believed that one should be renewed day by day because of the death *and* the resurrection of Jesus. In 1905 and in reference to this, she questioned,

> Why do so many of God's dear children fail to glorify Him by an abundant health and strength and go about sick and faint and miserable? Because they are manifesting the death and forgetting that it is 'the life also of Jesus' that is to be made manifest in their bodies. Believe it, claim it, dear one, that the constant death of all your own natural strength shall continually make a way for that marvelous resurrection life of Christ to be manifested in your mortal flesh until all shall see His life more abundant filling and sustaining you.[106]

According to Carrie, divine health was proof and an outcome of walking in faith. Her teaching suggests that since she saw sickness as a result of sin, she also correlated health with spiritual fullness and saw that it was dependent upon one's faith. Abundant health came when one walked through healing in the atonement and into the 'resurrection life of Christ'. Her view of people 'failing to glorify God' also adds a new dimension of sickness. Did this mean that Carrie believed if people were sick, then they were not glorifying God? Or that they were sick because of their limited faith to appropriate divine health? This appears to be what Carrie is referring to here. If sickness could be caused by sin, then much of the responsibility for divine health rested upon the individual to appropriate his or her own healing by taking hold of it in faith or else calling the elders to come and pray.

After 1908, Carrie's stance remained the same.[107] Being in God's presence and receiving divine healing could go beyond just a cure, it could also provide a sense of sustainability to keep sickness away as well as provide strong health. Alexander rightly notes that for Carrie, 'healing has already been accomplished at the cross; this position of healing should be accepted; and once accepted, there should

---

[106] Carrie Judd Montgomery, 'The Life Also of Jesus', *TF* 25.2 (Feb 1905), p. 26.

[107] Carrie Judd Montgomery, 'Separated Unto God', *TF* 36.12 (Dec 1916), p. 266. She believed that 'the fulness of the Lord's presence will give you not only Divine Healing, but also Divine Health. His presence, and continual obedience to Him, will bring you life more abundant'.

be an ongoing growth in health through the Spirit of Life'.[108] Even beyond this, however, Carrie noted that not just the death of Christ but also his resurrection should be appropriated as well. For Carrie, since sickness could come as a result of sin, so could divine health come as a result of obedience and walking in faith. But to say that Carrie believed that all sickness was a result of sin would be a mistake; she also saw sickness in terms of a spiritual battle against Satan.

4.3.2 Sickness: An Affliction of the 'Enemy'

Besides sin and disobedience as potential causes of sickness, Carrie also believed that sickness was caused by Satan and could be used to bring affliction. In 1888, she asked her readers, 'Does your faith accept Jesus as the all-conquering One? Do you believe that He was manifested to destroy the works of the devil in your soul and body? Have you taken Him at His word, and believed that He has rebuked the disease which was consuming your life?'[109] This implies using authority to disarm spiritual power behind the disease. In 1902, Carrie wrote that 'all our lives most of us have heard sickness spoken of as a blessing in disguise, but it is good to know that our God has called it a curse, for this will help us to claim freedom from it on the ground of Christ's redemption'. In this same article Carrie continued that 'the enemy would hurt and destroy our lives. Jesus, our great Redeemer, has taken our infirmities and borne our sicknesses (Matt. viii:16,17), and therefore He lays His healing hand upon us, renews our strength'.[110] In this light, sickness was seen as a 'curse' and more as an affliction brought on by the 'enemy' that could be overcome by laying hold of God's promises. Therefore, Satan was

---

[108] Alexander, *Pentecostal Healing*, pp. 49, 149, 171.

[109] Carrie F. Judd, 'While Yet Coming', *TF* 8.5 (May 1888), p. 100.

[110] Montgomery, 'Redeemed from the Curse', pp. 170-71. Additionally see Carrie's '"I Will Take Sickness Away From the Midst of Thee"', *TF* 28.2 (Feb 1908), pp. 25-26 where referring to Exod. 23.25, she wrote,

Diseases of Egypt are not for God's children, but if their hearts they go down into Egypt, God cannot meet them there in blessing or healing. He longs to deliver us from the diseases ... The text referred to in the beginning of this article contains the promise that God will take sickness away from the midst of us. If we have, through failure of consecration of faith, failed to accept the healing from God, which is our portion, and if there is sickness in the midst of us to-day, let us stand upon this blessed Word, 'I will take sickness away from the midst of thee'.

the author of sickness, and sickness was a battle directly connected to his power over someone who needed to be freed.[111]

Carrie saw that it was the responsibility of the Christian to loose the bonds of the devil that sometimes came in the form of sickness. She used Isaiah 58 to emphasize this time and time again.[112] In Carrie's paradigm, health and sickness were a part of a spiritual battle. She emphasized the importance of believing God's truth found in His word, standing on that, and declaring healing in the atonement even if feelings did not come right away. On this subject in 1907 Carrie said, 'but it remains for you to claim your freedom, to take it, to rise up in that liberty wherewith Christ has made you free, and to declare it by faith'. Carrie urged people to have faith in things unseen and to 'stand' on the word of God. She wrote that Satan 'will make symptoms in our body contradict the word of God upon which we have taken our stand'. She went on to say that if one has fulfilled all the necessary conditions of the promise but a person still does not see physical results, then 'all things which contradict that promise are lies of the enemy, and must be resisted by the blood, and in the Name above every name. As we thus resist the devil, he flees, even as God has promised that he shall do.'[113] So not only was sin and disobedience something that brought on sickness, the devil was also at work to bring affliction if God allowed it. Carrie believed that Satan afflicts with disease but God's hand heals.

---

[111] A Bible reading that Carrie printed gives a great overview of the kind of thinking that she supported. See Abbie C. Morrow, 'A Bible-Reading on Healing', *TF* 22.10 (Oct 1902), pp. 225-27, where she claimed that God is 'not the Author of sickness', and also questioned, 'Did Jesus ever make anybody sick?'. She then used the Scriptures to show that he did not. She further asked, 'Is Satan the Author of sickness?' followed by a reference to Job 2.7 where it says, and 'Satan ... smote Job with sore boils'. She also asked, 'What will always bring healing?' followed by a reference to the James 5 prayer. 'Connections between sin and sickness', 'Obedience associated with health', 'The will of God to heal', 'Divine healing resting on Christ's atonement', and 'Gifts of healing' were other themes highlighted. 'Promises for healing' and 'Divine healing in this dispensation' and the questions 'What hinders the work of God?', 'Why are not all healed?', were a few of the other one's mentioned.

[112] Carrie referred to Isaiah 58 in these articles, among others: 'Satisfied," *TF* 1.8 (Aug 1881), pp. 121-22; 'Ministry', *TF* 2.11 (Nov 1882), p. 173 (see also Appendix 3, below); 'The Ministry of Faith', *TF* 9.12 (Dec 1889), pp. 274-76; 'The Word and the Workers', *TF* 10.3 (March 1890), p. 64; 'Thou Art Loosed', *TF* 39.12 (Dec 1919), pp. 265-70.

[113] Carrie Judd Montgomery, 'Freed to Serve', *TF* 27.7 (July 1907), p. 146.

After her Pentecostal Spirit baptism, Carrie continued to speak about sickness as a battle in spiritual warfare terms and emphasized power and authority even more. In 1912, she referred to Maria Woodworth-Etter by saying that 'We have never seen anyone else rebuke demons and disease with such Heaven-sent authority and power'.[114] Carrie saw that the believer had authority in Christ to cast out sickness when she wrote about 'How to Resist the Devil'.[115] She also related illness to demon possession when she referred to Dr Finis Yoakum casting out demons of alcoholics.[116] There was a fight going on against demons and diseases but she saw that God had the power to overcome. One example of this is when her husband was sick in 1914 with pneumonia. Using Jn 10.10 as her inspiration, she rebuked Satan because he was trying to 'kill, steal, and destroy' the health of her husband; she fought in faith for his life and he was eventually healed.[117]

If one knew his or her position in Christ and walked in that authority, sickness was a battle that could be overcome. Carrie wrote in 1919 that 'years ago we did not know how to loose people that were bound by the Devil. We thought that we could only pray for them. It is right to pray, but often our prayers cannot be answered until we are able to speak with authority and loose the one whom Satan has bound'.[118] A sense of added authority and commanding prayers are seen here. However, while Carrie claimed to walk in this greater power after her 1908 tongues experience, she did not refer to that experience as the source of that power. Rather, she referred to this same power being available to all who believed what was

---

[114] Carrie Judd Montgomery, 'The Mighty Power of God at Dallas, Texas', *TF* 32.7 (July 1912), p. 269.

[115] Carrie Judd Montgomery, 'How to Resist the Devil', *TF* 32.7 (July 1912), pp. 145-49. This article also referenced Jas 4.7.

[116] Carrie Judd Montgomery, 'The Work in Los Angeles', *TF* 27.1 (Jan 1907), p. 15 and 'Brief Stay in Los Angeles', *TF* 33.12 (Dec 1913), p. 277. See also Alexander Boddy who references Yoakum, 'Best of all known for his "Faith healing …" a Bishop of the Drunkards and the Harlots', *Confidence* 5.11 (Nov 1912); and also Alexander, *Pentecostal Healing*, p. 101.

[117] Montgomery, '"Who Redeemeth Thy Life From Destruction"', p. 50. The continuing nature of healing versus instantaneous healing will be looked at in Chapter 5.

[118] Carrie Judd Montgomery, 'Thou Art Loosed', p. 266. See also the 1911 letter Carrie received from John G. Lake for similar themes.

spoken to Peter in Mt. 16.19.[119] Scripture, not her 1908 tongues experience, was what she claimed was the foundation for this new authority. Apart from this, however, there was an increase in spiritual warfare language emphasizing power and authority which was likely influenced at least in part as a result of her Pentecostal experience and her association with others within the forming movement. Besides seeing that sickness came as a result of sin, Carrie also saw that it could come as a result of a spiritual attack. In light of this, she regularly viewed it in terms as a spiritual battle against Satan to be fought and won. Her belief of healing in the atonement informed the way in which she interpreted sickness and also how she dealt with suffering.

4.3.3 Suffering

The name of Carrie's periodical, *Triumphs of Faith,* not only shows some of her Keswick influences, but it also reveals how she viewed suffering.[120] In an example from 1905 in relation to Mk 7.27 and the woman who begged for crumbs from Jesus, Carrie likened healing to the bread. She saw that the crumbs the Israelites threw away were enough to feed and heal the Gentiles. She moved on to Mt. 8.16-17 and rephrased it by saying, 'Here it is distinctly stated that Jesus healed all the sick ones in order to fulfill the prophecy of Isaiah, saying "Himself took our infirmities and bare our sicknesses"'.[121] Building on healing in the atonement, and while quoting Scripture, Carrie stated boldly that 'Jesus healed all the sick', which suggests that she was implying that this is true for all time. Later in 1917, she wrote, 'God's Word declares that "the prayer of faith shall save the sick." (Jas. v. 15) If the prayer of faith is really offered, the effect will always be healing from the hand of the Great Physician, for the Scripture cannot be broken'.[122] Note how much emphasis she put

---

[119] Carrie Judd Montgomery, 'Thou Art Loosed', pp. 265-70. Jesus says to Peter, 'And I will give you the keys of the kingdom of heaven, and whatever you bind on earth will be bound in heaven, and whatever you loose on earth will be loosed in heaven' (Mt. 16.19, NKJV).

[120] Keswick influences will be developed more in Chapter 6.

[121] Carrie Judd Montgomery, 'Why We May Be Healed', *TF* 25.7 (July 1905), p. 147, wrote, 'If the Lord bore their sicknesses, He has also surely borne ours, and He does not want us to bear what He has borne for us'.

[122] Carrie Judd Montgomery, 'One Hindrance to Divine Healing', *TF* 37.12 (Dec 1917), p. 265. She continued by saying, 'But it must be a prayer of FAITH to obtain such results'.

on the weight of Scripture here rather than on the gift of healing. From these two examples, with healing in the atonement as a foundation and looking through James' paradigm, Carrie believed that if the prayer of faith was offered, then healing would 'always' be the result.[123]

In reality, however, does Jesus heal all the sick all of the time? Carrie's belief in the 'James 5 prayer' and her extreme view of healing in the atonement caused her to understand that Jesus did 'always' heal. Because of this, there was no room to deal with suffering if healing did not come.[124] For Carrie, suffering implied a lack of faith. If one was sick, that sickness was already paid for in the atonement, and one simply needed to claim healing on those grounds. If one acted in faith according to the prayer of faith, Carrie saw that healing was complete whether there was visible evidence of that or not yet. As will be demonstrated further in the next chapter, if symptoms still existed, Carrie taught that people should deny those symptoms and believe what God's word said about their healing whether they experienced the physical improvement or not. In some instances, denying symptoms and acting on faith regardless of one's state produced healing like in the example of the woman with the sore foot who got up and was healed as she walked.[125] For others, this likely caused confusion when they chose to believe they were healed according to the finished work on the cross while continuing to live in pain. In this regard, Carrie's views in relation to how she viewed sickness prove to be somewhat problematic for those who claimed to be healed but never experienced a physical result of that healing in their bodies. In reality, her view of sickness does not account for suffering in any significant way other than to deny it or believe that it has come as a result of a lack of faith, affliction from the 'enemy', or discipline from God because of sin. This view created concerns for people in her time like R.K. Carter and brings up similar concerns today. Because of her extreme view of healing in the atonement, Carrie's theology did not have a sub-

---

[123] Montgomery, 'One Hindrance to Divine Healing', p. 265.

[124] Montgomery, 'One Hindrance to Divine Healing', p. 265.

[125] Montgomery, 'Continue in My Word', p. 74. See also years later in her 'Overcoming', *TF* 38.1 (Jan 1918), p. 3, a similar reference: 'It is a question of believing God's word, or the Devil's symptoms'. She also wrote about the need to reckon ourselves dead to sin and sickness and, in reference to Rom. 8.11, to stand in faith.

stantial paradigm to address the realities of suffering. Further discussion in relation to this will come in Chapter 5.

4.4 Healing

4.4.1 God's Will to Heal

If Carrie saw that sickness resulted from sin and also Satan's affliction, her perspective on God's will in relation to healing is also important to understand. Carrie believed that 'it is first necessary to be convinced from the Word that it is God's will to heal His people'.[126] With this perspective, she went against other common views that saw that 'sickness and death were part of God's inscrutable will'.[127] Jonathan R. Baer rightly believes that many in Evangelicalism during Carrie's time 'inherited a long tradition of theodicy that suggested that God willed or permitted the sickness of those he loved for their greater good, though his purposes might be unclear in the midst of suffering'.[128] Carrie and others in the Divine Healing Movement stood against this belief. Because of this paradigm shift, prayers transformed from mere petitions to commanding prayers. Rather than asking God to heal if it was his will or asking for patience to endure suffering, Carrie encouraged people to command healing to come by praying the prayer of faith.[129] She did not teach people to 'beg' God for healing as if they were unsure if he would come through. Rather, she encouraged people to use the authority they had already been given in Christ to rebuke and command sickness and disease to go in light of what Jesus had accomplished on

---

[126] Montgomery, 'Evidence of Things Not Seen', p. 49. She also stated this earlier in a chapter entitled 'God's Blessed Will for His Children' in her *The Prayer of Faith*, p. 68. A.B Simpson stated this as well in 'Divine Healing', *TF* 19.6 (June 1899), pp. 127-28.

[127] Jonathan R. Baer, 'Redeemed Bodies: The Functions of Divine Healing in Incipient Pentecostalism', *Church History* 70.4 (Dec 2001), p. 748. Dowie also believed as Carrie did along these lines at this time. See also Curtis, *Faith in the Great Physician* for an overview of the commonly held view of suffering at that time.

[128] Baer, 'Redeemed Bodies', pp. 760-61. Because sickness was seen as a battle against Satan, Baer further suggests that 'the healing experience thus overturned the idea that God had willed illness which helps explain the powerful sense of liberation and peace of mind that so often accompanied it'.

[129] Carrie F. Judd, 'Asking Amiss', *TF* 4.7 (July 1884), pp. 153-55.

the cross.[130] She wanted people to recognize their position in Christ and take hold of their healing. She taught that it was God's will to heal 'all' diseases and afflictions.[131] Since sickness was a battle with the 'enemy', speaking commanding prayers with authority became one way of bringing healing. Going against the accepted views of the day, Carrie moved beyond passive resignation and acceptance of suffering and instead chose to believe that God wanted all to be healed.[132]

4.4.2 Purposes of Healing

Service

For Carrie, there was always a purpose behind healing. Being set free from affliction and sickness was not just a means to an end but it was so that people could better serve Christ.[133] Carrie highlighted that deliverance from bondage or sickness was for the purpose of service and for glorifying God; once someone had been 'lifted up', they should go out and lift others up.[134] Evidenced in 'Freed to Serve' and in reference to the atonement, Carrie stated in 1907 that 'God wants to free us from the bondage of the enemy that we may be free to serve Him'.[135] She went on to reveal that the reason and motive that people should seek to be freed from physical bondage was for the purpose of serving God. Even years after her Pentecostal Spirit baptism experience, in 1919, Carrie said,

> If people ask why we want to loose those who are bound by Satan, it is because our blessed Lord, who created them, and redeemed them, and to whom they belong, has need of them in His service. He has need of every one, and wants every one to be loosed: loosed from our sins, loosed from our sicknesses, loosed

---

[130] Montgomery, 'Freed to Serve', p. 146. On this subject in 1907 Carrie said, 'but it remains for you to claim your freedom, to take it, to rise up in that liberty wherewith Christ has made you free, and to declare it by faith'.

[131] Montgomery, 'One Hindrance to Divine Healing', p. 265.

[132] See discussion in Chapter 2 in relation to Heather D. Curtis' *Faith in the Great Physician: Suffering and Divine Healing in American Culture, 1860-1900* (Baltimore: The John Hopkins University Press, 2007).

[133] Montgomery, 'Freed to Serve', pp. 145-46.

[134] Carrie F. Judd, 'Ye Serve the Lord Christ', *TF* 4.6 (June 1884), pp. 121-23, and Carrie Judd Montgomery, '"There is Lifting Up"', *TF* 21.5 (May 1901), pp. 97-99.

[135] Carrie wrote emphatically, 'God wants us to be freed that we may serve Him' (Montgomery, 'Freed to Serve', pp. 145-46).

from our prejudices, loosed from our own thoughts and reasonings, loosed from every bondage and made free to serve Him and to show forth His glory. Is not that a blessed motive for being set free and for setting others free?[136]

Further, in reference to Lazarus being raised from the dead, Carrie continued that 'God wants us not only to be made alive, but to be set free, that the grave clothes may be loosed, that we may walk, and talk and work for Jesus'. In reference to Isa. 58.6, Carrie summed up the motives for being healed when she said, 'God has set you and me free for one thing supremely, and that is because the Lord hath need of us in His service'.[137]

Evangelism

Beyond service, there were also other purposes of healing. In an article entitled 'Why We May Be Healed', written in 1905, Carrie explained, 'He healed the sick that the unbelieving ones might know His spiritual power to save souls ... So we must ask Him for healing, that others may know His power to save their souls'.[138] Carrie saw evangelism as another purpose to be healed. Additionally, articles like 'God Confirming His Word by Signs and Wonders' and 'Healed for God's Praise' reveal further insights into her view for the purpose of healing.[139] She said that 'far above the mere fact of being healed for our own comfort, or for the sake of our friends, we must want healing for the Lord's glory'.[140] Besides service, healing was also for the purpose of evangelism, confirming God's word, and glorifying God. This evangelistic aspect to healing that could

---

[136] Carrie Judd Montgomery, 'Thou Art Loosed', p. 267.

[137] Montgomery, 'Thou Art Loosed', pp. 268-69. See also her '"Who Redeemeth Thy Life From Destruction"', p. 50.

[138] Carrie Judd Montgomery, 'Why We May Be Healed', *TF* 25.7 (July 1905), p. 146. This article comes from notes of an address delivered at a Christian Alliance meeting in Oakland. Utilizing Mk 1.40-41, she began her article by noting how Jesus was moved with compassion when He had healed the leper. Moving on to Mk 2.10, she wrote that Jesus healed the crippled man as a sign of His power and salvation.

[139] Carrie Judd Montgomery, 'God Confirming His Word by Signs and Wonders', *TF* 33.5 (May 1913), pp. 97-99, and 'Healed for God's Praise', *TF* 38.2 (Feb 1918), pp. 25-28.

[140] Carrie Judd Montgomery, 'Some Hindrances to Healing', *TF* 33.12 (Dec 1913), p. 269. Many in the Divine Healing Movement taught about salvation before they introduced the topic of healing at conferences.

also draw people to salvation resonated with the Divine Healing Movement at the time.

4.4.3 The Gift of Healing

While Carrie printed articles by others who spoke about 'the gift(s) of healing',[141] she struggled to highlight this gift in her writings, mentioning it only a few times, once in relation to Woodworth-Etter's ministry in 1917[142] and once in 1941 when she said that God 'is ready to bestow upon us the priceless gift of healing for the body'.[143] Because Carrie's paradigm for healing rested so heavily upon the finished work of Christ which could be appropriated by

---

[141] She did, however, print many articles by others who referred to this gift, most associating it with healing that should not have ceased in the early Church but should be practiced in their day. Some articles that reference this gift in her periodical are: Mrs Edward Mix, 'Holding Fast', *TF* 1.1 (Jan 1881), pp. 4-5; A.J. Gordon, 'The Testimony of Scripture', *TF* 2.12 (Dec 1882), pp. 179-81; R.L. Stanton, Gospel Parallelisms: Illustrated in Healing of Body and Soul', *TF* 3.8 (Aug 1883), pp. 179-84; William C. Stevens, 'The Lord's Healing, *TF* 11.2 (Feb 1891), pp. 25-30; Asa Mahan, 'Healing Through Prayer', *TF* 12.4 (April 1892), pp. 81-82; no author, 'The Gift of Healing in the Holy Spirit', *TF* 12.4 (April 1892), pp. 88-91; H.C. Waddell, 'How to Receive Divine Healing', *TF* 16.2 (Feb 1896), pp. 35-40; E. Sisson, 'A Call to Prayer for a World-Wide Revival', *TF* 26.3 (March 1906), pp. 57-60; George Soltan, 'The Power of Faith and Prayer', *TF* 28.3 (March 1908), pp. 57-61; A.B. Simpson, 'Divine Healing through the Holy Spirit', *TF* 30.9 (Sept 1910), pp. 196-99; and Andrew Murray, 'Because of Your Unbelief', *TF* 45.2 (Feb 1925), p. 34, where he says that 'the entire Scriptures declare that these graces [which he mentioned earlier was the gift of healing] will be granted according to the measure of the Spirit and of faith'. Hardesty also notices that 'while Allen, the Mixs, and Montgomery all emphasized the importance of helping the sick person pray the prayer of faith, Mix did speak of Allen as having the gift of healing' (Hardesty, *Faith Cure*, pp. 10-11).

[142] Carrie Judd Montgomery, 'Precious Revival Meeting in San Francisco', *TF* 37.1 (Jan 1917), p. 20. Carrie wrote that one was 'able to receive healing through the "gift of healing", which it is quite evident God has given Mrs. Etter'. Through this statement, Carrie admitted that while faith was still necessary for healing to be appropriated, the faith did not necessarily have to come from the one who sought the healing but could could come from someone who had the 'gift of healing'.

[143] The other time Carrie specifically wrote about the gift of healing was in 'Divine Healing in the Book of Proverbs', *TF* 61.9 (Sept 1941), p. 194, where she said that 'We receive Jesus Christ Himself, "Who of God is made unto us Wisdom," and love Him for Himself, and not for His gifts, but we find His right hand, so to speak, is ready to bestow upon us the priceless gift of healing for the body. His ministry on earth was full of healing mercy to all who came to Him, and He is "the same yesterday, and today, and forever"'. Carrie mentioned 'gifts of healing' in 'The Unity of the Body', *TF* 2.6 (June 1882), p. 88. In 'By This All Men Know', *TF* 28.11 (November 1908), p. 241, she mentioned the 'gifts of healing, miracles, gifts of tongues, etc' but emphasized that love is greater.

anyone who applied the prayer of faith, the gift of healing was irrelevant.[144] Because at that time many others also emphasized prayer for healing in accordance to their understanding of the James 5 instructions, Carrie was not alone in leaving this gift out of the conversation about healing.[145] If healing was always available to anyone who believed and activated God's word, there was no need to single people out who had the gift of healing. Carrie's positional understanding of the atonement made her see that any and all who walked in faith were able to appropriate healing.

Moving forward, one might wonder if Carrie believed that she had the gift of healing. However, since her main hermeneutic for interpreting healing did not come from Pauline literature, she never referred to herself as having the gift. In light of the absence of language used in her periodical referring to this gift, it is highly doubtful that Carrie believed she had this gift, even though many today might look at her life and say that she did. People like Dorothy Trudel and her successor also never claimed to have this gift.[146] Because of Carrie's paradigm, she likely saw things similarly to Lee Chin, a Christian Alliance missionary sent out from the Oakland branch who said, 'I have no gift of healing, but I pray to the Lord alone who has the power to raise you up'.[147] If Carrie did believe she had the gift of healing, she never publicly identified herself with it.

---

[144] Carrie Judd Montgomery, 'The Work of the Holy Spirit', *TF* 32.11 (Nov 1912), p. 242. In relation to Mt. 8.17, she said that 'When the Spirit shows us this it is so real and blessed, and we have no difficulty in appropriating the healing for our bodies provided through His cross'. See also Petts, 'Healing and the Atonement', and John Wimber, *Kingdom Suffering: Facing Difficulty and Trial in the Christian Life*, Christian Essential Series (Ann Arbor, MI: Vine Books, imprint of Servant Publications, 1988), pp. 23-26. For contemporary scholarship on the New Testament texts related to healing, see John Christopher Thomas, *The Devil, Disease and Deliverance,* pp. 20-21. In relation to the themes of sickness and suffering with regard to Jas 5.14-16, Thomas notices that in Pauline literature there might have been a call for someone who had the 'charism of healing', but such a call is not part of James' instructions.

[145] Alexander admits that her research 'revealed a surprising lack of discussion of spiritual gifts, especially the gift of healing, in early Pentecostal discourse' (*Pentecostal Healing*, p. 226).

[146] Kydd says that 'Neither Trudel nor [her successor Samuel] Zeller believed they possessed the biblical gift of healing; rather, they believed bodily healing was provided for in the atonement' (*Healing through the Centuries*, p. 153).

[147] F.J. Masters, 'Good News from China', TF 16.9 (Sept 1896), p. 201.

4.5 Conclusion

In conclusion, the major healing themes that emerged in Carrie's writings were healing in the atonement and the prayer of faith. Her interpretation of these informed her view of sickness and healing. These foundations remained the main hermeneutic through which Carrie interpreted sickness and healing both before and after her 1908 tongues experience. Additionally, her teachings on healing in the atonement as early as 1880 demonstrate her significant contribution to the forming of the doctrine itself as she was one of its earliest advocates. By creating space in her periodical for others also to teach on the subject, she helped spread the doctrine globally, strengthened the Divine Healing Movement's understanding of it, and infiltrated Pentecostal theology with it. Since many within Charismatic and Pentecostal circles have adopted the doctrine of healing in the atonement or variations of it, Carrie's participation not only in the formation, but also in the spreading of the doctrine demonstrates her important contribution to Pentecostalism and beyond.

5

From Theology to Practice: Implications of Carrie's Theology of Healing

Carrie's belief of healing in the atonement appropriated through the 'James 5 prayer' informed her theology of healing, but pragmatically, what difference did it make in her own life and in her healing ministry? This chapter will discuss those implications as well as explore her methods of application. What Carrie saw as the necessary spiritual posture to pray the 'James 5 prayer' and to receive healing will be highlighted along with her additional models of healing. Further, how Carrie practically approached some of the tougher questions in relation to healing and sickness along with a discussion on whether Carrie thought that people could lose their healing will be explored. Specific movements or streams where Carrie's theology has emerged will be identified along with a discussion of where she might fit within present day healing paradigms.

5.1 In Carrie's Life

Carrie's own experiences will essentially foreshadow the themes to be discussed in more detail throughout the rest of the chapter. One early instance where Carrie's belief in healing in the atonement was actualized was in 1882. Despite her deteriorating physical state, she continued to hang on to her belief that she was already healed in the atonement. In regards to this, she wrote,

Let me illustrate these truths by an experience of my own, through which many points, formerly perplexing, were made clear to me. Suddenly attacked one day by a physical ailment which occasioned great suffering, and which, humanly speaking, *required* a certain course of treatment and nursing to give any relief, I took the case to my 'Great Physician' in prayer, and pleaded for relief from pain. But the hours passed by and I was conscious only of increased suffering, while by degrees the conviction forced itself upon me that I must make a direct *claim of faith* before my prayer would be granted. Glancing at my watch, I said, 'It is four minutes past ten (A.M.), and I *now* accept the blessing which is already mine by the merits of my Saviour's Atonement. In the name of the Lord I am healed'.[1]

Claiming faith for her healing because of what Christ had already accomplished in the atonement provided a basis for her authority when she proclaimed herself healed.

During this same account, Carrie believed that regardless of persisting symptoms, she was already healed. She said,

Having made this declaration by faith, and on the authority of God's truth, without reference to my feelings, there began a trial or proving of my faith. For several hours longer I engaged in my customary duties growing more and more worn with suffering, but responding meanwhile to every taunt of the enemy, 'I was healed at four minutes past ten this morning, and so I am healed now'.[2]

While reality showed that the physical effects of Carrie's sickness increased during this time, she denied those feelings and chose to live in a different reality that had not yet manifested itself in her body. She experienced turmoil in her mind and her thoughts claiming that the 'enemy' was taunting her. Her rebuttal to the 'enemy' was to claim that when she prayed the very first time, she was indeed healed, whether she felt the results of that or not. She reflected further in relation to this incident by saying, 'As I realized with thanksgiving and joy the perfect healing, so wondrously wrought, the thought came to my mind, "Although I am only now *conscious* of

---

[1] Carrie F. Judd, 'Trial of Faith', *TF* 2.3 (March 1882), p. 37.

[2] Judd, 'Trial of Faith', p. 37.

being made whole, the healing was accomplished at the very moment I first made my claim of faith before God'".[3] Regardless of
how long it took for her to experience and feel a measure of healing
in her body, because of the atonement, she chose to believe that it
had been accomplished the moment she claimed it by faith.

As noticed from the example just given, the prayer of faith was
also actualized in her personal experiences of healing even after her
initial account. In Carrie's 1879 healing, the anointing of oil mentioned in James 5 was absent from her experience. Struck so much
by the significance in the prayer of faith, however, she later found it
a privilege to use oil when she was sick so that she could 'follow all
that the Lord commanded'.[4] In 1901, when asked if there could be
some other way to be healed without being anointed with oil, she
responded by encouraging people to follow the whole command
and to include the oil. She reflected upon this theme in regard to
her initial healing:

> At the time of my first healing I had never understandingly read
> this passage in James, so I was healed by the touch of God in
> answer to the prayer of faith, without any such service of conse-
> cration as the anointing implies. But as time went on I became
> so impressed with the beautiful significance of this ceremony
> that I longed for the opportunity to present my body after this
> sacred manner. I was even glad when a severe touch of illness
> came upon me, that I might yield as one of the sick to this sweet
> and blessed rite ... I felt that the anointing was significant of the
> Holy Spirit, who would come in healing power upon my body,
> and I rested there in faith, without any care at the moment as to
> whether I felt better or not.[5]

During the illness mentioned above, after people prayed and
anointed her with oil, she went up to her room to rest. She admitted
that she 'was not looking for any particular manifestation of healing,
but I was occupied with the Healer Himself, and enjoying sweet rest
in my soul as I leaned my whole weight upon His promise. I had

---

[3] Judd, 'Trial of Faith', p. 37.
[4] Carrie Judd Montgomery, 'The Path of Obedience', *TF* 21.9 (Sept 1901), pp.
194-95.
[5] Montgomery, 'The Path of Obedience', pp. 194-95. Carrie saying she was
glad when sickness came contradicts most of her other claims in relation to sickness. Notice also her Episcopalian roots in her choice of terminology.

fulfilled my part of the covenant, and had He not met me in it, even though I did not yet see or feel it?' Relying on God's word and the fact that she had already trusted Him for her healing, she chose to 'rest' upon 'His promise'.[6] She later claimed that she felt God's touch and was healed. Timing between believing God for healing and actually experiencing it was not a huge issue for Carrie; she believed it was already accomplished through the finished work of Christ the moment she acted in faith to appropriate it.

In another example in 1907, Carrie explained how she dealt with the tension of believing she was healed when she had not yet felt it in her body:

> When we covenant to trust God it must not be with the thought of experiment for a limited time. I remember my own experience, during a time of great physical testing, when I was standing on God's promise, and yet had no evidence in my body that my prayer was answered, the enemy craftily inquired how long I would be willing to endure the present suffering and helplessness, and still believe that God had been true to His promise. I was enabled by His grace to reply that I would trust to the end of my life, even if I never saw. The enemy then retired, completely vanquished, and soon afterward the Lord graciously manifested His healing power in my body, enabling me at once to rise and walk, though I had been seriously crippled by a most severe attack of sciatic rheumatism.[7]

This example continues to demonstrate how Carrie dealt with the effects of illness and suffering in her own life by believing she was healed even when she still experienced sickness in her body. The sickness remaining was just the 'enemy' wanting to use those symptoms to shake her faith. Healing for a specific time period as the responsibility of the individual is highlighted here but will be developed more later on. It has been shown through these examples that Carrie integrated the doctrine of healing in the atonement and the prayer of faith into her own situations. Now we will turn to see the practical implications of her theology within her ministry of healing.

---

[6] Montgomery, 'The Path of Obedience', pp. 194-95.
[7] Montgomery, 'Evidence of Things Not Seen', p. 50.

5.2 Positioning Oneself to Receive Healing

Right Attitude

Carrie believed that there were specific things people could do to posture themselves to pray the prayer of faith and to receive healing. One of these things was getting right with God. She expounded on this in her 1914 article, 'The Right Attitude of Heart to Receive Healing'.[8] Having the right motivation to approach healing was crucial, as she believed it was important that one's heart and determination was 'to find the blessed Healer, Jesus Himself, far more than merely to be healed by Him'. She continued that when one becomes 'well acquainted with Him, He will not only assure you of forgiveness and healing, but He will lead you on unto unspeakable heights and depths of His love'.[9] The right perspective had to be taken when approaching the 'Great Physician' for healing, which was to keep one's eyes on him above all else.

Forgiveness

Before being able to pray the prayer of faith properly, one had to deal with unforgiveness or a 'root of bitterness' in his or her heart. Carrie wrote in relation to this, 'so we see how absolutely necessary it is to be filled with forgiving love before we can pray the prayer of faith'.[10] Because Carrie saw that sickness and sin were connected, 'either directly or indirectly,' she also saw that 'repentance and healing have also the same intimate connection'.[11] In 1918, she advised,

> Ask God to cause you to remember your sins and inconsistencies, and ask Him to give you grace to confess them. Begin at once to pray that the Lord will bless the people who have been

---

[8] Carrie Judd Montgomery, 'The Right Attitude of Heart to Receive Healing', *TF* 34.10 (Oct 1914), pp. 217-19. Also see her '"To-Day If Ye Will Hear His Voice"', *TF* 34.11 (Nov 1914), pp. 241-42, where she encouraged people not to harden their hearts for 'He is the Lord that Healeth Thee (Ex. 15:26, 23:21,25, Deut. 7:12,13,15, Romans 8:11)'.

[9] Carrie Judd Montgomery, 'Diligent Harkening', *TF* 35.2 (Feb 1915), p. 26.

[10] Montgomery, 'Some Hindrances to Healing', p. 268.

[11] Montgomery, '"Touch Not Mine Anointed"', pp. 51-52. She added, 'We find that not only does our great Intercessor instruct us to pray "the prayer of faith" for healing and to confess our faults one to another as a means of humbling ourselves to a place where we may receive healing, but most of all our blessed Saviour has made provision for our healing by Himself bearing our sickness and infirmities'.

stumbled through you, and to turn their hearts toward you, so that they will be ready for your confession. 'Get right with God,' and then faith for the healing of your sick body will spring up spontaneously.[12]

From the above example, much of the responsibility for healing was laid upon the individual and it was imperative to 'get right with God' and confess one's sins so that faith for healing would come as a result.

Confession

For Carrie, the act of confession mentioned in James 5 was also an important part of preparing one's heart to receive God's healing.[13] In 1910, she wrote,

> [N]ot only does our great Intercessor instruct us to pray 'the prayer of faith' for healing and to confess our faults one to another as a means of humbling ourselves to a place where we may receive healing, but most of all our blessed Saviour has made provision for our healing by Himself bearing our sickness and infirmities.[14]

Confession was a means of humbling oneself to be better postured to receive healing.[15] It also played an integral part in stirring up faith for healing. Carrie continued to emphasize the need for confession when she wrote that 'part of the breaking process is to confess our faults one to another. It is easy to tell them to Jesus, for He knows all about us, but it is very humbling to confess to each other, and God blesses to us this process of breaking down our pride and self-

---

[12] Carrie Judd Montgomery, 'The God That Answereth by Fire', *TF* 38.10 (Oct 1918), p. 220.

[13] Carrie Judd Montgomery, 'Confession and Restitution', *TF* 17.9 (Sept 1897), pp. 193-95, and 'Our Lord's Directions About Prayer', *TF* 18.3 (March 1898), pp. 49-54, are additional places where Carrie mentioned confession.

[14] Montgomery, '"Touch Not Mine Anointed"', pp. 51-52. The passage started out with, 'As we study God's blessed Word cover to cover we find that while sickness and sin have a most intimate connection, either directly or indirectly, yet repentance and healing have also the same intimate connection'. This was followed with quotes from Mt. 8.16-17.

[15] Montgomery, 'The God That Answereth by Fire', p. 220.

sufficiency'.[16] Confession could bring a person to the place where they could liberally pray the prayer of faith. Carrie saw that confession was a key to release healing.[17]

Obedience

Obedience also played a crucial role for receiving healing. In 1901, Carrie referred to the story of Naaman to illustrate this. She saw that he was willing to do some great thing to be healed but struggled with his pride to do something as low as wash himself in the murky waters of the Jordan. She said, 'Beloved, the path of obedience is that which you must pursue if you would receive healing for your diseased body, and greater light for your longing soul'.[18] Over 15 years after this article, Carrie used Naaman again as an example in an article entitled 'Healing Through Obedience', where she re-emphasized the importance and connection of obedience with healing.[19] Obedience unto God was a way of putting oneself in the right position to receive healing.

Faith

Once someone was in the right posture to pray for healing, Carrie believed they also needed to believe that at the moment they acted in faith, they then received healing from God according to His word. In 1888 when referring to Mk 11.24, she said that 'when you

---

[16] Carrie Judd Montgomery, '"The Prayer of Faith"', *TF* 39.6 (June 1919), pp. 123-24. Her thinking resonates with a phrase I heard many years ago that 'confession to God brings forgiveness but confession to others brings healing'.

[17] Montgomery, 'The God That Answereth by Fire', p. 220. Carrie quoted Finney here who said,

> A revival of religion may be expected when Christians begin to confess their sins one to another. At other times, they confess in a general manner, as if they were only half in earnest … But when there is an ingenuous breaking down, and a pouring out of the heart in making confession of sins, the floodgates will soon burst open, and salvation will flow over the place.

[18] Carrie Judd Montgomery, 'The Path of Obedience', *TF* 21.9 (Sept 1901), p. 194.

[19] Carrie Judd Montgomery, 'Healing Through Obedience', *TF* 38.11 (Nov 1918), pp. 241-44. See also her '"For This Cause"', *TF* 30.12 (Dec 1910), pp. 265-68, where Carrie also suggested that if one took the Lord's Supper in a wrong manner, sickness and death could result. In her 'Full Redemption for Spirit, Soul and Body', *TF* 39.3 (March 1919), pp. 49-53, in relation to Isa. 43.1 and Deuteronomy 28, she wrote that curses which included sickness, are the result of disobedience. In 'Glorifying God', *TF* 40.7 (July 1920), pp. 145-48, using Mal. 2.2, she wrote that if people do not listen to his commands he will bring a curse.

pray, you are to believe that you *then* receive the very things for which you ask, He is not requiring anything unreasonable or impossible'. In the same article, she also wrote,

> Some of you have been living very miserable lives, defeated constantly by the enemy ... Will you begin from this moment, dear ones, to take this new position of trust, crowning Jesus King of your whole life, of that sin which has conquered you in the past, of that burden which has been crushing your life, of that disease which no human power can reach, of that pain which wearies the brain, of that heartache which is known to no friend but Jesus, and which no hand but His can touch? Will you crown Him by faith? Then shall He crown thee 'with loving-kindness and tender mercies;' then shall the government of your life so rest upon His shoulder that all burdens shall be lifted from yours; then shall soul, and mind, and body come into complete subjection to the King of kings.[20]

Taking one's 'position' in Christ and trusting in his promises for healing was a strong foundation for Carrie. Notice, too, that Carrie was not just concerned about physical healing; emotional and spiritual healing were also important throughout her whole ministry as well.

Helping Others

The Scripture on Carrie's gravestone is Ps. 41.1-3 which talks about how when people help the poor, the Lord will strengthen them on their beds of illness and restore or sustain them on their sickbeds. Ironically, this was never one of Carrie's major theological texts used when supporting divine healing. In light of her gravestone, it is quite possible that she saw helping the poor as another means of receiving healing. Her many references to Isaiah 58 also suggest that helping others can release healing.[21] In 1889, Carrie demonstrated this with a story of when she had prayed for herself but had not felt any relief. A woman came to visit her more on business matters but

---

[20] Judd, 'Jesus Crowned', p. 122.

[21] Judd, 'Ministry', *TF* 2.11 (Nov 1882), p. 173 (See Appendix 3, below). See also her 'Satisfied', *TF* 1.8 (Aug 1881), pp. 121-22; 'The Broken Heart', *TF* 6.2 (Feb 1886), pp. 25-27; 'The Ministry of Faith', *TF* 9.12 (Dec 1889), pp. 274-76; 'The Word and the Workers', *TF* 10.3 (March 1890), p. 64; and 'Thou Art Loosed', pp. 265-70, to name just a few.

who was suffering from a severe headache. Carrie hesitated at first to pray for her because the woman's original intention of coming was not for prayer, as well as the fact that Carrie herself was having trouble listening to her because of her own pain. Nevertheless, Carrie said she felt the Spirit leading her to pray for this woman. It was in this process that Carrie experienced healing in her own body. The other lady was also healed at the same time. In light of this, Carrie remarked, 'Again, and again, in my life, in many different ways, have I been called in deep spiritual poverty to water others by faith, and have found myself watered'.[22]

Hindrances to Healing

Besides correctly positioning oneself (in a spiritual sense) to invite healing, Carrie saw that there were also things that could hinder one from receiving healing.[23] In 1913, she wrote that disobedience and a failure to 'harken' to the voice of God could prevent healing. She believed that a 'jealous, critical spirit will also hinder faith'. In relation to the children of Israel, she continued to say that 'a murmuring spirit is often a cause of lack of victory'. She also saw that it was relatively easy to receive healing the first time from God 'but when one has been thus healed, and has failed to stand as a faithful witness, or has not given that restored life to the Lord, to be used as He directs, it is not so easy to find the Great Physician the next time'. Even if the hindrances just mentioned were removed, Carrie still suggested that 'a lack of zeal in pressing through to claim their inheritance along the line of healing' could also inhibit healing to come.[24] And finally, she proclaimed that 'there are many hindrances that might be spoken of, but one which surely prevents the faith which brings healing, is lack of love and compassion for other

---

[22] Carrie F. Judd, 'The Ministry of Faith', *TF* 9.12 (Dec 1889), pp. 275-76. Notice how Carrie felt the Spirit led her to pray. It was not only being led by the Word, but there was an interplay between the foundation of the Word and the Spirit's leading.

[23] Carrie later wrote about hindrances in 'The Conditions of God's Covenant of Healing', *TF* 39.5 (May 1919), pp. 97-101; '"The Prayer of Faith"', *TF* 39.6 (June 1919), pp. 121-24; and 'What Hinders Your Healing?', *TF* 40.9 (Sept 1920), pp. 193-96, where she used Exod. 15.26, Ps. 103, and Isaiah 40 to write about how asking amiss, with wrong motives, pride, or unforgiveness could also hinder healing.

[24] Montgomery, 'Some Hindrances to Healing', pp. 268-69. This also references the previous quotes in the paragraph.

members of the body'.[25] According to Carrie, love was essential for faith to arise for healing.

From all the preparations given, it appears that Carrie put the majority of the weight on the individual to exercise faith to receive healing. If people were closed off to healing because they had not prepared their heart, they could choose to miss out on receiving their healing. People had to want to be healed and spiritually position themselves correctly for it to happen. Healing was dependant upon God but appropriated through the faith of the individual much more than on those who were praying. The resurgence of the gift of healing along with accounts like Jesus' healing the paralytic because of his friends' faith in Mark 2 do not easily fit within Carrie's focused James 5 and healing in the atonement paradigm.[26]

5.3 Models and Methods of Healing Practice

While Scripture greatly influenced Carrie's theology of healing, it was her healing experience that significantly informed her models of healing. This section will examine how Carrie practically administered healing as well as additional models of healing that have not yet been explored. Already mentioned in Chapter 2 was an analysis of the model of healing homes that Carrie ran throughout her life. The main purpose of her homes was to teach on healing and to encourage people to act in faith so that they could take hold of what God had already given to them. Because divine healing was not a popular subject in the church, healing homes provided a safe place for people to come and learn about this 'new' truth and also pray for and receive healing. This model, that some refer to as a 'pastoral model of healing', spanned the majority of Carrie's life.[27]

---

[25] Montgomery, 'One Hindrance to Divine Healing', pp. 265-69. Earlier Carrie wrote that 'The sick one may say, "I do not know of anything wrong in my heart or life." But if there is a delay in healing, if there is difficulty, if faith does not spring up in the heart, there must be a yielding to God in great humility, and brokenness of spirit, for God to search the very inmost being. He alone can show the reason why faith does not spring up and take full possession of the heart.' See also her 'Divine Healing as Related to Our Tongue', *TF* 38.4 (April 1918), pp. 73-76.

[26] See Carrie Judd Montgomery, '"The Promise of the Father." A Personal Testimony', *TF* 28.7 (July 1908), pp. 145-49.

[27] Storms, 'Carrie Judd Montgomery: The Little General', p. 277. Storms also saw Carrie as a forerunner amongst the Charismatic movement. Storms recogniz-

5.3.1 Long Distance Healing

Another model of healing came in the form of prayer meetings and long distance prayer. Carrie would pray for people who attended her gatherings but also for people at a distance who sent in letters requesting prayer. Modeled to her by Sarah Mix, many were healed through Carrie's ministry of long distance praying.[28] An example of this can be seen in 1882 when at one of her meetings, Carrie and the others prayed for a specific request sent in by Mrs C.M. Dutcher, who 'had been severely ill for nineteen years with disease of the spine'.[29] A few days after the prayer meeting, Dutcher was strengthened enough to walk a quarter of a mile to her church. Another example of this model comes from a local newspaper article about Richard Huffman. He was told by physicians that his sickness of a paralyzed nervous system and hardening in his spinal column was incurable. Not too long after that, he got a hold of Carrie's *Prayer of Faith*. A reporter notes that 'he was so much struck by its contents that he wrote to her and proposed that she should pray for him at her weekly prayer meetings'. She agreed and organized a time when she would pray 'at the same time' as him. Shortly after prayer was given, he began to grow stronger and could walk up the stairs for the first time in three years. Ever since his healing, he claimed that he had been 'leaping and walking and praising'.[30]

Because of this particular model, to the public eye, Carrie was termed the 'Long Range Faith Curer' or someone who 'performs Faith Cures by Correspondence'.[31] In 1896, a writer in *The Brookfield*

---

es that Carrie used a 'pastoral model of healing'. And while there was an element of pastoral support, Carrie still expected healings to come immediately even if the manifestations arose at a later time.

[28] See *Word, Work and World* 9.4 (Oct 1887), pp. 136-39, to read one account by Major R. Chamberlain written September 6, 1887.

[29] *Troy Times,* reprinted in *The Daily Eagle* (NY), August 14, 1882. She heard an account of a 'miraculous cure' in answer to prayer in a nearby town and 'believed that she would be cured if Christians prayed for her'. She also 'attributed her cure to the efficiency of prayer'.

[30] 'Alleged Miracle', *Buffalo Courier*, April 23, 1883. Another example of how Carrie prayed for someone at a distance was mentioned in a newspaper in Minnesota. And while this time the person was not healed, she felt 'easier and is trusting in the mercy of God' after the prayers were offered for her ('Faith in Prayer', *The St. Paul Sunday Globe* [MN], February 5, 1882, p. 8).

[31] 'Long Range Cures: Mrs. Montgomery Rivals Schlatter', *The Sunday Herald* (Syracuse, NY), December 1, 1895, p. 14, 'Healing at Long Range: Mrs. Mont-

Courier quoted Carrie as saying, 'It has always been my belief that the Lord could heal as well when I was at a distance from the object of my prayer as when we were together'. The reporter went on to say that Carrie claimed to be 'the champion long distance faith

MRS. CARRIE JUDD MONTGOMERY.
(The Long Range Faith Curer.)

Figure 19
'The Long Range Faith Curer'
Taken from 'Long Range Cures: Mrs. Montgomery Rivals Schlatter,'
The Sunday Herald (Syracuse, NY), December 1, 1895, p. 14.

curist'.[32] However, the public's perception of Carrie was different from her own. In her writings, there is no mention of her making any such claims. In 1895, Carrie did have to defend her 'Long Range Theory' publicly in *The San Francisco Call* when someone opposed her.[33] And while Carrie practiced and encouraged long dis-

gomery Performs Faith Cures by Correspondence', *The Brookfield Courier* (NY), January 15, 1896.
[32] 'Healing at Long Range: Mrs. Montgomery Performs Faith Cures by Correspondence', *The Brookfield Courier* (NY), January 15, 1896.
[33] 'Testing Faith Healing, Newly Arrived Minister Says It Is the Work of the Devil, Opposes Mrs. Montgomery', p. 9.

tance praying, it was the public who highlighted this aspect of her ministry. Carrie's weekly prayer meeting, which included praying for people at a distance, was one of the models of healing she practiced throughout her life.

5.3.2 Methods of Prayer

Stanley Frodsham's recollection of Carrie adds insight to how she practically ministered at times. He recalled an account of how Mrs Norton came to the Home of Peace straight from India and was a 'nervous wreck'. He said that Carrie

> never waited for people to ask her for prayer, she just always would go over and lay hands upon them and pray for them. And she went over to Sister Norton and laid her hands upon her and began praying, praying in tongues. And Sister Norton had just come back from India and she said, 'You're praying in Hindustandi,' you're saying 'Take, my little one, take, take, take, take, take.' So Mary believed and began to take and in a few days she was absolutely restored, she said 'I've just been taking, taking, I've been taking'.[34]

Carrie's boldness and faith is revealed here with the inclusion of praying out in tongues during ministry. While it is not completely clear whether Carrie was encouraging her to 'take' of her healing or of more of the Spirit, this description is helpful in understanding more of how Carrie might have actually prayed for people.

While Carrie wrote about various ways healing could come, her basic methods of practice were heavily rooted in the 'James 5 prayer'. Even though the confession of sins, the anointing with oil, and the laying on of hands were absent in her first healing account, they became important in her methodology. In 1907, she referred to Jas. 5.14-15 and Mk 16.17-18 and encouraged her readers to 'follow out God's commands, call for the elders to anoint you, or ask some believing ones to lay hands upon you in the name of Jesus'.[35] If one

---

[34] Stanley Frodsham, 'Abiding Under God's Shadow', audio recording at <http://brothermel.com/stanleyfrodshamrecordings.aspx>. His account confirms the article in Carrie's periodical by Mary Norton, 'Returning to India', *TF* 37.10 (Oct 1917), pp. 231-32 where Norton shared about her time in the Home of Peace. Carrie's emphasis on 'taking' resonates with her own 1908 experience of Pentecostal baptism and all other spiritual blessings.

[35] Montgomery, 'Evidence of Things Not Seen', p. 50. '[T]hen take God at His Word, and believe that He meets you in the covenant, and that you are

was struggling to believe along these lines, she challenged them to 'ask Him to fill you with faith by the power of the Holy Ghost'.[36] She believed that physical touch could be used as a channel of the Great Physician's healing power. In 1912, she wrote of instances where Jesus laid hands on the sick and they were healed.[37] This method, however, was never a prerequisite to receive healing as many times circumstances prohibited this. People could still receive prayer without the laying on of hands as was demonstrated through her long distance model. Further, if there was no one around to lay hands on the sick, Carrie encouraged her readers to lay hands on themselves in faith and to pray in the name of Jesus.

While Carrie was significantly influenced by Mix's methods of healing and saw many get healed as a result, was that the only way she believed that one could be healed in light of the many different ways in which Jesus healed people in the Bible?[38] Carrie did recognize that there were other ways to receive and administer healing. One example of this is in Carrie's periodical when there is mention of how Dr Yoakum prayed over handkerchiefs before sending them to the sick; many who received these were later healed.[39] At the end of Carrie's Pentecostal Camp meeting in 1914, participants also prayed over and sent out handkerchiefs to sick people and recorded some positive results.[40] Carrie was open to this and various other

---

healed because He says so. You may not feel healed. In fact, you must not look at your feelings (the things seen) to confirm the truth of God's Word … so we must have faith that we are healed because God is true, and not because our feelings say so'.

[36] Montgomery, 'Evidence of Things Not Seen', p. 50.

[37] Carrie Judd Montgomery, 'The Healing, Helping Hands of Jesus', *TF* 32.2 (Feb 1912), pp. 25-30.

[38] Sometimes Jesus spit into the ground and rubbed dirt on people's faces. Sometimes it was when people responded and acted in response to Jesus' declarations that they were healed. Paul at times grabbed people by the hand and raised them up, pronouncing healing. Sometimes healing came in conjunction with the sick person's faith and at others times, it had to do with the faith of the people praying for the sick person.

[39] 'A Wonderful Work of Faith', *TF* 27.1 (Jan 1907), p. 17. This excerpt on the Pigsah home was from a letter of a visitor to the home. 'Taking his authority from Acts xix:12, Dr. Yoakum prays over handkerchiefs and they are sent to the sick. Instances are constantly occurring in which wonderful healings take place, or character and habits are so changed as to transform the vicious and depraved into respectable and even godly people'.

[40] Elizabeth Sisson, 'Incidents from Elim Grove Camp Meeting', *TF* 34.8 (Aug 1914), p. 181.

ways that people could receive and pray for healing even if it was not incorporated into her methods of practice. Even though she was open to other ways of administering healing, her primary methods were heavily informed by the prayer of faith, her belief in healing in the atonement, and the foundations that Mix laid for her.

Because of the emphasis of the 'James 5 prayer', Carrie's healing theology and practice, along with many of the early leaders in the Divine Healing Movement, advocated that everybody could take part in healing the sick. Aimee Semple McPherson, Kathryn Kuhlman, William Branham, Oral Roberts, and others who came later operated more as solo healing evangelists partly because the gift of healing was emphasized more in their day. They transferred faith for healing from the individual receiving it to those who administered healing through the gift of healing. That Carrie and others so heavily relied on healing in the atonement appropriated through the 'James 5 prayer' meant that anybody could pray for healing, not just a charismatic healing evangelist who had the gift of healing. While Carrie many times supported solo healing evangelists of her day, her theology and models of healing were built to be broad and inclusive for as many people as possible to be involved in praying for the sick.[41]

5.4 How Healing Comes

5.4.1 Does Healing Come Instantly or Over Time?
In regards to the question of whether healing came instantly or over time, in 1911 Carrie reflected on her first healing by saying that it 'was instantaneous, but strength came gradually'.[42] In light of her understanding of healing in the atonement, Carrie believed that healing came immediately when one chose to act in faith, even if the effects and evidence of that healing in the body came at a later time. Alexander rightly notes that for some of the people who share Carrie's beliefs, 'gradual healings were likely interpreted as healings

---

[41] Simpson and many others in the Divine Healing Movement also operated in a similar way.

[42] Montgomery, 'Some Secrets of Faith', p. 76.

which had already been obtained, but gradually manifested themselves'.[43]

To demonstrate this further, Carrie said that when Miriam got
leprosy, Moses cried out to the Lord, saying, "'Heal her now, O
God, I beseech thee." This prayer was a heart cry, and it was a cry
not only for healing, but for instantaneous healing; "Heal her
NOW'".[44] Notice how this type of thinking closely resembles
Phoebe Palmer's altar theology.[45] Heather D. Curtis notices this
connection as well when she says,

> Just as Palmer's 'altar terminology' overturned the expectation so
> prevalent among some proponents of revivalism that ecstatic
> emotions always accompanied the experience of sanctification,
> so Judd's explanation of acting faith unsettled the assumption
> that tangible physical sensations necessarily attended to the expe-
> rience of healing.[46]

---

[43] Alexander, *Pentecostal Healing*, p. 214. Alexander argues that many in the Finished Work stream of Pentecostalism which Carrie greatly influenced, commanded the sick to be healed and that 'this approach, which called for an immediate
response, emphasized the instantaneous nature of healing. Though Finished
Work Pentecostals allowed for gradual healings, probably based upon their observations of how these healings did take place, it is clear that their theology
called for an instantaneous work'. Note that her view is greatly biased by her
Wesleyan Holiness Pentecostal background and the reality is that there are varying views within the Finished Work tradition that may or may not agree with her
statement.

[44] Montgomery, "'Touch Not Mine Anointed'", pp. 51-52.

[45] Phoebe Palmer, *The Way of Holiness, with Notes by the Way; being a Narrative
Religious Experience Resulting from a Determination to be a Bible Christian* (New York:
200 Mulberry Street, Printed for the author, 1854), pp. 34, 36.

[46] Heather D. Curtis, *Faith in the Great Physician: Suffering and Divine Healing in
American Culture, 1860-1900* (Lived Religions, ed. David D. Hall and Robert A.
Orsi; Baltimore: The John Hopkins University Press, 2007), pp. 92-93. She writes,
'Both women found a way to uncouple the quest for assurance from sensible
experience by shifting the emphasis onto faith in action'. Curtis additionally con-
nects some of Carrie's theology with that of Palmer when she says (p. 92),

> Employing rhetoric reminiscent of the Holiness Movement, and particularly
> of Phoebe Palmer's 'altar phraseology,' Judd opposed faith (defined in terms
> of profession put into practice) to feelings or emotions as well as to sensory
> manifestations or appearances ... In 'Faith's Reckonings,' Judd echoed Palm-
> er's teachings regarding spiritual blessings, emphasizing the need to act in
> faith rather than the need to feel some specific emotion.

Curtis rightly recognizes that for Carrie, feelings or manifestations of the healing were not necessary to acknowledge that the work of healing was complete.

If one acted in faith *now*, according to how Carrie understood the Bible, that person could immediately be healed even if it took some time for the physical effects to be felt.[47] In her *Prayer of Faith*, she wrote,

> [O]ne great step toward gaining the victory is to believe that we *have* the blessing for which we pray; not that we shall have it at some indefinite, future time, but that it belongs to us just as soon as we have fulfilled the condition, and asked for it in Jesus' name, Christ said: 'What things soever ye desire when ye pray, *believe that ye shall receive them*, and ye shall have them.' – St. Mark xi:24.[48]

Carrie further illustrated this concept with a story of a woman who had used crutches for many years because her foot was severely disabled. One morning this woman was stirred to pray for healing. She had the impression that if she was to believe that God had already answered her prayer, she needed to stand firm on His promises and walk. As she was 'resting' on her faith in God's promises alone, she experienced a 'crushing pain' as she began the journey to church without her crutches. She endured intense pain in her foot as she attempted to continue to walk and by the time she arrived, her foot was completely healed.[49]

Another example Carrie used to illustrate this is in Mk 11.20-21 when Jesus rebuked the fig tree but the disciples did not see any immediate result. It was not until several days later that the disciples saw the outcome of Jesus' spoken words evidenced by the withered fig tree. Carrie compared this to standing on the finished work of Christ and believed that what he promised was already complete even if the visible results were not yet evident.[50] Regardless of feelings, Carrie believed it was important to 'stand on' God's word and

---

[47] Carrie Judd Montgomery, 'The "Now" of God', *TF* 24.2 (Feb 1904), pp. 25-26.

[48] Judd, *The Prayer of Faith*, pp. 96, 155. When referring to God's promises, she wrote to 'bear in mind that they are all *conditional*. It is always "according to thy *faith* be it unto thee".'

[49] Judd, *The Prayer of Faith*, p. 100.

[50] Montgomery, 'Continue in My Word', p. 74.

then 'evidence' for healing would eventually follow. She said that 'we stand upon this truth, not because we feel it, but because the Lord has said it, the Holy Spirit will witness to the truth, and we shall have the evidence in our body'.[51] Whether or not results were immediately felt, just as the root of the fig tree was dead the moment Jesus cursed it, so for Carrie, because of the finished work, the root of sickness was destroyed the moment one prayed the prayer of faith. For Carrie, healing came instantly, even if manifestations might come gradually.

5.4.2 What About When Symptoms Persist?

As early as 1880, Carrie admitted that sometimes suffering can even get worse immediately following one's healing as the body might remain sore from the sickness leaving. She said that sometimes 'increased pain and weakness are ours after prayer has been offered, feeling sure that it is the departing struggle of the disease which Jesus has rebuked'.[52] Carrie's teachings suggest that if symptoms of sickness persist after acting in faith, one should simply deny or rebuke them and continue to 'stand on His word' in faith. In 1904, she wrote about a friend who had an attack of 'sciatica' that caused her limb just below her knee to become crippled. In relation to praying for this woman, Carrie said, 'Fulfilling all the conditions as far as I knew, I took my stand upon the promises and believed for the great Healer's touch of power to come to the very root of the trouble'.[53] Carrie went on to share her story of 'Jesus the Healer':

> I explained my position of faith and confessed the Lord's healing. I remember well the look of astonishment and incredulity which passed over her face, as she pointed to the crippled limb, upon which she could see the foot hanging so helplessly, and exclaimed almost fiercely, 'What's that, then?' … I replied with calm assurance, 'That is the devil's lie.' I knew God could not lie, and I knew I was standing with Him on His word, so that must be the lie of the enemy which had not yet manifestly fallen before His truth. God would deal with the lie, as I should continue to stand with Him by faith, and to abide in his word … Did He fail His trusting child? No, verily. Soon after this I heard His

---

[51] Montgomery, 'Healing in the Atonement', pp. 121-22.
[52] Judd, *The Prayer of Faith*, pp. 102-103.
[53] Montgomery, 'Continue in My Word', p. 74.

sweet and all-powerful whisper in my soul, 'Arise and walk,' and she went on to walk triumphantly on her crippled foot that became healed.[54]

For Carrie, any symptoms of continued illness were merely the 'devil's lie'. Just because sickness was a fact did not mean that it was the truth. Carrie said that 'surely, it is God's truth which sets us free, and as we continue in that word which He declares His truth, all lies of the enemy will fade and the glorious truth of His finished redemption for soul and body shall be manifested in us'.[55] In 1918 and in relation to Rom. 8.11, Carrie wrote about the necessity to claim the promise of healing and to realize that one must fight, as the 'enemy' too was going to battle all along the way. She wrote that 'it is a question of believing God's word, or the Devil's symptoms'.[56]

Carrie used the healing of the ten lepers to demonstrate this principle further. Jesus asked them to show themselves to the priest before they were healed. Carrie described that their cleansing took place as they were on their way in faith to the priest. They had to act in obedience and it was in the midst of that action that healing resulted.[57] Utilizing the 'James 5 prayer' to establish the work of healing in the atonement, she urged her readers to receive healing and to recognize that 'You may not immediately see all the symptoms removed, but you can reckon the work accomplished according to His word, and it shall be done unto you according to your faith'.[58] When contradictions or confusion came for people in rela-

---

[54] Montgomery, 'Continue in My Word', p. 74. See also years later in her 'Overcoming', *TF* 38.1 (Jan 1918), p. 3.

[55] Montgomery, 'Continue in My Word', p. 75.

[56] Carrie Judd Montgomery, 'Overcoming', *TF* 38.1 (Jan 1918), p. 3. People were to 'reckon' themselves dead to sin and to the 'Devil's symptoms' of sickness and stand in faith upon God's promises regardless of how they felt. She saw it important to release people from sickness who were 'bound by the Devil'.

[57] Judd, *The Prayer of Faith*, p. 101.

[58] Montgomery, 'Healing in the Atonement', p. 123. She started this out with,

Dear suffering ones, ask God to reveal to you that Christ has really borne away your sickness and pain. Wait upon Him until this point is clear, and then the rest will be easy. Then you can call for the elders of the church, as commanded in James v:14, 15, and be anointed with oil in the name of the Lord, and the groundwork of your faith will become so solid you will only have to fulfill your part and know that the work is done.

tion to this issue, Carrie encouraged her readers to take a stand and believe wholeheartedly on his word. She said,

> You are on a different plane and as you trust God's word He will deal with these obstacles, and make all fall in line with His truth. The question for you to settle is this: 'Is God true, or are these circumstances true which seem to make Him untrue? Since He is true, He has done what He said He would, and all things will be subdued unto Him as I continue trusting'.[59]

The obstacles and circumstances she was referring to were the symptoms of illness still present in people's lives even after they prayed the prayer of faith. If healing truly was already accomplished in the atonement, then by the means of activated faith, it was obtained instantly regardless of how long it took for the symptoms to disappear.[60] For those with whom this was problematic because they prayed the prayer of faith but their symptoms of sickness continued to persist, Carrie encouraged these to deny or rebuke their symptoms and to strengthen their faith by 'standing on' the promises found in the Bible. This was Carrie's antidote to deal with suffering. There is a fine line here, however, because at the same time, Carrie did not encourage a denial of reality, but of a paradigm of what she understood was truth. She said, 'We are not of course, to say we *feel* better, unless we do, but we may state the fact that we *are* being made whole, on the authority of God's word'.[61]

---

[59] Montgomery, 'Continue in My Word', p. 74, in reference to Jn 8.31-32. Carrie also printed an earlier article about this same thing by A.B Simpson, entitled, 'The Withering of the Fig Tree', *TF* 23.9 (Sept 1903), pp. 208-209. A.B. Simpson also taught along a similar line much of the time, as seen in his 'How to Receive Divine Healing', *TF* 8.2 (Feb 1888), pp. 36-39, where he wrote that there should be no questioning, no 'if's' or 'perhaps' but instead full reliance on the already written word of God and what it says about Christ's death and resurrection. In reference to divine healing, he encouraged people to stand on God's truth claim their healing, to 'put a stake down, and mark it forever; and date from this afternoon till the great day of His coming, as an epoch in your life when something was settled, and passed out of your hands forever'. He later exhorted people not to depend on the anointing, the touch, the feeling, or the thrill, but rather to simply 'reckon' that the work was finished.

[60] Alexander, *Pentecostal Healing*, p. 214.

[61] Judd, *The Prayer of Faith*, pp. 97-98.

5.4.3 What About Partial Healing?

While Carrie believed that the moment one claimed the promises of God their healing was accomplished, she also realized that the effects of this might show up differently for different individuals. She encouraged her readers along this line when she wrote that 'He is content to await the "fullness of the time" for you'.[62] So while Carrie believed that healing was accomplished *now* through the atonement of Christ, she also realized that the effects of that fulfilled promise might come at different times and in different measures; this however did not deter from the fact that she believed that healing was already accomplished.[63]

While Carrie did mention that sometimes healing came in different degrees, she also believed that when one did not receive the full effects of healing from the start, it was because of that person's lack of faith. This is demonstrated in a 1906 article where she wrote about the story of how Daniel was touched three times by the Lord before being fully healed and strengthened. The first few times he was touched, he was only partially healed. Carrie expounded on this by writing,

> To those who, in the past, have only had the first touch, or even the second touch also, and who have experienced only a partial deliverance in their spiritual life, or have been partially healed in the physical life, this message may come, perhaps, with fresh encouragement to trust for all God has for them.[64]

It was not until the third touch by God that Daniel was healed. Carrie saw that it was Daniel's fault that he was not healed the first time when she said that 'there was nothing lacking in [God's] first touch. The lack is in us. We only partially believe, and therefore only receive in a limited way'.[65] This example demonstrates that at the time, Carrie believed that complete healing had to do with individuals acting in faith. It also shows that if someone was only partially

---

[62] Judd, 'Trial of Faith', p. 36. This she said in reference to the healing of a woman who was blind and experienced some healing but then the blindness came back again before it was fully healed.

[63] Montgomery, 'Continue in My Word', p. 74. How she interpreted the fig tree demonstrates this.

[64] Carrie Judd Montgomery, 'The Touch of His Healing Hand', *TF* 26.1 (Jan 1906), p. 2.

[65] Montgomery, 'The Touch of His Healing Hand', p. 3.

healed, she believed that it was because of their lack of faith that they were not fully healed.

Further, in 1907, Carrie wrote of the story found in Mark 8 of the blind man. Jesus spat and touched the man, and at first he could see what looked like trees walking. Carrie commented, 'How sweet the compassion of the Lord Jesus as He gives him that touch and that partial evidence of sight, to encourage him to trust for the fullness of the blessing'. After that, Jesus touched him again and he could fully see. Carrie went on to relate this to healing in the atonement when she said that 'He is waiting to lay His hands again upon you and to cause all spiritual blindness to disappear until you shall see as never before that He Himself has taken your infirmities and borne your sicknesses, and that therefore, by His stripes you are healed'.[66] Carrie encouraged people to press on to the 'fullness of the blessing'. She saw that partial healing came as a result of a person only having partial faith; one needed to have 'full' faith to appropriate total healing.[67] Carrie regularly encouraged people to take hold of 'all' that God had for them and not to be content with anything less. If they had not experienced the fullness of the healing manifestations in their bodies, they could stop and be content with partial healing, but for Carrie, they would be missing out on so much more that was freely available. In the situation with her mother, Carrie called upon others saying, 'Will our dear friends continue to pray for increased strength, a natural appetite; in fact, for complete healing?'[68] While Carrie saw that one was already completely healed in the atonement, she also recognized that sometimes that person needed strength and support to stand in faith to receive the fullness of their healing.

5.4.4 When Should Someone Stop Praying?
Since Carrie believed that at the time one acted in faith they were healed whether they felt the effects or not, she regularly taught that there was no need to continue praying specifically for healing after

---

[66] Carrie Judd Montgomery, 'Grace Yet Again', *TF* 27.8 (Aug 1907), pp. 171-72.

[67] Carrie Judd Montgomery, 'A Forward Movement', *TF* 40.3 (March 1920), p. 60.

[68] Carrie Judd Montgomery, 'A Note of Praise', *TF* 30.3 (March 1910), p. 72.

that, but rather for strength to stand in faith.[69] In reference to the story in John 4 of the nobleman who came to Jesus to ask for his son to be healed, Jesus said the word and the man believed and went his way. This nobleman had no other proof that his child was living except the *word* of Jesus. Because of this, Carrie saw no reason for the nobleman to continue to entreat Jesus. She wrote,

> Here is a case which proves to us that it is right and consistent to cease praying for a certain blessing, when the Lord's own word assures us it is ours for the asking. Had the father continued his entreaty, it would have shown lack of faith. 'But the man believed the word that Jesus had spoken unto him,' and therefore showed his faith by the only act which was consistent with his belief, and 'went his way'.[70]

Further, in relation to divine healing and referencing Heb. 11.1, Carrie said in 1907 that 'if we have real, living faith we have the conviction in our own heart that our prayer is answered, that the work is done, that we need not therefore pray again for the answer, because it is already ours'.[71]

In May of 1908, Carrie continued along similar lines emphasizing that the prayer of faith needs to be prayed only once:

> Will you believe it, not watch to see or feel, but because God is true? Believe that recovery, deep and real, comes immediately into the very root of the trouble, causing the very taproot of the disease to wither. No, you must not look at your pain to see if it is less. If you do, you are not really believing. If you truly believe God's word, you will have witness in your own heart, and you will know the work is done **because He says so** ... You will not want to pray that prayer again, because you will know it is answered. Remember that when Jesus cursed the barren fig tree, the disciple afterward beheld it 'withered from the root.' Have

---

[69] The previous example of her mother indicates some inconsistencies here. This may be because she recognized her mother had already been healed but had not fully received the complete manifestation of that healing yet.

[70] Carrie F. Judd, 'Except Ye See', *TF* 6.4 (April 1886), p. 36.

[71] Montgomery, 'Evidence of Things Not Seen', p. 49. Carrie believed similarly in relation to finances. In her autobiography and in relation to Mk 11.24, she believed that when she prayed, she received from him her request, 'not asking again, as I felt that to pray further for that particular thing would be unbelief' (*Under His Wings*, p. 86).

we not in our unbelief looked for our trouble to be withered from the top, and because leaves and twigs were as green as ever, we did not believe in the power of Christ to deliver? O, beloved, do not deceive yourselves into thinking that you have faith, if you are depending upon any sign or symptom instead of upon Christ's sure word.[72]

After the prayer of faith had been prayed, one only needed to trust and rely on God's word to know that what they prayed for had already been answered. If symptoms or 'lies of the devil' still persisted, it was important to persist in prayer and overcome these battles; this, however, did not take away from the fact that she believed healing had already been accomplished.

Overall, Carrie saw that praying the prayer of faith once for healing would suffice if it was followed by actively receiving, appropriating, and taking hold of that healing already promised through the Bible. If sickness was simply a battle against Satan, once that battle was won through the atonement, the destruction of the sickness was already complete.[73] When symptoms, or the 'devil's lies,' did continue to persist, Carrie resolved to deny or rebuke them and to 'stand' on God's promises. This was something different than continuing to pray for healing as that would imply a lack of faith or disbelief that he had already accomplished what he promised.[74]

5.5 Losing one's Healing

Carrie's perspective of 'standing' on God's word to believe that healing was accomplished is evident throughout her writings. But could people lose their healing after having received it? Carrie remembered receiving an early exhortation from Mrs Mix's husband along these lines,[75] and in 1903, Carrie claimed that people could

---

[72] Carrie Judd Montgomery, 'The Power of His Name', *TF* 28.5 (May 1908), pp. 98-99. (Emphasis in original)

[73] Carrie Judd Montgomery, 'Not Fainting', *TF* 23.5 (May 1903), p. 97. There was one noticeable time where Carrie believed it was important to continue praying until deliverance was experienced. The following example however, was not in relation to sickness but rather in reference to the persistent widow in Luke 18 who wanted justice from her adversary. She wrote, 'Instead of fainting we are to pray, and to *keep on praying* until deliverance comes'.

[74] Judd, 'Asking Amiss', p. 153-55.

[75] In her autobiography, Carrie referred to a letter she received from Mr Mix where 'he warned me that if I did not give myself up to the Lord to be used in

lose their healing if they 'believe the testimony' of their feelings rather than chose to trust in the promises in the Bible.[76] Carrie encouraged her readers:

> Believe that He then and there does His part; that the prayer of faith does then and there save the sick; that you are saved from your sickness at that moment of meeting God in His covenant … You cannot see the change He has already worked in the physical organism, but we can see His promise. Keep standing right there. He has healed you. Trust Him to keep you from wavering, and you will have great 'recompense of reward.'[77]

---

this ministry of healing I would be apt to lose my own health' (*Under His Wings*, pp. 81, 117). Many others during Carrie's time also believed this. See F.F. Bosworth, *Christ the Healer* (Grand Rapids, MI: Chosen Books, 1924), reprint 2008, p. 131, where he writes, 'Many lose the manifestation of healing already in operation, by turning their attention from Christ and the Word of God to their feelings'. John G. Lake also believed this ('Sin in the Flesh', in Roberts Liardon, *John G. Lake on Healing* [New Kensington, PA: Whitaker House, 2009], p. 102). E.W. Kenyon says that if one does not confess their healing, then they 'will lose the blessing that belongs to' them (See his and Don Gossett's *Words that Move Mountains*: Revised and Expanded version of *The Power of Spoken Faith* [New Kensington, PA: Whitaker House, 2003], p. 63). Others in the current Faith Movement also discuss this. People like Benny Hinn, Gordan Lindsay, and Kenneth Copeland include John G. Lake's teachings in their works as well.

[76] Montgomery, 'Cast Not Away Your Confidence', p. 25, writes,

We have seen people commit their bodies to the Lord, calling for the elders to anoint them (James v:13, 14) or receiving the laying on of hands in Jesus' Name (Mark xvi:17,18); we have known them to accept Christ's promise, and to receive by faith the blessing held out to them; we have seen them stand in this attitude of faith for a short time, and then we have known them to cast away their confidence, as though Christ's promises were worthless, and as though they had proved that it did not pay to trust Him … You began to look at your feelings to see if they would support God's Word, and, when they did not, you would rather believe the testimony of your feelings than the testimony of God's Word. If you had continued to believe God's Word even when your feelings did not confirm it, He would have made all within you to conform to His truth sooner or later.

[77] Montgomery, 'Cast Not Away Your Confidence', p. 26, adds,

You must get God's facts and stand upon them. He tells us that Jesus 'Himself took our infirmities and bare our sicknesses' (Matt. viii:17). How many times in my own experience this fact has made healing very easy to accept. If He had borne this sickness, then it was no longer mine to bear, and I would reject it in His Name and through the blood of His cross. Standing on this truth of God, the Holy Spirit would witness it in my body, and pain and weakness would disappear. The 'shalls' of God in James v:14, 15 and Mark xvi:17,18, are sufficient for the whole universe to stand on. We do our part in

This implies that if one chose to stop 'standing there' in that place of faith, then they might lose their healing.

Was being healed solely for the purpose of service a good enough reason to be healed in light of Carrie's beliefs? What about being healed simply to be made whole? And if people were healed but then chose not to serve God or even thank Him for their healing, would their sickness return? According to Carrie, if people did not respond to healing with service, they ran the risk of losing their healing. In reference to Mk 1.30 where Jesus healed Peter's mother-in-law and she immediately served Him, Carrie wrote,

> Here we see that Jesus raised her up for ministry … We may not all be called to preach, but if we are healed by Him, He will surely show us some place of lowly service; and if we do not go on ministering, we shall be very apt to get sick again. Our Master 'went about doing good and healing all that were oppressed of the devil,' and we are to walk in His footsteps.[78]

Carrie made it clear that if one decided not to serve God after being healed, then the sickness was likely to return. But what would happen if someone did get healed and served God but then their sickness returned to them? Would they be riddled with guilt because they believed that the sickness returned from some fault of their own? Carrie's healing theology presents these and other possible dilemmas.

Carrie also believed that 'one reason why God's children do not get their full inheritance from the Lord, is because they do not seek to help other Christians into their inheritance'.[79] She saw that it was the healed person's responsibility to help others receive their inher-

---

calling the elders, in being anointed, in receiving the laying on of hands, then God's Word is pledged.

[78] Carrie Judd Montgomery, 'Why We May Be Healed', *TF* 25.7 (July 1905), p. 146.

[79] Carrie Judd Montgomery, 'The Lord's Hand is Not Shortened', *TF* 39.7 (July 1919), pp. 147-48. She said, 'If you will promise God to be perfectly obedient to Him, and to use your health and strength for Him, He will show you how to receive the healing brought to you by the prayer of faith'. After telling the story of the Israelites she continued, 'After we get our spiritual possessions, if we do not go over Jordan and help our brethren to get theirs, God says to us, "Be sure your sin will find you out"'. Further, 'Beloved, when you are healed by the Lord, or receive great spiritual blessing from Him be sure to help others into their inheritance, or else, "Your sin will find you out"'.

itance or else it was a sin. There were times people would come to Carrie's meetings, get healed there, and then disappear for awhile before coming back with another or the same illness re-emerging. In Carrie's view, one of the possible reasons for this was because they did not tell others what the Lord had done for them.[80] Carrie also believed that people could lose their healing because of their limited faith, or lack of endurance in faith. In relation to Heb. 11.1, she wrote that 'a great many people lose the blessing of healing, or rather fail to take it because they are not definite in their faith'.[81] She also spoke about waging war against the 'Devil's rage' to hang on tight to one's healing.[82] According to Carrie, lack of endurance in faith, not being thankful or confessing what God had done, not standing upon God's word but rather looking at physical feelings, or simply losing the battle against the devil, were some of the possible reasons people might lose their healing.[83]

5.5.1 Carrie's Interpretation of her Second Major Illness

The fact that Carrie believed people could lose their healing puts her second major illness into a new perspective, one that might suggest that she lacked faith. In 1897, Carrie became severely ill again for nearly six months. It is interesting to notice that she displayed many of the same symptoms she had twenty years earlier in her initial intense sickness. She even referred to her later sickness as 'hy-

---

[80] Montgomery, 'The Lord's Hand is Not Shortened', p. 148 in reference to Exod. 15.26.

[81] Montgomery, 'Evidence of Things Not Seen', p. 49.

[82] Judd, 'Trial of Faith', pp. 37-38. She told the following story:

A dear sister, well known to me through a mutual friend, was healed of nearly total blindness, of many years' duration, in answer to the prayer of Dr. Chas. Cullis, of Boston. For a short time she rejoiced in the possession of sight, sounding God's praises on the right hand and left, proclaiming Him her all-sufficient Healer and Saviour. Then, to her amazement and consternation, she again became blind. Concealing as much as possible from the outside world this new manifestation of the Devil's rage, she continued as before to claim her healing as accomplished, and for three long and weary months held on in the darkness. And then came the victory, and such a victory as only our God can give! For years since then she has enjoyed perfect sight, and has used her eyes, as well as the rest of her consecrated powers, to the glory of God.

[83] Montgomery, 'The Power of His Name', p. 100. She also said to 'resist in Jesus' Name any pain which may still be present. It does not belong to you because you are healed'.

peraesthesia'.[84] In light of her belief that one could lose their healing, did she believe that she had lost her healing somehow? Did this
second severe illness have any connection with her initial sickness
when she was 18 years old? Had she fought to lay hold of her healing for nearly twenty years and then all of a sudden could not quite
hang on? While Carrie never publicly connected these two accounts
together, I notice a possible connection.

During her illness, Carrie's husband fought hard in prayer for
her. She recalled that 'Again and again, when I seemed almost at the
point of death, he would lay his hands on me in Jesus' Name, resisting the enemy with steadfast faith, and relief would soon follow'.[85]
There is the possibility to see this as a contradiction to Carrie's theology of praying once for healing and believing it has been accomplished. However, George's prayers here were of resisting the enemy and his symptoms and lies, not praying the prayer of faith for
healing; this stands in accordance with her theology.[86] Several
branches of the Christian Alliance and the Salvation Army in the
area also had days of fasting and prayer for Carrie's healing. It was
around 2.00-4.00 am one morning that Carrie claimed to feel 'a
mighty but very gentle power' go through her body. During the
same time that people were fasting and praying, she claimed 'the
work of healing was accomplished'.[87] While she went to bed that
evening very ill, once she had the assurance and heard the Spirit's
voice, she got up and was healed.[88] The way in which she was

---

[84] Montgomery, 'A Miracle of Healing', pp. 142-46. Read full account in
Chapter 3.

[85] Montgomery, 'A Miracle of Healing', p. 145. 'And then, hardest of all, was
the fact that I could enjoy but little of my dear husband's society, for even the
vibrations of his tender voice jarred my suffering nerves, so that the most he
could do to comfort and help me was to retire to his own room and pour his soul
out in prayer for me'.

[86] See also how Carrie attempted to prevail in prayer in a similar way when
George was sick and near death ('"As Dying, and Behold We Live"', *TF* 34.5
[May 1914], pp. 97-100).

[87] Montgomery, 'A Miracle of Healing', p. 146. 'At the same time there came a
mighty conviction of the Holy Ghost like a deep, tender voice, pervading all my
spirit, that the work of healing was accomplished. In one sense I had trusted God
for healing from the first but I had not before received the assurance of the Spirit
that the work was done'. She was talking about how assurance came along with
the manifestation when the healing was complete.

[88] She mentioned that after the 'Lord laid His hand in healing upon' her, that
she was so blessed that 'she could not even tell her [friend who was in the same

healed very shortly after these surges of prayer and fasting on her behalf strengthen her belief that the sickness indeed *was* tied to a direct spiritual attack.

But how did Carrie interpret this account for her own life? Had she let go of her first healing? In 1880, Carrie said that 'faith is laying hold of a blessing [while] doubt is just the opposite – *letting go* of it ... Having once laid hold of a promise, by faith, we must *keep hold* of it'.[89] If the two sicknesses were connected in any way, according to her theology, it appears that she lost faith to stand in her initial healing. However, Carrie did not believe this second sickness was connected to her first major illness but rather interpreted it purely as a spiritual battle of 'resisting the enemy' to take hold of the ground that God had already given her through the atonement.[90] She did not think that she had 'lost' her initial healing because she lacked faith, but instead saw that a new sickness came upon her as a result of a battle with the 'enemy'. This presents another possibility of how someone might lose their healing.

In part from her theology, but more from observations, it is possible that her healing ran out and needed to be renewed.[91] In other words, maybe her healing was for a specific amount of time and once that time ran out, a new battle needed to be fought to reclaim it.[92] Another possibility is that the 'enemy' stole her previous healing and she had to fight to regain it. Regardless, the facts demonstrate that Carrie was healed a second time of sickness that greatly resem-

---

room] about it for about two hours because [she] was lost in the presence of [her] lovely Jesus' (*Under His Wings,* p. 160).

[89] Judd, *The Prayer of Faith*, p. 48.

[90] Montgomery, 'A Miracle of Healing', p. 145.

[91] Montgomery, 'Evidence of Things Not Seen', p. 50. Carrie did mention that healing could be for a time period. Not referring to her own experience here, she said, 'When we covenant to trust God it must not be with the thought of experiment for a limited time'.

[92] Carrie's second healing experience of a similar sickness brings up some significant questions for today. Is healing only for a time period? Is healing like the Promised Land in the way that one must take hold of it, where things might be going really well there but then every so often an enemy comes in to try and fight for the land and take it captive. See Carrie Judd Montgomery, 'The Lord's Hand is Not Shortened', *TF* 39.7 (July 1919), pp. 145-48. Does one need to be prepared to guard the 'land' that God has already given? What about cancer? Are some people healed from cancer for a time period and then whenever that measure of healing for a certain time period is over, they relapse and must re-claim and renew their initial healing once again?

bled her first major illness. Whether Carrie realized it or not at the time, there may have been some connection between her first major illness and her second one twenty years later that had nearly all of the same symptoms. While Carrie did believe people could lose their healing, she did not relate this to her own situation.

5.6 Locating Carrie within Contemporary Studies of Healing

5.6.1 Ronald Kydd: Models of Healing

Now that Carrie's theology and practice of healing have been laid out, it will be interesting to place her within present day conversations. Ronald Kydd's *Healing through the Centuries: Models for Understanding* will be the first classification to be explored. He looks at several different people involved in healing ministry and classifies them within one of his six models.[93] He places Johann Cristoph Blumhardt and John Wimber in a Confrontational model where the main battle is a power encounter and where Jesus is emphasized as the Victorious One. He additionally presents the Incubational model, where healing occurs over time, the Revelational model where Kathryn Kuhlman and William Branham are classified, and the Soteriological model where Oral Roberts and Smith Wigglesworth are emphasized. Because of the way he defines the Intercessory and Reliquarial models as praying to saints or using their relics, these are left out of the discussion since they are not applicable to Carrie.

Confrontational Model

Beginning with the Confrontational model, Kydd suggests Blumhardt and Wimber fit here. There was a mark of Triumphalism in Blumhardt's ministry where 'the belief that Jesus had overcome evil became the dominant fact of his ministry'.[94] According to Kydd, Blumhardt 'did not look for instantaneous healing, and he referred people to doctors without hesitation'.[95] He also believed that if one was healed, it was from God, but if one was not, God would give

---

[93] Kydd, *Healing through the Centuries*. Kydd, formerly a Pentecostal minister, is now an Anglican priest <www.tyndale.ca/person/ronald-kydd>.

[94] Kydd, *Healing through the Centuries*, p. 45.

[95] Kydd, *Healing through the Centuries*, pp. 43-44. It must be noted that even though he did not look for instantaneous healing, it would often happen in services while he was speaking.

that person the strength to bear the illness. In this way, he allowed room to deal with suffering in his model. While Carrie also saw Jesus as victorious over Satan, she interpreted this differently and saw that healing was instantaneous, even if the manifestations came at a later time. Contrary to his views, she also understood that healing was always available in the atonement and that God alone should be the great Physician.

Under the same Confrontational model, Kydd introduces John Wimber. In relation to healing in the atonement, he claims that Wimber saw that healing occurs *through* the atonement.[96] He points out that Wimber brought a greater 'democratization' of healing to the common people since he taught healing in such a way to equip lay people to 'do the stuff' and participate in praying for healing rather than restricting that to a leader.[97] Kydd is in agreement with Margaret Poloma's recognition of Wimber and notices that previous healing ministries were tied to the 'healing evangelist' until Wimber revolutionized and trained the common person to pray for healing.[98] Wimber expected healing and deliverance to come instantly and also modified the doctrine of healing in the atonement to allow room to deal with suffering more extensively.[99]

Rather than adopt the extreme version of healing in the atonement like Carrie, Wimber did not claim that 'Jesus always heals' but allowed room to deal with the realities of suffering when people did not experience the full manifestations of healing. Because of this, some might claim, as they also did with Cullis, that Wimber did not truly believe in healing in the atonement. While this is still debatable, Wimber was influenced by and did apply the doctrine in a modified form in his ministry, where many healings have also been rec-

---

[96] Kydd, *Healing through the Centuries*, p. 52.

[97] Kydd, *Healing through the Centuries,* pp. 55-56, referring to White's *When the Spirit Comes*, notices that 'John White, not surprisingly, sees John Wimber and the Vineyard as a challenge to Evangelical Christianity to live by the Spirit rather than by programs'.

[98] Margaret Poloma also claims that 'perhaps no single individual did more to promote this democratized belief [of healing] during the last decades of the twentieth century than John Wimber, the founder of the Association of Vineyard Churches' ('Old Wine, New Wineskins', p. 62). See also Ronald A.N. Kydd, 'Healing in the Christian Church', in *NIDPCM*, pp. 698-711, 702.

[99] John Wimber, *Kingdom Suffering: Facing Difficulty and Trial in the Christian Life.* (Christian Essential Series; Ann Arbor, MI: Vine Books, imprint of Servant Publications, 1988), pp. 27-28, and Kydd, *Healing through the Centuries,* p. 141.

orded. While Wimber was more open to deal the realities of suffering than Carrie, similar strands ran through both of their ministries in the way that they both taught and empowered the average person to pray for the sick.[100] While Carrie many times supported solo healing evangelists of her day, her theology and models of healing were built to be as broad and inclusive for as many people as possible to participate. Carrie differs from both Wimber and Blumhardt because she taught to deny the 'lies' of sickness and instead to lean upon God's truth, while they both admitted that when one did not experience the manifestations of healing, sometimes there was no way to explain this.[101]

Incubational Model

For the Incubational model, Kydd suggests Dorothy Trudel's faith homes, where there was no time pressures in relation to healing. Contrary to the previous model, people could be taught in a safe environment where many received healing over the course of time rather than being healed instantly.[102] Carrie's healing homes were very similar to Dorothy Trudel's homes in that there was teaching and prayer where people were not rushed for an immediate result. This allowed Carrie to teach others how to pray the prayer of faith and receive healing rather than just pray for them and send them on their way. In this, however, Carrie still believed that healing came instantly even if the manifestations came at a later time.

---

[100] Wimber, *Kingdom Suffering*, pp. 27-28. A.B. Simpson and many others in the Divine Healing Movement also did the same thing. Additionally, Wimber influenced Bill Johnson in various ways as well.

[101] Wimber expected healing and deliverance to come instantly. He also modified the doctrine of healing in the atonement to allow room to deal with suffering more extensively. In response to questions about why a righteous person who is sick might get prayed for and not be healed, Wimber, *Kingdom Suffering*, pp. 27-28, wrote the following:

> The fact that we are living between the first and second comings of Christ, what George Ladd calls living between the 'already and the not yet', provides the interpretive key for understanding why the physical healing that Christ secured for us at the cross is not always experienced today. His sovereignty, lordship, and kingdom are what bring healing. Our part is to pray 'Thy kingdom come' and trust him for whatever healing comes from his gracious hand. And if in this age it does not come, then we still have assurance that it will come in the age to come. We have no right to presume that unless God heals in every instance there is something wrong with our faith or his faithfulness.

[102] Kydd, *Healing through the Centuries*, p. 153.

Revelational model

For the Revelational model, Kydd suggests Kathryn Kuhlman fits here. She did not do anything until she received revelation from God and the anointing fell. Rather than depend upon Biblical truth, Kuhlman instead depended upon revelatory truth in that moment from God. Kydd mentions that Kuhlman had a foundation of theology based on healing in the atonement which was likely influenced from her time spent at a Christian and Missionary Alliance Bible school stemming from A.B. Simpson's ministry. While faith was an important ingredient, because of the fact that not everyone got healed and also that she noticed more and more within her Bible reading that healing came as one was led by the Holy Spirit, she began to adapt her thinking. When someone was healed of a tumor as she was preaching in April of 1947, it brought a shift in her ministry and made her decide to rely exclusively upon the Holy Spirit to lead her in relation to healing.[103]

Contrary to Kuhlman's approach in the Revelational model, Carrie approached healing by appropriating the already finished work of Christ through praying the prayer of faith. In relation to faith, while Kuhlman saw that it was important for healing, she also saw that it was 'a gift of God'.[104] Carrie connected faith more with the will to act on Biblical truths to appropriate what was already freely available; even in this though, she also claimed to be led by the Spirit. Kuhlman, however, believed that 'faith is not a condition of the mind. It is a divinely imparted grace to the heart'. Kuhlman also wrote that 'we have made faith a product of a finite mind when all of the other gifts of the Spirit we have attributed to God. To many people, faith still is their own ability to believe a truth, and is often based on their struggles and their ability to drive away doubt and unbelief through a process of continued affirmations'.[105] Kydd rightly believes that Kuhlman stood in contrast to others from the Divine Healing Movement. He says that they

> taught a different understanding of faith and saw it as the responsibility of those who wished to be healed. For them, the sick

---

[103] Kydd, *Healing through the Centuries*, pp. 190-95.

[104] Kathryn Kuhlman, *I Believe in Miracles* (Englewood Cliffs, NJ: Prentice-Hall, 1962), p. 199, in Kydd, *Healing through the Centuries,* p. 191.

[105] Kathryn Kuhlman, *God Can Do it Again* (Englewood Cliffs, NJ: Prentice-Hall, 1969), 252, in Kydd, *Healing through the Centuries,* p. 191.

had to discipline their minds and spirits to force out any doubt about God's willingness to heal. The sick had to cling to the 'promises of God,' which were understood as God's commitment to heal those who came to him with perfect faith, regardless of pain or other symptoms.[106]

Kuhlman stood against some aspects of the theology of the Divine Healing Movement which also some times got confused with positive thinking.

When asked why all are not healed, Kuhlman responded,

[T]he only honest answer I can give is: I do not know. And I am afraid of those who claim they do know. For only God knows, and who can fathom the mind of God? Who can understand His reasoning? I think there are some simple matters we can look into, but the ultimate answer as to who is healed and who is not healed lies with God alone.[107]

Kuhlman did not deny suffering but also did not provide a solution. Carrie's approach to healing differed from that of Kuhlman's. Carrie's model was based more on appropriating the Biblical promises of God coupled with being led by the Spirit, with greater emphasis on the former.[108] Kuhlman's model was based more exclusively on the revelatory leadings of the Spirit. Carrie was led by the Spirit in a more disciplined fashion to act on God's truth, while Kuhlman was led most often by intuitions in hearing the Spirit in that moment. Kuhlman made space to discuss the uncertainties around when someone did not get healed while Carrie's spiritual warfare perspective saw that one should always be victorious because of what Christ had done on the cross.

---

[106] Kydd, *Healing through the Centuries,* p. 196. Kydd also mentions that Charles S. Price was a great influence for Kuhlman in relation to this thinking.

[107] Kuhlman, *God Can Do it Again*, p. 250 in Kydd, *Healing through the Centuries,* p. 191.

[108] Carrie F. Judd, 'The Ministry of Faith', pp. 275-76. In the example here, Carrie was not only being led by the Word, but there was an interplay between the foundation of the Word and the Spirit's leading. See also Carrie's 'Led by the Spirit' poem and many instances of being led by the Spirit throughout her *Under His Wings*.

Soteriological Model

For the Soteriological model, Kydd suggests that 'people can be miraculously cured through the same means by which they become Christians, through the atoning work of Christ'.[109] Healing in the atonement is a known slogan for people classified in this model where Kydd identifies Oral Roberts as a strong advocate.[110] He says that Roberts believed that 'healing is in the atonement therefore it includes all'. Roberts said that 'Each one of us has a perfect right to God and just as He will forgive all our sins, He will heal our diseases'. He further encouraged people to 'know that God's will is to heal you'. This would be done 'by faith alone'. He convinced people that 'God wants to heal you now'.[111] If Carrie's name was substituted as the author of the above quotes instead of Roberts, one would likely not notice any difference.

Kydd also places Smith Wigglesworth in this model since he also held to healing in the atonement. In 1924, Wigglesworth wrote,

> There is healing through the blood of Christ and deliverance for every captive. God never intended His children to live in misery because of some affliction that comes directly from the devil. A perfect atonement was made at Calvary. I believe that Jesus bore my sins, and I am free from them all. I am justified from all things if I dare to believe. He Himself took our infirmities and bore our sicknesses; and if I dare believe, I can be healed.[112]

This is very close to Carrie's theology. Kydd says that healing in the atonement means that 'everyone can be healed instantly. People such as Wigglesworth and Hagin have held that position without

---

[109] Kydd, *Healing through the Centuries*, p. 199.

[110] In understanding origins, Kydd turns to Dayton, *Theological Roots of Pentecostalism*, who 'traces the concept of healing in the atonement through people such as Carrie Judd Montgomery, R.L. Stanton, A.B. Simpson, A.J. Gordon, and R. Kelso Carter' (Kydd, *Healing through the Centuries*, p. 200).

[111] Oral Roberts, *If You Need Healing, Do These Things* (New York: Country Life Press, 1952), p. 39, cited in Kydd, *Healing through the Centuries*, pp. 205-206. Roberts also spoke about 'points of contact', which was to be a set apart time when faith would be released for healing.

[112] Smith Wigglesworth, *Ever Increasing Faith* (1924; reprint; Springfield, MO: Gospel Publishing House, 1971), p. 43, cited in Kydd, *Healing through the Centuries*, p. 206. See also Smith Wigglesworth, 'Filled with God', *TF* 42.8 (Aug 1922), pp. 184-87.

qualification. Like most Pentecostals, however, Roberts does not'.[113]
Kydd describes that while Roberts believed in healing the atonement, when he could not explain why people did not experience
healing, he also believed in God's sovereignty. Roberts believed that
in some cases where God did not heal, maybe it was because God
was at work to perform an even greater work in that person's life.
R.K. Carter also experienced a similar change of opinions as time
went on.[114] What sets Carrie apart from Roberts is that she, and
people like Wigglesworth, took a hard and absolute stance in relation to healing in the atonement. There was no room for God to
deny His word. She and Wigglesworth held to an extreme view of
this doctrine which Roberts decided to modify to make room to
deal with suffering.

Conclusions

Out of the models Kydd suggests, different aspects of Carrie's ministry resonate with several of them. It is obvious that Carrie did not
fit into the Revelational model with Kuhlman because it appears
that Kulhman relied more on her intuitions of the Spirit and Carrie
more on God's written word as her basis. In the Confrontation
model, like Blumhardt, Carrie saw Jesus as victorious and like
Wimber, she too believed that healing came instantly. Carrie also
contributed to the democratization of healing during her time as
Wimber did later. However, unlike Carrie, these two admitted that
when one did not experience the manifestations of healing, sometimes there were no answers to explain that. Carrie, however, taught
to deny the symptoms of suffering.

Carrie's healing homes were also very similar to Trudel's homes
in the Incubational model in that there was teaching and prayer
where people were not rushed for an immediate result. This allowed
Carrie to teach more on the doctrine behind healing rather than just
pray for someone and send them on their way. In fact, she spent
much of the time teaching them how to pray effectively the prayer
of faith. In this, however, Carrie did believe that healing came instantly even if manifestations came at a later time. Finally, the Sote-

---

[113] Kydd, *Healing through the Centuries*, p. 207.
[114] Kydd, *Healing through the Centuries*, p. 209. Kydd claims that in the end
Carter came to see 'healing not as a right that could be demanded but as a special
favor from God'.

riological model is the one that Carrie most resembles and also a model she greatly shaped since it is based mostly around healing in the atonement. While Oral Roberts and others adapted the view of healing in the atonement to deal with suffering in one way or another, Wigglesworth and Carrie held to the original and extreme view of healing in the atonement without making modifications. While Carrie's theology resonates in one way or another with Kydd's Confrontational, Incubational, and Soteriological models, within these, aspects of her ministry most resonate with Wimber, Trudel, and Wigglesworth because of similarities mentioned above.

5.6.2 Henry H. Knight: God's Faithfulness versus God's Freedom

God's Faithfulness

The model of healing that Henry Knight presents has to do with a pendulum swing from whether certain people put more weight on God's faithfulness or his freedom and sovereignty. From a Wesleyan perspective, Knight based his research on more contemporary theologies of healing when he wrote his article in 1993.[115] He classifies Carrie within the 'faith confession,' or 'word of faith' movement (Faith Movement) category which he places at one extreme of God's faithfulness and Kathryn Kuhlman on other extreme of God's sovereignty. The likes of Francis McNutt, John Wimber, and even John Wesley are somewhere in the middle of these two poles.

Knight notices that teaching in the Faith Movement connects with the 'early healing ministers like Elizabeth Mix and Carrie Judd Montgomery'.[116] It is important to note that many see roots of the present day Faith Movements (including Word of Faith and Prosperity Gospel) within the theology of the Divine Healing Movement, and even more specifically within Carrie's theology.[117] Carrie's

---

[115] Henry H. Knight, III, 'God's Faithfulness and God's Freedom: A Comparison of Contemporary Theologies of Healing', *JPT* 2 (1993), p. 69. Knight is currently part of a United Methodist Church. See also Dayton *The Theological Roots of Pentecostalism*, who connected this thinking to the holiness movement as well.

[116] Knight, 'God's Faithfulness and God's Freedom', pp. 68-69.

[117] D.R. McConnell in his *A Different Gospel* (Peabody, MA: Hendrickson, 1988) believes that this type of thinking was rooted in E.W. Kenyon while B. Barron in his *The Health and Wealth Gospel* (Downers Grove, IL: InterVarsity Press, 1987) connects this thinking as also having possible roots in A.B. Simpson's teachings. In reference to the 'word of faith', also known as 'faith confession' movement, Knight recognizes that some see that this type of 'New

healing theology has indeed emerged in different forms within the current Faith Movement and many other streams within Pentecostal and Charismatic Christianity.[118] Similar to the teachings of both Palmer and Carrie, many in this stream stress acting in faith and positive confession even if manifestations have not yet come.[119] Knight says that the Faith Movement's 'extreme view would claim that, if God has promised healing, and God is faithful to that promise, one will instantly be healed'.[120] He classifies the Word of Faith Movement as believing that 'to pay attention to symptoms which persist after you have claimed your healing is to invite negative confession, doubt God's word, and thereby lose your healing'.[121] He

---

Thought' originated with E.W. Kenyon while others see A.B. Simpson teaching the same thing but not in any connection with Kenyon. In Paul L. King's research into the CMA, *Genuine Gold: The Cautiously Charismatic Story of the Early Christian and Missionary Alliance* (Tulsa: Word & Spirit Press, 2006), p. 34, he recognizes that Kenyon was friends with Simpson and F.F. Bosworth and held to a similar theology, but then later in life was a proponent of things that would likely not be embraced by the CMA. Interestingly enough, the Montgomerys were good friends with E.W. Kenyon and actually came up against some of the similar criticisms as he did in his early ministry. Kenyon's biographer Joe McIntyre even notes that Carrie is 'another direct link with today's Faith Movement. Her ministry has striking parallels with E.W. Kenyon's ministry, both in her teachings on faith and healing, and her spiritual evolution' (*E.W. Kenyon and His Message of Faith: The True Story* [Lake Mary, FL: Charisma House, 1997], p. 46).

[118] McIntyre says that 'F.F. Bosworth, John G. Lake, Carrie Judd Montgomery, and E.W. Kenyon closed the gap and connected the Faith-Cure, or Divine Healing Movement into Pentecostalism and the Faith Movement'. Further, he says that these four 'carried the torch of divine healing into the next generation and into the Pentecostal Movement' (McIntyre, *E.W. Kenyon and His Message of Faith*, p. 61). Storms additionally claims that 'as the only survivor of the faith-healing movement who lived to see the beginnings of a fresh wave of divine healing and revival through the ministries of Oral Roberts and William Branham, Montgomery acted as an important organic link to the faith-healing movement of the late nineteenth century' (Storms, 'Carrie Judd Montgomery: The Little General', p. 287). King explains that present day faith teaching originated in the Wesleyan, Keswick, Higher Life holiness, and healing movements of which Carrie was very much a part (King, *Genuine Gold*, p. 34).

[119] It must be noted that Carrie would not readily fit with the 'name it and claim it' teaching. There is a fine line here because she did believe in positive confession if it was in relation to specific things she felt that God had revealed to her like opening up a healing home or starting a periodical or believing for healing. This was not for everything though, only things she felt that God was revealing to her through the Spirit or through Scripture.

[120] Knight, 'God's Faithfulness and God's Freedom', p. 63.

[121] Knight, 'God's Faithfulness and God's Freedom', p. 68, says that they believe 'when our sense perceptions contradict the teachings of Scripture, a positive confession requires us to affirm Scripture and deny our senses'.

suggests that they teach this denial of symptoms so that they do not lose their healing. Additionally, many in this stream believe that they only need to pray once because to pray a second of third time for healing is to doubt God.[122] That Knight places this group on the opposite side from Kuhlman continues to demonstrate, as was shown in Kydd's model, that Carrie's approach differs.

Knight is accurate in that there are several theological roots that have emerged within the present day Faith Movements that stem from Carrie's theology and that of the Divine Healing Movement. While Carrie was friends with the significant Faith leader, E.W. Kenyon, and contributed to some foundational theology on which the Faith Movements built, many added to these foundations in ways in which she did not initially teach or intend.[123] Carrie never emphasized the prosperity gospel or some of the other interesting and controversial theologies that have emerged in some current Faith teachings.[124] Regardless of these differences, Carrie fits closest and is classified with this group in Knight's paradigm.[125]

---

[122] While there may have been a denial of symptoms in Carrie's theology, she still believed that the claims of healing were absolutely true even if the manifestations came at a later time. Her reference to when Jesus rebuked the fig tree demonstrates this point. She believed that the tree died the minute Jesus rebuked it even if the outward results of that came at a later time (Montgomery, 'Continue in My Word', p. 74).

[123] Carrie also printed several of his articles over the years in her periodical: W.E. Kenyon, 'Legal Authority', *TF* 34.12 (Dec 1914), pp. 281-85 and 'The Master's Love Slaves', *TF* 64.12 (Dec 1945), pp. 280-81. Just after George Montgomery died, Carrie also received a letter from E.W. Kenyon (E.W. Kenyon, Letter to Carrie, *TF* 50.10 (Oct 1930), p. 234). In reference to George he said that 'he meant more to me than I can ever tell you'. He recalled that he was drawn to George and 'wanted to sit near him' when he was near. He also said that 'Oakland will not be the same when I go back' and that he 'loved him very tenderly'. McIntyre, notes in *E.W. Kenyon and His Message of Faith: The True Story* (Lake Mary, FL: Charisma House, 1997), pp. 46, that 'many of the people who greatly impacted Kenyon's life were touched by Phoebe Palmer's ministry, including Charles Cullis, Carrie Judd Montgomery, and A.B. Simpson'.

[124] Thomas Smail, Andrew Walker, Nigel Wright, '"Revelation Knowledge" and Knowledge of Revelation: The Faith Movement and the Question of Heresy', *JPT* 5 (1994), pp. 57-77. They write from an unsympathetic perspective and seek to pin the Faith Movement down as a heresy.

[125] D.R. McConnell, 'The Faith Movement: New Revelation or Charismatic Cultism?', a paper delivered to the European Pentecostal Theological Association in Erzhausen, West Germany, March 31, 1989, pps. 19-20. Petts, 'Healing and the Atonement', p. 80, provides a helpful overall sketch of the theology of the Faith Movement when he says,

In relation to his classification of the Faith Movement, Knight says that 'there is no question of God's not healing instantly; the only question is whether we believe and not doubt that God has done so'. He goes on to say that to them 'faith is essentially trusting in God's promises in Scripture rather than trusting in God. Indeed, the believer is assured of healing because, given the spiritual laws and scriptural promises, a faithful God has no choice in the matter'. Knight argues that people who subscribe to the Word of Faith Movements 'emphasize God's faithfulness at the expense of God's freedom'.[126] Saying that people within this paradigm believe that faith is 'trusting in God's promises' rather than 'trusting in God' might be an overstatement. While that is one way to interpret their theology, another way to look at it might be that a person's word is their honor and one might wonder if taking a person's promise at face value does not also place a lot of trust in that individual, expecting that he or she will come through as promised? Is there the possibility that these people are putting their trust in the Author of these words and not in the words themselves? While it appears that many who subscribe to this type of Faith theology emphasize and place more weight on God's written general word (*logos*) than his words of revelation (*rhema*), does that mean that they are not also 'trusting in God'?[127] Trusting and acting on God's words may indeed prove to strengthen one's trust in the Author of those words rather than diminish it. Charles Spurgeon noticed that God's sovereignty was not only about taking hold of his word. He said,

---

The Faith eschatology is 'hyper-realized' because of its extreme promises to the believer of a life which is absolutely invulnerable to any type of evil. It claims that 'the powers of the age to come' have *completely* come in this life and that these powers can be used *at will* by the believer with enough faith and knowledge to operate them. There is no process of realization in the lives of those who exercise Faith principles. We see evidence of this hyper-realized eschatology in the Faith doctrines of healing, authority, and prosperity. The hyper-realized nature of Faith eschatology emphasizes the 'now' of the kingdom of God to the exclusion of the 'not yet'.

They see that in light of the past, the full Kingdom of God can and should come now to believers. This present day theology is similar to Carrie's teachings. The question to ask might be, just because people are not fully experiencing the Kingdom completely today, does that mean that one should not expect and believe for the Kingdom to come in every instance?

126 Knight, 'God's Faithfulness and God's Freedom', p. 69.
127 See Appendix 6 to read Carrie's poem 'Led by the Spirit'.

Before [God] pledged His word He was free to do as it pleased Him; but after He had made a promise, his truth and honor bind Him to do as He said. To Him, indeed, this is no limiting of His liberty; for the promise is always the declaration of His sovereign will and good pleasure, and it is ever his delight to act according to His word.[128]

Spurgeon's perspective does not limit sovereignty at the expense of liberty but rather integrates the possibility of both in more equal measures. Joe McIntyre also offers some helpful distinctions. He says,

Some maintain that sickness in the believer's life is an expression of God's sovereignty and that healing is also at His sovereign discretion. To demand healing is to 'give orders' to God. Others understand the atonement of Christ to cover sickness as well as sin; therefore, they believe God wants to heal everyone. But they do not demand healing of God. Rather they demand that the devil remove his demonic affliction. In this approach, they imitate the ministry of Jesus.[129]

Because of potential fanaticism, people in both the Divine Healing and the Faith Movements regularly can be seen as 'demanding' things from God when, from their perspective, they understand that there are certain things that are freely available through the finished work of Christ; because of this, they simply assert their authority over 'the devil' to reclaim what God has *already* given. Placing emphasis on acting according to God's word might not necessarily diminish one's view of His sovereignty; it might just reinter-

---

[128] Charles H. Spurgeon, *According to Promise* (London, UK: Passmore and Alabaster, 1890; reprint Grand Rapids, MI: Baker Book House, 1964), p. 43, cited in McIntyre, *E.W. Kenyon and His Message of Faith,* p. 266

[129] McIntyre, *E.W. Kenyon and His Message of Faith,* p. 266. He says that 'most of the Faith-Cure advocates [Carrie was included here] believed God wanted to heal all, but certainly aware that not all were healed. Many insisted, however, that the failure to be healed was not necessarily an expression of God's sovereignty, but rather the result of some other known or unknown hindrance to healing'. His book is a defense of Kenyon's misrepresentation by others who have classified him within the metaphysical cults. McIntyre overviews the Faith-Cure movement and presents many comparisons and parallels between Kenyon's theology and others like Cullis, Simpson, Pierson, Gordon, and also Carrie to demonstrate that his roots are in the divine healing movement that began before Christian Science and other metaphysical cults.

pret and broaden it. There is much controversy in relation to the Faith Movement and even the Divine Healing Movement with some valid concerns.[130]

The Prosperity Gospel and other streams within the Word of Faith Movement have adapted theological elements that Carrie helped to popularize in her day which has caused some concern. After adopting Carrie's theology, some people remained sick and as a result got disillusioned. At the same time, it is important to realize that many healings did come in response to people acting out in faith both in Carrie's time and also today within the Faith Movements. While some criticisms might be deserved, there might be other aspects of their theology that can be valuable if understood more fully. It is important not to throw away the 'wheat' because there are some 'tares' mixed in, or what Carrie might say as letting fear of the 'wild fire' cause one to miss the 'true fire'.[131]

While Knight classified Carrie along with the others in the Faith Movement at the pendulum swing towards God's faithfulness, that does not mean that both she and the newer movement disregarded God's sovereignty, they just had a different paradigm for understanding it.

5.6.3 Kimberly A. Alexander: Wesleyan or Finished Work Pentecostal?

From her Wesleyan-Holiness Pentecostal perspective, Kimberly Alexander distinguishes between a Wesleyan-Pentecostal and a Finished Work Pentecostal stream in her research of models and theology within Pentecostal Healing. Even though both groups held to the doctrine of healing in the atonement, the way these groups appropriated it caused her to notice some differences. She believes that 'from 1906 to 1910, the Pentecostal Movement fit decidedly

---

[130] Hank Hanegraaff is also a longstanding critic of the Faith Movement. See his *Christianity in Crisis: 21ˢᵗ Century* (Eugene, OR: Harvest House Publishers, 1993). John Wolf heavily criticizes Bill Johnson's ministry (who some categorize in the Faith Movement), associates him with Benny Hinn, and also comes from the place where he does not believe that the gifts of the Spirit are for today ('The Word of Faith Movement', Church Education Resource Ministries found at <www.cerm.info/bible_studies/Apologetics/WordofFaith.html>. Assessed January 2, 2011).

[131] Carrie Judd Montgomery, 'The Work in Los Angeles', *TF* 27.1 (Jan 1907), p. 14

within the Wesleyan stream of theology'.[132] After William Durham began teaching a newer Finished Work soteriology in 1910 however, splits over the doctrine occurred.[133] Alexander rightly recognizes that this teaching was not original to him when she says that 'while Durham said little about healing in relation to his Finished Work view, it is clear that his followers, and even some of his predecessors who were already proposing a Finished Work Theology (e.g. Carrie Judd Montgomery), linked their understanding of "healing in the atonement" to a Finished Work soteriology'.[134] And while Carrie was a part of the healing movement which was influenced by Wesleyan thought, Alexander believes that her healing theology was very different from Wesleyan-Pentecostals in that she advocated the Finished Work.[135]

---

[132] Alexander, *Pentecostal Healing*, pp. 150, 233. She continues,

Those who came into the Pentecostal experience from non-Wesleyan (usually Baptistic) backgrounds, came via the door of an experience of sanctification as a second work definite work of grace. However, in 1910, William Durham, who had traveled this route, began to rethink his theology. Though he had testified to and preached an experience of baptism in the Holy Spirit in 1907, in 1910 Durham modified his theology, accommodating it to his Baptist roots. This new Pentecostal soteriology disclaimed sanctification as a second definite work of grace, seeing justification and sanctification as occurring at the moment of conversion. He based his theology on what he termed the Finished Work of Christ on the cross.

[133] Alexander, *Pentecostal Healing*, pp. 183, 210-11.

[134] Alexander, *Pentecostal Healing*, pp. 151, 211, and p. 156, n. 197. Carrie taught on the finished work as early as 1880. See Chapter 4. Durham also later claimed that the Montgomerys endorsed his theology and revival work ('The Work of God in Los Angeles: How God overruled the Attempt of the Devil to Stop It', *Pentecostal Testimony* 1.8 [1911], p. 11, cited in Alexander, *Pentecostal Healing*, p. 151).

[135] Alexander's research in *Triumphs of Faith*, focused on 1906-1910. That is a crucial time but demonstrates just a small sample of Carrie's theology. While some rejected this doctrine, others who came from a Baptism background or from Alexander Dowie's Zion Church in Illinois embraced it. This finished work soteriology as well as the racial divide continuing to grow in Charles H. Mason's Church of God in Christ led to a meeting in Hot Springs, Arkansas in 1914 where the Assemblies of God branched off. The Assemblies of God, of which Carrie became a part of early on, embraced Durham's 'finished work' soteriology and became part of the Finished Work stream. Very similar to Carrie's view, the newly formed Pentecostal group believed that healing was 'provided for and finished in the atonement' and thus it only needs to be 'appropriated by a faith claim'. Carrie's influence within the Finished Work stream also reveals her impact upon the Assemblies of God (Alexander, *Pentecostal Healing*, pp. 73, 151, 160, 166).

Alexander sees that emphasis of the Finished Work stream is more on its 'already' aspect than upon the 'not yet'. Because of this, she sees a danger in that the Finished Work stream believes that the Spirit brings 'full resurrection life now to the believer, as a result of a finished work. The dilemma becomes one of: For what does one pray if the healing work, indeed health, is already present?'[136] However, Carrie and other others classified in the Finished Work stream believed that one *does* need to pray because while healing is already present and freely available, one must still take hold of and appropriate it for it to become actualized. In a similar way that Joshua and Caleb had to engage in a battle to take hold of and inherit the Promised Land that God had *already* given them (Numbers 13), so Carrie acted similarly in relation to healing. Healing was 'already' given and simply needed to be 'taken hold of'.[137]

Alexander claims that the two streams interpreted signs (referring to Mk 16.17-18) differently in that for the 'Wesleyan camp, the signs were the inbreaking of the Kingdom to come; for the Finished Work camp, they pointed backward to the cross'.[138] While Alexander makes an important point, for some within her classification, like Carrie, the signs came as a result of a finished work but for a purpose of the Kingdom's breaking into the present. For Carrie, it was not an either/or question in regards to if the signs were the 'inbreaking Kingdom' or 'signs of a work already finished'.[139] It was both. She saw that because of what Jesus had done on the cross, signs that released His kingdom into the present would be released. She saw that the inbreaking of the Kingdom was necessary for people to walk in all the fullness God had for them in the present.[140] An

---

[136] Alexander, *Pentecostal Healing*, pp. 233-34.

[137] Carrie's writing is saturated with this type of language. These are just a few examples of this: Carrie F. Judd, 'Ministry', *TF* 2.11 (Nov 1882), p. 173; 'Wilt Thou Be Made Whole?', *TF* 4.3 (March 1884), pp. 53-56; 'Except Ye See', *TF* 6.4 (April 1886), pp. 83-84; 'Exceeding Wise', *TF* 6.8 (Aug 1886), pp. 169-72; and 'Praises at Midnight', *TF* 9.4 (April 1889), p. 90, where she says, 'Oh, that all the strained and weary eyes might cease their sad watch of the things seen, and look unto Jesus and the blessed verities which He has *already given* us, and which He is inviting us to *take* by simple faith'. See also Jennifer A. Miskov, *Silver to Gold: A Journey of Young Revolutionaries* (Birmingham, UK: Silver to Gold, 2009) for this similar theme told through the form of an allegory.

[138] Alexander, *Pentecostal Healing*, p. 234.

[139] Alexander, *Pentecostal Healing*, p. 234.

[140] Carrie used Isaiah 58 many times to describe this kingdom's coming to bring freedom and healing. See Chapter 4, n. 112.

example of this is when she wrote about the importance of abiding in Christ:

> Thus shall we glorify the Father. Soul and body filled with the abounding life and health of Jesus Christ, we shall go forth strong in His might to proclaim 'deliverance to the captives' whom Satan hath bound. Then shall they indeed realize that the Kingdom of God hath come nigh unto them. And how is this union attained? Simply by receiving His word where He assures us that having died in His death we are now risen together with Him and that henceforth we are to live in 'newness of life.' Yielding unto Him as 'alive from the dead,' and reckoning by faith the truth of His finished work for us, we begin to realize the cessation of all self-effort as a new and wonderful life-power takes possession of us, thinking, speaking, moving through us, bringing into captivity every faculty of soul and body to the obedience of the Christ-life within.[141]

What has happened in the past enables and empowers one to bring the Kingdom into the present. When Carrie spoke about the quickening life that the resurrection brings, 'lifting us above the natural plane, and causing us indeed to "taste of the powers of the age to come"', she pointed to the future, not to the past.[142] For Carrie, it appears that the signs came as a result of the past, but they did not point there but rather acted as a launching pad to bring the Kingdom into the present.[143] The first quote above came from before Carrie's Pentecostal Spirit baptism while the second one came after

---

[141] Carrie F. Judd, 'Abide in Me', *TF* 3.9 (Sept 1883), p. 202.

[142] Carrie Judd Montgomery, 'The Whole Body Full of Light', *TF* 29.8 (Aug 1909), p. 189:

> His quickening life means purity, rest, healing, freedom from nerve strain and weariness. The law of the Spirit of life in Christ Jesus makes us free in a larger way than we have known in the past ... if we are deeply baptized into that quickening of the Spirit we shall not only be able to take this attitude by faith, but He will also respond to our faith that we shall sensibly realize in our mortal bodies the streams of glorious, resurrection life lifting us above the natural plane, and causing us indeed to 'taste of the powers of the age to come'.

[143] Carrie F. Judd, 'The Lord Our Healer', *TF* 5.12 (Dec. 1885), pp. 270-71. Additionally, if the Lord's prayer suggests that believers pray, 'Let Your kingdom come (Matt. 6:10)', what is wrong with a person's attempting to live in that place at an extreme level (in the 'not yet')? Would trying to balance out the 'now' in that equation help someone to live in reality, or contribute to crippling their faith?

showing she retained a similar strand. And while Carrie greatly helped to shape the Finished Work stream, because of her Wesleyan influences, Holiness roots, and views on sanctification which will be discussed further, these suggest that she should not exclusively be classified in this one stream alone.[144]

5.6.4 Synopsis

Carrie's influence on the doctrine of healing in the atonement contributed to many of the models surveyed in one way or another. While Smith Wigglesworth, the Faith Movement, and the Finished Work Pentecostal stream were the closest to retain healing in the atonement as Carrie taught it, many of the others mentioned also integrated it into their ministries to some extent, even if adaptations were made. Several in Carrie's time like R.K. Carter, also saw problems associated with the extreme view of healing in the atonement and adapted their views.[145] While some could not explain suffering, rather than say that it came from the lack of faith of the individual, they admitted they did not have the answers. This at least made room to deal with the realities of suffering where Carrie did not. Many of these leaders were still successful in their healing ministries even if the extreme view of healing in the atonement was modified. This shows that utilizing this doctrine or even an adaptation of it *and* making room to deal with suffering does not necessarily diminish the effects of healing.[146] This insight can provide those who

---

[144] This will be demonstrated more in Chapter 6 where some of Carrie's pneumatology and her view of sanctification is shown to have Wesleyan influence.

[145] See 4.2.1.

[146] While many others also adopt a similar stance, especially those within the Faith Movement, one close current example to Carrie's view of healing in the atonement lived out today can be seen in Bill Johnson's ministry. He leads a revival movement at Bethel Church in Redding, California and has recorded many healings. He claims that healing is 'in the Atonement – The price that Jesus paid for my sins was more than sufficient for my diseases'. See <http://www.bjm.org> and <http://www.ibethel.org/site/>. Bill Johnson, 'Healing: Our Neglected Birthright' audio teaching with transcriptions online, no date, found at <http://www.ibethel.org/store/> assessed January 11, 2011. See also his *Strengthen Yourself in the Lord: How to release the Hidden Power of God* (Shippensburg, PA: Destiny Image Publishers, Inc., 2007), p. 46, where he says that 'In reality, He already *has* won. Our job is to align our hearts with the reality of the victory of the Cross so that we can see His purposes and redemption at work around us'. See also his *When Heaven Invades Earth: A Practical Guide to a Life of Miracles* (Shippensburg, PA: Destiny Image Publishers, Inc., 2005). 'Commanding prayers' or similar views of healing in the atonement to that of Johnson's can also be seen in the Healing on

have integrated and/or adapted the doctrine a deeper understanding of the implications, both positive and negative, that can come as a result of applying it to their ministries.

5.7 Implications

Laying out Carrie's theology of healing provides a snapshot of one of the earliest and more extreme forms of healing in the atonement lived out along with its implications. One of the biggest problems with Carrie's extreme belief in healing in the atonement is that there was no room to deal with the reality of suffering other than to deny it. This resulted in guilt if one did not experience the manifestations of his or her healing and it also put most of the responsibility on the individual. While Carrie's healing theology lacks a paradigm to deal adequately with suffering, it is also important to realize that many people were healed as a result of applying her teaching. Some of these may not have had the energy to hope or pray any longer, but in response to her theology, they had been stirred to believe again, and as a result, many of them experienced healing. While Carrie's life and theology caused confusion and disillusionment for some, it also brought hope and healing for others. In light of this study and the success that has come even after making adaptations to the doctrine, to decrease the guilt and confusion left when one does not experience manifestations of their healing, people applying a similar theology today could make room to deal with the reality of suffering in a more tangible way than what looked like denial on Carrie's part.

---

the Streets model that originated by Mark Marx from a Vineyard church in Ireland within the last 10 years <http://www.out-there.org>.

6

ANALYSIS AND EVALUATION OF PENTECOSTAL THEMES WITHIN CARRIE'S PNEUMATOLOGY

Now that the foundations and implications of Carrie's theology of healing have been laid out, the development of her pneumatology both before and after her 1908 tongues experience will be examined. I will trace how Carrie viewed the work of the Spirit from within her varied Holiness framework, and then later within her Pentecostal perspective. Carrie's views on sanctification and Spirit baptism will also be shown as they developed within these separate paradigms. A discussion in relation to Carrie's approach to the initial evidence doctrine will also be explored. The key questions that will be investigated throughout the chapter are: How did Carrie's view of Spirit baptism develop? What effect did her 1908 tongues experience have on her life, ministry, and pneumatology? And, what is the significance of her Pentecostal Spirit baptism experience for today?

6.1 Pre-1908 Language and Influences

6.1.1 Pentecostal Language in *Triumphs of Faith* before 1908

Carrie was no stranger to Pentecostal terminology before her 1908 Spirit baptism experience, even if her understanding of these terms adapted with the times. The frequency of Carrie's Pentecostal language, specifically in relation to Spirit baptism themes, filled her periodical years before the new movement emerged.[1] As early as 1885, Carrie spoke at a conference that encouraged people to seek 'a special baptism of the Holy Spirit' and by 1886, the term 'Pentecostal' started appearing in Carrie's periodical.[2] In 1887, she printed an article by Ada Coolidge entitled 'The Baptism of the Holy Ghost'.[3] In 1891, and in reference to two YMCA meetings in San Francisco, Carrie claimed there was sweet unity and all present 'experienced a precious baptism of the Holy Spirit'.[4] Warren Collins also wrote that since Carrie had spoken at his church a year before, they had 'been receiving a constant baptism of the Holy Spirit … The city has been blessed with almost a constant revival ever since'.[5]

By 1895, Carrie published her own article called 'Pentecostal Blessing' where she introduced a letter about the 'unusual waves of glory' that fell in the Home of Peace. There is a sense of a greater and more concentrated measure of the Holy Spirit evidenced in these accounts. In this same article, she asked, 'Is your soul hungry for the baptism the Holy Ghost? If so, then he is ready to fill you'. to which she followed by saying, 'Oh, I am sure that it is our privilege not to be half full, but to be *filled to overflowing*, and *that all the time*, and the overflowing rivers will then be poured out to a thirsty, lost world'.[6] There is an essence here of being able to live in a place of a continual baptism that constantly allows the Spirit to overflow. An emphasis on measures and a desire to be filled to overflowing

---

[1] This is not surprising as Pentecostal themes were already present in other areas such as in the first National Camp Meeting Association for the Promotion of Holiness in July 1867 in New Jersey that had the goal to realize the Pentecostal Spirit baptism. See Dayton, *Theological Roots of Pentecostalism*, p. 90.

[2] Judd, 'A Convention for Christian Life, Divine Healing, Evangelistic and Missionary Work', p. 240. See also C.A. Fox, 'How Pentecostal Lives are Spoilt', *TF* 6.11 (Nov 1886), pp. 254-59.

[3] Ada S. Coolidge, 'The Baptism of the Holy Ghost', *TF* 7.7 (July 1887), p. 153.

[4] Montgomery, 'The Work and the Workers', *TF* 11.12, p. 276. YMCA is the Young Men's Christian Association but acted more as a Christian charity for both men and women.

[5] Warren Colins, 'The Work at Home: The Work of the Lord in Ft. Worth, Texas', *CAMW* 6.16 (April 17, 1891), p. 250.

[6] Montgomery, 'Pentecostal Blessing', pp. 60-62. She recorded this account of what she heard had happened there during a time when she was away holding meetings with the Salvation Army.

with the Holy Spirit '*all the time*' was a part of Carrie's life for many years before her own 1908 experience.[7]

Continuing with Pentecostal themes, in 1895, Carrie gave an address at the Cazadero Camp meeting on 'The Work of the Spirit' where she spoke about the baptism of the Holy Spirit.[8] The next year at the camp meeting, she recorded that people received the 'baptism of the Spirit to go forth in His service with renewed power' and also that 'droppings of Pentecostal showers' came during those meetings.[9] Rather than emphasizing the continual nature of baptism here, she spoke about it as an empowering experience in people's lives. Throughout the years leading up to her own 1908 Pentecostal Spirit baptism, Carrie's growing interest in the subject continued to emerge within her periodical.[10] In 1896, it was reported that the Pentecostal Prayer Union had formed.[11] In August 1897, she printed 'Baptism of the Holy Spirit' by E.V. Baker where the author wrote that 'when you get it, you'll know it'.[12] Carrie also printed an interesting article by A.E. Davis in that same issue entitled 'The Sin of Not Being Baptized with the Holy Ghost'.[13] In 1900, F.B. Meyer wrote in Carrie's periodical that Pentecost is different from 'regeneration' because 'in regeneration the Holy Spirit is described as being *within*, but in Pentecost and ever after the Holy Ghost is described as being UPON. He anoints. He equips'.[14]

During Carrie's own searching time over the subject of the new Pentecostal Spirit baptism in 1906-1907, she continued to print arti-

---

[7] Carrie Judd Montgomery, 'Filled', *TF* 15.7 (July 1895), pp. 145-52.

[8] Carrie Judd Montgomery, 'The Work of the Spirit', *TF* 15.9 (Sept 1895), pp. 193-99.

[9] Carrie Judd Montgomery, 'Cazadero Camp Meeting', *TF* 16.9 (Sept 1896), p. 216.

[10] E.g. Bishop Hamlin's teaching on Spirit baptism was explored twice by unknown authors: 'The Baptism of the Holy Spirit', *TF* 24.2 (Feb 1904), p. 47, and 'The Baptism of the Spirit', *TF* 26.10 (Oct 1906), p. 209, which was based on his own account of Pentecostal Spirit baptism.

[11] Waddell, 'The Home of Peace'. Waddell instituted three half hours of silence and waiting on God during the day which later formed into this prayer union.

[12] E.V. Baker, 'Baptism of the Holy Spirit', *TF* 17.8 (Aug 1897), p. 183.

[13] A.E. Davis, 'The Sin of Not Being Baptized with the Holy Ghost', *TF* 17.8 (Aug 1897), pp. 189-90.

[14] F.B. Meyer, 'Pentecost', *TF* 20.7 (July 1900), p. 167.

cles in relation to Pentecostal themes.[15] In 1906, she wrote of an 'inbreathing' of the Spirit to transform lives where she also discussed the Spirit coming from outside the believer; here she also prayed that the Lord 'would baptize us with His blessed Spirit'.[16] In 1907, she published accounts of Pentecostal Spirit baptism at Pandita Ramabai's orphanage as well as John Salmon's experience.[17] Articles in relation to Carrie calling out to God and inviting Him to baptize her and her readers with His Spirit, to printing testimonies about people's Pentecostal Spirit baptism experiences, occurred with more regularity during these years leading up to her own experience.[18]

This small sample of Carrie's use of Pentecostal terms before the movement emerged shows that she was already using language that was easily transferable. It also shows a lack of clarity of her understanding as at times she referred to Spirit baptism as a distinct empowering experience and other times as a continual overflowing of the Spirit. This was not unusual at that time as many in the Holiness Movement also lacked precision when describing Spirit baptism. Carrie's literature also reveals that even before 1908, she had already sought and prayed multiple times for 'a special outpouring of His Holy Spirit' and 'a special baptism of the Holy Spirit for service'.[19] She had also already experienced some of these 'outpourings' before as well. As will be developed further, before 1908, Carrie used

---

[15] Carrie introduced Mrs Marshall to share her experience of Spirit baptism in 'Deliverance of an Insane Sister', *TF* 27.1 (Jan 1907), pp. 11-13. See also B.H. Irwin, 'My Pentecostal Baptism – A Christmas gift', in *TF* 25.5 (May 1907), pp. 114-17.

[16] Carrie Judd Montgomery 'The Touch of His Healing Hand', *TF* 26.1 (Jan 1906), pp. 1-3.

[17] In *TF* 27.12 (Dec 1907), both 'Showers of Blessing' by Pandita Ramabai (pp. 267-69) and 'My Enduement' by John Salmon (pp. 269-71) were printed which both were records of Pentecostal Spirit baptism accounts.

[18] Carrie Judd Montgomery 'The Touch of His Healing Hand', *TF* 26.1 (Jan 1906), pp. 1-3.

[19] Carrie F. Judd, 'A Convention for Christian Life and Work', *TF* 5.10 (Oct 1885), p. 240. In 1885 she announced a conference saying, 'We know that many dear ones are hungering for a fuller manifestation of Christ in their souls and bodies, will be glad of this opportunity to meet together in the name of the Lord, and wait upon Him for a special outpouring of His Holy Spirit'. She was also due to speak at another conference for 'All who desire a deeper Spiritual Life, a special baptism of the Holy Spirit for service, a quickening in the truth, life, and work of the Lord, and in the hope of His appearing' ('Christian Convention in Philadelphia, PA', *TF* 5.10 [Oct 1885], p. 240).

to see her 1879 healing account as her Spirit baptism. In addition to her healing, she also had enjoyed other powerful experiences with the Spirit as well. Later, reflecting through her fresh Pentecostal perspective, she wrote,

> I remembered an experience which I had a few years after my healing, while kneeling with a dear sister, and asking for the Spirit's fullness. He had then come upon me in much greater power than at the time of my healing, and so manifested His sweet presence that it had been almost overpowering.[20]

In a section called 'Ocean Depths of Blessing' in her autobiography, she shared further about this experience in language that nearly matches how she described her 1908 experience; the only real difference being that it did not include the manifestation of tongues.[21] These pre-1908 'overpowering' experiences demonstrate that Carrie's pursuit of being baptized with the Spirit was a common thread even before her intersection with Pentecostalism. That she recognized similar stirrings of the Spirit makes Carrie a true proto-Pentecostal who was just waiting for the sparks of the new revival fire to start before she was ready to engage with a familiar flame.

6.1.2 Holiness Paradigms

While the Pentecostal understanding of Spirit baptism and the gift of tongues was not common in the Church before the twentieth century, there were developing views of sanctification within various strands of the Holiness Movement that contributed to its terminology and understanding. Methodism, specifically the teachings

---

[20] Carrie Judd Montgomery, '"The Promise of the Father." A Personal Testimony', *TF* 28.7 (July 1908), pp. 145-46. See Appendix 4 for full article.

[21] Montgomery, *Under His Wings*, pp. 96-98. She similarly journeyed to a friend's home to pray for this deepening of the spiritual life since her 'hunger seemed to deepen more and more'. When Carrie arrived there and her friend offered her something to eat, she replied: 'Oh, I do not want anything to eat; I want God'. She continued,

> All at once I experienced a blessing that is difficult to put into words. It seemed as though God manifested Himself in a cloud of Heavenly dew which descended gently upon my head and entered my being, taking full possession of me. At the same time a sweet, restful feeling almost overpowered me ... for His presence seemed to surround me, and at the same time fill me ... While waiting on the Lord a few more days ... the manifestation of the Lord's presence about me, and within me, became still more glorious until my whole being seemed to be filled with 'rivers of living water'.

of John Wesley, John Fletcher, and Phoebe Palmer, greatly influenced developments of sanctification and/or Spirit baptism within Holiness streams heading into the twentieth century.[22] A brief analysis of some of these streams (Wesleyan, Reformed/Calvinist, Keswick) alongside the development of Carrie's view of sanctification reveals that Carrie's theology was a conglomeration of all these streams since she integrated different aspects of them in one way or another.[23] Like the Wesleyan-Holiness view, Carrie saw sanctification as a crisis experience and also applied Phoebe Palmer's methods of sanctification to other areas of her ministry. Like the Reformed view, Carrie saw Spirit baptism more as an experience for empowerment than for holiness.[24] Like the Keswick view, Carrie saw that the 'fullness of the Spirit' enabled one to be victorious over sin, not to eradicate it.[25] Because of Carrie's great emphasis on

---

[22] The Wesleyan-Holiness stream in the late 1800s saw sanctification as something that would remove the sin and that could come in a process over time. Keswicks saw that sanctification could come in an instant but that the process of fullness might come over time. This stream also took a positional understanding that they were already sanctified at the moment of their crisis experience even if the manifestations were not yet completed. While these two streams developed more fully later on into Wesleyan-Holiness Pentecostals and the group most resonating with Keswick became the Finished Work Pentecostals, they both have their roots in Methodism; Keswick just adapted those roots into their own non-Methodist backgrounds.

[23] In Bebbington's assessment of the Holiness Movement in England, he broke down his categories into four streams: The High Church, Calvinist, Wesleyan, and Keswick traditions. In the High Church classification he mentions the Anglican influence, in the Calvinist tradition, Finney, and C.H. Spurgeon were key shapers, and in the Wesleyan tradition, it was John Wesley, James Caughy, Phoebe Palmer, and the Salvation Army. Finally, and similarly to Dayton, Bebbington sees that the Keswick stream is 'a synthesis' of Calvinist and Wesleyan traditions. As is evident through Carrie's life and literature, all of the above influences Bebbington states affected her in one way or another (David Bebbington, *Evangelicalism in Modern Britain: A History from the 1730s to the 1980s* [London and New York: Routledge, 2002 reprinted from Unwin Hyman Ltd 1989], p. 73).

[24] Asa Mahan, 'Questions Answered', *Divine Life* 6 (Dec 1882), pp. 109-10, cited in Dayton's *Theological Roots of Pentecostalism*, p. 96. Palmer equated the two together by believing that 'holiness is power'. Others like Baptist Holiness evangelist A.B. Earle also believed that one must have a 'clean heart' as preparation for the baptism of the Holy Spirit. Mahan used the metaphor of needing to be an empty vessel and be pure before one can be filled with power. R.A. Torrey also believed the purpose of Spirit baptism was to empower people for service. See also C.E. Jones, 'Holiness Movement', in *NIDPCM*, p. 727.

[25] Dayton, *Theological Roots of Pentecostalism*, p. 105. See also Bebbington, *Evangelicalism in Modern Britain*, p. 173. In *TF* 29.3 (March 1909), p. 60, the following was mentioned by unknown author: 'Sanctification means more than eradication,

measures, the most dominant influence on her developing Pentecostal pneumatology appears to be the Keswick stream because of its similar emphasis and continual pursuit for the 'higher Christian life'. However, because there is inconsistency and lack of clarity within both Keswick's and Carrie's developing pneumatology, and because all of the various Holiness streams have roots within Methodism, these are loose boundaries rather than bold identifications.

Keswick Theology

The Keswick tradition was a mixture of both the Wesleyan and Reformed/Calvinist views as well as a mixture of English and American influences, especially Anglican.[26] Total dependence on God was a way 'to triumph over temptation' and one of the best known catchwords for the movement was 'victory'.[27] This influence is easily seen in the title of Carrie's periodical, *Triumphs of Faith*. At some of the early Keswick meetings, the theme of Spirit baptism was overshadowed with themes of 'the fullness of the Spirit' and the 'Spirit-filled life'.[28] While inconsistencies exist within Keswick pneumatology, some of its advocates saw that after a defining crisis moment, the fullness of sanctification could continue to come in an ongoing process.[29] David Bundy notes that these believed that the 'normative Christian life is characterized by "fullness of the Spirit" [which is] a definite act of faith, distinct from but usually coincident with regeneration. The actualization of this power usually develops throughout the Christian life' and can also come with repeated experiences and fillings of the Holy Spirit.[30] This view was attractive to those who did not come from a Wesleyan tradition. C.E. Jones also notices that the Finished Work stream within Pentecostalism

---

or suppression of the old nature; it is death and resurrection'. See also David D. Bundy, 'Keswick Higher Life Movement', in *NIDPCM*, p. 821 and David Bebbington, *Holiness in the Nineteenth-Century England: The 1998 Didsbury Lectures* (Glasgow, Great Britain: Paternoster Press, 2000), p. 83.

[26] David Bebbington, *Evangelicalism in Modern Britain,* p. 73. Similar to Dayton, Bebbington sees that the Keswick stream is 'a synthesis' of Calvinist and Wesleyan traditions.

[27] Bebbington, *Evangelicalism in Modern Britain,* p. 170. Additionally, Keswick was also premillennialist rather than the Wesleyan postmillennial perspective at the time.

[28] Dayton, *Theological Roots of Pentecostalism*, p. 105. He says that this happened in a more Christocentric framework.

[29] Bebbington, *Holiness in the Nineteenth-Century England*, p. 79.

[30] Bundy, 'Keswick Higher Life Movement', p. 821.

'bears the closest resemblance to Keswick'.[31] This is not a surprising connection as Carrie's influence on that stream has already been shown.

Along with Carrie's Episcopal background, that many of her friends or influences like Charles Finney, Asa Mahan, Phoebe Palmer, Dwight L. Moody, Robert Pearsall Smith and Hannah Whithall Smith, W.E. Boardman, Andrew Murray, A.J. Gordon, Alexander Boddy, Otto Stockmayer, A.B. Simpson, R.A. Torrey, F.B. Meyer, and A.T. Pierson either shaped Keswick theology or were also influenced by it, made it easy for her to assimilate it. Even in this however, it must be noted that several themes in the other holiness streams also influenced her in one way or another, specifically empowerment themes from the Reformed view and Wesleyan influences from Palmer and the Salvation Army.[32]

6.1.3 Carrie's View of Sanctification before 1908

While Carrie taught on sanctification before this,[33] she claimed that Charles Cullis, who was also an Episcopalian, first introduced her to the 'Methodist' doctrine of sanctification. Mixing Keswick and Wesleyan terms, in 1887 she recounted,

> We must know from God's own Word that there is a higher life than the up and down experiences of most Christians. I wonder if any of you were as much astonished as I was when I first

---

[31] Jones, 'Holiness Movement', p. 727.

[32] Miskov, 'Missing Links: Phoebe Palmer, Carrie Judd Montgomery, and Holiness Roots within Pentecostalism', pp. 8-28. This article traces similarities of Palmer's and Carrie's theology.

[33] Carrie Judd, 'The One Offering', *TF* 1.12 (Dec 1881), pp. 182-83. In 1881, Carrie believed that consecration and sanctification had similar Old Testament meanings 'to set apart, or devote as holy' and that 'when anything is wholly consecrated to God it must also be sanctified'. These two terms were closely related and she saw that the main purpose of being consecrated was so that one might be sanctified to 'serve the Lord'. She saw that people did not need to strain to be consecrated but just had to acknowledge the consecration that God had already made for them. She also associated this work with salvation saying, 'And here [Heb. 10.14] we see that our consecration is Jesus' work as well as the rest of our salvation'. Like consecration, Carrie also believed that there was no need to strive for sanctification but rather a need to 'acknowledge' that which 'our great high Priest has made for us'. At this early time, she understood that a person was sanctified because of the atonement of Christ and that sanctification was something that simply needed to be realized, as a position one already had in Christ. Palmer also saw that sanctification was available in the atonement. See also Phoebe Palmer, *Faith and Its Effects* (New York: Published for the author, 1852), p. 53.

found it out. I wrote to Dr. Cullis for his prayers about some matter, and in answering he enclosed a little tract reference to the life of holiness which a Christian could live by being wholly yielded up to the Spirit, and letting Him live and reign entirely within us. I had always thought that the most we could ask for was forgiveness after committing some sin, and I was very much surprised by the tract. I suppose some of you feel like asking, 'Why, are you not a Methodist?' No, I am an Episcopalian, and I did not know the Methodist or Bible doctrine about sanctification until I read the tract.[34]

Following this and after initial hesitation, she went to a Methodist holiness meeting to learn more. She also searched the Bible for deeper understanding, and after wading through the 'seas of perplexity' in relation to this issue, she decided to let her 'faith [take] hold of God's Word on the subject'. After she did that, she said, 'I soon found that it was not a great mass of holiness I had to get into my soul to last all my life, but that I was to breathe it in moment by moment as I did the air'.[35] Before she had received Cullis' tract, Carrie saw holiness as something that needed to be complete in a moment and that would last her whole life. After this new introduction to sanctification, she saw that it could also continue to come in an ongoing process.

Carrie further connected this process with healing by saying, 'The same thing is true also about Divine healing. I am healed and continue to be healed physically by drinking in His life moment by moment. I am as little and foolish and empty myself as ever, but the Lord is dwelling in me'. Notice that she recognized that the 'Lord' was already dwelling in her at this point. Reflecting Keswick think-

---

[34] Carrie F. Judd, 'Address Monday to Wednesday: Address by Carrie F. Judd', in *Report of the Christian Convention at Old Orchard Beach, ME held July 31 to August 9, 1887* (New York, NY: Word, Work and World Publishing, 1887), p. 23, accessed from C&MA Archives <https://apas.box.net/shared/tvjm06q2vo>. She continued,

> There was one prayer in our sweet church service which I never understood. It was this: 'Vouchsafe, O Lord, to keep me this day without sin.' I did not see anyone that I believed had been kept without sin, and I was puzzled to know what it meant. I thought I could be kept in a degree, but not entirely; but the Holy Spirit within me was reaching out after the fulfilment of the prayer long before I knew anything about the doctrine of holiness.

[35] Judd, 'Address Monday to Wednesday', pp. 23-24.

ing, for both healing and sanctification, she recognized an initiation point followed by a continual process. Although a specific date could not be found of when Carrie claimed her sanctification, she shared that 'If any of you have not taken Him in His fullness then I know that you are very hungry, and I want to tell you of the step of faith you have got to take to know Christ as your Sanctifier, you must step right into the swelling waters, and you will find they will open as you go through till you reach the other side'.[36] This statement suggests that one would know when they had their sanctification experience. Carrie also saw that proof of having this experience would be evident in righteous living.[37]

In 1894, Carrie also weaved conversion themes into her discussion about sanctification. She said 'And just as we believe in Jesus for salvation we must believe in Him for sanctification'. She developed her argument further by saying 'How are you to get sanctified? Let Jesus reign in your heart, and He, the Sinless One, will continually live out His holiness in and through you. This blessing of sanctification is a most precious and definite work of grace in the heart, and it is necessary that we should testify definitely to this blessing if we want to abide in such a precious experience'.[38] There was a crisis moment when a new level of holiness began but it also continued to develop. This reflects a Wesleyan-Holiness view of sanctification. Additionally, how Carrie chose to appropriate sanctification heavily resonated with Palmer's teachings. Carrie said,

> With the heart we believe, and with the mouth we confess, as in every other blessing. If you are not willing to confess that Jesus Christ has saved you, you have not salvation, or have so little that it will all leak away. When you get sanctified you must confess it as definitely as you confess salvation. People have come to me in great sorrow, saying, 'I used to have the blessing of sancti-

---

[36] Carrie F. Judd, 'Address Monday to Wednesday', pp. 24-25. She also printed A.B. Simpson's view in his, 'Sanctification', *TF* 8.1 (Jan 1888), pp. 11-13.

[37] Judd, 'Address Monday to Wednesday', p. 25. She said that 'The test will come in daily living. The people you live with will know whether you are sanctified or not. They are the best judges of that'.

[38] Carrie Judd Montgomery, 'Believing and Receiving', *TF* 14.5 (May 1894), pp. 98-100, also found in her *Life of Praise*, pp. 68-69.

fication, but I have lost it'. And when we probe deep to find the reason, we find very often that it is because of failure to testify.[39]

In a similar way that the lack of confession in relation to salvation meant that it could be lost or begin to 'leak away', the failure to testify or confess one's sanctification meant that it too could be lost.

Building upon conversion and sanctification themes, Carrie continued to integrate healing within this same paradigm when she said, 'And it is the same with divine healing. If people are not willing to testify to the healing power of the Great Physician, they are very apt to lose their health again'. Following this, she expounded on the importance of standing upon the 'naked' Word of God despite feelings or emotions and that at some later time these would become manifest.[40] She also believed that it was through the atonement of Christ that one could receive their sanctification.[41] How Carrie already approached healing was also applied to how she approached sanctification: Act in faith to take hold of what was already available, confess what has been received, and stand on God's Word as the evidence. If confession was not made, one ran into the problem of potentially losing what had been received. Carrie applied Palmer's methods of obtaining sanctification to much of her own theology, including healing.[42]

By 1900, Carrie wrote that 'sanctification means to make holy' and that 'He wants me to get a better experience, so that I will just be filled with Himself, and so that nothing can move me'. People could not become holy by themselves, they needed fully to 'surrender and trust Him to do it all'. Further, she warned, 'Do not resist the call, but yield humbly and lovingly to it, and you shall prove Him "faithful," for He "will do it." The above verse [1 Thess. 5.23] speaks of such a full sanctification that it reaches "spirit, soul and

---

[39] Montgomery, 'Believing and Receiving', pp. 98-100. This also shows that Carrie believed that people could lose their salvation, not just their healing.

[40] Montgomery, 'Believing and Receiving', pp. 98-100. See also Carrie Judd Montgomery, 'Sanctification', *TF* 20.5 (May 1900), p. 97, where she says 'It is not that we have to work up some kind of feeling'. Carrie associated sanctification with an 'experience' and made sure not to emphasize feelings. The term 'naked' connects with Palmer's influence.

[41] Montgomery, 'Sanctification', pp. 97-99. 'Back to the cross we are taken, and made to see that not only was our salvation wrought out there "once for all," but also our sanctification'. In reference to 2 Thess. 2.13 and in regards to obtaining one's sanctification, she wrote that it 'comes through the Spirit of God'.

[42] See Miskov, 'Missing Links'.

body," so that the whole being shall be "preserved blameless"'.[43] By using the term 'full' here, this reveals that Carrie saw sanctification not only as an experience but also in terms of measures. Sanctification could be reached partially, but one should not stop until they had 'fully' received it. This resonated with how she viewed the manifestations of healing.

Immediately following the article above, Carrie made an interesting announcement where she said that 'A brother in the Lord desires to hear from those who have had clear experiences of anointing and sealing of the Holy Ghost, separate and distinct from the experience of sanctification. Please address, Major J.N. Parker, Quarry, Ohio'.[44] This is important not only to point out that Parker was searching for a distinct experience beyond sanctification before the early Pentecostal revivals, but also how some viewed sanctification and Spirit baptism at that time. Carrie also printed other articles of varying views in relation to these themes at this time.[45]

---

[43] Montgomery, 'Sanctification', pp. 97-99. She also said, 'If you try to make or keep yourself holy, it will be a miserable failure. You must make a full surrender and trust Him to do it all'.

[44] Montgomery, 'Sanctification', p. 99.

[45] A.M. Mills, 'Entire Sanctification – What it is and How Obtained', *TF* 22.5 (May 1902), pp. 99-104 and Author unknown, 'Entire Sanctification', *TF* 28.5 (May 1908), p. 106. In Mills' article, she described sanctification as 'a deeper and more radical work of grace, an enlargement of soul and an enduement of power'. She also likened it to a 'blessing' that was for 'each child of God' as well as referred to it as the 'promise of the Father'. Further, she said that 'You can pray for the baptism of the Holy Ghost till your tongues are tired, but so long as you fight sanctification as a possible experience of the children of God, He will not come to your souls'. In relation to the timing of knowing that entire sanctification had been obtained, Mills said that 'ordinarily the witness comes promptly'. She also suggested that it could take a few days, even a week, but those cases were rare. Quoting Andrew Murray who encouraged to 'Wait upon God and He will give you the filling of the Holy Ghost', Mills concluded that 'to be filled with the Spirit means to be sanctified'. In the other article, the unknown author described 'entire sanctification' as something that was more than justification but was not to be included in the already complete new birth. This author described a two-fold outlook of 'blessings' of conversion and entire sanctification or 'perfect love'. This person distinguished between a 'primary sanctification' that is 'instantaneous, distinct, and perfectly bounded' and is also 'included in conversion', with 'entire sanctification', which is seen as a 'second and distinct work of grace [which] is a necessity to complete purity of heart'. So while Mills' earlier article blended sanctification and Spirit baptism meanings, other articles in Carrie's periodical clarified the work of sanctification as separate and distinct in its different measures. This demonstrates some of the inconsistencies surrounding terms and definitions in relation to sanctification and Spirit baptism preceding the Pentecos-

Before 1908, while Carrie saw sanctification as an experience towards increased holiness that one needed to receive 'fully', she also noticed that there were different degrees to which people could be sanctified. Additionally, while she may have overlapped meanings, Carrie's own writings did not readily interchange sanctification with Spirit baptism but kept these terms separate.[46] Up to this point, Carrie emphasized that holiness was the result of sanctification and saw that it was a 'definite work of grace' that began with a crisis moment but continued on in a process. She saw that one's sanctification experience was an initiation point to greater holiness in which one should continue to 'abide'.[47] How Carrie's view of sanctification developed after her 1908 experience will be looked at shortly.

6.2 Development of the Purpose of Spirit Baptism

6.2.1 Power for Service

While Carrie's understanding of Spirit Baptism developed over the years, both before and after her 1908 experience, she saw that one of its main purposes was for empowerment. Early evidence of this came in 1885 when she encouraged people to seek Spirit baptism for the purpose of service.[48] In 1896, she continued to build upon this theme by encouraging those at her Cazadero Camp meeting who received their Spirit baptism experience, 'to go forth in His service with renewed power'.[49] R.A. Torrey, whose writing influ-

---

tal revivals. See also J.W. Beeson, 'After Sanctification What?' *TF* 23.3 (March 1903), pp. 51-55; and Carrie Judd, 'The One Offering', *TF* 1.12 (Dec 1881), p. 183.

[46] 'Testimonies to the Fact of Sanctification', *TF* 11.9 (Sept 1891), pp. 203-206. However, she did overlap meanings. An example of this is in her title, 'Testimonies to the Fact of Sanctification', which she introduced by saying 'I give the following testimonies of eminently holy and reliable witnesses to the truth, reality, and fullness of sanctification by the power and indwelling of Christ by the Holy Spirit'. Fletcher, Wesley, Upham, Palmer, and Finney were a few of those quoted. Being dead from sin, receiving perfect love, and being assured of sanctification were some themes here.

[47] Carrie Judd Montgomery, 'Believing and Receiving', *TF* 14.5 (May 1894), pp. 98-100.

[48] Judd, 'A Convention for Christian Life, Divine Healing, Evangelistic and Missionary Work', p. 240.

[49] Montgomery, 'Cazadero Camp Meeting', p. 216.

enced Carrie, also emphasized empowerment for service in his 1895 book *The Baptism of the Holy Spirit* when he said,

> [T]he Baptism with the Spirit is not intended to make us happy but to make us effective. We should not look and long for ecstatic experiences, but for power and efficiency from God. The Baptism with the Holy Spirit is not even primarily for the purpose of cleansing from sin, but for the purpose of empowerment.[50]

Greatly influencing Keswick theology, he saw the primary purpose of Spirit baptism was for empowerment. While Carrie also held a similar view, she did not remain exclusive to that.

6.2.2 Power and Eradication

In 1903, Carrie mentioned a secondary purpose of Spirit baptism as having a ridding effect of sin. In relation to a hardness of heart in believing God and His miracles, she wrote, 'Praise God that the Pentecostal baptism of the Holy Spirit is able to remove this unbelief and hardness of heart' from the disciples' lives.[51] At this time for Carrie, one of the additional purposes of Spirit baptism was not to suppress sins, unbelief, or other hindrances but rather to eradicate, remove, and bring a softening of the heart. Her association with the Salvation Army may have influenced her in this way. While this does not represent her primary take on Spirit baptism, this view fit more in line with the Wesleyan-Holiness view of sanctification and Spirit baptism than it did with the Keswick view.[52]

6.2.3 Power from on High

Heading towards early Pentecostalism, some saw Spirit baptism as providing an 'enduement of power', a means of bearing more fruit

---

[50] R.A. Torrey, *The Baptism with the Holy Spirit* (New York: Fleming H. Revell Company, 1895), pp. 14-15. See R.A. Torrey, 'How a Sceptic Became a Believer', *TF* 24.12 (Dec 1904), pp. 273-74; 'The Message of the Earthquake', an extract from a sermon given by R.A. Torrey in Philadelphia, *TF* 26.4 (April 1906), p. 92; and his 'Hindrances to Prayer', *TF* 49.7 (July 1929), pp. 151-55.

[51] Carrie Judd Montgomery, 'A Hardened Heart', *TF* 23.8 (Aug 1903), p. 170, and in reference to passage by Mk 3.5 when Jesus was grieved at the hardness of people's hearts toward the man with the withered hand being healed.

[52] Carrie printed an article that varied in views. See Author unknown, *TF* 29.3 (March 1909), p. 60 said that 'Sanctification means more than eradication, or suppression of the old nature; it is death and resurrection. The believer's death to the old life in Adam, and his resurrection to the new life in Christ'.

in Christ, or a way towards increased holiness. Minnie Abrams, who influenced Carrie's thinking, wrote in 1906 that Spirit baptism empowered people to be effective witnesses for Christ. She questioned her readers by saying,

> Are you able to give witness day by day in your daily life, and by your words, of Jesus' power to save? If not, then you need to be empowered by the baptism of the Holy Ghost and fire to live a victorious life, and to obey the command to Jesus to make disciples.[53]

Abrams also wrote that Peter became a bold witness for Christ only after Pentecost. Before Acts 1.8, she said that Peter was a 'coward', but afterwards, he was a courageous witness for Christ. For Abrams, there was a new authority and power for preaching God's word in those who had received their Spirit baptism. She continued on, 'Let us seek the fulness of the baptism of the Holy Ghost and fire, that we may serve God acceptably, and have power to witness, and to win souls for Christ'.[54] Finney's earlier emphasis on power additionally contributed to Carrie's views as she printed several of his articles in relation to this theme, one entitled 'Power from on High'.[55]

Even before Carrie had her 1908 Spirit baptism experience, she observed its purpose played out in other's lives. While in Los Angeles in 1907, Carrie heard of Mrs Marshall's account and asked her to write it for the periodical. Carrie introduced the article by saying

---

[53] Minnie F. Abrams, *The Baptism of the Holy Ghost and Fire* (Kedgaon: Pandita Ramabai Mukti Mission, 1906), pp. 1-4, 11. When this book was first published in April 1906 there was no mention of speaking in tongues. In her December 1906 edition, however, she included a section on it. At that point, people in India were already speaking in tongues, and she had also read accounts from Azusa Street. See Robeck, *The Azusa Street Mission and Revival*, p. 253. For more on Abrams, see Gary B. McGee, 'Baptism of the Holy Ghost and Fire! The Revival Legacy of Minnie F. Abrams', *The Enrichment Journal* (Springfield, MO: The General Council of the Assemblies of God, 2011). Note that Carrie met Abrams a few years after this book was published.

[54] Minnie F. Abrams, *The Baptism of the Holy Ghost and Fire*, pp. 9, 10, 45.

[55] Montgomery, 'The God that Answereth by Fire', p. 220. In this article, Carrie includes a quote by Finney in reference to the need for true repentance in relation to revival. See Finney's 'Power from on High', *TF* 26.10 (Nov 1906), pp. 217-20; and 'The Baptism of the Holy Ghost', in *TF* 30.10 (Oct 1910), pp. 226-29. See also H. Ray Dunning, 'A Wesleyan Perspective on Spirit Baptism', in Chad Owen Brand (ed.), *Perspectives on Spirit Baptism: Five Views* (Nashville: Broadman and Holman Publishers, 2004), p. 206.

that Marshall and her daughter 'became convinced there was a greater spiritual fulness for them, and taking hold of God's promises they claimed the baptism of the Holy Spirit by faith'. Following this, Marshall wrote that shortly after her tongues experience, she cast out a 'devil' from her neighbor 'and it was done by and through the power of the Holy Ghost in the name of Jesus'.[56] The immediate effect of the Pentecostal Spirit baptism for Marshall was that she moved in power like she never had before. This account likely stirred up questions for Carrie as she was being drawn to seek the Pentecostal experience for herself at that time. With healing, Carrie saw that one was freed from bondage and from the oppression of the 'enemy' so that one could serve Him.[57] With Spirit baptism however, one was not necessarily freed from anything but rather filled, receiving an 'enduement' of power from on high for service. Power themes were already integrated into Carrie's view. How her view further developed following her 1908 experience will be demonstrated below.

6.2.4 Power for Witnessing

By 1917, Carrie added to the purpose behind Spirit baptism to be 'endued with power for witnessing'.[58] Note that after 1908, Carrie spoke about Spirit baptism through a Pentecostal paradigm which meant that the manifestation of tongues was readily associated with it. At this time, she saw that Spirit baptism was for service specifically tied to mission and to Acts 1.8 in relation to being witnesses. By 1918, when referring to Acts 2.1-4, Carrie went so far as to write, 'Why did God send His Spirit in Pentecostal power? That they might be witnesses unto the power of the risen Christ, and when you want the baptism of the Holy Ghost for this purpose, you will receive'.[59] Was she implying that if that was not their sole purpose, then they would not receive it? That is a possibility since she saw that if Christians failed to be faithful witnesses and serve God, then their Pentecostal blessing could fade away. She demon-

---

[56] Carrie Judd Montgomery, 'Deliverance of an Insane Sister', *TF* 27.1 (Jan 1907), pp. 11-13.

[57] Montgomery, 'Freed to Serve', pp. 145-46.

[58] Carrie Judd Montgomery, 'Endued with Power for Witnessing', *TF* 37.10 (Oct 1917), pp. 217-21. Even before this Carrie referred to the fullness of the Spirit and 'Pentecostal power' in Carrie Judd Montgomery, '"The Latter Rain"', *TF* 34.1 (Jan 1914), p. 5.

[59] Montgomery, 'The God That Answereth by Fire', p. 221.

strated this in 1920 when she wrote about the purpose of receiving the Holy Spirit in relation to Acts 1.8, 4.33, and Lk. 24.29 saying,

> Thus we see that God's great purpose in sending the Holy Ghost was to raise up witnesses who would testify of Christ. After we have received the Holy Spirit in Pentecostal power, we must be faithful witnesses, letting the streams of living water ever flow through us for the salvation and blessing of men, or the waters will fail to flow and we shall be set aside from His service with only a memory of past blessing, and no liberty or fresh anointing in our lives.[60]

Just as if people stopped walking in their faith for healing, they might lose it, so it was imperative that they be faithful witnesses to allow the Spirit to freely flow in their lives or else the flow might be cut off.

6.2.5 Analysis

Before Carrie's 1908 experience, she mainly saw that the purpose of Spirit baptism was empowerment for service (influenced from the Reformed and Keswick Holiness views) with hints of eradication included (a Wesleyan influence). Following her own Pentecostal Spirit baptism and in congruency with others during that time, she placed more emphasis on the purpose being empowerment to witness. Her immediate international ministry trip following her 1908 experience reveals this development put forth into action. The main thread that was integrated throughout Carrie's development of the purpose of Spirit baptism from the Holiness and into the Pentecostal Movement regularly included some aspect of power. As the purpose of Spirit baptism has been laid out, a look at the fruits of the experience now follow.

6.3 Development of Carrie's View of Speaking in Tongues

6.3.1 'Tongues of Fire'

Even before her 1908 experience, as early as 1892, Carrie wrote about 'tongues of fire' when referencing Rev. B. Fay Mills' talk on

---

[60] Carrie Judd Montgomery, 'A Letter from the Editor', *TF* 40.5 (May 1920), p. 115.

Pentecostal baptism at a prayer meeting she attended. According to Mills, God was preparing people for the 'in-filling of the Spirit', and his mention of 'tongues of fire' was in reference to the power of the Holy Spirit in ministry. This talk was given at a Salvation Army prayer meeting where they prayed to see revival and 'a wave of salvation' shake the city of San Francisco. The connections between prayer, revival, Pentecostal baptism, tongues of fire as 'illustrative of the power of the Holy Ghost', and the filling of the Spirit were all things that were familiar to Carrie before her own 1908 experience.[61]

As Pentecostal themes at Pandita Ramabai's orphanage in India and at Azusa Street became more prominent, Carrie began to allow articles in relation to tongues be printed in her periodical.[62] Still before her own experience, Carrie printed a letter by Frank Bartleman about the manifestation of tongues. She introduced his letter by encouraging people to humbly consider what God might want 'to pour out on His children'.[63] Bartleman's letter followed where he said, 'Hitherto I have been led to say but little regarding the "tongues," for there is always danger at such a time as this of diverting the attention from the great Giver to the gift, nor do I intend now to unduly exalt them'.[64] By early 1907, in relation to her trip to Los Angeles, Carrie commented on a meeting in Pasadena where she noticed 'the quiet but powerful manifestations of the Spirit of God in the speaking with tongues, and interpretations of the messages'.[65] Carrie later invited a friend to share her experience of the baptism of the Holy Spirit with the manifestation of tongues for

---

[61] Montgomery, 'The Work and the Workers', *TF* 12.9, pp. 211-12.

[62] B.S. Taylor, 'Work at the Altar', *TF* 24.4 (April 1904), pp. 85-88, taken from the *Christian Standard*. He writes about Acts 19 and being filled with the Holy Ghost and speaking in tongues.

[63] Carrie Judd Montgomery, 'Letter from Los Angeles', *TF* 26.12 (Dec 1906), p. 247. This is an extract 'from a remarkable letter from Frank Bartleman' that was earlier published in the *Way of Faith*. She may have felt at liberty to print his letter because her husband had brought back a good report of Azusa Street.

[64] Frank Bartleman, 'Letter from Los Angeles', *TF* 26.12 (Dec 1906), p. 248. He also wrote of an account of a 'colored woman' who spoke in perfect German when she spoke in tongues though this woman did not speak any German herself. He claimed that this instance caused some skeptics to be more open to this manifestation.

[65] Carrie Judd Montgomery, 'The Work in Los Angeles', *TF* 27.1 (Jan 1907), p. 14. She wrote that sweet unity was present but also cautioned against the devil's counterfeits.

Triumphs of Faith.[66] That same year Carrie printed an excerpt that celebrated the conversion of a 'Hindoo' man. The unknown author wrote that after his conversion, he 'received the baptism of the Holy Spirit and the English language was given him instantly, when before this he had "only known enough English to ask for something to eat." [Carrie responded by saying] Praise God for this new evidence of the "latter rain"'.[67] Carrie began to print things like this more consistently in her periodical which demonstrates that even before she spoke in tongues, while still cautious, she was open to discovering more about the manifestation. She claimed that she did not want to miss out on any of the 'blessing' God wanted to pour out in her day.[68]

All the way up to her May 1908 edition of *Triumphs of Faith*, Carrie printed testimonies of people who had their Pentecostal Spirit baptism experiences and spoke in new tongues; many of these reports came from overseas.[69] She printed articles in support of the manifestations of tongues as well as ones more skeptical of it.[70] Carrie also mentioned several of her friends in whom she noticed an increase in 'intercessory prayer', 'a baptism of divine love', and 'depths of sweetness, humility and power' evident in their lives since they had received their new language. During Carrie's searching time, even while she wanted her focus to be on seeking God rather than seeking the manifestations, she admitted that she 'kept on tarrying at His feet for the manifestation of His gracious presence'.[71]

---

[66] Mrs Belle Marshall, 'Deliverance of an Insane Sister', *TF* 27.1 (Jan 1907), pp. 11-13.

[67] *TF* 27.5 (May 1907), p. 105.

[68] Carrie Judd Montgomery, 'Letter from Los Angeles', *TF* 26.12 (Dec 1906), p. 247.

[69] Pandita Ramabai, 'Showers of Blessing', *TF* 27.12 (Dec 1907), pp. 267-69; Cecil Polhill's 'This is That', Mrs Gustava Selander's 'A Sister's Experience', and Bertha Pinkham Dixon's 'The Latter Rain" in *TF* 28.5 (May 1908), pp. 100-104, are other examples of this.

[70] B.H. Irwin, 'My Pentecostal Baptism, A Christmas Gift', *TF* 27.5 (May 1907), p. 114, A.S. Worrell, 'The Pentecostal Movement in Los Angeles', *TF* 27.8 (Aug 1907), pp. 179-81, taken from the *Gospel Witness* and his 'An Open Letter to the Opposers [sic] of this Pentecostal Movement', *TF* 27.11 (Nov 1907), p. 249.

[71] Carrie Judd Montgomery, '"The Promise of the Father." A Personal Testimony', *TF* 28.7 (July 1908), pp. 146-47. See Appendix 4.

6.3.2 Narrowing Down the Date of her True Pentecostal Spirit Baptism Experience

The defining moment when Carrie believed she had her *full* Spirit baptism experience is important because it sheds light onto how she viewed tongues at that time. A week before Carrie received the manifestation of tongues, she had an intense spiritual experience while praying with some friends in Cleveland. She claimed that she 'took' her Spirit baptism by faith even though the manifestation of tongues did not follow at that time.[72] For the several days following her experience in Cleveland, she believed that she had experienced her Pentecostal Spirit baptism even though there were no manifestations. Roughly a week later however, she had another experience after Lucy E. Simmons prayed for her; this resulted in her speaking in tongues for the first time. Not too long after this, she narrowed down the date of her Pentecostal Spirit baptism experience and tied it to the same date she spoke in tongues (June 29, 1908) rather than the time of her intense experience a week before.[73] She did a similar thing with her 1908 experience as she did with healing. She took them both by faith but then celebrated the date of the fullness of either her healing or Pentecostal Spirit baptism experience as the time when she experienced the actual manifestations of it.

Before 1908, Carrie often referred to 'fullness' in terms of receiving more of the Spirit. After 1908 however, she began to relate it more specifically to the manifestation of tongues that many times accompanied one's Pentecostal baptism.[74] How she approached this topic as her husband sought this manifestation illustrates this further. In September of 1908, she wrote that 'the cloud of blessing which has been rising for several weeks in answer to special prayer has now broken over Beulah, and several of our Orphanage children have received the baptism of the Holy Spirit, and God has been singing and speaking through them in tongues'. Further, she recounted,

---

[72] See Chapter 3.3.3 for full account.

[73] Montgomery, '"The Promise of the Father." A Personal Testimony', p. 148. Carrie Judd Montgomery, 'A Year with the Comforter', pp. 145-49.

[74] Montgomery, '"The Promise of the Father." A Personal Testimony', p. 146. She referred to one who 'received the fullness' of their Pentecostal Spirit baptism as one who also received the manifestation of tongues.

Eight of these children voluntarily laid hands on Mr. Montgomery's head that he might receive a greater fullness of the Holy Spirit. He had lately received his Pentecostal baptism, but not in the fullness which he desired. These children were all praying most fervently in different languages, as the Spirit gave utterance to each.[75]

At that time, Carrie wrote that her husband had already received his 'Pentecostal baptism' but not in its fullness (referring to the manifestation of tongues). She did not discount her husband's experience here, but she did believe that there was still more and that with the manifestation of tongues, his Spirit baptism would be 'full'. As an aside, George did receive the manifestation of tongues, entering into 'the fullness which he desired' not too long after Carrie's experience.[76]

These examples in 1908 demonstrate that during this time in her life, Carrie believed that even without the manifestation of tongues, people still could have had their Pentecostal Spirit baptism experience, just not in its fullest measure. For people to receive the 'fullness' of their Pentecostal Spirit baptism, it needed to be accompanied with the manifestation of tongues. Once a person had both the experience and the manifestation tongues, even if the gap between those was a week or even longer, Carrie believed that was when they had received their full Pentecostal baptism. At this time in her life, the sign of tongues measured the fullness of one's Pentecostal baptism experience rather than validated it.

---

[75] Carrie Judd Montgomery, 'Pentecostal Outpouring at Beulah', *TF* 28.9 (Sept 1908), pp. 195-96. In 'Going East', Carrie mentions 'Our dear friend, Mr. S. R. Break, has recently received the Pentecostal fullness of the Spirit, and speaks with tongues, magnifying God'. Tongues was still a part of the Pentecostal fullness here. In another article entitled 'A Precious "Latter Rain" Worker', Carrie went on to write how Sister Daniels helped lead many children at the orphanage 'into the fullness' as well as had 'marked results and great outpouring of the Spirit of God' in several meetings she did in Oakland.

[76] Carrie recalled that 'Not long after my return from the East my dear husband also received this blessed outpouring' (Montgomery, *Under His Wings*, p. 170). See also Carrie Judd Montgomery, 'Recent Trip to Mexico', *TF* 33.12 (Dec 1913), p. 271. It was likely in the late summer of 1908 when George had received the manifestation of tongues. Once while in Mexico, George spoke out in tongues and someone there who spoke Chinese could understand him. See Carrie Judd Montgomery, 'Letter from Mrs. Montgomery', *TF* 29.8 (Aug 1909), p. 176.

6.3.3 Re-interpreting her Healing in light of her 1908 Experience

Leading up to the twentieth century, Carrie believed that she had already had her Spirit baptism experience at the time of her earlier healing. Shortly after her 1908 experience however, she re-adjusted her previous understanding and through her newer Pentecostal lens, reflected,

> For some time I have been thirsting for the fullness of the Holy Spirit's presence and power. At the time of my miraculous healing, when a young girl, I was first made conscious of the Holy Spirit's work in revealing Jesus in and to me. At this time a power to testify came into my soul, and the Word of God was wonderfully opened to me, so that He has greatly blessed my ministry in the Word since that time. This experience I have always referred to as the baptism of the Holy Ghost until a few months ago, when I began to watch what God was doing in pouring out His Pentecostal fullness upon some of His little ones. At first I was perplexed. I knew my experience, above referred to, was most real and lasting in its effects. How could I cast it away? Then I came to understand that I was not to depreciate His precious work in the past, but to follow on to receive the fullness of the same Spirit. Before Pentecost Jesus 'breathed on His disciples and saith unto them "Receive ye the Holy Ghost" (John xx:22).' I believe they then received a foretaste, or earnest, of what they afterwards received in fullness at Pentecost.[77]

While Carrie previously associated her healing with Spirit baptism, following her 1908 tongues experience, she no longer connected the two in that way. Instead, she re-interpreted her healing account as just one portion of the Spirit's fullness for her life.

Further, Carrie also re-interpreted her experiences of the Spirit before her 1908 experience by saying they were 'tiny streams' but not yet 'rivers'.[78] She believed that her Pentecostal experience was

---

[77] See Appendix 4 for full article. Montgomery, '"The Promise of the Father." A Personal Testimony', pp. 145-46.

[78] Montgomery, '"The Promise of the Father." A Personal Testimony'. See also Carrie Judd Montgomery, 'Miraculously Healed by the Lord Thirty Years Ago', *LRE* 2.1 (Oct. 1909), p. 8, where she described measures of hunger in relation to her experiences with the Spirit: 'I came to the place a few years after my healing

the 'fullness of the Holy Ghost' similar to what the disciples experienced at Pentecost.[79] One might wonder if the only difference between her Pentecostal Spirit baptism and all her previous 'baptisms' was the reception of tongues. If it was not for the impinging Pentecostal perspective all around her, it is a possibility that she may not have even named her 1908 experience as being her full Spirit baptism. Instead, she may have just seen it as yet another significant intersection with the Spirit or another one of her many 'Spirit baptisms' as she had in years past. Regardless, after her 1908 experience, she immediately claimed to feel empowered and satisfied by God in a way that she had not yet experienced before, referring to that experience as her 'fuller baptism'.[80] The measure of the Spirit that Carrie claimed to experience then was greater than any of her previous Spirit 'baptisms'.[81]

6.3.4 Foreign Languages

Many people during Carrie's time claimed to speak in a foreign language when they spoke in tongues so it is not surprising that when she finally received the manifestation in 1908, she claimed to speak in Chinese and Mandarin.[82] Later in 1914, a missionary from Pales-

---

where I was looking out for more of God; but now, after a few years comes a greater cry, a longing cry that might be filled with all the fullness of God'.

[79] Montgomery, '"The Promise of the Father." A Personal Testimony', p. 145.

[80] In one sermon, she said,

I cannot begin to tell you what God has done in my mind since I have had this fuller baptism of the Holy Ghost ... This is a part of the life on wings. In all the many years of blessedness before this fuller baptism, I did not know what I am talking about now, this freedom of the mind from all care; of course, I had a great deal of blessing and a great deal of freedom from care, and felt that God had guided me and blessed me wonderfully, but I didn't know what I am talking about now. Now I feel that the Holy Spirit holds my brain just as He does the rest of my being, but it is just as loving and tender as it is strong. (Montgomery, 'The Life on Wings', p. 174)

See also Montgomery, 'A Year with the Comforter', pp. 145-49.

[81] Montgomery, 'Miraculously Healed by the Lord Thirty Years Ago', p. 10 and section in *TF* 28.7 (July 1908), p. 145. She added that it felt like her 'head went under ... The cry in my heart became satisfied, and I have been satisfied ever since ... I do not know what it is to thirst, the source of supply meets me every instant'.

[82] Carrie Judd Montgomery, 'Speaking in Tongues (A Personal Testimony)', *TF* 30.11 (Nov 1910), pp. 253-55, and *Under His Wings*, p. 169. See also 'With Christ', *PE* (August 17, 1946), p. 7, where the author wrote that when Carrie was in Ohio at a camp meeting sharing a room with Harriette Shimer, a missionary to China, she began to sing in tongues and what came out was a Chinese dialect. Mrs Shimer could only speak Mandarin and Carrie was apparently speaking in

tine asked Carrie to join with her in prayer for the girls at her school. Carrie recalled that the 'Holy Spirit presently prayed through me fervently in other tongues'.[83] When they were done praying, the missionary was surprised because she had heard Carrie pray in Arabic and in Turkish. Additionally, it was recorded that Carrie prayed in tongues over Mary Norton in another known language.[84] Some early Pentecostals believed that because they spoke in a foreign language when speaking in tongues, that God was leading them to be a missionary to that land and that He would enable them to speak the new language upon arrival.[85] However, that Carrie studied Chinese before going to China and also took Spanish lessons demonstrates that she did not rely upon the manifestation of tongues to enable her to speak foreign languages.[86]

6.3.5 Proper Use

While one of Carrie's main New Testament healing texts came from the book of James, it was primarily Paul's writings that she relied on to understand and interpret tongues. She also distinguished between tongues used for the assembly and tongues which were used on a more personal level.[87] Shortly after her own experience in 1908, she referred to 1 Corinthians 14 and shared how Paul had exhorted the Church not to forbid the personal use of tongues because one was

---

other dialects. When Carrie was made aware of this she is reported to have said 'I will ask the Lord to let me speak in Mandarin'. The next day during the meeting Carrie sang in Mandarin where Mrs Shimer interpreted. Twice though, the 'Lord gave Sister Montgomery the interpretation before Mrs. Shimer could translate what she said, and in each instance the interpretation was verified by Mrs. Shimer'.

[83] Carrie Judd Montgomery, '"The Latter Rain"', p. 3. The missionary told Carrie that it takes weeks for people to learn how to say 'Jesus' in Arabic when they come out to the mission field, yet she said that Carrie did it easily when she prayed.

[84] Stanely Frodsham, 'Abiding Under God's Shadow', and Mary Norton, 'Returning to India', *TF* 37.10 (Oct 1917), pp. 231-32.

[85] See Anderson, *Spreading Fires*, where this theme comes up throughout his book.

[86] It appears that Carrie may have spoken more with 'Xenolalia (i.e., known tongues [languages] recognized by hearers)' than 'Glossolalia ("unknown" tongues)'. See McGee, 'Baptism of the Holy Ghost and Fire!' where he distinguishes between the two types of languages. See also Mark J. Cartledge, *Encountering the Spirit: The Charismatic Tradition* (London: Darton, Longman and Todd Ltd., 2006) for more in relation to speaking in tongues.

[87] Because speaking in tongues was a newer thing during her time, terms surrounding it got interchanged and there was not precision when speaking about it.

speaking mysteries to God and also 'edifieth himself'.[88] She further wrote that 'the Word of God tells us that when we speak in an unknown tongue we speak unto God, and that we speak "mysteries". We are also told that when we speak in tongues (between God and ourselves) we are edified, or built up, even when there is no interpretation'.[89] Carrie additionally explained that using tongues in the assembly must be accompanied with an interpretation. She believed that God was 'not the author of confusion, but of peace (1 Corinthians 14:33)' and that there were guidelines when speaking out in tongues in the context of a public community.[90] To stay true to her understanding of this, occasionally when Carrie did speak out in tongues in a gathering, it was recorded that there was also an interpretation following.[91] According to Carrie's interpretation of Pauline literature, this was the correct order of things.

Dealing with Excess

Even after speaking in tongues for the first time, Carrie believed that too many overemphasized it. She complained that she had heard of services where tongues were given publicly and not followed with interpretations, and also that some churches were failing to manage this gift well.[92] She warned that no matter how wonderful the manifestations become, 'if we get our eyes upon these instead of upon Himself and His glorious redemption they will

---

[88] Montgomery, '"The Promise of the Father." A Personal Testimony', p. 146.

[89] Carrie Judd Montgomery, 'Our Bodies Preserved Blameless Unto His Coming', *TF* 37.8 (Aug 1917), p. 172. She followed this with a reference to 1 Cor. 14.2-4.

[90] Montgomery, '"The Promise of the Father." A Personal Testimony', p. 146.

[91] Carrie Judd Montgomery and letter from a friend, 'Life at the Home of Peace', *TF* 32.1 (Jan 1912), p. 15. Carrie's friend said that Carrie had, up to this time, only been 'led to speak in public meetings in tongues twice, and each time with interpretation'. See also 'With Christ', *PE* (August 17, 1946), p. 7.

[92] Montgomery, '"The Promise of the Father." A Personal Testimony', p. 146. Carrie's view of tongues appears to be two-fold. She recognized that there was the gift, or manifestation of tongues that usually came following one's Spirit baptism and was for personal use and edification. She also recognized the gift of tongues that was for the edification of the Church and administered in the public assembly. Her understanding was that when tongues was administered in this way that it must be accompanied by an interpretation; when used at a personal level, no interpretation was necessary. The language she used to describe the tongues that came after one's Spirit baptism was not precise and included terms such as sign, manifestation, and gift all to describe the same thing of one's personal new spiritual tongues.

cease'.[93] Carrie did not necessarily have a problem with tongues, but had more of an issue with the fanaticism and misuse in the Church. Because of this, she regularly sought balance. She celebrated one 'lady' to her readers because 'she spoke in tongues, but kept the gift in its proper place'.[94] Likely in part as a response to the 'misuse' of the public use of tongues in many churches, Carrie made sure to emphasize love as the cornerstone and crucial thing to have over and above tongues.

Instructions

Similar to her approach to healing, Carrie believed there was a spiritual posture people could adopt in order to better receive their 'new tongues'. She said that if one desired to be a witness for Christ and sought Spirit baptism, they might not immediately see a result, but as they continued trusting, God would give them 'fruit, and fruit that shall remain'.[95] In relation to Jn 7.39 about Jesus not yet being glorified because the Holy Spirit had not yet been given, she said that 'as this was true dispensationally, it is also true of us individually. When Christ is not fully enthroned in us, we cannot receive the baptism of the Holy Ghost'. She continued to instruct that if people take 'the mind of Christ' and fall 'into His arms', then He will 'baptize them in His Spirit'.[96] Carrie also mentioned that people could receive their Pentecostal Spirit baptism much sooner 'if they forget themselves and begin to glorify the Lord Jesus with the voice of praise … so first of all you must yield to Him your whole being to do His will and enthrone Him as your King'. She continued, 'As you forget yourself, and, are lost in praise to Jesus, He will baptize you with the Holy Ghost and fire, and give you "new tongues" with which to express the wondrous new adoration which will take possession of you'.[97] In a later article on this same theme she wrote that 'some people do not want the Pentecostal Baptism because they are not willing to let God take such complete control of their minds

---

[93] Carrie Judd Montgomery, 'Christ's Quickening Life for the Mortal Body', *TF* 28.8 (August 1908), p. 170.

[94] Montgomery, '"The Promise of the Father." A Personal Testimony', p. 146.

[95] Montgomery, 'The God That Answereth by Fire', p. 221. Notice her emphasis on fruit, not gifts.

[96] Carrie Judd Montgomery, 'The Promise of the Father', *TF* 37.1 (Jan 1917), pp. 2-3. See also her 'A Life of Triumph Through Praise', *TF* 37.3 (March 1917), p. 52.

[97] Montgomery, 'A Life of Triumph Through Praise', p. 52.

that He can talk through them in the unknown tongues'.[98] Forget-
ting oneself, letting go, getting lost in praise, completely surrender-
ing, and enthroning Him as King all contributed to one getting
closer to having their full Spirit baptism experience, which after
1908, Carrie regularly associated with the reception of tongues.

6.3.6 Tongues, Love, and Forming Doctrines

Early views in *Triumphs of Faith* (1907-1908)

As the movement continued to develop, early Pentecostals debated
whether the manifestation of tongues was one of several signs of
Spirit baptism or if it was the initial physical evidence of it. How
Carrie approached these conversations is important because it reveals the weight she placed on this manifestation in light of other
issues. Even before she spoke in tongues, Carrie printed varying
articles in relation to the forming doctrine. In 1907, B.H. Irwin proclaimed that not only does the baptism of the Holy Spirit include
speaking in tongues, but also that it is 'not simply the sign or evidence of the baptism, but a part of the divine baptism itself'.[99] A
few months later, an article by A.S. Worrell also appeared in her
periodical about the dangers in overemphasizing the 'gift of
tongues', when referring to using it in the assembly. He noticed that
no one was allowed to lead any of the Los Angeles meetings unless
they spoke in tongues. It was there that he observed how the 'gift of
tongues' had eclipsed all others and that Christian character had
been overlooked. His conclusion was that while there were many
counterfeits, there were also many good things happening at the
same time.[100] The following month, Carrie printed another article by
Worrell in defense of the Pentecostal Movement where he called
for a balanced view on the 'gift of tongues' that was regulated by
the Bible.[101]

---

[98] Montgomery, 'Our Bodies Preserved Blameless Unto His Coming', p. 170.

[99] Irwin, 'My Pentecostal Baptism, A Christmas Gift', p. 114.

[100] A.S. Worrell, 'The Pentecostal Movement in Los Angeles', *TF* 27.8 (Aug
1907), pp. 179-81, taken from the *Gospel Witness*. He said that 'The ability to speak
in some unknown tongue seems to inflate many with manifest pride, and cause
them to depreciate persons who may have a number of other gifts of the Spirit
far more valuable than the gift of tongues'.

[101] A.S. Worrell. 'An Open Letter to the Opposers of this Pentecostal Movement', *TF* 27.11 (Nov 1907), p. 249.

In the early days of the revival, several in Carrie's extended network rejected that the sign of tongues was the only evidence of the baptism of the Spirit. Minnie Abrams was one of these who wrote in *Triumphs of Faith* in 1908,

> It is true that a part of those who have received this Baptism with tongues claim that speaking in an unknown tongue is the only sign of the Baptism of the Holy Ghost, while others of us feel the unknown tongue is a sign of the Baptism of the Holy Ghost, but feel that while all may and should receive this sign, yet we dare not say that no one is Spirit baptized who has not received this sign.[102]

At this time, Abrams believed that regardless of what one believed, there still should be a shared sense of unity when working together to spread the Gospel. But what stance, if any, did Carrie take on the developing initial evidence doctrine that became prominent in many early Pentecostal circles of which she was a part, and at the same time was rejected by some of her close friends? As has already been shown, shortly after Carrie's own 1908 experience, she tied the manifestation of tongues closely to and in conjunction with her own *full* Spirit baptism experience. While early on Carrie connected the fullness of Spirit baptism with the manifestation of tongues, she made sure to emphasize that the most solid evidence of having the experience was love.[103] A further look at how her view developed will help to clarify the emphasis she put on tongues and where she stood in regards to the forming doctrine.

Unity in Love

One of Carrie's highest priorities was unity in love. This emphasis became a greater reality when she attempted to hold the middle ground and bring understanding between non-tongues speakers and those who had received the manifestation of tongues.[104] Carrie saw

---

[102] Minnie Abrams, 'India: A Message from Mukti' (Ramabai's Work), *TF* 28.11 (Nov 1908), pp. 260-61.

[103] Carrie Judd Montgomery, 'Pentecostal Conference, Sunderland, Eng.', *TF* 29.7 (July 1909), p. 152. Following a reference to Spirit baptism, many times she added 'and' or 'with' tongues in the same sentence as seen here: 'Many seeking the baptism of the Holy Spirit in Pentecostal fulness came into blessed liberty, and praised God in new tongues'.

[104] Carrie Judd Montgomery, 'The Oil and the Dew', *TF* 32.10 (Oct 1912), pp. 217-20. The article called for unity in love. Carrie wrote how this was possible

that tongues was profoundly beautiful in the life of the believer, but also realized that if one did not receive it, that did not invalidate their Christian faith, it only made it less full.[105] If she had taken any other stance, it likely would have put a strain on her friendships with people who had not received the manifestation of tongues. While she was passionate about sharing her experience and urging others to taste of God's highest and the 'marvelous manifestations of His grace and love', she also directed others not to judge those who had not yet received tongues.[106]

Without Love

In 1910, while recounting the end of her national trip, Carrie said that she had come across division in churches over the issue of tongues. In defending those who had not yet received this manifestation, Carrie wrote that the 'real test is Divine love;' without this love, even though people may speak in tongues, they 'become as sounding brass and a tinkling cymbal'. She went on to write that this lack of love was a reason that 'some of the "tongues" heard in these days are brassy and metallic and without the sweetness and benediction of the Spirit in them'. After she shared about this disillusionment in relation to tongues speakers, she narrowed in on what 'true tongues' really was when she said, 'Praise God for the true "tongues" of heavenly adoration proceeding from a heart filled with love to God and man, which glorify Him'.[107] For tongues to be

---

because at the Home of Peace, even when people have minor doctrinal issues, they dwelt together in love as one family. She also included articles by others who supported her view as in Ellen M. Winter, 'A Plea for the Love and Unity of the Spirit', *TF* 32.9 (Sept 1912), pp. 195-99. This article was based on 1 Corinthians 13 and called for unity in love between those who believed in tongues as initial evidence and those who did not. Another way in attempting to bring balance, Carrie also printed articles or letters by people who did not speak in tongues to give another perspective. See her 'Life at the Home of Peace', *TF* 32.1 (Jan 1912), pp. 12-16.

[105] This is evident in how she viewed her husband's pursuit of the manifestations. In relation to his full Spirit baptism, Carrie wrote that 'Eight of these children voluntarily laid hands on Mr. Montgomery's head that he might receive a greater fullness of the Holy Spirit. He had lately received his Pentecostal baptism, but not in the fullness which he desired. These children were all praying most fervently in different languages, as the Spirit gave utterance to each' (Carrie Judd Montgomery, 'Pentecostal Outpouring at Beulah', pp. 195-96). See also 6.3.2.

[106] Montgomery, 'A Year with the Comforter', p. 148.

[107] Carrie Judd Montgomery, 'Service for the King', *TF* 30.10 (Oct 1910), p. 220.

valid for Carrie, love had to be the foundation and the main 'fruit'. The primary lens she looked through to interpret tongues was 1 Corinthians 13 where Paul encouraged the Church to refocus on love.[108] She also wrote that 'while all the gifts [tongues was included here] of the Holy Ghost are most desirable and precious and useful, yet the main thing, the most mighty thing, which must be the foundation for every other equipment for service, is the love of God shed abroad in our hearts by the Holy Ghost'.[109] Years later she continued to emphasize that 'genuine tongues are always attended with the Divine love which is shed abroad in the heart by the Holy Spirit's indwelling'.[110] This love theme remained strong both before and after her Pentecostal baptism.

Fruit

For Carrie, proof that someone had a 'close union with God which comes with this Pentecostal baptism', was marked by humility, a deeper love, and a change in character.[111] She also said that 'the "Pentecostal" people are a very humble people if they have received the deep and real blessing of the "latter rain" fullness. And if any are not humble, there is surely something wrong with their experience'.[112] At this time in her life, tongues alone could not validate the fullness of the Spirit baptism experience for Carrie any longer; it also had to be accompanied by 'fruit'. In 1913, when Carrie was on a trip to Mexico she mentioned that five 'received the baptism of the Holy Ghost with the precious sign of speaking in tongues. When the Spirit came down in power upon the seeking ones, baptising them and filling them with wonderful joy' others were drawn

---

[108] Carrie also used Jas 3.13-18 as another grid in helping to discern if someone had a true Pentecostal Spirit baptism experience. See her 'Service for the King', *TF* 30.10 (Oct 1910), pp. 217-20, and 'Life at the Home of Peace', *TF* 32.1 (Jan 1912), pp. 12-16. See also her 'Together in Love', *TF* 28.9 (Sept 1908), pp. 193-95, and '"By This All Men Shall know"', *TF* 28.11 (Nov 1908), pp. 241-43.

[109] Montgomery, 'By This All Men Shall Know', p. 241. Included here are 'gifts of healing, miracles, gifts of tongues ...' See also Carrie Judd Montgomery, 'Knit Together In Love', *TF* 28.9 (September 1908), p. 193.

[110] Montgomery, 'The God That Answereth by Fire', pp. 220-21.

[111] Carrie Judd Montgomery, '"The Latter Rain"', p. 3. See also her 'The Work and Worker', *TF* 31.5 (May 1911), p. 118.

[112] Carrie Judd Montgomery, '"Pentecostal" Friends in Scotland and England', *TF* 29.8 (Aug 1909), p. 170. She was referring to the humility of Cecil Polhill here.

in to the meeting.[113] Speaking of joy in this account demonstrates that while Carrie saw tongues as a sign of Spirit baptism, to avoid excess and fanaticism, she quickly moved on from the possible signs that followed, to the fruit of the Spirit that should be evident in a person's life as a result.

The Sign of the Latter Rain (1914-1917)

Edith Blumhofer rightly notes that many early Pentecostals 'used the term *latter rain* to describe the 20th century outpouring of the Holy Spirit', putting weight on Joel 2.23 and Zech. 10.1 as key prophecies for this.[114] Carrie was no exception. In early 1914, she printed an article called 'The Latter Rain' where she explained that the 'early rain of the Holy Spirit' fell on the 120 who tarried in Jerusalem and it was during this time that 'there was a certain Sign manifested which has not been given before in all of Christ's miracles, and this was the speaking with other tongues as the Spirit gave utterance'. She went on to write that 'God has poured out His Spirit' on the earth in her day with the same 'wonderful Sign'. Carrie believed that those in her generation were experiencing the Latter Rain and were receiving the same sign as the 120 at Pentecost in the 'early rain'.[115] At this time in her life, Carrie saw that tongues was the sign of receiving the outpouring of the Spirit.

'The Promise of the Father' (1917)

In a 1917 article entitled 'The Promise of the Father', Carrie shared how she spoke in tongues for over an hour but also added,

> When you have the full baptism of the Holy Spirit you are satisfied; but do not rest satisfied merely with speaking in tongues,

---

[113] Carrie Judd Montgomery, 'Recent Trip to Mexico', *TF* 33.12 (Dec 1913), pp. 270-71. She also mentioned 'backsliders returning to the Lord' and people being 'blessedly saved'. This is likely the same meeting where Chonita Morgan Howard had her Pentecostal Spirit baptism which will be mentioned further in Chapter 7.

[114] Blumhofer, *The Assemblies of God*, p. 156.

[115] Carrie Judd Montgomery, '"The Latter Rain"', pp. 1-2. She based this on Jas 5.7 here: 'We cannot help but see that the mighty down-pouring of the rain of the Holy Spirit has been coming all over the world during the past few years. This chapter [James 5] clearly proves when is the time of the Latter Rain, and what will be occurring when it is due'. It must also be noted that in other articles Carrie did rely on the Joel passage in reference to these theme of Latter Rain. Cf. e.g. her 'The Outpouring of God's Spirit', *TF* 37.7 (July 1917), p. 145.

because in the last chapter of Mark we read 'these signs shall follow them that believe,' and speaking in new tongues is one of the signs that might follow any believer (who had faith for it), so one could speak in tongues without receiving the baptism of the Holy Spirit. Do not be satisfied until you have the indwelling Spirit HIMSELF as a witness. You will not need any human being to tell you that you are filled. His blessed Presence will permeate your whole being, and you will continually feast upon Christ in adoring love.[116]

This passage touches on several significant themes. First, it shows that at this time Carrie saw 'full baptism' with speaking in tongues as lacking until one was fully satisfied with 'the indwelling Spirit HIMSELF as a witness'. Speaking in tongues was not the end or stopping point, but rather another means to connect with God at a deeper level; it was entering into additional extended measures of the Spirit's presence that would continually permeate one's whole being. This means that one could have had their Pentecostal Spirit baptism with speaking in tongues, but there was still even more of the fullness of the Spirit freely available for them. In this passage, Carrie moved beyond empowerment themes by also adding the element of intimacy. Second, Carrie saw that tongues could have been just *one* of the signs following Spirit baptism rather than the *only* sign. Third, she saw that there was the possibility that people could speak in tongues without having had their full baptism experience. This was likely written in reaction to those who spoke in tongues but who lacked love. Furthermore, for Carrie, added measures of the Spirit's love and presence superseded the popular manifestation of the Pentecostal Spirit baptism. Carrie saw that the indwelling Spirit continually abiding in one's life was even greater than speaking in tongues.[117] She believed that there would be a time

---

[116] Montgomery, 'The Promise of the Father', p. 5. In relation to the ten young virgins, Carrie implied earlier that those who neglected pursuing God for their Spirit baptism were like the five foolish virgins who did not have enough oil. Carrie's quote was similar to F.F. Bosworth's stance at that time. See Cecil M. Robeck, 'An Emerging Magisterium? The Case of the Assemblies of God', *Pneuma* 25.2 (Fall 2003), pp. 181-86.

[117] Albrecht agrees. In relation to this article he says that 'the baptized believer should be satisfied because the indwelling Spirit Himself abides continually to make the things of Christ more real' ('The Life and Ministry of Carrie Judd Montgomery', p. 151).

one day when people would be so overwhelmed by God's glory that even tongues would cease.[118]

Doctrinal Changes (1918)

As time went on and the doctrine of initial evidence was being further shaped, Fred F. Bosworth argued against it and decided to resign from his post as one of the leaders in the Assemblies of God just before the 1918 General Council.[119] It was at that meeting where the stamp of tongues as initial evidence became embedded for the Assemblies of God. A.B. Simpson also eventually concluded that the sign of tongues should not be the only thing that can be counted as 'initial evidence' of the baptism of the Holy Spirit.[120] In 1918, Carrie still wanted people to embrace tongues regardless of controversies and she cautioned people who did not understand 'other tongues' to be careful not to despise it when she said,

> [I]f God saw that [tongues] was good enough to attend the outpouring of the Spirit on the Day of Pentecost, are we too good to receive it now? Can we talk against this holy Sign, this manifestation of the Spirit, and be blameless? There are multitudes of God's dear saints all over the world today who have received this baptism, with the sign of speaking in tongues.[121]

Here she mentions tongues as *the* sign of Spirit baptism and shows how it is accessible to all. The lack of precision in Carrie's language was not uncommon during that time.

---

[118] Montgomery, 'The Life on Wing', pp. 175-76.

[119] Robeck, 'An Emerging Magisterium?' pp. 181-86, and Blumhofer, *The Assemblies of God*, p. 52. Interestingly enough, Bosworth was one of the few who went from the Assemblies of God to the CMA as a result of this decision; many of the other prominent leaders went the other way. See Paul King's *Genuine Gold: The Cautiously Charismatic Story of the Early Christian and Missionary Alliance* (Tulsa: Word & Spirit Press, 2006) for a comprehensive list.

[120] Charles Nienkirchen, 'Albert Benjamin Simpson' in *NIDPCM*, pp. 1069-70. Nienkirchen sees that Simpson charged that the 'initial evidence doctrine' brought a 'preoccupation with spiritual manifestations rather than cultivating a devotion to God'. A.B. Simpson also held to a four-fold gospel view (Christ as Savior, Sanctifier, Healer, and Coming King) in which Carrie was influenced. See her 'Letter from Mrs. Montgomery', *TF* 29.9 (September 1909), p. 207.

[121] Montgomery, 'The God That Answereth by Fire', pp. 220-21.

Under His Wings (1936)

In her autobiography, Carrie remembered that while in Los Angeles in 1911, she believed that God had led her to start a weekly healing meeting for 'all God's children' in Oakland to bring unity. She recalled,

> [A]t this time there did not exist as much harmony among the Lord's children in Oakland as we felt there should be, misunderstandings often coming up between different assemblies and groups of people, who believed alike on essentials but differed on non-essentials. I felt that the Lord wanted to unite all these dear ones in His own love.[122]

Unity in love was once again her emphasis. While it was not directly stated, the possibility exists that she could have been referring to the manifestation of tongues as 'non-essentials' here. Further in her 1936 autobiography, Carrie added an extra paragraph to the reprint of her 1917 article, 'The Promise of the Father', in which she stressed 1 Corinthians 13 and the importance of unity in love.[123] This is significant because it demonstrates that towards the end of her life, while she still greatly valued tongues, she saw unity in love and humility as the most essential aspects to focus on in relation the manifestation.

In Perspective

One thing that is prevalent in Carrie's practice over the years is that she regularly connected the fullness of one's Pentecostal Baptism with speaking in tongues. She did this when she associated the date of her own Spirit Fullness as the same time she received the manifestation of tongues. She also linked the two together in her husband's experience and in countless others. Additionally, she joined a denomination that put the two together.

---

[122] Montgomery, *Under His Wings*, p. 165.

[123] See Appendix 4. 'The 13th chapter of 1 Corinthians speaks of tongues of men and angels, but shows us that without divine love the people who speak are "become as sounding brass, or a tinkling cymbal." So let all who have this experience see that they keep low at the feet of Jesus, being filled with His own humility and love' (Montgomery, *Under His Wings,* p. 170).

In light of her 1908 experience, which also resonated with several other Assembly of God ministers of her time,[124] Carrie could agree with the General Council's fundamental statement at the time (1916) that 'the full consummation of the baptism of believers in the Holy Ghost is indicated by the initial physical sign of speaking with other tongues as the Spirit of God gives them utterance'.[125] And while Carrie did not use words such as 'initial physical sign' or evidence, she regularly associated the two together.

Another noticeable thing that emerged from this study is that while Carrie personally associated one's Spirit Fullness with tongues, her teaching was sometimes inconsistent with this. This is not surprising as her view was developing while the doctrine was forming. On the one hand, that she named the date of her full Spirit baptism as the same date that she spoke in tongues demonstrates that in practice, she connected Spirit baptism with the manifestation tongues in her own life. On the other hand, in her teachings, she inconsistently referred to the manifestation of tongues as 'the sign' and also as 'one of the signs' of Spirit baptism; at one point she even said that it was possible that people could speak in tongues without having had their Spirit baptism.[126]

Allan Anderson says that 'others like A.B. Simpson, Pandita Ramabai, Carrie Judd Montgomery, William H. Piper and some of the Holiness periodicals accepted that speaking tongues was one of the gifts the Spirit needed in the contemporary church, but that to

---

[124] Donald Gee's experience is very similar to Carrie's except that he recorded the date of his Spirit baptism as the intense experience he had two weeks before he spoke in tongues. Though Gee did not combine the date of his Spirit baptism and the date of his manifestation of tongues several weeks later, Carrie did for her experience. J. Roswell Flower also had a similar experience. See Robeck, 'An Emerging Magisterium?', p. 195.

[125] 'A Statement of Fundamental Truths Approved by the General Council of the Assemblies of God (October 2-7, 1916)' in the Combined Minutes of the General Council of the Assemblies of God in the United States of America, Canada and Foreign Lands- 1914-1920, p. 13. Article 6. 'The Full Consummation of the Baptism in the Holy Ghost', Accessed at <http://ifphc.org/DigitalPublications/USA/Assemblies%20of%20God%20USA/Minutes%20General%20Council/Unregistered/1920/FPHC/1914-1920.pdf>. '... Acts 2:4. This wonderful experience is distinct from and subsequent to the experience of the new birth, Acts 10:44-46 ; 11:14-16; 15:7-9. The speaking in tongues in this instance is the same in essence as the gift of tongues, 1 Cor. 12:4-10, 28, but different in purpose and use'.

[126] Montgomery, 'The Promise of the Father', p. 5.

insist on speaking in tongues as "necessary evidence" of Spirit baptism was unscriptural'.[127] While Carrie did not publicly make a statement that supports Anderson's assumptions and her practice differed, her 1917 article shows that, at the time, she broadened her view to see tongues as just 'one' of the potentially many signs of Spirit baptism.[128] This shows that there was some disconnect between Carrie's practice and her teaching on the subject of tongues.

In looking at the emphasis Carrie placed on tongues, while she signed papers in agreement with the fundamental truths of her denomination, she never publically advocated or promoted the doctrine of initial evidence. Her silence here suggests that the issue of initial evidence was something which she did not believe was important enough to try and convince others of and that it was a battle not worth fighting. Carrie regularly stayed away from issues that could cause unnecessary controversy and division and for her, unity in love took a higher priority than trying to prove if someone had experienced their Spirit baptism or not. While Carrie never publically tried to convert people to the 'doctrine of initial evidence', she did invite many to be baptized by the Spirit and to speak in tongues.

There are a few varying views in relation to the emphasis Carrie put on the doctrine of initial evidence that need to be weighed. J.N. Gortner, who received his Spirit baptism and spoke in tongues under Carrie's ministry and then later became a Pentecostal minister, gave a tribute at a Christian and Missionary Alliance church for Carrie's funeral in 1946. He said that 'as a natural result of her having received the baptism in the Spirit according to the original pattern, our sister became a firm believer that speaking in other tongues is the initial physical evidence of the baptism of the Holy Spirit. She stood firmly in this tenet of faith'.[129] However, Carrie's account of Spirit baptism did not fit the original pattern since she had an intense Spirit baptism-like experience a week before she actually received the manifestation of tongues. Additionally, the language of initial physical evidence is absent from Carrie's writings. While

---

[127] Anderson, *Spreading Fires*, p. 53 and taken from *Live Coals* 5.6 (Feb. 13, 1907), p. 2.

[128] Montgomery, 'The Promise of the Father', p. 5.

[129] J. Narver Gortner, 'Carrie Judd Montgomery – A Tribute' Eulogy: article comes from an 'address delivered at the funeral service of the late Carrie Judd Montgomery in the Christian and Missionary Alliance Tabernacle in Oakland, August 29, 1946'.

speaking in tongues became an important aspect of Carrie's spirituality and something she encouraged others towards, she was more concerned that people partook in all that God had for them rather than trying to prove if they had had their Spirit baptism experience or not. While Gortner highlighted this in Carrie's life, it was never something that she chose to emphasize. That Gortner received the manifestation of tongues under Carrie's ministry and was himself a public advocate of initial evidence likely contributed to him putting focus where Carrie otherwise would not. Another possible reason he highlighted this aspect of Carrie's spirituality might be because he was trying to challenge those from the Christian and Missionary Alliance who did not hold to the doctrine, while his denomination did.

Daniel Albrecht similarly states that eventually 'with her initial reservations satisfied, Carrie became an enthusiastic advocate for the doctrine of the baptism of the Holy Spirit with the accompanying sign of tongues'.[130] While in practice, Carrie inspired many people to have their 'full' Spirit Baptism experience and speak in tongues, she never became an advocate for the 'doctrine' of it; rather she wanted people to experience the fullness of the Spirit in every way that she had. While Carrie greatly valued tongues, she tended to put more emphasis on love (1 Corinthians 13). Throughout the years, unity in love between other believers and spiritual encounters with God were more important to her than 'doctrines'. It appears that she never pressed the issue in regards to the initial evidence doctrine because she saw that it could be at the expense of love being demonstrated more fully.

Possibly influenced through her strong connection with A.B. Simpson, who did not speak in tongues or embrace the doctrine, Carrie remained moderate in her public views in relation to initial evidence.[131] This position strengthened her ecumenical platform by allowing her to be inclusive to those who had not received the manifestation of tongues. Instead of getting caught up in debates over

---

[130] Daniel E. Albrecht, 'Carrie Judd Montgomery: Pioneering Contributor to Three Religious Movements', *Pneuma* 8.2 (Fall 1986), p. 111.

[131] G.B. McGee, 'Initial Evidence' in *NIDPCM*, pp. 784-91. Carrie also never separated herself from the A.B. Simpson and the C&MA even after these things took place. It is interesting though, that many left the C&MA and later became prominent leaders in the Assemblies of God because of their disagreement over this very doctrine.

initial evidence, she refused to become dogmatic in relation to the issue. While she did engage in other debates like the Oneness controversy,[132] her main concern in relation to the manifestation of tongues was not if it was the initial evidence or not, but that its greatest fruit was love. While Carrie picked and chose her battles throughout the years, one she fought strongly for was unity in love above all controversies.[133]

More important than the lack of public emphasis Carrie put on the doctrine of initial evidence is how she maneuvered through the debates surrounding the issue. Carrie invested her time more into bringing people into the fullness of their Pentecostal Spirit baptism than she did in engaging in what she realized were unnecessary battles.[134] This is one of Carrie's legacies. She gave honor to the movements that she was a part of, while at the same time did not enter into public debates with others over 'uncritical issues' where division rather than love was to be the likely outcome. In this way,

---

[132] D.A. Reed, 'Oneness Pentecostalism' in *NIDPCM*, pp. 936-44. The Jesus Only controversy emerged within Assemblies of God in 1914 before it split off and developed into Oneness Pentecostalism in 1917. Carrie tackled the Oneness controversy head on by directly disagreeing with while at the same time attempting to support her erring 'brothers' by 'standing' for them in intercession ('Perilous Times; and False Doctrines', *TF* 35.3 [March 1915], pp. 69-70). Beginning with 2 Tim. 3.1, Carrie refuted the baptism in Jesus Name argument as well as other new heresies of people who thought they were not saved until they were baptized and spoke in tongues. She wrote on the Trinity, 'See the marvelous oneness of the Trinity, and yet the distinct personality of the Father, Son and Holy Ghost', and about Jesus as the 'fulness of the Godhead bodily'. She later also wrote 'Spiritual Discernment Versus Judging' in *TF* 35.5 (May 1915), p. 99, which demonstrates the way in which she approached the issue.

[133] See Appendix 17 to see how Carrie's emphasis on unity in love resonates with Heidi Baker's present day ministry.

[134] See 'A Statement of Fundamental Truths Approved by the General Council of the Assemblies of God (October 2-7, 1916)' in the Combined Minutes of the General Council of the Assemblies of God in the United States of America, Canada and Foreign Lands- 1914-1920, p. 18. Accessed at <http://ifphc.org/DigitalPublications/USA/Assemblies%20of%20God%20USA/Minutes% 20General%20Council/Unregistered/1920/FPHC/1914-1920.pdf>. ADDENDA:

Our Distinctive Testimony. Courtesy. The resolution was adopted as follows: Resolved, That this Council considers it a serious disagreement with the Fundamentals for any minister among us to teach contrary to our distinctive testimony that the baptism of the Holy Spirit is regularly accompanied by the initial physical sign of speaking in other tongues as the Spirit of God gives the utterance, and that we consider it inconsistent and unscriptural for any minister to hold credentials with us who thus attacks as error our distinctive testimony.

she remained open and inclusive to a wide range of people, and through her spiritual, rather than dogmatic approach, introduced many to the Pentecostal Spirit baptism with the manifestation of tongues.

6.4 'Sanctification and Baptism of the Holy Spirit' through her Pentecostal Perspective

Carrie's emphasis on measures of the Spirit will now be explored within the development of her view of sanctification alongside Spirit baptism after 1908. Through her new Pentecostal perspective, Carrie's writing reveals that she believed Spirit baptism, which she also referred to at times as the 'fullness of the Spirit' or the 'glorious infilling of the Holy Ghost', helped people to experience extended measures of the Spirit beyond what they could without it.[135] In her 1911 article entitled 'Sanctification and the Baptism of the Holy Spirit', Carrie demonstrated the difference in measures between sanctification and Spirit baptism by beginning with Old Testament imagery. Referencing Lev. 14.1-18, she said that before the man with leprosy went to the priest, he was '"healed" but not "cleansed"'.[136] She connected this healing as only a measure of Christ's finished work.[137] She explained that even after healing, a person must still be purified and cleansed through the blood. She described that the anointing oil went on top of the blood and then

---

[135] Carrie Judd Montgomery, 'The Whole Body Full of Light', *TF* 29.8 (Aug 1909), p. 176. See also her 'The Work and the Workers', *TF* 31.5 (May 1911), p. 118. After her 1908 Spirit baptism experience, Carrie referred to Spirit baptism in a variety of ways: 'outpouring of the Spirit', people being 'filled with the Spirit', and even 'a gracious visitation of the Spirit'. See also her 'The Work of the Holy Spirit', *TF* 32.11 (Nov 1912), p. 244, where she says, 'How necessary then that we be filled with the Spirit, and having received Him, to recognize and honor His indwelling presence continually, that He may show us how to possess and use the glorious riches which are ours through the cross of Christ'. See also her '"Be Filled with the Spirit"', *TF* 29.9 (Sept 1909), pp. 193-95.

[136] Carrie Judd Montgomery, 'Sanctification and the Baptism of the Holy Spirit', *TF* 31.11 (Nov 1911), p. 241. Carrie likened leprosy to sin and referred to healing as a type of 'new birth'.

[137] Montgomery, 'Sanctification and the Baptism of the Holy Spirit', pp. 241-42. She said that 'here we see that all separation between the soul and God, caused by sin, must be bridged over by a further recognition of the atonement of the Lord Jesus Christ'. Further, Carrie referred to the leper's offerings (including washing, shaving off of hair, and complete separation from the camp) that followed as 'showing different aspects of Christ's full atonement for sin'.

the priest poured out the remaining oil all over the person receiving the cleansing. Further, she said,

> [I]t is a sad thought, in view of our glorious privilege in Christ, that it is possible for our faith to stop at some point along the way before all has been wrought out IN us, that Christ has wrought out FOR us. Many receive the touch of the blood that do not receive the anointing upon the blood, and many who have received the anointing do not realize that there is anything further for them.[138]

Carrie saw that beyond healing and sanctification, there was even more available through Christ's atonement for those who 'realize' this.

She continued with this theme by using the example of when Jesus breathed on His disciples after His resurrection (Jn 20.22) where she explained that 'without a doubt they then received a measure of the Holy Spirit which would answer to this anointing of oil upon the blood. We can see from this type in Leviticus, as well as from their experience afterwards on the day of Pentecost, that there was much more of the oil to follow'.[139] She said that the first breath of the Spirit brought joy and victory to the disciples but while

> this touch of the oil brings a certain amount of joy, praise and victory, but there is much more for them. How sad it would be for the cleansed leper to be content with that finger – dip of the oil, when the 'remnant of the oil' was waiting in the priest's hand to be poured upon the head of the cleansed leper. Exalted privilege – marvellous blessing – to receive not only a touch of the oil, not only a breath of the Holy Spirit from the risen Christ; but also to receive from Him 'the rest of the oil' (Leviticus xiv:29) not merely applied to us by His dear finger, but poured, actually POURED, upon our head (Leviticus xiv:18).[140]

Here Carrie interpreted sanctification as the first small touch of oil or the first breath of Jesus upon his disciples, and Pentecostal Spirit

---

[138] Montgomery, 'Sanctification and the Baptism of the Holy Spirit', p. 243.

[139] Montgomery, 'Sanctification and the Baptism of the Holy Spirit', pp. 243-44.

[140] Montgomery, 'Sanctification and the Baptism of the Holy Spirit', pp. 243-44.

baptism as the 'remnant of oil' to be poured out, or what happened
to the disciples at Pentecost. She further described that it is 'even
the cleansed leper whom He calls to this glorious blessing of cleansing, anointing and baptism of the Holy Spirit. "The rest of the oil"
is for each one, [will you] come in an attitude of childlike faith and
receptivity and let Him pour it upon you to your full joy and satisfaction, and to His glory'.[141] In light of the leper, Carrie believed
that regardless of if people had already been healed, cleansed, and
anointed or sanctified with a small touch, there was still a fuller expression of God's anointing to be poured out. This article is significant because it emphasizes her understanding of Spirit baptism as a
fuller *measure* of something that has already been given in small portions (sanctification being one of these).[142]

6.4.1 Beyond Stages and into Measures

Carrie continued on this same theme in 1911 with an article entitled
'The Remnant of the Oil'. Utilizing the example in Lk. 24 of the
two walking on the road to Emmaus, Carrie wrote that '"The
BETTER often stands in the way of receiving the BEST," and thus
it seems, as we talk with many of God's dear children; they have
already received such a blessed touch of Christ's resurrection life,
that they do not realize how much more is waiting for them'.[143] In
relation to the disciples' process of seeing Jesus more fully, she said
that at one time 'there came a still clearer manifestation of their res-
urrected Lord'.[144] The picture she painted was of a process of fuller
manifestation that came gradually in degrees and measures *and* additionally came in a divine moment of deeper revelation.

Carrie also believed that there were certain things that the Christian could do to be in a position to receive Spirit baptism and being
sanctified was one of those things.[145] If people were not 'truly

---

[141] Montgomery, 'Sanctification and the Baptism of the Holy Spirit', p. 244.

[142] It also shows that in addition to sanctification, healing was also seen as an
integral and necessary part of the Christian's life.

[143] Carrie Judd Montgomery, 'The Remnant of the Oil', *TF* 31.12 (Dec 1911),
p. 265.

[144] Montgomery, 'The Remnant of the Oil', p. 266 when referring to Lk.
24.33, 35.

[145] Albrecht, 'The Life and Ministry of Carrie Judd Montgomery', pp. 147-49.
He concludes that 'sanctification was a necessary part of baptism in the Spirit for
Carrie Judd Montgomery'. Quoting Carrie in 'The Promise of the Father', pp. 3,
5, he claims that Carrie believed that Spirit baptism came after sanctification in
light of her mentioning that the Spirit can not be poured out on 'carnal nature'.

cleansed and anointed', 'wholly surrendered', or if they 'lack[ed] complete obedience', they needed to remove their hindrances and then go to God in 'simple faith'.[146] If one was merely satisfied with the first touch (sanctification) and not hungry to receive the full outpouring (Spirit baptism), Carrie saw that this person was missing out on more.[147] She said of the leper in Leviticus 14 who already had the 'full atonement' made for him in the offerings and who had received the 'sanctified touch of the blood and oil;' that he

> was now by that very process in a position to receive 'the rest of the oil'; saved, sanctified, anointed, he does not make the mistake of considering the work complete, and therefore does not withdraw himself from the place of blessing. As we implied before, we would be robbed of the best if we remained satisfied with only the better portion.[148]

Additionally, it was the leper's responsibility 'not to go away satisfied with the partial blessing, but to wait for the larger inheritance which belonged to him, as much as the lesser'.[149] For Carrie, the question was always about *how much* of one's inheritance in Christ a person was willing to take hold of and *how much* of the 'fullness of the Spirit' one was willing to pursue.

Carrie further compared Jesus' breathing on His disciples as the 'first anointing of the Spirit'. This resulted in 'great joy', praise and worship for God. Carrie also carefully pointed out that all this happened 'BEFORE PENTECOST' and that there was even more of the 'fulness of the blessed Spirit' freely available to all who would

---

[146] Montgomery, 'The Remnant of the Oil', p. 268. She believed that the condition to receive the Pentecostal fullness changed from the disciple's need to tarry, to having faith according to Gal. 3.14. Notice the similarities here to how Carrie believed people should prepare themselves to receive healing. See Chapter 5.

[147] Montgomery, 'The Remnant of the Oil', p. 267. Pentecostal Spirit baptism contributed to keep the joy alive inside and without it, their joy might fade. She said,

> Oh, what hungry hearts we find everywhere as we go on about the Master's business! Hearts that have truly received an abundance of the Lord's grace, and even a touch of His glory; but because they have not gone the rest of the way in full obedience to His command, because they have not received that glorious PERSONAL HOLY GHOST, who was to keep them evermore from being orphaned or comfortless, their first rapturous joy has largely died away.

[148] Montgomery, 'The Remnant of the Oil', p. 267.
[149] Montgomery, 'The Remnant of the Oil', p. 267.

ask.[150] Regardless of the 'blessings' one had already experienced, including the cleansing of the blood and the touch of anointing oil, Carrie saw that there was still more. She did not want people to be content with just a small blessing, but she wanted them to continue on to partake of the limitless measures of the Spirit freely available.

Post-Pentecostal Spirit Baptism Experiences

Even beyond one's Pentecostal Spirit baptism experience, for Carrie, the possibility existed that even more intense subsequent experiences with the Spirit could come. In a message she gave in 1910, she admitted that earlier that same morning, her spirit, soul, and body was 'pervaded with His presence;' this was something so 'marvelous' that she could not even speak with tongues at that time. About this post-Pentecostal Spirit baptism experience, she said there are times 'when His presence is so all-pervading and the atmosphere so heavenly that I cannot talk at all in any language, but the power of His blessed Spirit upon me is so marvelous that it seems as though I were almost dwelling in heaven'.[151] This speaks of an experience that moves beyond mere 'fillings of the Spirit'. Her perspective is closer to being baptized or completely overwhelmed in the Spirit again. Her language in this article demonstrates that these like 'Spirit baptisms' or floodings of the Spirit were a continual part of her life even after her 1908 experience.[152]

---

[150] Montgomery, 'The Remnant of the Oil', p. 266. Her emphasis on Pentecost. She also wrote:

if you have received from the risen Lord the cleansing of blood, and the touch of oil, which the cleansed leper received in Leviticus 14, or, to put it in New Testament phrase, if you have had your eyes opened to see Jesus ... if you had deep peace and joy in His presence, and the glorious manifestation of His blessed person ... and yet if you have not, after all this, received the outpouring of the oil upon your head in the 'promise of the Father'; will you not ask Him here and now, not to let you miss the fulness of the blessed Spirit because of all the great spiritual blessings He has given you hitherto?

[151] Montgomery, 'The Life on Wings', pp. 175-76. 'Usually it is a blessed experience to be able to speak in tongues, to let the heavenly song flow out, but there are times when even tongues cease, when His presence is so all-pervading and the atmosphere so heavenly that I cannot talk at all in any language'.

[152] The following are a few of the articles in relation to this theme written by Carrie after her 1908 Spirit baptism experience: 'Christ's Quickening Life for the Mortal Body', *TF* 28.8 (Aug 1908), pp. 169-70; 'Pentecostal Outpouring at Beulah', pp. 195-96; 'The Quickening Life of the Indwelling Spirit', *TF* 28.10 (Oct 1908), pp. 217-19; 'Pentecostal Healing At Beulah', *TF* 28.10 (Oct 1908), pp. 229-30; 'A Year with the Comforter', pp. 145-49; '"Be Filled with the Spirit"', *TF* 29.9

Continuous Nature

Carrie also believed that there should be a continuous process to 'keep drinking from him' so that there would never be a need to thirst.[153] This, however, did not diminish or take away from the fact that she believed that she had already 'received Him' prior to her 1908 experience.[154] That 'Spirit baptism' in the Bible refers to a verb rather than a noun supports Carrie's understanding of continuously being overwhelmed in the Spirit.[155] Further on this theme, she said,

---

(Sept 1909), pp. 193-95; 'Sanctification and the Baptism of the Holy Spirit', pp. 241-44; 'The Remnant of the Oil', pp. 265-68; 'The Life on Wings', pp. 169-77; 'The Work of the Holy Spirit', *TF* 32.11 (Nov 1912), pp. 241-44; '"The Latter Rain"', pp. 1-5; 'Outpouring of the Spirit at Beulah Heights', *TF* 34.1 (Jan 1914), pp. 5-6; 'Some of the Offices of the Holy Spirit', *TF* 36.10 (Oct 1916), pp. 217-21; 'The Promise of the Father', pp. 145-49; 'The Outpouring of God's Spirit', *TF* 37.7 (July 1917), pp. 145-49; 'Endued with Power for Witnessing', pp. 217-21; 'The Temple Filled with God's Glory', *TF* 40.4 (April 1920), pp. 73-77; 'Be Filled with the Spirit', *TF* 41.2 (Feb 1921), pp. 25-28; and 'Revelation of the Spirit', *TF* 43.9 (Sept 1923), pp. 193-96.

[153] Carrie Judd Montgomery, 'Temples of the Holy Ghost', *TF* 32.4 (April 1912), p. 74. She said that

> it is a conscious realization of the presence of Christ by the power of the Holy Ghost in the whole temple of the body, which causes not only life and strength, but a holy awe and rejoicing in this manifestation of His presence. We have a touch of the power of his endless life welling up like a fountain, and it is wonderful to live; there are no more common moments ... By continuous acts of faith we keep drinking from him, and we do not thirst, even as Christ said. Why should we thirst, if we keep drinking every moment from Him?

See also Montgomery, 'The Promise of the Father', p. 5, where she said 'some people think they receive enough for time and for eternity, and they stop drinking. But after receiving the baptism there must be a continuous act of faith, always drinking of Christ in order to keep filled'. See also her 'Endued with Power for Witness', pp. 217-21.

[154] Carrie Judd Montgomery, 'The Outpouring of God's Spirit', *TF* 37.7 (July 1917), p. 148. Keswick influences are also seen here in the crisis event or actualization followed by the process that also comes with repeated experiences and fillings of the Holy Spirit (Bundy, 'Keswick Higher Life Movement', p. 821). See also Albrecht, 'The Life and Ministry of Carrie Judd Montgomery', p. 147, in reference to the quote of Carrie in 'The Promise of the Father', *TF* 37.1 (Jan 1917), pp. 3, 5.

[154] Montgomery, 'Endued with Power for Witness', pp. 217-21.

[155] Walter C. Kaiser Jr., 'The Baptism in the Holy Spirit as the Promise of the Father: A Reformed Perspective', in Chad Owen Brand (ed.), *Perspectives on Spirit Baptism: Five Views* (Nashville: Broadman and Holman Publishers, 2004), p. 36. See also Norbert Baumert, '"Charism" and "Spirit Baptism"': Presentation of an Analysis', *JPT* 12.2 (2004), pp. 153-54.

'And as God is Love, and He fills us with His own life, we shall be continually baptized into a mighty sea of Divine Love; and flowing out it will bathe the weary ones around us'.[156] Though she was referring to love here, the continuing nature of baptism is evident once again. While Carrie recognized that her 1908 experience was specific and significant, even beyond this, she continually sought similar Spirit baptism-like experiences where she purposed to dwell in limitless measures of the Spirit.[157]

Limitless Measures

Carrie not only saw things in terms of measures, she also saw a limitless supply of the Spirit freely available to the extent that one would not even be able to measure this fullness.[158] She used the passage in Ezekiel 47 to illustrate this:

> When we first step into the holy waters (as seen in Ezekiel's vision) they are very shallow, but we go on from ankle-deep to knee-deep, and then to loin-deep, but we are never out where God wants us to be until we get swept off our feet. Finally the prophet found the waters risen, 'waters to swim in, a river that could not be passed over.' Ezekiel 47:5. When we are swept off our feet, we cannot longer measure our experience, but can go on and on in the boundless fulness of the Spirit of God.[159]

When a person begins to walk into deep waters, it appears that they are at different stages as the water comes up to their feet, then knees, waste, chest, and neck. However, Carrie's paradigm moves

---

Although going against more popular views, J.L. Gresham, *Charles G. Finney's Doctrine of the Baptism of the Holy Spirit* (Peabody, MA: Hendrickson Publishers, 1989), p. 86, concluded that Charles 'Finney believed in repeated Baptisms in the Spirit as a normal part of the Christian life'. See also Miskov, *Spirit Flood, passim*.

[156] Carrie Judd Montgomery, 'The Whole Body Full of Light', *TF* 29.8 (Aug 1909), p. 189.

[157] Albrecht, 'The Life and Ministry of Carrie Judd Montgomery', p. 146. To Carrie, her understanding of Pentecostal Spirit baptism was the promise of the Father ('Be Filled with the Holy Spirit', *TF* 29.9 [Sept 1909], pp. 193-95), Carrie emphasized the command to be filled with the Holy Spirit in Ephesians 5, and she exhorted believers to ask God to make them thirsty.

[158] See Carrie Judd Montgomery, 'Filled', *TF* 15.7 (July 1895), pp. 145-52.

[159] Carrie Judd Montgomery, '"The Tongue of the Wise is Health"', *TF* 36.4 (April 1916), p. 74. This was from an address given at Bible Reading at Home of Peace, recorded by Sadie Cody and revised by Carrie. See also S.P. Jacobs, 'The Spirit Before Pentecost' taken from his book *The Real Christian* (*TF* 31.9 [Sept 1911], pp. 213-14).

beyond these stages and calls for full immersion. Notice that Carrie said that there was no way to measure this limitless experience. She wanted people to move beyond measurements and comparisons of experiences, stages to achieve, or crisis points, and simply dive into the rivers of living waters.

Carrie interpreted that it was at Jesus' water baptism when the Dove descended that 'the Spirit was poured upon Him without measure'.[160] She, too, claimed that *she* had experienced the 'gushing forth of those [same] living waters'. She believed that the first time she went 'all the way under' was when she also spoke in tongues.[161] With her tongues experience ushering her into even greater fullness, metaphorically, Carrie moved from wading in 'tiny streams' to swimming in floods of living water. She wanted everything that was available in those waters whether it was healing, sanctification, tongues, or some other blessing. And whatever she experienced in those waters, she sought to give away freely. She continually entreated 'dear hungry and thirsty souls who have not yet received the fullness of their inheritance in Christ, to likewise come and drink'.[162]

Once someone dived completely into these waters (where the manifestation tongues would be initiated), Carrie saw that they could also live in that place continually. She called for others not to stop at that one experience, but simply to allow that to be their entry point into deeper measures. She admonished people to continue to be 'swept off' their feet into the limitless measures of the Spirit, not simply in one great experience but continually. She wanted people to live in the 'deep end' rather than in the shallow waters where their feet could touch the ground. Total surrender to the Spirit gripped her life. Carrie's theology was marked by a hunger to live in the deepest place possible with the Spirit and she believed that it was possible to thrive where the living waters flooded, overwhelmed, and baptized one's life continuously.

---

[160] This is when she believed that He had His Spirit baptism experience ('The Remnant of the Oil', pp. 268-70).

[161] See Carrie's 'Miraculously Healed by the Lord Thirty Years Ago', p. 9, where she wrote, 'I remember when Mr. Simpson literally baptized me ... I was bound it would be a thorough work ... and that was the way I felt about the Spirit's baptism. I wanted God to put my head under, and He did'.

[162] Montgomery, 'The Remnant of the Oil', pp. 268-70. See her full account in Chapter 3.

6.5 Situating Carrie within a Present Day Pentecostal Perspective of Spirit Baptism

While Carrie was a part of the early Pentecostal Movement, her pneumatology was in development long before then. Because of this, not all of her theology resonates with present day views of Pentecostalism. It is important to point out that during her time, Carrie's view fit within the developing view of the Assemblies of God. However, as changes occurred within fundamental truth statements, not all of Carrie's developing views or experiences would fit perfectly with current statements.[163] Carrie would agree with Pentecostal scholar and Assembly of God member since 1935, Stanley Horton, that Spirit baptism opens one up to a greater realm of spiritual possibilities and that the manifestation of tongues is normative for every believer to access and receive.[164] However, she would differ in that she recognized that tongues did not have to come immediately following one's Spirit baptism but could come at a later time; since the view of initial evidence was continuing to develop during her time, her view did not go outside of her denomination's beliefs at that time.

In agreement with Horton, through her Pentecostal perspective, Carrie saw that Spirit baptism was a distinct experience that came after conversion. She would differ though, in that she believed that sanctification could be a distinct experience as well (a more Wesleyan-Holiness Pentecostal view). While many in the current day Assemblies of God hold to a two-crisis view of conversion and Spirit baptism, Carrie would not readily fit here because she also mentioned sanctification. Though some scholars place her in three-stage process because of this, she can not easily be classified here ei-

---

163 While Carrie's developing view fit with her denomination at that time, since the changes in 1960, some of her views would no longer readily fit within the fundamental truths for the Assemblies of God today. See Montgomery, 'The Promise of the Father', p. 5 and The General Council of the Assemblies of God 'Statement of Fundamental Truths', Accessed May 23, 2011 <http://agchurches. org/Sitefiles/Default/RSS/AG.org%20TOP/Beliefs/SFT_2011.pdf>. See also Stanley M. Horton, 'Spirit Baptism: A Pentecostal Perspective', in Chad Owen Brand (ed.), *Perspectives on Spirit Baptism: Five Views* (Nashville: Broadman and Holman Publishers, 2004), pp. 54, 78.

164 Horton, 'Spirit Baptism: A Pentecostal Perspective', p. 69. See also Frank D. Macchia, 'Pentecostal Theology', in *NIDPCM*, p. 1129.

ther.[165] Carrie recognized many significant 'Spirit baptism-like' experiences throughout her life both before and after 1908. And while she mentioned some of these important crisis experiences in her own life (though she did not clarify a date for her conversion or her sanctification), it is important to point out that any and all stages or crisis experiences that did exist, were encompassed in overall expanded degrees and measures of the Spirit which made up her overarching pneumatology.[166]

Ultimately, Carrie's paradigm was one of measures, not of stages. She claimed to encounter the Spirit in varying crisis experiences, degrees, and measures throughout her life. Whenever a newer revelation or manifestation of the Spirit was introduced, she added it to her previous experiences whether that was healing, sanctification, speaking in tongues, or some other blessing. If anything, Carrie would need to be categorized as a 'many-fold' Christian because she consistently sought after whatever she saw was freely available in and through the Spirit.[167] Because Carrie pursued the 'fullness of the

---

[165] Based on Carrie's articles, 'Sanctification and the Baptism of the Holy Spirit' and 'The Remnant of the Oil', Diana Chapman says that 'Carrie sets out clearly her belief that the Baptism in the Holy Spirit accompanied by the sign of tongues is a third work of grace' (*Searching the Source of the River*, p. 77). Terry Arnold and Mike Claydon also believe that Carrie wrote of 'a three stage process consisting of Salvation, Sanctification and the Holy Spirit baptism, with faith as the only condition'. However, they go on to state how her understanding of this resonated more with the Holiness tradition than it did with the new Pentecostal approach of a 'subsequent baptism with the evidence of tongues', and they later compare Carrie's view with the newer Charismatic approach to Spirit baptism which 'does not view tongues as necessarily "the evidence" of the "Baptism with the Spirit" but a likely consequence' ('The Foundation and History of the Pentecostal Movement', *Diakrisis Australia* 2.26 [Jan/Feb 2004], p. 10). Jeannette Storms' emphasis on dimensions, or measures of spirituality rather than stages is helpful. She says that a 'survey of editorials published in [Carrie's] first phase of ministry revealed a primary focus on the higher Christian life with faith healing being treated in a secondary way. This reflected her belief in an experience subsequent to salvation, popularly known as Holy Spirit baptism, which ushered the believer into a deeper dimension of spirituality and empowerment for victorious Christian living' ('Carrie Judd Montgomery: The Little General', p. 277).

[166] This was also true with degrees of faith. See Carrie Judd Montgomery, 'Different Degrees of Faith', *TF* 38.7 (July 1918), pp. 145-50. She named the date of both her healing and Pentecostal Spirit baptism but not her conversion or sanctification experience which suggests a mixture of both crisis experiences and processes.

[167] Montgomery, 'The Work and the Workers', *TF* 12.2, p. 34. While Carrie supported Simpson's Four-fold Gospel even before her Spirit baptism experience, in reference to Isaiah 58, she said that 'If we go out to sin-bound souls and

Spirit', in which she saw the Spirit was without measure, and intimacy with God within the context of a relationship with Him, intimacy increased rather than stages to achieve. Therefore, trying to place Carrie within a paradigm of stages or crisis events is like trying to pour oceans of water into a cardboard box.

6.6 Effects of Carrie's Pentecostal Spirit Baptism Experience

6.6.1 Life and Ministry

Carrie was fifty years old and already a well known and influential writer, 'healer', and itinerant minister by the time she had her Pentecostal Spirit baptism experience. But how did that experience affect her life and ministry? Through a Pentecostal perspective, Carrie personally claimed that her 1908 experience with tongues brought a great increase of love, joy, peace, intimacy, power for service, freedom from care, and even physical strength.[168] The way that Carrie reflected upon and wrote about her Pentecostal Spirit baptism throughout the years reveals that she believed it was a profound experience that greatly marked her life. Whether she overemphasized the importance of this experience in light of her newer Pentecostal paradigm is hard to judge because of the personal nature of her claims. However, from her perspective, it is evident that she believed that her 1908 tongues experience played an important role in greatly enhancing and taking her spirituality to a new level.

In relation to her ministry however, did Carrie simply absorb the Pentecostal experience into what she was already doing or did it radically alter her ministry? Within several months after she received the manifestation of tongues, Carrie abruptly decided to participate

---

break their chains through Christ our "light shall break forth as the morning" and our "health shall spring forth speedily," and all the blessings of the "Four-fold Gospel," yea, of the many-fold Gospel, shall be ours'. To say that Carrie later moved from a Four-fold position to a Five-fold position adding Jesus as Spirit baptizer would limit her. For her, there were 'many' folds of the Gospel that could be embraced without categorization.

[168] Montgomery, 'A Year with the Comforter', pp. 145-49. In one sermon, she described her 'fuller baptism' experience as resulting in 'freedom of the mind from all care', which she said she had previously yet to settle. See also her 'The Life on Wings' and Miskov, *Spirit Flood*, p. 33. Carrie also claimed to have received 'greater power for service, and increased fellowship in prayer and praise' (Montgomery, *Under His Wings*, p. 170).

in foreign missions when before that she mainly supported them from home. She also ended her orphanage work so that she could spend more time exclusively in the ministry of the Gospel. Besides teaching and praying for healing, Carrie additionally began to advocate and pray for people to have their Pentecostal baptism and to speak in tongues. She did this by sharing her own testimony of Pentecostal fullness as well as writing about it in her periodical. Carrie wanted people to pursue all that the Spirit had for them and from her personal experience, she realized that not only was healing 'freely' available to all who took hold of it, but an experience where other tongues was initiated was available as well. She wanted to share with others what she had received whether it was clothed under the heading of Pentecostalism or not. In other words, she wanted people to speak in tongues whether or not they decided to join the Pentecostal Movement afterwards. Instead of her Pentecostal experience becoming a whole new ministry, it rather expanded her boarders and was absorbed and integrated into her already effective ministry.[169] Overall, Carrie's 1908 experience brought deeper satisfaction to an already influential healing evangelist, added a new flavor her ministry, and took her to a deeper level of intimacy than she had claimed to experience thus far. While her reception of tongues built upon, rather than completely transformed her life and ministry, her experience proved to have significant ripple effects for early Pentecostalism.

6.6.2 Theology of Healing

Carrie's foundational healing theology had already been formed for many years before the newer interpretation of Spirit baptism with the manifestation of tongues was widely known. While some smaller and enhancing changes occurred in her theology of healing as a result of her 1908 experience, there were no huge paradigm shifts.[170]

---

[169] Albrecht, 'The Life and Ministry of Carrie Judd Montgomery', pp. 141-42, agrees and says that 'while some points of view changed preceding and immediately following Carrie's baptism, many foundational things in her life and ministry remained the same'. Albrecht also notices that 'another area in Carrie's life that did not shift radically but was perhaps enhanced following her baptism was the focus on Christian love'.

[170] Albrecht, 'The Life and Ministry of Carrie Judd Montgomery', p. 142. Albrecht also sees that there was no major change in Carrie's theology of healing when he says that because of Carrie's previous experiences with the Holy Spirit,

One thing she did notice was that the experience could also bring healing to people. She recorded during the Sunderland convention that 'Pentecostal fulness has in many cases brought new life and healing to wornout and sick bodies'.[171] A potential new model for healing was introduced here as she noticed that the effects of the Pentecostal experience not only included spiritual deepening and empowerment, but also healing for the body. She also saw that the Pentecostal baptism could magnify his healing presence within the body. Shortly after her 1908 experience, she said, 'We have experienced and taught Divine healing for many years, but never have personally known such a constant indwelling of the Healer as since we received our Pentecostal baptism'.[172] Another slight modification came in the way she prayed for others. After her 1908 experience she began to emphasize authority and power even more when rebuking sickness.[173]

In agreement with other scholars, I would argue that while Carrie's 1908 experience did enhance other areas of her life and ministry, it did not change her theology of healing in any major way.[174] In fact, it was her healing methodology, in part, that informed her approach to taking hold of the Pentecostal baptism and the manifestation of tongues. Building upon Palmer's methods, the similar themes of acting faith that Carrie applied to healing she also applied to Pentecostal baptism. 'Taking hold' of the Pentecostal Spirit baptism could be appropriated as easily as 'taking hold' of one's healing

---

'the emphasis on the indwelling Spirit and His role in the healing process was perhaps a slight shift'.

[171] Carrie Judd Montgomery, 'Pentecostal Conference, Sunderland, Eng.', *TF* 29.7 (July 1909), p. 152.

[172] Carrie Judd Montgomery, 'Christ's Quickening Life for the Mortal Body', *TF* 28.8 (Aug 1908), p. 170, continued, 'After taking this position, accepting by faith the deadness of our own body, that the life of Christ may reign within, we will find that any failure to yield to the indwelling Spirit will cause weakness and even illness'. See also her, 'The Quickening Life of the Indwelling Spirit', p. 217.

[173] Carrie Judd Montgomery, 'The Quickening Life of the Indwelling Spirit', p. 218, referring to her 1908 experience said, 'For this Holy Ghost baptism is not only one of light and life and power, but also of fire'. This was also in reference to Isaiah 6 and the coals, where Carrie wrote that 'the fire of God's holiness would consume us, if it were not from the altar of Jesus Christ'. She wrote in 1919 that 'years ago we did not know how to loose people that were bound by the Devil', however, she did not directly relate this to her 1908 experience though. See her 'Thou Art Loosed', p. 266.

[174] Alexander, *Pentecostal Healing*, p. 154. Alexander's conclusions are mainly based from a sample (1906-1910) of *Triumphs of Faith*.

in light of the finished work on the cross.[175] While Carrie's 1908 experience was significant and did have an influence in her life, it never ultimately defined her ministry or transformed her theology of healing. Carrie's desire to see people healed, both spiritually and physically, remained a prominent and foundational theme in her life even after her 1908 experience. Evidence of this comes from her life story which was published in 1936 when she was 78 years old; this was more than 25 years after she spoke in tongues for the first time. The major threads woven into *Under His Wings* were unity in love, divine healing, and fullness of the Spirit, but not specifically the Pentecostal Spirit baptism. The agreement in love and the testimonies of divine healing saturating her book more frequently than the manifestation of tongues further demonstrates the role the experience had in her life; it enhanced and added new depths to her life and ministry, but at the same time it did not bring any major shifts or overshadow her theology of healing.[176]

6.6.3 Pneumatology

Carrie's early pneumatology already included a hunger for 'fullness of the Spirit', which she also referred to as Spirit Baptism, before the manifestation of tongues was readily associated with it.[177] She had already spoken of the Spirit, even in Pentecostal terms, years before her 1908 experience. While the meaning of terms was adapted through the years, the similar ethos of wanting to be overwhelmed with the Spirit was consistently present in her pneumatol-

---

[175] Alexander, *Pentecostal Healing*, p. 213. Alexander rightly notes that 'much of Montgomery's theology of healing remained the same after her Pentecostal experience. She continued to maintain that divine healing was provided in the atonement and continued to teach that healing could be obtained through faith'.

[176] One of the reasons she likely downplayed tongues was because of the fanaticism associated with tongues as well as her desire to maintain unity. She also continued in this way throughout her life because, like John Wesley in many ways, she was more concerned with the fruit of the Spirit than the gifts of the Spirit.

[177] See, for example, the following articles that Carrie wrote before her 1908 Spirit baptism experience: 'Rivers of Living Water', *TF* 1.4 (April 1881), pp. 57-58; 'Led by the Spirit', *TF* 2.10 (Oct 1882), pp. 145-46; 'The Temple of the Body', *TF* 4.2 (Feb 1884), pp. 25-27; 'The Anointing of the Spirit', *TF* 4.8 (Aug 1884), pp. 181-82; 'Quickened by the Spirit', *TF* 4.9 (Sept 1884), pp. 193-94; 'Living Water', *TF* 7.3 (March 1887), pp. 67-68; 'Rivers of Living Water', *TF* 13.10 (Oct 1893), pp. 241-46; 'Filled', *TF* 15.7 (July 1895), pp. 145-52; 'The Work of the Spirit', *TF* 15.9 (Sept 1895), pp. 193-99; 'Living Waters', *TF* 16.10 (Oct 1896), pp. 217-20; and 'Receive Ye the Holy Ghost', *TF* 18.1 (Jan 1898), pp. 1-7.

ogy within the contexts of Wesleyan-Holiness, Keswick Higher Life, Reformed, and then later, Pentecostalism streams.

Since Carrie was already headed in the direction of Pentecostalism and because seeking the 'fullness of the Spirit' was already an important aspect of her life, the biggest change that occurred in her pneumatology after her 1908 experience was that speaking in tongues was then integrated into her spirituality. She claimed that this experience greatly deepened her faith in ways she had yet to know before. Her 1908 experience also caused her to adopt a Pentecostal paradigm for re-interpreting her past 'Spirit baptism' experiences as well as had a great impact on early Pentecostalism.[178] While Carrie personally recognized that her 1908 experience enhanced her spirituality in new ways and was a significant experience in her life, from the outside looking in, her 1908 Pentecostal experience did not look drastically different from her previous experiences with the Spirit except that speaking in tongues was now added. It was this new language that marked her 1908 experience as a significant and deeper encounter than she had realized up until that point. Using Carrie's terminology, it appears that she was already moving deeper in the waters of the Holy Spirit throughout her life but then in 1908, she let her head go all the way under those waters. After that, she felt as if she was able to swim in the waters of the Holy Spirit at new depths and with a greater freedom than she realized before.

Throughout Carrie's life, she was continually drawn towards and pursued intimacy with God and a 'deeper spiritual life'. It was speaking in tongues that allowed her to communicate at a new level that she had yet to experience beforehand. She recognized that 'close union with God' increases as a result of one's 'Pentecostal baptism'.[179] Carrie's 1908 tongues experience opened a new door and initiated a deeper level of intimacy with God than she had realized before. To explain this further, it is similar to the defining

---

[178] Montgomery, '"The Promise of the Father." A Personal Testimony'. See also her 'Miraculously Healed by the Lord Thirty Years Ago', p. 8, where she described measures of hunger in relation to her experiences with the Spirit: 'I came to the place a few years after my healing where I was looking out for more of God; but now, after a few years comes a greater cry, a longing cry that might be filled with all the fullness of God'.

[179] Carrie Judd Montgomery, '"The Latter Rain"', p. 3. See also her 'The Work and Worker', *TF* 31.5 (May 1911), p. 118.

moment when two are united in a new level of vulnerability and intimacy within the context of a love relationship. This becomes a special moment to remember but at the same time that intimacy did not start, nor does it stop there; it continues to develop and progress over time where even after the initial union, there are other special moments of intimacy shared beyond that. Carrie had significant experiences with the Spirit both before and after 1908. Speaking in tongues for the first time ushered her into a new level of intimacy and vulnerability with God. Carrie's pneumatology suggests that for her, the reception of speaking in tongues was a significant entry point into deeper measures with the Spirit.

6.7 Implications of Carrie's 1908 Tongues Experience for Christians Today

Because Carrie contributed in ecumenical ministry both before and after her 1908 experience, her life lends to several significant questions for Christians from various backgrounds: Does someone who is already successful in Christian ministry need to add the Pentecostal Spirit baptism with speaking of tongues to their life? And will the experience and addition of tongues broaden or enhance their ministry? Carrie's life up to 1908 demonstrates that even if someone has not been Spirit-baptized in the Pentecostal sense, they can still be effective in ministry. However, the personal impact that her 1908 tongues experience had on her spirituality also suggests that even flourishing ministers can receive greater personal fulfillment, satisfaction, blessing, and intimacy with God through speaking in tongues.[180] Carrie's 1908 experience caused her to believe that regardless of age, reputation, previous experiences, or denominational ties, speaking in tongues was worth seeking and something that would draw one closer to God. Carrie's interpretation of her 1908 experience serves as an invitation for Evangelicals and Christians from all different backgrounds to pursue speaking in tongues as one way that might enhance and deepen their spirituality.

At the same time, Carrie's views can challenge Pentecostal streams today that hold to an uncompromising doctrine of initial evidence, to allow room to embrace others who cannot wholeheart-

---

[180] Miskov, *Spirit Flood*, p. 34.

edly agree on that issue or who do not emphasize it. That a leader within the Assemblies of God did not enter into the public debate over initial evidence suggests that there might be a need to reconsider the weight given to this issue within present day doctrinal statements and discussions. Her approach can also encourage Pentecostals and others to focus more on practice than on doctrine in this area. Carrie's ability to maintain unity in love with Christians from various traditions is also an example that she leaves behind for present day ministers. Her legacy can encourage people in Christian leadership to major on the majors and not let minor disagreements over doctrine divide. Carrie saw that the purest demonstration of religion is love. If leaders within Christian movements followed in Carrie's footsteps and similarly chose to live this out today, the results could be astounding. Carrie's pursuit of the 'fullness of the Spirit', regardless of what that looked like throughout her life, can also inspire Pentecostals to seek even greater measures of the Spirit beyond their Spirit baptism experience.

Furthermore, in light of Carrie's experiences with the Holy Spirit and her relentless pursuit of the 'fullness of the Holy Spirit' throughout her entire life, I suggest a need for redefinition and expansion of the Pentecostal Spirit baptism. Presently, the general Pentecostal understanding of Spirit baptism with the sign of tongues makes Spirit baptism sound like something that is attainable.[181] The emphasis on one major and attainable crisis experience is a great start, but to end there would be limiting because it suggests mere 'fillings' of the Spirit to come after that. However, as high-

---

[181] See Miskov, *Spirit Flood* for a full discussion on this theme. Some of the sources used here are J.R. Williams, 'Baptism in the Holy Spirit', in *NIDPCM*, p. 358, Frank D. Macchia, *Baptized in the Spirit* (Grand Rapids, MI: Zondervan) 2006; Stanley M. Horton, 'Response by Stanley M. Horton', in Chad Owen Brand (ed.), *Perspectives on Spirit Baptism: Five Views* (Nashville: Broadman and Holman Publishers), 2004; Walter J. Hollenweger, 'Rethinking Spirit Baptism: The Natural and the Supernatural', in A. Anderson and W. Hollenweger (eds.) *Pentecostals After a Century: Global Perspectives on a Movement in Transition* (JPTSup, 23; Sheffield, England: Sheffield Academic Press, 1999); Walter J. Hollenweger's *Pentecostalism: Origins and Developments Worldwide* (Peabody, MA: Hendrickson Publishers, 1997); Anderson, *Spreading Fires*; Baumert '"Charism" and "Spirit-Baptism": Presentation of an Analysis', pp. 147-79; Larry Hart, 'Spirit Baptism: A Dimensional Charismatic Perspective', in Chad Owen Brand (ed.), *Perspectives on Spirit Baptism: Five Views* (Nashville: Broadman and Holman Publishers, 2004); and Donald E. Miller and Tetsunao Yamamori, *Global Pentecostalism: The New Face of Christian Social Engagement* (Los Angeles: University of California Press, 2007).

lighted in Carrie's writings, since the Spirit can never be fully attainable, 'the fullness of the Spirit' is without measure. The ethos of the Pentecostal Spirit baptism as an overwhelmed experience should captivate Christians not only in one heightened experience, but also continually *throughout* their entire lives. If one disassociates the term Spirit baptism from the reception of tongues, speaking in tongues could be something to pursue and take hold of alongside other gifts or manifestations of the Spirit like prophecy, healing, and so on. It also means that moving beyond one distinct experience, there can be a hunger for the Spirit to continue to draw one deeper into His limitless measures and to even greater spiritual encounters beyond that. 'Spirit baptisms' then, in a sense, can be redefined not just as one crisis experience, but rather as fresh floodings of the Spirit. This redefinition can stir the believer to dive into both an initial flooding of the Spirit with speaking in tongues *and* also to continue to call for overflowing measures of the Spirit on a regular basis. Because 'Spirit baptism' as a noun does not even exist in the Bible but is in verb form, that the Spirit might want to baptize one afresh continually in multiple flooding experiences both before and after one has received the manifestation of tongues exists.

Perhaps it is time for a paradigm shift in relation to this term. Think of what transformations might take place when Christians from various traditions are drawn to be fully possessed by the Spirit, when they are stirred to be overwhelmed and baptized not just in one crisis experience but again and again in the rivers of living water. What might it look like when a new generation arises to pursue pursue the fullness of the Spirit and live in a place where the floods of living water are unstoppable, when they choose to move beyond that one intense experience to dive even deeper into more abundant measures of the Spirit after that?[182] For those who are hungry to *live* in the place of the Spirit's abundance, not just in one experience but on a regular basis, the floodgates of the Spirit are waiting to be poured out.

---

[182] The point is not that Pentecostals do not seek for more of the Spirit following their Spirit baptism experiences, but the emphasis here is on what measures of the Spirit are emphasized. A redefinition can move people from praying for mere 'fillings' of the Spirit to praying for the limitless measures of the Spirit to overwhelm one's life completely, even after their Pentecostal Spirit baptism experience. See Miskov, *Spirit Flood*, pp. 35-39.

7

SIGNIFICANCE AND IMPACT

7.1 Significance for Scholarship

7.1.1 Why has Carrie been Under-examined?

One of the possible reasons that Carrie has not been given much attention in academic circles today is because of her temperament. Because she was not 'charismatic' in personality or controversial in her moral affairs, she has received little sustained attention. Carrie was likely more introverted, and because of this, her ministry looked different from the more outgoing personalities like Maria Woodworth-Etter, Aimee Semple McPherson, and Kathryn Kuhlman, who get more exposure.[1] As these female evangelists get mentioned again and again, it has been easy to dismiss and overlook Carrie, Sarah Mix, Elizabeth Sisson, and others who have also had a significant impact. In light of this, one might wonder whether having an outgoing personality is necessary for one's influence within the Pentecostal Movement to be rightfully acknowledged. This study, however, has demonstrated that in addition to the more charismatic personalities that regularly get noticed, there are also other powerful voices within Evangelicalism and Pentecostalism whose contribution deserves recognition.

---

[1] Blumhofer, Aimee *Semple McPherson*, and Warner, *Maria Woodworth-Etter*. Kathryn Kuhlman has been the subject of several biographies including those by Benny Hinn (1999), Wayne E. Warner (1993), Roberts Liardon (1996).

7.1.2 Contribution to Scholarship

This research has expanded upon the limited work done on the life, ministry, and theology of Carrie Judd Montgomery. Over twenty years ago, Daniel Albrecht noticed a need for Carrie's story to be recovered when he wrote that 'although little is remembered or known about Montgomery in religious circles today, as an evangelical pacesetter and a Pentecostal forerunner, her life and work deserve renewed reflection and serious study'.[2] This research has just begun to answer that call. Building upon previous foundations, this is the first study to have analyzed specific Pentecostal themes within Carrie's pneumatology as well as organize her theology of healing together with a historical biography.

This study was also specifically shaped around Carrie's public presentation of herself and how she interpreted the moves of God in her day. Just as Frank Bartleman's account of Azusa Street is important because it adds one perspective to the history of the revival, so Carrie's perspective of the Holiness, Divine Healing, and Pentecostal Movements is significant.[3] That Carrie's periodical spanned through several generations means that she chronicled the histories of many important developments within North American Evangelicalism and Pentecostalism. For example, this research traces the enduring friendship between Carrie and A.B. Simpson before, intersecting, and after the early Pentecostal revivals. Her perspective provides a snapshot of how Simpson approached the early Pentecostal revivals and gives Christian and Missionary Alliance historians a deeper understanding into the early developments of their movement. How Simpson intentionally opened doors and created space for Carrie to speak can also contribute to conversations surrounding the role of women within the CMA today.

Additionally, this research provides a picture of several Holiness roots lived out within Pentecostalism. Carrie's life and writings provide a trajectory of holiness/healing theology as it intersected with early Pentecostalism.[4] Carrie brought aspects of Reformed, Wesley-

---

[2] Albrecht, 'Carrie Judd Montgomery: Pioneering Contributor to Three Religious Movements', p. 101.

[3] Frank Bartleman, *Azusa Street: The Roots of Modern-day Pentecost* (Los Angeles 1925; reprint, S. Plainfield, NJ: Bridge Publishing, Inc., 1980).

[4] Miskov, 'Missing Links: Phoebe Palmer, Carrie Judd Montgomery, and Holiness Roots within Pentecostalism', pp. 8-28. See also Petts, 'Healing and the Atonement', p. 26, n. 14. Petts rightly believes that Carrie's life alone 'is at least

an, and Keswick themes with her into the new movement. While Carrie never personally met Phoebe Palmer, she did know prominent holiness healing evangelists Maria Woodworth-Etter (1844-1924), Elizabeth Sisson (1843-1934), and others from similar Holiness streams who also later joined the Pentecostal Movement. By outliving the women mentioned, Carrie (1858-1946) stands out as one of the strongest links of a holiness female healing evangelist who integrated various strands of Holiness theology deepest within Pentecostalism.[5]

7.1.3 Further Topics for Research

This research has served to lay a foundation and act as a catalyst for further dialogue. With over sixty years of articles in *Triumphs of Faith*, there were only a few topics that could adequately be focused on in this study. There is more research that needs to be done by anyone who is a pioneer like Carrie and willing to take up the challenge. Some possibilities of this could be looking more specifically at her faith, not only in relation to healing but also for finances and other areas. One could explore her ecumenism and how she attempted to keep unity when movements that she was a part of forming later became institutionalized. A deeper look at her emphasis on 'total surrender' and her model for initiating ministries would be worthy of note. Tracing the theme of unity in love throughout

---

one very clear evidence that the origins of Pentecostalism lie in the Holiness Movement'. See also Abraham Ruelas, *Women and the Landscape of American Higher Education: Wesleyan Holiness and Pentecostal Founders* (Eugene, OR: Wipf & Stock Publishers, 2010), p. 78. Ruelas also sees Carrie as a link between proponents of the earlier healing movement with people like Oral Roberts and William Branham.

   [5] Note that McPherson, and even Kuhlman, came after the Holiness Movement but are regularly included in conversations in conjunction with Woodworth-Etter or Palmer, while Carrie regularly gets left out. See Stanley James Grenz and Denise Muir Kjesbo, *Women in the church: A biblical theology of women in ministry* (Downers Grove, IL: InterVarsity Press, 1995), p. 54, and R. Marie Griffith, 'Kathryn Johanna Kuhlman', in Susan Ware (ed.), *Notable American Women: A Biographical Dictionary Completing the Twentieth Century* (Radcliffe Institute for Advanced Study; Cambridge, MA: Harvard University Press, 2004), pp. 354-56. See also Joe McIntyre, *E.W. Kenyon and His Message of Faith: The True Story* (Lake Mary, FL: Charisma House, 1997), p. 61, where he names Carrie as the only female in list of similar connections. He says that 'F.F. Bosworth, John G. Lake, Carrie Judd Montgomery, and E.W. Kenyon closed the gap and connected the Faith-Cure, or Divine Healing Movement into Pentecostalism and the Faith Movement'. Note that Carrie also outlived Sarah Anne Freeman Mix (1832-1884) and Aimee Semple McPherson (1890-1944) as well.

Triumphs of Faith, seeing how her intersection with the Salvation Army affected her soteriology, or an analysis of her life purely through the perspective of her readers would be interesting. A chronological and geographical analysis of the children in her orphanage or the people healed in her ministry and where they ended up would also be a fascinating study. Mix's life also needs to be explored further. Building on this research, an analysis of the healing testimonies or of the other authors she chose to publish or how she distinguished between miracles and healing would be helpful. An in depth discussion of all of her spiritual experiences throughout the years or the development of her theology from 1921 to the end of her life would also prove satisfying. An analysis of Carrie's healing theology in relation to that of Maria Woodworth-Etter, Elizabeth Sisson, Aimee Semple McPherson, and Kathryn Kuhlman would also be a fascinating study that can now be more fully developed. While there is not enough space to include this in my study, how Carrie's theology has further been integrated, modified, or resonates within present day Charismatic and Pentecostal Movements would also be important for future research. I await these studies with anticipation.

7.2 Significance of Carrie's Life and Ministry: Breaking Through Barriers

Carrie broke through cultural stereotypes, denominational barriers, and geographical boundaries, and additionally participated in two major moves of God during her lifetime. The network Carrie created in the Divine Healing Movement through her periodical, healing homes, camp meetings, and speaking tours provided her with a ready made platform to influence the nations with Pentecostal themes. One of the most prominent and significant vehicles she used for this was her *Triumphs of Faith.* Carrie's periodical acted as a global network that spread early revival fires around the world and also provided space for ecumenical voices from different backgrounds to interact. Her periodical also carried holiness, divine healing, and Pentecostal themes across denominations and throughout generations.[6] Furthermore, it provided an important platform for women to speak out on theological themes. The expansive network Carrie built is a remarkable accomplishment considering this was years before the internet was even invented. Her periodical is one of the most important things she leaves behind today as it provides insight and history into the spiritual currents within Evangelicalism and Pentecostalism during her time. Through the vehicle of her periodical, camp meetings, and healing homes, Carrie's strong desire to freely share what God had done in her life regardless of gender, religious, or geographic classifications, proved to greatly multiply her influence.[7]

7.2.1 Usurping Cultural Stereotypes: Women in Ministry

Carrie not only broke through racial barriers by choosing to minister to African Americans early on, but she also usurped cultural stereotypes when she emerged as woman in ministry in her day.[8] The potential controversy of women in ministry was never a big issue for Carrie. From my research up until 1920, she did not write in defense of women in ministry, but rather continued in the ministry to which she believed God had called her.[9] Her faith in following through with the things she felt God had called her to regardless of her gender inspired many women to do the same, especially in relation to healing homes and itinerant preaching.[10] Carrie played a key role in Emma Whittemore's healing who later went on to 'establish ninety-seven Door of Hope rehabilitation homes for destitute girls'

---

[6] Cavaness, 'Spiritual Chain Reactions', p. 25. Cavaness believes that throughout her ministry, Carrie was potentially in contact with over one hundred missionary boards that she spread healing themes to besides helping to raise support for them and disseminate their stories internationally.

[7] See her 'The Work and the Workers', *TF* 9.5 (May 1889), p. 118.

[8] See Chapter 2 for more on the significance of engaging in ministry as a woman during Carrie's time.

[9] She did include other authors at times though. See also Mr Judd, 'Should Women Prophesy?', *TF* 6.12 (Dec 1886), pp. 270-72; and Katherine Bushnell, 'Women Preachers; Why Obscure the True Reading?', taken from *Peniel Herald* in *TF* 24.11 (Nov 1904), pp. 259-61, where Bushnell uses Ps. 68.11-12 to demonstrate that God wants women to preach.

[10] Carrie Judd Montgomery, 'A New Faith Home in Los Angeles', *TF* 31.6 (June 1911), pp. 143-44. Dora Griffin Dudley was one of these who first discovered healing through one of Carrie's books and then later opened up a healing home that Carrie was called on to dedicate. Clara Miner and Inga Thorgeson were first groomed by Carrie when they ran the Home of Peace before being sent off to start their own healing home in Los Angeles.

around the world.[11] It was through Carrie's inspiration that Anna W. Prosser began to speak about her healing as well as open up a healing home.[12] Carrie Bates, who later went to India as a missionary, was healed while at Carrie's Buffalo home.[13] Countless other women were healed through Carrie's ministry and went on to influence those around them.[14] Additionally, when Carrie first opened up her Bible school, it was exclusively for training women for ministry.

Carrie's impact on women continued within the Pentecostal Movement. Her one time assistant editor, Elizabeth Sisson, later went on to facilitate her own revival campaigns as well as preach alongside Woodworth-Etter and McPherson.[15] Mina Ross Brawner also spent some time working with Carrie in Oakland before going to Australia as a Bible Standard missionary and planting 14 churches.[16] Carrie's impact on women additionally spread beyond national borders as can be seen in Mexican American Concepción (Chonita) Morgan Howard (1898-1983). She was 'marvelously filled with the Spirit, in Pentecostal fullness' during Carrie's trip to Mexico in 1913 and was inspired to begin evangelistic work.[17] Her ministry lasted

---

[11] *CAMW* 3.1 (Aug 1, 1889), Mrs N. Wood, 'Personal Testimonies, The Lord My Healer', *CAMW* 7.11 (Sept 11, 1891); *CAMW* 8.1 Jan 1, 1892; and Barbara Cavaness, 'Spiritual Chain Reactions: Women Used By God', *AGH* (Winter 2005-06), p. 24.

[12] Montgomery, *Under His Wings*, p. 68. Carrie also provided space for Prosser to contribute regularly to her periodical and ironically, Prosser's healing home ended up being the same Buffalo home where Carrie earlier had her healing home. While Prosser was older than Carrie, she was greatly influenced by her example, claiming that she followed 'in her very footsteps' in Anna W. Prosser, 'Faith Home and Missionary Training School in Buffalo', *TF* 16.12 (Dec 1896), p. 277.

[13] Carrie Judd Montgomery, 'Poor India/Return to India', *TF* 17.3 (March 1898), pp. 70-72. See also *The Christian Alliance* 16.7 (Feb 14, 1896). Bates was said to have been healed from dyspepsia March 25, 1883 while staying with Carrie there.

[14] Mrs W.A. Shappee, 'A Glimpse of the Past and the Present', *TF* 17.8 (Aug 1897), pp. 179-82. This is a testimony about Carrie praying for her and then she was healed.

[15] Sisson was also one of the only women invited to deliver the main address for the Assemblies of God council in 1917 (Hardesty, *Faith Cure*, p. 63).

[16] Robert Bryant Mitchell, *The History of Open Bible Standard Churches* (Des Moines, Iowa: Open Bible Publishers, 1982), p. 106.

[17] Montgomery, 'Recent Trip to Mexico', pp. 270-71; 'A Trip into Mexico', *TF* 36.3 (March 1916), p. 65; and her 'A Trip into Mexico, Etc.', *TF* 37.7 (July 1917), p. 157. In 1917, Carrie visited her again and they did ministry together. See

over 50 years and impacted many Hispanic women in the USA and Mexico where she also helped to establish work with the Assemblies of God.[18]

One of the main vehicles that Carrie used to create space for women to engage in ministry, besides her meetings and healing homes, was by giving them the opportunity to speak on theological themes in her periodical. This platform acted as a catalyst for many women to initiate and advance their ministries. Additionally, Carrie's public promotion of other women like Woodworth-Etter, McPherson, Sisson, Prosser, and Baxter strengthened and celebrated the somewhat controversial role of women in ministry. Throughout her life, Carrie broke through the social and cultural constraints of her time to advance the revolution and cause of women in ministry. By determining to share what God had done in her own life, she paved the way for future generations of women to enter into Christian ministry with more receptivity than in the past.

7.2.2 Transcending Denominational Barriers: Ecumenical Impact

Throughout the years, Carrie has been referred to as an author, teacher, poet, first woman to itinerant preach across North America, long range curer, social worker, philanthropist, editor, little general, faith healer, radical Evangelical, pioneer, religious entrepreneur, fire starter, and even the first Charismatic.[19] As can be seen, it is

---

Jennifer Stock, 'George S. Montgomery: Businessman for the Gospel', *AGH* 9.2 (Summer 1989), pp. 12-14, 20, where there are photographs of Howard with the Montgomerys. See also Gastón Espinosa, 'LIBERATED and EMPOWERED: The Uphill History of Hispanic Assemblies of God Women in Ministry, 1915-1950', *AGH* 28 (2008), pp. 44-48. Howard's father was connected to George in relation to business.

[18] Espinosa, 'LIBERATED and EMPOWERED', pp. 44-48. She also went on to become a 'pioneer Latina Pentecostal evangelist, pastor, and women's leader in the US and Mexico'. By 1928, Howard was recognized and ordained by the Assemblies of God and sent out to work with Mexicans living near the border. She also served as the second president (after Sunshine Marshall Ball) of the *Concilio Misionero Femenil* (Women's Missionary Council) from 1941 to 1962.

[19] Willard and Livermore (eds.), *A Woman of the Century*, p. 512, where Carrie was referred to as a 'church worker and poet'. Carla C. Waterman in 'Montgomery Carrie Judd (1858-1946)', in J.D. Douglas (ed.), *Twentieth-Century Dictionary of Christian Biography* (Grand Rapids, MI: Baker Books, 1995), p. 258, refers to her as a 'Pentecostal writer, social worker, and teacher'. Diana Chapman in *Searching the Source of the River*, p. 66, refers to her as 'a speaker and teacher who was said to be the first woman to itinerate across the America ... Carrie was a remarkably gifted religious entrepreneur'.

hard to put Carrie into a box. In light of her various roles and her ecumenical nature, she was able to reach a variety of people from many different backgrounds. Throughout her ministry, Carrie transcended ecclesiology boundaries and operated more through a relational network than she did under a system. She was more concerned about advancing the Kingdom of God than she was about fitting into Church structures.[20] A friend of hers, J.N. Gortner, rightly noticed that she 'did not belong exclusively to any particular section of the world or to any particular denomination' but that her ministry 'was too worldwide in its scope, and too interdenominational in its character, to confine her to the limits of any man-made society or organization'.[21] Not only did Carrie transcend denominational barriers, but Albrecht rightly notices that she also became a 'spokesperson, leader and molder of three important religious streams: the faith healing movement, the Christian and Missionary Alliance, and the Pentecostal Movement'.[22]

Most significantly through her connection with founder A.B. Simpson, Carrie influenced the early stages of the Christian and Missionary Alliance. She also planted several of their churches and later introduced many members to their Pentecostal Spirit baptism experience.[23] That Carrie was a part of the early development of this movement as well as close friends with the founder reveals the im-

---

[20] See Waddell, 'The Home of Peace', pp. 232-33, in relation to training at the missionary school they had there. He said that the school provided 'daily teaching in the riches of the kingdom. This will fully carry out the original idea of the Home in the mind of Brother and Sister Montgomery, and fulfill the ideal of a complete work of the Holy Spirit.'

[21] J. Narver Gortner, 'Carrie Judd Montgomery – A Tribute'. He said she was 'internationally and interdenominationally known, and loved, and honored'. He later expanded and likely exaggerated here that her periodical has gone 'to every section of the inhabited globe' and that she 'has been known in every country on the face of the earth'. Because Carrie was a part of the initial formations of several organizations before their structures were crystallized, she had freedom to move within other networks as well.

[22] Albrecht, 'Carrie Judd Montgomery: Pioneering Contributor to Three Religious Movements', pp. 101, 112; and Alexander, *Pentecostal Healing*, p. 25. Jeannette Storms also correctly sees Carrie not only as an 'evangelical entrepreneur and theological groundbreaker' but also as a 'respected voice in evangelical and Pentecostal circles whose experience and wisdom contributed valuable perspective and direction' ('Carrie Judd Montgomery: The Little General', p. 286).

[23] These were initially started as branches and then later became churches. Carrie was well connected with many CMA missionaries who later came to stay with her at her Home of Peace. See Chapter 2.

portant role she played in influencing the foundations of a network of churches that is still in existence today. Carrie's contribution to the Salvation Army through supporting several of their ministries is also significant. Carrie additionally acted as a Pentecostal ambassador. Besides influencing major theological foundations within Pentecostal streams, especially the Assemblies of God, through her influence on leaders like Francisco Olazábal, she also provided support to other Pentecostal structures as well. Key leader of the Bible Standard Churches, Mrs Everett J. Fulton, even referred to Carrie as 'our dear little "spiritual mother"'.[24] Furthermore, this spiritual entrepreneur also acted as a 'fire starter' to inspire new ministries to begin.[25] The Union Bethel Gospel Mission in Texas was just one project that was started in response to her encouragement.[26] Additionally, spending time with the Montgomerys meant that their church planting heritage and entrepreneurial spirit might rub off. And to many, that is precisely what happened.

7.2.3 Moving Beyond Geographic Boundaries

Carrie's connections with many different international leaders also helped to strengthen and expand both the Divine Healing and early Pentecostal Movements. Her friendship with Alexander A. Boddy, Smith Wigglesworth, Elizabeth Baxter, and others allowed her teachings to spread further within Britain and beyond.[27] In addition to her friendship with A.B. Simpson, she also connected to Canadi-

---

[24] Mrs E.J. Fulton, 'Not Under a Bushel Now!', *Bible Standard Overcomer* (Oregon) 15.11 (Nov 1934), p. 13. For more information on this, see 'Introducing E.J. Fulton, Pastor of Lighthouse Temple, *The Open Standard Overcomer* 15.10 (Oct 1934), p. 2; and Mitchell, *The History of Open Bible Standard Churches*, p. 93. See also Carrie Judd Montgomery, 'Willows by the Water Courses', *Bible Standard* 8.5 (Nov 1927), p. 11; and 'The Trial of Faith', *Bible Standard* 9.7 (July 1928).

[25] Storms, 'Carrie Judd Montgomery: The Little General', p. 287. Clara Miner and Inga Thorgeson were first groomed by Carrie when they ran the Home of Peace before being sent off to start their own healing home in Los Angeles.

[26] W.E. Shepherd, 'Mission and Rescue Work in Texas', *TF* 16.1 (Jan 1896), p. 16. He told a story of how in 1890 when Carrie was passing through, she encouraged them to start a 'Gospel Mission' in which they 'immediately acted upon'.

[27] Boddy also subscribed to *Triumphs of Faith* and encouraged his readers to do so as well. When he came out to California, he made sure to attend Carrie's camp meetings and stay at her Home of Peace. One of the last articles of Carrie's in *Confidence* was entitled 'A Message to the Sick', and it was printed in May 1915. In relation to attending her World Wide Pentecostal Camp Meeting in 1914, Boddy saw that Carrie's name alone was an assurance against fanaticism. Carrie also connected with Baxter and the Boardman's who were in London as well as many others involved in the Keswick conventions.

an Pentecostal leaders Andrew H. Argue and his daughter Zelma Argue, and Aimee Semple McPherson.[28] Carrie's influence through Francisco Olazábal, Chonita Morgan Howard, and Juan L. Lugo had a significant impact on Latino Pentecostalism.[29] Additionally, Carrie's support of Pandita Ramabai's India ministry was important for dispersing her revival stories.[30] And while Carrie did go on an international missionary journey as well as to Mexico, the majority of the time the nations flocked to her base either in Buffalo or in Oakland where she ministered. It appears that Britain and Latin American experienced some of the most significant international ripple effects from Carrie's ministry.

7.2.4 Influencing the Apostolic[31]

As has been shown throughout this research, Carrie's significant influence extended beyond the regular participants of the Divine Healing and Pentecostal movements and reached to key apostolic leaders who initiated, influenced, or shaped their movements in profound ways.[32] Several key Pentecostal leaders were first introduced to divine healing or the Pentecostal Spirit baptism through Carrie's ministry.[33] Francisco Olazábal was one of these whose story

---

[28] Home of Peace Guest Book (Aug. 14, 1928-1938), July 8, 1931, p. 87, comment left by Bro. A.H. Argue. See also 1931, p. 85, comment left by Zelma Argue: 'The refreshment, perfume, and inspiration of this happy visit will accompany me to far fields'.

[29] Ruelas, *Women and the Landscape of American Higher Education*, p. 77, when referring to Victor De Leon's *The Silent Pentecostals: A biographical history of the Pentecostal Movement among the Hispanics in the twentieth century* (De Leon, 1979), p. 33. Lugo was taught under the Montgomerys before planting a Pentecostal church in Puerto Rico.

[30] The editors of *Confidence, PE, AGH, The Overcomer, Bible Standard*, and other periodicals with an international reach, chose to reproduce many of Carrie's writings over the years.

[31] I am using this term generally to describe influential leaders who lay down foundational structures for networks or movements to be built upon. Understanding of this term is based upon and influenced by Bill Johnson's view that 'Apostles carry a blueprint in their hearts concerning the church and God's purposes on the earth. They are used to bring fresh revelation to the church' ('Apostolic Teams', by Bill Johnson, found on www.bjm.org, accessed February 24, 2011). See also David Cannistraci's *The Gift of Apostle* (Regal Books, 1996).

[32] Carrie influenced many from the CMA to have their Pentecostal Spirit baptism experiences who later joined the Pentecostal Movement.

[33] Carrie Judd Montgomery, 'Notice', *TF* 43.1 (Jan 1923), p. 23. Mr and Mrs George Beal opened a Pentecostal Mission in Detroit Michigan as a result of Mrs Beal receiving her 'Baptism of the Holy Spirit' at Carrie's Beulah Chapel several years before.

is significant because it shows Carrie's influence in his life on three different levels: salvation, healing, and Pentecostal Spirit baptism. Because of the Montgomerys' influence, he went on to become one of the most significant figures in early Latin America Pentecostalism. It was also specifically through Carrie's writings that A.J. Tomlinson, who eventually founded the Church of God of Prophecy, was introduced to the doctrine of divine healing.[34] These along with John G. Lake, Alexander Boddy, and earlier non-Pentecostal A.B. Simpson are just a few examples of Carrie's influence on apostolic leaders. While I mention a few specific leaders whom Carrie influenced, these just scratch the surface as there are many more who were affected by her ministry.[35] That Carrie influenced many leaders within the Pentecostal Movement, even several who started their own movements under that umbrella, demonstrates the magnitude of her contribution to global Pentecostalism.

7.3 Significance of Carrie's Theology

7.3.1 A Radical Evangelical

It was Carrie's healing account in 1879 and her early literature that acted as a 'tipping point' for the national and global expansion of the Divine Healing Movement. The rapid spread of her healing story contributed to a major shift within Evangelicalism from the belief that God wanted one to endure suffering patiently to the belief that God wanted to heal. Her *Prayer of Faith* (1880) was revolutionary as it was one of the early theological books on divine healing. As a forerunner in her country, Carrie can easily be called the mother of healing homes in North America.[36] Carrie's pioneering contribution of healing homes is a valuable foundation and resource for any involved or interested in a similar healing ministry today. Additionally, by encouraging the common person to pray the prayer of faith, Carrie contributed to the democratization of healing.

---

[34] Shattuck, 'Ambrose Jessup Tomlinson', p. 991.

[35] Carrie was also personal friends with other apostolic leaders like Charles Cullis, William Booth, Minnie Abrams, Pandita Ramabai, Maria Woodworth-Etter, William J. Seymour, Smith Wigglesworth, Aimee Simple McPherson, and many others.

[36] I would call Dorothea Trudel the grandmother but it most be noted that she did her work in Europe, not North America.

7.3.2 Healing in the Atonement

While Carrie did not originate the doctrine of healing in the atonement, she was one of the early advocates to teach, popularize, and spread it through her networks as early as 1880.[37] This doctrine has become a cornerstone for many streams within Charismatic and Pentecostal Movements. Because of the many streams that have integrated the doctrine of healing in the atonement in one way or another, Carrie's influence on its formation is one of her most significant theological contributions not only for the Divine Healing Movement but also for Pentecostalism.

By laying out Carrie's theology of healing, this study has demonstrated one of the earliest and extreme forms of healing in the atonement lived out with its implications, difficulties, and results. This can be helpful for those who also adopt or have modified this doctrine when seeking to understand origins and also in learning how to approach the topic of suffering. Introducing a theology to deal with suffering along side of the doctrine of healing in the atonement might help to bring balance to the disillusionment of those who do not receive the immediate effects of their healing. Furthermore, Carrie moved beyond Palmer's positional understanding of sanctification to include not only healing, but everything else she saw that was in Christ's inheritance as well. This included finances to provide for ministry projects she felt the Spirit led her to initiate as well as her Pentecostal Spirit baptism. Just as Joshua and Caleb saw that the Promised Land was already theirs to take hold of, Carrie also understood that there were many things in the Christian life that had *already* been given and simply needed to be taken hold of. Understanding and integrating this principle today might similarly stir up strong faith in people to see the unseen and bring revolutionary changes as a result. Her thinking also provides space for further dialogue in relation to what specifically is freely available in the atonement of Christ. Carrie's theology of healing is also helpful for discussions in relation to if one can lose their healing. This research has begun these conversations and provides the opportunity for people to dialogue further on this and other themes related to healing.

---

[37] See Chapter 2 where I mention the others who also contributed to the early formation of the doctrine.

7.3.3 Pneumatology

The main effect that Carrie's 1908 experience had on her pneumatology was the integration of speaking in tongues along with adopting a newer Pentecostal paradigm for interpreting previous experiences. In Carrie's life, both before *and* after her initial speaking in tongues experience, her message was to act in faith to receive divine healing, to be unified in love above all controversies, and to pursue the fullness of the Spirit. The addition of tongues simply built on and added an extended element to the last one listed. Throughout the years, Carrie called people to dive into the limitless measures of the Holy Spirit and not to settle for anything less. It was not her 1908 experience that radically altered or empowered her life; it was her hunger for the 'fullness of the Spirit', in *whatever* way that looked, which caused her to continue to be effective in ministry both before and after her Pentecostal Spirit baptism experience. Even in that however, her interpretation of her 1908 experience demonstrates that she believed that speaking in tongues was an important aspect of the Christian life to pursue which would enhance one's spirituality and open them up to even deeper measures with the Spirit. Additionally, for Carrie, the manifestation of tongues brought her closer to God more than it empowered her for ministry. These are important things to consider in relation to the place of Pentecostal Spirit baptism and the manifestation of tongues within spirituality.

Further, this research on Carrie's pneumatology is significant because it shows that one of the early people involved in the formation of the Assemblies of God did not publicly enter into debates regarding the doctrine of initial evidence.[38] That she saw this as a non-essential of the faith can spark deeper conversations in relation to initial evidence and its place in the Christian life and in doctrinal statements. Additionally, throughout her ministry, Carrie emphasized the fruit of the Spirit more than the gifts or manifestations of the Spirit, without throwing either out. Her pneumatology was not 'either/or' in relation to the gifts and experiences of the Spirit, but 'both/and more'.[39] Carrie actively sought the fullness of

---

[38] Montgomery, *Under His Wings,* p. 165. Even later on in life she still referred to it as a sign.

[39] Heidi Baker, Interview by Jennifer A. Miskov, February 26, 2011 at St. Aldates Church in Oxford, England. This was originally 'both/and' until an inter-

the Spirit in continuous flooding measures both before and after 1908 *and* also pursued the distinct experience of Pentecostal Spirit baptism and the reception of tongues. The limitless measures of the Spirit that Carrie described in her writings, which encompassed both a distinct Pentecostal experience of Spirit baptism with the manifestation of tongues *and* included continual similar flooding experiences of the Spirit, presents a new paradigm of limitless measures, not stages. Furthermore, this research suggests a need for a reinterpretation of what Spirit baptism is and calls for people take hold of speaking in tongues *and* also to pursue the fullness of the Spirit relentlessly and consistently in overwhelming measures.

7.3.4 A Legacy worth Remembering

Carrie contributed to the growth and strength not only of the Divine Healing Movement, but also the early Pentecostal Movement in a profound way that deserves recognition. Through her networks, she influenced the expansion of both movements by spreading their themes throughout the world. Carrie had an ecumenical and global heart; she was not content to minister just in 'Galilee', she wanted to minister to the 'ends of the earth', and in fact, she did both.[40] Her life can easily be summed up by Mt. 10.8 where Jesus says, 'Freely you have received, freely give', because whatever Carrie received from God, she sought to give away freely whether that was salvation, healing, Pentecostal Spirit baptism, or some other blessing. Her literature, healing homes, role in the formation and advancement of the doctrine of healing in the atonement, active pursuit of the fullness of the Spirit, and passion for unity in love all contribute to her legacy. Furthermore, she not only inspired women in ministry, advocated on behalf of minorities, but she also influenced significant leaders within both movements. Carrie was a prophetic pioneer who had a global, ecumenical, and theological impact on the Divine Healing Movement, Pentecostalism, and beyond; her unique and powerful contribution need no longer be underestimated.

---

view with Heidi Baker in relation to Carrie Judd Montgomery where she mentioned the added element of 'both/and more'.

[40] In reference to Acts 1.8 and John 2.

7.4 Significance for Christian Leaders Today: A Prophetic Voice for a Revival Generation

Carrie's voice can continue to inform, guide, and challenge movements today as it did in the past century. We can learn from the *way* in which Carrie approached the newer manifestations of the Spirit and maneuvered through revivals or spiritual awakenings in her time.[41] On a pragmatic level, she used discernment, *actively* pursued what she discovered as valuable, and then disseminated it to others. She did all this while maintaining unity in love. It is important to recognize that Carrie was not simply 'open' to new moves of the Spirit as some suggest, but she was 'hungry' for and *actively* pursued the 'fullness of the Spirit', however that might have looked both before and after 1908.[42] Regardless of age, reputation, or previous experiences, Carrie chose to look beyond fanaticism and to the heart of what she believed the Spirit was doing in her day. Carrie was not merely open to the Spirit, but she actively pursued all that she believed the Spirit had for her in her generation.

Furthermore, Carrie's ability to maintain unity in love can be significant for present day Evangelicals interacting with Pentecostals, for traditional Catholics intersecting the Charismatic movement, or for Christians from any tradition when approaching the newer things of the Spirit.[43] Despite excesses or fanaticism in relation to the manifestations of the Spirit, Carrie continued to press into what she believed God was doing in her day while keeping love as the central theme. When the work of the Holy Spirit comes in all different packages, sizes, shapes, sounds, and expressions, for Carrie, the *way* in which a person approaches these things can be important so that they do not miss out on all that the Holy Spirit

---

[41] Miskov, *Spirit Flood*, pp. 30-39.

[42] Montgomery, 'Pentecostal Blessing', p. 62, and her 'Miraculously Healed by the Lord Thirty Years Ago', p. 8. Alexander, *Pentecostal Healing*, p. 151. Alexander notices that Carrie 'was characterized by an openness to new experiences, especially those of a spiritual nature'. If she was merely 'open' to the 'fullness of the Spirit' during the early 1900s however, she would not have gone on a trip to search these things out or ask her friends to pray with her for the Pentecostal experience. See also Montgomery, *Under His Wings,* p. 42.

[43] Paul L. King *Genuine Gold: The Cautiously Charismatic Story of the Early Christian and Missionary Alliance*, p. 311. In light of King's speculations of where A.B. Simpson might fit today, I would not place Carrie in the category of one who chases after signs and wonders but rather one who chases after the fullness of the Spirit. Signs and wonders were welcomed by Carrie, but not overemphasized.

might want to do in their lives. Carrie never wanted to be like 'many conservative Christians [who] are so afraid of "wild fire" that they are apt to miss the true fire'.[44] Having an openness *and* hunger to pursue the fullness of the Spirit regardless of what it might look like is a legacy that Carrie leaves behind. Her wisdom can continue to inspire people from any background to do the same today. In December 1906 and in relation to her own spiritual journey towards the newer manifestations of the Spirit in her time, Carrie said, 'Let us all bow low before God, and be as humble and simple as little children, that we may miss nothing of the blessing God wants to pour upon His children in these last days'.[45] She also later encouraged,

> Now who is going to trust God for the winged life? You can crawl instead if you wish. God will even bless you if you crawl; He will do the best He can for you, but oh how much better to avail ourselves to our wonderful privileges in Christ and to 'mount up with wings as eagles, run and not be weary, walk and not faint.' O beloved friends, there is a life on wings. I feel the streams of His life fill me and permeate my mortal frame from my head to my feet, until no words are adequate to describe it. I can only make a few bungling attempts to tell you what it is like and ask the Lord to reveal to you the rest. May He reveal to you your inheritance in Christ Jesus so that you will press on and get all that He has for you.[46]

May Carrie's words indeed stir a new generation to take hold of all that God has for them and may her own passionate pursuit of the Spirit inspire an unquenchable thirst for the fullness of the Spirit within our hearts today.

---

[44] Carrie Judd Montgomery, 'The Work in Los Angeles', *TF* 27.1 (Jan 1907), p. 14.

[45] Carrie Judd Montgomery, 'Letter from Los Angeles', *TF* 26.12 (Dec 1906), p. 247. This is how she introduced an extract 'from a remarkable letter from Frank Bartleman' that was earlier published in the *Way of Faith*. See also her 'The Work in Los Angeles', *TF* 27.1 (Jan 1907), p. 14, where she says, 'May God keep us from any deception of the enemy, and yet keep us so humble at the feet of Jesus' cross that we may miss nothing of the fulness of blessing which He has in His heart for us'.

[46] Montgomery, 'The Life on Wings', p. 176.

Appendix 1

Timeline of Carrie Judd Montgomery's Life (1858-1946)

(Dates that are significant and that receive attention in this volume are listed in boldface type.)

1858 April 8, Carrie Frances Judd born in Buffalo, New York

1868/9? Carrie's sister Emma died

1869/70 Carrie's brother Eddie got sick. She prayed alone her room and he was later healed

1872 Carrie was confirmed at St. Mary's Church by Bishop Arthur Cleveland Coxe

1873 Moved with brother Charlie to Dansville, NY, and worked for an editor of a health magazine

Returned home to help with ill father and sister Jennie. Father was healed, but Jennie died

1875? Moved to Linden, NY with brother Charlie for a year. Started Sunday school in her home there.

1876 Jan. 6, Carrie had an accident that caused her to be bedridden for two years. Carrie 17 years old at the time.

1879 Feb. 20, Thursday, Carrie's father read newspaper article on Mrs Mix/ family mailed letter to Mrs Mix

Feb 25, Tuesday, Carrie received response letter from Mrs Mix

Feb 26, Wednesday at around 3:30 pm, Carrie was healed. She was 20 years old at this time.

1880 *Prayer of Faith* book published, one of the early books that taught on healing in the atonement

June, she began Thursday prayer meetings 7:30-9:00 pm. In the summer, she opened Faith Sanctuary

1881 January, *Triumphs of Faith* begins with 'Faith Reckonings' as first article. Carrie was 22 years old.

1882 April 3, Carrie's healing home, Faith-Rest Home in Buffalo, NY opened

1883 Carrie met A.B. Simpson. In May, he established his healing home

1885 May 1, Carrie's Faith-Rest Cottage opened (a larger home was rented and opened)

1887 Sept., establishment of The Christian Alliance at Old Orchard Convention with Carrie, recording Secretary

1888 George Montgomery healed through the prayers of Alexander Dowie

1889 May, a church shut doors to Carrie because she was a woman preacher and she preached to 'negros'

Oct., Carrie met George in Chicago at one of Simpson's conventions and invited her to convention in CA

Carrie traveled with Elizabeth Sisson to West Coast where they encountered Woodworth's ministry

1890 April/May, E. Sisson no longer assistant editor, confusion over Woodworth's ministry

May 14, Carrie married George with A.B. Simpson there to help officiate wedding in Buffalo, NY

May 24, Carrie's father died/Honeymoon trip to the West Coast/ Carrie met up with Charles Cullis in Boston

She temporarily moved to San Francisco, CA (at 32 years old)

1891 May 25, baby Faith born

July/Aug. Montgomerys initiated Oakland branch of the Christian Alliance

Nov., On Thanksgiving Day, Carrie and George become 'National Specials' in Salvation Army

1892 While in New York, Carrie joined the SA's 'Slum Sisters' in their outreaches

May 1, Faith Rest Cottage (Buffalo, NY) officially closed down/Carrie moved to Oakland, CA permanently

Sept/Oct, she established a mission in the slums to reach out to prostitutes, this lasted about a year

Oct/Nov, visited Cazadero for first time

1893 June 20-31st first Cazadero Camp meeting with mostly Holiness teachers, Christian Alliance, and SA

Nov. 7, Home of Peace dedicated

1894 Dec., Montgomerys met William Booth

Cazadero Camp Meeting

1895 Cazadero Camp Meeting

Oct. 5, 1895, Shalom Training School initiated

Sept. 6, dedication of Beulah Orphanage (she ran her orphanages from 1895-1908)

1896 Cazadero Camp Meeting

1897 The Christian Alliance and Missionary Alliance merged to form The Christian and Missionary Alliance

Cazadero Camp Meeting

Nov. 19, Bird's Nest (home for young children) dedicated, Rose Bud (babies), Sunshine Home later

1898 Canceled Cazadero Meeting because too sick to organize

June 11, Carrie was healed again shortly after surges of prayer/fasting by SA and CMA

1900 Cazadero Camp Meeting

1901 Cazadero Camp Meeting

1902 Cazadero Camp Meeting

1905 Beulah Chapel Church dedicated

1906 April 18, Carrie woke up early, prayed the blood of Jesus over home, then San Francisco earthquake hit

1st article in *TF* mentioning Azusa Street

George went to Azusa Street to investigate revival

Cazadero Camp Meeting

1907 Carrie mentioned her visit to Azusa Street in *TF* and also connected with Yoakum, founder of Pigsah home

1908 Carrie took a trip east to clear her head and search out new Pentecostal stirrings

April 1, Frank Bartleman and family stayed in Home of Peace

Carrie prayed with friends in Cleveland, Ohio for her Pentecostal Spirit baptism and took it by faith

About a week later in Chicago, on June 29, while with Simmons, Carrie (50 yrs old) spoke in tongues

Carrie closed down her orphanage work

1909 Carrie supported Woodworth-Etter's ministry, even sharing the stage with her

Missionary journey (Jan. 23-Sept. 16) to China, India, England then New York back to the West Coast

1910 April 7, Carrie's mother died (1822-1910). William Durham started teaching on Finished Work of Christ

1911 Inga Thorgeson and Clara Miner branched off to start a healing home in L.A.

1912 May-Sept? William J. Seymour to Alexander Boddy stayed in Home of Peace.

1913 Trip to Texas also Woodworth-Etter's meetings

1914 'World Wide Pentecostal Camp Meeting' in Cazedero (Pentecostals, Evangelicals/Holiness, Wigglesworth)

Carrie registered as an Evangelist with the forming Assemblies of God

Oneness Controversy

1916 Maria Woodworth-Etter meetings. Carrie traveled to Mexico, L.A.

1917 Assemblies of God officially formed

1918 May 27, Judd Finley Berry born to Faith Merrill H. Berry, Carrie became a grandmother

A.B. Simpson still inviting her to preach, Carrie took trip back east with George

1919 March 17, Aimee Semple McPherson spoke at Carrie's Monday meeting

Oct. 29, A.B. Simpson died

1921 She wrote *Secrets of Victory*

1922 She wrote *Heart Melody, The Life of Praise*

1923 Meeting in Fresno at Full Gospel Tabernacle where she met Zelma Argue

1930 George died (1851-1930)

1931 Andrew H. Argue with wife and daughter, Zelma Argue, stayed in Home of Peace

Carrie took trip back east, also to Toronto, Canada and spoke there

1936 She wrote her life story in *Under His Wings*

1946 July 26, she died (at 88 yrs)

Appendix 2

Mix's Healing Account in 'Miraculous Cures in Connecticut', *The Buffalo Daily Courier*,

(Thursday Morning) February 20, 1879

MIRACULOUS CURES IN CONNECTICUT.

Springfield Republican.

Mrs. Edward Mix, a Wolcottville colored woman of 45, is creating quite a sensation in Litchfield county by her cures from the laying on of hands. She says she does nothing without God's help; that her patients must have implicit faith to insure success; and that she herself was cured, after years of ill health by the prayers and the laying on of hands of a second advent preacher of this city, named Allen. He suggested that she had the power of healing in her, and her first experience was in curing a troublesome wart under her eye. After laying her hand on the protuberance and praying for its removal it withered away and dropped off in a night. Then she began with other persons and has treated 200, some of them with wonderful success. A Mrs. Burr, of Burrville, who had been sick for 30 and confined to her room for 25 years, was treated on one Sunday and has been well and strong ever since, while a Wolcottville boy, who had never walked on account of weak ankles, was similarly cured. The doctors in the vicinity say Mrs. Mix has wonderful power of some kind, but they claim that she is successful only with functional or chronic diseases, and that the most of her cures are effected among the lower and more superstitious classes. Mrs. Mix never asks for any pay from her patients, as she says it would be wrong to do so while doing God's work, but she takes what is offered her. Sometimes, however, she has to pay her own expenses when going to see people and gets nothing in return.

This is the newspaper article about Mrs Mix's healing account that Carrie's father read just before her healing (Microfilm accessed at Buffalo State University, NY). This article was originally printed in the *Springfield Republican* and reprinted in *The Buffalo Daily Courier*

Appendix 3

Carrie F. Judd, 'Ministry', *Triumphs of Faith* **2.11 (Nov 1882), p. 173.**

To obtain great spiritual blessings for ourselves we must pour out our souls for others. There is a form of spiritual selfishness which keeps us so conscious of our own needs that, in seeking spiritual supplies for ourselves, we become almost oblivious of the needs of others, and forget the apostle's injunction, 'Let no man seek his own, but every man another's wealth'. – (1 Cor. 10:24).

We often feel justified in this selfishness by the argument that we cannot help others without first being filled ourselves. While in one sense this is true, yet as those who walk by faith and not by sight, we must take by faith our position in Christ, claiming that He is to us each moment all we need, for in Him are 'hid all the treasures of wisdom and knowledge', and then out of His abundant wealth which we thus claim because He has given *Himself* to us, we must by faith dispense to others. God tells us in His Word that if we draw out our soul to the hungry, and satisfy the afflicted soul, then shall our light rise in obscurity and our darkness be as the noon-day. – (Isa. 58:10).

Human wisdom would tell us first to fill ourselves before we try to fill others; *Divine* wisdom takes her stand as *already filled*, by faith in Christ's fullness, and realizes that as she gives to others of this hidden wealth it shall be made manifest. The promise goes on, 'And the Lord shall guide thee continually, and satisfy thy soul in drought and make fat thy bones and thou shalt be like a watered garden and like a spring of waters, whose waters fail not' – (Isa. 58:11). Guided, as, by faith in our Guide, we guide others; satisfied, as, by faith, we satisfy the afflicted souls around us; made fat, as we give of Christ's overflowing fullness to those who seem even less needy than ourselves, until at last we are no longer conscious of receiving the former, and latter rains moderately, but our souls become like watered gardens and like springs of never-failing water. *Filled continually*, as by faith we *pour out continually*. Beloved, let us in all our service, in the ministry of prayer as well as in work or exhortation, be like the Son of Man Who came not to be ministered unto, but to minister and to give His life a ransom for many. Then shall we stand with Him, our great High Priest, in our office of royal Priesthood, 'consecrated for evermore'.

Appendix 4

Carrie Judd Montgomery, '"The Promise of the Father." A Personal Testimony', *Triumphs of Faith* 28.7 (July 1908), pp. 145-49.

'That we might receive the promise of the Spirit through faith'. Gal. 3:14.

'If any man thirst, let him come unto Me and drink. He that believeth on Me, as the Scripture hath said, out of his inner man shall flow rivers of living water. But this spake He of the Spirit, which they that believe on Him should receive.' John 7:37-39.

For some time I have been thirsting for the fullness of the Holy Spirit's presence and power. At the time of my miraculous healing, when a young girl, I was first made conscious of the Spirit's work in revealing Jesus in and to me. At this time a power to testify came into my soul, and the Word of God was wonderfully opened to me, so that He has greatly blessed my ministry in the Word since that time. This experience I have always referred to as the baptism of the Holy Ghost until a few months ago, when I began to watch what God was doing in pouring out His Pentecostal fullness upon some of His little ones. At first I was perplexed. I knew my experience, above referred to, was most real and lasting in its effects. How could I cast it away? Then I came to understand that I was not to depreciate His precious work in the past, but to follow on to receive the fullness of the same Spirit.

Before Pentecost Jesus 'breathed' on His disciples and saith unto them, 'Receive ye the Holy Ghost' (John 20:22). I believe they then received a foretaste, or earnest, of what they afterwards received in fullness at Pentecost. I watched the so-called Pentecostal work carefully and prayerfully. There was much that did not appeal to me. People who claimed to have received the baptism seemed to get in the way of the Spirit. Beginning in the Spirit, they often seemed to fail to walk in the Spirit. They became lifted up, or let self get the ascendency. Many of the manifestations did not seem at all like the work of the calm, majestic Spirit of God. In many meetings there was much confusion, where God tells us He is not the author of confusion, but of peace (1 Cor. 14:33, 40). The people often failed to walk in Scriptural lines in regard to unknown tongues, using them in the general assembly, 'the whole church,' where there was no interpreter, contrary to the Word of God. See 1 Cor. 14, for careful direction about this matter. In 1 Cor. 12:28, we see that 'diversities of tongues' are 'set' in the church, and Paul says not to forbid them (1 Cor. 14:39). He also tells us that he who speaks in an unknown tongue, speaketh not unto men, but unto God, and that 'in the spirit he speaketh mysteries' (1 Cor. 14:3); also that he 'edifieth himself'. We are told, however, most plainly, that 'greater is he that prophesieth than he that speaketh with tongues, except he interpret, that the church may receive edifying'. And yet, in spite of all this, Paul says, 'I would that ye all spake with tongues,' and he thanks God that he speaks with tongues more than they all. (Why did he thank God for this gift, if it was not truly to be desired?) This chapter is so very clear, we need not refer to it further, but commend it to the careful attention of our readers.

I have stated some of my objections to the so-called Pentecostal work, but God began to work among some of my personal Christian friends, and it compelled my closest attention. One lady I had known for years as a sanctified and anointed teacher of God's Word. She was not satisfied, and pressed on by faith into the fullness of the Holy Ghost. Her experience was most satisfactory, such appreciation of the blood, such power to witness, increased intercessory prayer, such a baptism of divine love. She spoke with tongues, but kept the gift in its proper place. One of the dear Beulah workers also received the fullness, and we could all realize the increased depths of sweetness, humility and power which took possession of her life. Other dear friends, whose lives I had fully known, pressed on by faith and received their baptism.

I began to 'thirst' for the fullness. I remembered an experience which I had a few years after my healing, while kneeling with a dear sister, and asking for the Spirit's fullness. He had then come upon me in much greater power than at the time of my healing, and so manifested His sweet presence that it had been almost overpowering. This experience had been so remarkable and so sacred that John 7:37-39 seemed to be verified to me then, only that I stopped short, I believe, of all that He desired to give me at that time, and so the oil was stayed. The effect of this Divine outpouring has always remained to some degree in my life, causing a separatedness unto Him which I did not know before. I had often longed for the sense of His presence to return, as I then experienced it, before I (to some extent) grieved Him by unbelief and failure to go on with Him. Recently I began seeking the fullness of the Holy Ghost but was kept very busy, and did not actually 'tarry' at His feet as I felt I should.

While on an eastern trip this summer, I met other precious friends whose sweet Christian life I had known in the past, but who had pressed on into God's best. I grew still more thirsty for the rivers of living water. I knew I had tiny streams, but not rivers. I tried to go to meetings where people were tarrying for the endurement [sic] of power from on High, but seemed again and again providentially hindered from going to them. I then prayed that if it were His will He would let me receive His fullness while waiting upon Him alone, or with some Christian friend. I asked Him also for quiet, sweet manifestations, which would reveal His majesty and dignity, and not such as might seem like excitement of the flesh.

In Cleveland I met a dear young lady whom I had known since she was six years old. Her face was beaming with the calm light and beauty of God's unmistakable seal. Several of her young friends had also received their baptism, but were being kept on quiet, Scriptural lines. I asked them to pray for me, which they did. I said, 'By the blood of Jesus my whole being is open to the fullness of God, and by that same precious blood I am closed to any power of the enemy'. As these dear ones prayed for me, the Spirit said, 'Take'. I waited and was afraid to do this, lest I should go back on this position of faith. The Spirit said again, and yet again, 'Take,' and finally I received the Spirit, by faith, to take complete possession of spirit, soul and body, and testified thus to the dear ones praying for me. I kept on tarrying at His feet for the manifestation of His gracious presence. I asked Him to teach me to 'drink'. Rom. 8:11 was vividly brought to me, and I saw in a most forcible way that my body, His temple, was to be filled with His resurrection Spirit. That same evening, in a measure, I began to experience His power, but He held me steadily to my position of faith, not letting me get my eyes on manifestations. The next day I returned to Chicago, and as soon as possible made my way to the home of Mrs. Lucy Simmons, of Oak Park, a dear friend of former years, whose Christian life has long been an inspiration to me, and whose recent experience of Pentecostal fullness had greatly impressed me. We tarried together at the Savior's feet. The cry was still in my heart, although I was standing by faith.

On Monday, June 29th, less than a week from the time I first took my stand by faith, the mighty outpouring came upon me. I had said, 'I am all under the blood and under the oil'. I then began singing a little song, 'He gives me joy instead of sorrow,' etc. To my surprise, some of the words would stick in my throat, as though the muscles tightened and would not let me utter them. I tried several times with the same result. Mrs. Simmons remarked that she thought the Lord was taking away my English tongue, because He wanted me to speak in some other language. I replied, 'Well, He says in Mark 16:17, 'They shall speak with new tongues,' so I take that, too, by faith'. In a few moments I uttered a few scattered words in an unknown tongue and then burst into a language and came pouring out in great fluency and clearness. The brain seemed entirely passive, the words not coming from that source at all, but from an irresistible volume of power within, which seemed to possess my whole being, spirit, soul and body.[1]

For nearly two hours I spoke and sang in unknown tongues (there seemed three or four distinct languages). Some of the tunes were beautiful, and most Oriental. I tried sometimes to say something in English, but the effort caused such distress in my throat and head, I had to stop after a few words and go back to the unknown tongues.[2] I was filled with joy and praise to God with an inward depth of satisfaction in Him which cannot be described. To be thus controlled by the Spirit of God and to feel that He was speaking 'heavenly mysteries' through me was most delightful. The rivers of living water flowed through me and divine ecstasy filled my soul. There was no shaking, and no contortions of the body. I felt that I drank and used up the life and power as fast as it was poured in. I became very weak physically under the greatness of the heavenly vision and staggered when I tried to walk across the floor. But when the exhaustion became very great, dear Mrs. Simmons asked the Lord to strengthen me, which He did so sweetly, letting His rest and healing life possess my weary frame. Passages from the Word of God came to me with precious new meanings. Not long after this I had a vision of the work of His Cross as never before. The blessing and power abides and He prays and praises through me in tongues quite frequently.

When His power is heavy upon me, nothing seems to give vent and expression to His fullness like speaking or singing in an unknown tongue. I pray that I may be kept as clay in His hands; that I may be kept very low at His feet, and never get in His blessed way. He keeps me continually standing by faith in His finished work, not walking by

---

[1] When Carrie reprinted this in her autobiography nearly 20 years later, she rephrased this sentence by saying that 'The words seemed to come from an irresistible volume of power within, which seemed to possess my whole being, spirit, soul and body' (Montgomery, *Under His Wings,* p. 169)

[2] Montgomery, *Under His Wings,* 169. In her autobiography, she deleted this sentence and inserted the following instead: 'A "weight of glory" rested upon my head, which I could distinctly feel and see in the Spirit'.

sight, and this is my answer to those who might accuse me of depending upon manifestations in my Christian life. He says, 'Ye shall be witnesses unto me'. Pray that I may be a faithful witness to His glory.

Reports of Pentecostal blessing are coming from all over the world. It certainly seems that it is the time of the 'latter rain' *mentioned* in Zech. 10:1.

If so, let the dear sanctified children of God heed the words, 'Ask ye of the Lord rain in the time of the latter rain; so the Lord shall make bright clouds, and give them showers of rain".[3]

---

[3] In recounting this in her autobiography, she added the following paragraph to the ending of the article:

The 13th chapter of 1 Corinthians speaks of tongues of men and angels, but shows us that without divine love the people who speak are 'become as sounding brass, or a tinkling cymbal.' So let all who have this experience see that they keep low at the feet of Jesus, being filled with His own humility and love. I might add that a number of times the Holy Spirit has spoken through me in languages which have been understood by missionaries who had learned those languages on the foreign field. At one time a family of four from China, the husband ad wide and two sons, heard me speak in the Chinese language, and readily understood what was said. At other times, in my private devotions, or with some friend of the same mind, I have been given sweet, ecstatic utterances which seemed indeed like the tongues of angels. Not long after my return from the East my dear husband also received this blessed outpouring. We both realized a greater power for service, and increased fellowship in prayer and praise (*Under His Wings,* p. 170).

Appendix 5

Carrie Judd Montgomery, 'The Life on Wings: The Possibilities of Pentecost'

First printed in *The Latter Rain Evangel* 3.3 (December 1910), pp. 19-24, and then later in *Triumphs of Faith* 32.8 (August 1912), pp. 169-77, the article was taken from an address delivered at the Stone Church in Chicago in 1910 and revised by the author (CJM).

I want to talk to you about 'The Life on Wings'. Read with me Deuteronomy xxxii:9-14. That the Lord's people are the Lord's portion is a precious thought, for He left everything in order that He might have this portion. So, I believe the Lord means for us to realize how very, very precious we are to Him. We remember how in our own experience He found us in a 'desert land' and in the 'waste howling wilderness,' and led us about and instructed us and kept us as the apple of His eye.

Then in this scripture there follows the picture of the eagle stirring up her nest. Many of you have probably read the description as has actually been witnessed by some who have climbed to the dizzy height of rocks and watched the mother eagle break up the nest of her young. The time had come when the mother-bird saw that the eaglets must learn to fly, and in order that they might learn to do this, she took her strong beak and made havoc of the nest; pulled it to pieces in order that the eaglets might no longer have a resting place there. Then she throws the young eaglets out of the nest down over the dizzy precipice, and of course, the little things think they will be dashed to pieces on the great rocks beneath, but with one great swoop the mother-bird sweeps down under them, and the little eaglets, instead of falling down to be dashed to pieces on the rocks below, fall upon the safe, strong wings of the mother.

This is the picture that God gives us as the actual way in which He deals with you and me. We can all of us think as we look back, how He stirred up our nests. We had such nice ones; all fixed up for ourselves. They were softly lined, and cozy and warm, and we expected to stay but God came, spoiled all our plans, broke in pieces the nest and tumbled us out. Why? In order that we might learn to fly; in order that we might find the wings which He had already caused to spring forth within our very hearts, but which we had not learned to use, the wings of faith. I look back and remember how He tore my nest to pieces. I had it all arranged. I had my aspirations and ambitions as a young girl. I knew just what I wanted and what would make me happy, and what, in a vague way, I trusted would make me useful, but God permitted the nest to be pulled to pieces. That awful sickness that followed after I had fallen and injured my spine, those days and nights of suffering, of anguish, of helplessness ; those days when the very room had to be darkened on account of the suffering in my head, were but a mere shadow of the darkness that had come into my life and into my very soul. Through this awful trial it seemed as though everything was lost; I could not see that there ever would be any brightness in life. I was a confirmed helpless invalid. For two years and two months I lay there, being taken down at the age of eighteen, at a time when a girl's life usually looks the brightest. Oh, how hard it was! Nobody knows how hard, and I was so hungry after God. My soul was utterly unsatisfied, but God was breaking up the nest of human ambitions, human hopes and aspirations. He knew what He was doing, although I did not.

Job said, 'He knoweth the way that I take; when He hath tried me I shall come forth as gold'. He knew the way for Job and He knew it for me also. Now, after all the years of blessing that have been mine since I was so wondrously healed by the Lord, I realize more and more it was because the snug nest in which I thought I was so secure, was broken up. Now I am able to encourage other hearts that are going through the shadow and through the valley. So take heart, dear friends; it is better farther on, for as some one has said, there are two openings to the tunnel. We go in at one end, but there is another end to come out. We may be in the tunnel today, beloved, but the other end is there, and you will go through if you go on with God.

What would my life have been without that stirring up? God only knows, but I know it would not have been what it has been. After the long period of suffering and anguish and the coming down to the very jaws of death, the Lord swept His great eagle wings under the poor little frightened eaglet and I found His great wings to rest upon.

He says in Exodus xix:4, 'Ye have seen what I did unto the Egyptians, and how I bare you on eagles' wings, and brought you unto Myself'. Oh, what a blessed goal! Unto Himself! On the strong eagle wings God bears us unto His very heart of love. Oh what a wonderful day that was when He answered prayer for me! The time had been set for prayer by that dear colored woman, Mrs. Mix. How wonderful it was that we heard about her at all! The Lord knew what the result would be when He let that little account of her healing of consumption in answer to prayer, be published in a Buffalo paper, and let it catch my father's eye. In those days very little was known, especially in this country, about Divine Healing. Do not think, beloved, we ever had such meetings as these we now enjoy. I would that you might realize your privileges!

When this dear colored sister in Connecticut wrote and said 'The prayer of faith shall save the sick, and the Lord shall raise him up,' I didn't know that was in the Bible. She said, 'This promise is for you as though you were the only person living. That was a wonderful thought, and the Lord gave me a mighty inspiration of divine faith I never had before. He revealed Himself to me, raised me up, caused all the diseases to depart in one instant of time, and gave me my first introduction to the Holy Spirit. Oh how wonderful it all was! No words can describe it.

Those days were days of praise when it seemed as though I should call upon everything around to help me praise the Lord. I found the eagle's wings. At first it seemed as though I only knew the dove wings; they were not very strong; the little attempted flights of faith, in certain directions had to be increased. You remember the Psalmist said, 'Oh that I had wings like a dove, that I might fly away and be at rest'. But the dove wings would not take us very far; we need the eagle wings. So through different teachings and especially through many testings and trials of faith, the Lord changed the dove wings into the eagle wings.

But some are saying, 'How are we to get this faith?' The only way God can develop our faith is through trial. You ask the Lord to give you a stronger faith, and what does He do? He puts a trial upon the faith you already have. He will take your faith and test it and try it, and you think all is lost, but that very testing and trying of your faith is what brings out the pure gold and causes you to have a stronger faith than ever you had before.

In California we have many gold mines even yet, although they are not so plentiful as they used to be. There are two kinds of mines: one is the placer mine which contains the loose gold mingled with the sand and which therefore can easily be separated; the other is a quartz mine, where the gold is in the rock. When it is free gold it can very easily be separated from the rock, but in many of the mines there is what the miners call rebellious ore; they also call it refractory ore, and when I first heard my husband call the ore rebellious and say it was a technical term they used, I said, 'That is just like some people, rebellious ore, refractory ore; the gold is there but very hard to get out'. This gold is so united with baser metals that they must have a different process to get the gold free from the baser ore; they do not care anything about the baser ores, they can be burned up or volatilized, but the miners are after the gold.

Now God is after the gold in us. 'I counsel thee to buy of Me gold tried in the fire, that thou mayst be rich'. They have different processes now, but one process which is used a good deal is a row of furnaces through which it is put one after the other and each one is hotter than the preceding. We ask to be delivered from one of God's furnaces and we may get into a hotter one. I visited a mine and I saw the whole process. First, they broke the rock in pieces and then pulverized it, then there were large canvas sheets spread out, slightly on an incline, and the pulverized rock and ore was put on there and a stream of water was run over it, and someone stood at the top and swept it down carefully. The pulverized rock which was light went off with the water, but the metal, which was heavier, stayed on the canvas and it was swept off in little piles. It didn't look at all like gold, and you know, beloved, it is only God that can see the gold in us sometimes; I am sorry we haven't more spiritual perception to enable us to see the gold in each other. May God help us to see the gold in each other's souls!

Those sulphurets, as they call them, look something like mortar; you couldn't see any gold at all, but it was there. We went into the furnace room, and saw where they were putting it into one furnace after another; my husband is a mining man and he took me to visit this large mine that I might see all the processes.

The superintendent stood by me and we saw a lot of little sparks flying in every direction, and he explained that that was the baser metals being burned or volatilized, and then, not knowing he was uttering a great spiritual truth, he said, 'When the sparks stop flying we take it out of the fire. It is finished'. That was so good I looked up at my husband and said: 'Why, that is the way it is with us; the Lord takes us out of the furnace when the sparks stop flying, the sparks of doubt, the sparks of fear, the sparks of impatience and of lack of love; when they stop flying then God the Great Refiner knows it is time to take US out of the furnace'. Let us ask God to do His work quickly that the sparks may stop flying, but when we do see the sparks flying in ourselves or in each other shall we not be more patient now that we know what the sparks are? that they are only flying because God is working with us or working with some other soul? May God help us to be patient with each other when the sparks fly! Sparks are not always agreeable especially when they fly upon us, but the Lord can make us patient.

Oh, I often think that if instead of getting impatient with the dear tried ones when perhaps their love fails, or their patience fails, or their faith fails, if we could only stand in love and tenderness and resist the enemy for them, claim the victory of the blood for their poor, tried souls how much better it would be and how much faster the Lord could work with our own souls. The Lord help us! He is trying to teach us to love one another with a pure heart fervently. I understand 'fervently' here, in the Greek, means to be 'boiling hot' in our love. You never can have the love that keeps up to the boiling heat all the time unless you first have a pure heart. 'Love one another with a pure heart fervently'.

We want to look again at the thought of the winged life. We get it in that well-known passage in Isa. xl:28-31. 'He giveth power to the faint; and to them that have no might He increaseth strength'. I wonder if there are any faint ones here tonight. He says He will give you power. The fainting are the very ones to whom He promises power, but to them that have no might at all He increaseth strength.

All that we have must be surrendered to Him to use as He wills. The one thing I found hardest to consecrate to the Lord when I was a girl and He was seeking to lead me to Himself, was a little talent I was born with, and that was a little gift of writing verses and also prose and when the Lord sought to lead me to Himself during that awful suffering, I gave God all but that one thing, and about that I said, 'No, it is good and I do not have to give it up'. He pressed it upon me that I had to surrender it to Him, and finally I told Him I would hold onto it as tightly as I could and that He would have to pull it away from me. That wasn't very pleasant for the Lord, nor for me, but He was faithful; He saw I had to take the hard way. So when I got to the place of full surrender, just before I was healed, I said 'Lord, I am willing to have Thee make me willing,' and He took me at that. When I got there I gave it all up to Him as best I could, and I never expected Him to let me write another thing.

I had written from a child and had a volume of poems printed, written before I had finished my eighteenth year, but I never expected to be able to write again, and so after my healing it was a wonderful joy to find that that which had gone to Calvary with Him was given back in resurrection power. There only was this difference: Instead of using it myself, the Holy Spirit uses it. God seems to keep it, as it were, locked up in a cupboard, and whenever He wants me to use it for Him, He enables me to use it in the power of His endless life, and then takes it back again for safe keeping. That is why the Lord is pleased to use the little book, 'The Prayer of Faith,' so greatly, because He wrote it through me. This is a little illustration to show you that everything you have, has got to go down into death, all your natural ability, all your natural talent, all your natural knowledge and wisdom. Everything! If He chooses to give you back anything in resurrection life, all right, and if He doesn't it is better not to get it back. It is an empty life, wherein you feel absolutely nothing; perfect weakness, emptied out for Jesus; you feel nothing but blankness and God causes you to stand before Him. It is just a question of trusting Him; letting Him take possession of your mind, and 'when our weakness leans upon His might, then all is right'.

People know very little about the mind being cleansed by the blood and being emptied of all its human thoughts. I cannot begin to tell you what God has done in my mind since I have had this fuller baptism of the Holy Ghost. He shows me that people are having their minds corrupted from the simplicity that is in Christ Jesus. He shows me that the weapons of our warfare are not carnal, but mighty through God to the pulling down of strongholds; casting down imaginations and every high thing that exalteth itself against the knowledge of God. He shows me I cannot reason in the old way. Oh the wonderful realization that God has emptied my own mind out, and that I have the mind of Christ. This is so restful; it feels as though my brain was having a holiday, and all the busy, wearisome thoughts are gone.

This is a part of the life on wings. In all the many years of blessedness before this fuller baptism, I did not know what I am talking about now, this freedom of the mind from all care; of course, I had a great deal of blessing and a great deal of freedom from care, and felt that God had guided me and blessed me wonderfully, but I didn't know what I am talking about now. Now I feel that the Holy Spirit holds my brain just as He does the rest of my being, but it is just as loving and tender as it is strong.

Now He tells us He exchanges our strength. We shall mount up with wings as eagles, and this is wonderfully true not only in the spiritual and the mental, but true in the physical, and since this mighty baptism in the Holy Ghost which I received over two years ago, I know what that mounting up with wings is in my physical being. I feel oftentimes when I walk along the streets as though I could hardly walk properly, I am so full of something which seems as though it was lifting me up on wings; wings on my feet, wings on my limbs, wings all over. I realize it as I run up and down the stairs. It is Romans viii:11, 'But if the Spirit of Him that raised up Jesus from the dead dwell in you, He that raised up Christ from the dead shall also quicken your mortal bodies by His Spirit that dwelleth in you'.

Early this morning as the power of God was upon me, and I was recognizing, as I so often love to do, the presence of the indwelling Comforter, and worshipping Him in His temple, with the Father and the Son, was led out in prayer for different things, but all at once He said to me, 'I want you to recognize definitely that I am filling the temple'. Of course, I know He always fills it, but this was something a little different and He wanted the recognition that every part of spirit, soul and body was pervaded with His presence, and that meant, as He revealed to me His meaning, that I should drop even prayer for the time and be occupied with the presence of His glory, and I said, 'Oh, God, the Holy Ghost, Thou art filling Thy temple,' and immediately, just as though a little vial of attar of roses had been broken in this room and every part of it would soon be filled with the perfume, so the presence of His glory, sensibly pervaded every part of my being and even love and prayer were lost in worship. Then I thought of the time in the Old Testament when the temple was so filled with God's glory that the priest could not even stand to minister.

There is, therefore, an experience beyond service and beyond prayer, and that is a revelation of His own personality to such an extent that there is nothing but adoring worship filling our being. Usually it is a blessed experience to be able to speak in tongues, to let the heavenly song flow out, but there are times when even tongues cease, when His presence is so all-pervading and the atmosphere so heavenly that I cannot talk at all in any language, but the power of His blessed Spirit upon me is so marvelous that it seems as though I were almost dwelling in heaven.

I hope this testimony will make someone press on for the fulness. The Word tells us, 'That the communication of thy faith may become effectual by the acknowledging of every good thing which is in you in Christ Jesus'. Philemon 6. Through our faithful testimony somebody else's torch may be lighted in the love and providence of God, and suppose we should hesitate for fear of persecution, should stop acknowledging every good thing which is in us in Christ Jesus and somebody's torch should fail to be lit. We have a great responsibility, and if we fail in testimony our own light will grow dim.

If you acknowledge everything that is in you in Christ Jesus He will be ready to give you more good things, and just so far as you have gone on with Him you will be able to help somebody else. I find a great many witnesses who have failed God. It means a great deal to be a witness for God in these deeper and higher things, because doing it means reproach; it means going outside the camp, and I have found some people that do not like reproach and draw back and try to compromise; but I pray that we may always be kept true. Beloved, keep true and testify faithfully to Him. He tells us in Revelation that because we have a little strength and because we have kept His Word and have not denied His Name, He has set before us an open door. I could go back and tell you of one door after another that God opened in my own life. When the little doors were opened He could open larger ones, until now the doors are so large and so many I never know which to enter, only as God makes it clear. So, beloved, be faithful and do not deny His Name.

In Ps. ciii :5, we read, 'Who satisfieth thy mouth with good things; so that thy youth is renewed like the eagle's'. Here is a reference to the eagle again, the youth renewed like the eagle's. Beloved, I do not believe in growing old, do you? I believe God means just what He says. Isn't it beautiful? I never expect to grow old. The years may slip over my head, but what of that? That has nothing to do with it. He who has eternal youth is my youth and my strength.

Now, who is going to trust God for the winged life? You can crawl instead if you wish. God will even bless you if you crawl; He will do the best He can for you, but oh how much better to avail ourselves of our wonderful privileges in Christ and to 'mount up with wings as eagles, run and not be weary, walk and not faint'. O beloved friends, there is a life on wings. I feel the streams of His life fill me and permeate my mortal frame from my head to my feet, until no words are adequate to describe it. I can only make a few bungling attempts to tell you what it is like and ask the Lord to reveal to you the rest. May He reveal to you your inheritance in Christ Jesus so that you will press on and get all that He has for you.

Appendix 6

'Led by the Spirit', a Poem by Carrie Judd Montgomery in Her *Heart Whisperings*

(Beulah, Mills College, CA: Office of Triumphs of Faith, 1897), pp. 48-49.

Led By the Spirit

'As many as are led by the Spirit of God, they are the sons of God'.
Romans 8:14

'Oh, what blessed freedom,
Led by Christ alone!
Through His precious leading
Cares and griefs have flown.

Led by Love unerring,
Led by Grace Divine,
Brightly in my spirit
Doth His beauty shine.

Led, but never driven,
By His Spirit dear,
All my path is restful,
Every step made clear.

Never need of planning,
For He has the care;
His the goal I'm reaching,
His to lead me there.

Led by God's own Spirit,
Can I ask for more?
And when life is ended,
On the other shore-

There the Lamb shall lead me,
By the fountains sweet;
Led by him forever,
Bliss shall be complete'.

Appendix 7

Sample of a Song Carrie wrote

TRIUMPHS OF FAITH.

A MONTHLY JOURNAL,

Now thanks be unto God, which always causeth us to triumph
in Christ.—II Corinthians ii. 14.

Vol. 16.   *FEBRUARY, 1896.*   *No. 2.*

OUR LORD'S PRAYER IN RHYME FOR THE LITTLE ONES.

BY THE EDITOR.

Father dear, who lives in Heaven,
  May Thy name most holy be,
May Thy Kingdom come most quickly,
  Come to all, and come to me.
May Thy will be done, dear Father,
  Just as it is done in Heaven;
Give us each our needful manna,
  Every day of all the seven.
All our crimson sins forgive us,
  Just as we forgive each other,
Let us not go near temptation,
  But from evil save us, rather.
All the power to Thee belongeth,
  And the Kingdom is Thine own,
All the glory's Thine forever,
  Thou shalt reign, and Thou alone.
          Amen.

Appendix 8

Sample of Books in Carrie's Personal Collection

(All original books, most of which were Carrie's personal books, although a few were her mother's, and some possibly her daughter's. Accessed at the Home of Peace)

Abrams, Minnie F., *The Baptism of the Holy Ghost and Fire* (Kedgaon, printed at the Mukti Mission Press 1906) (Carrie inserted a note that said 'Please keep this for me ...')

Argue, Zelma, *Strenuous Days: Choice Thoughts for Daily Meditation* compiled by Argue in The 'Garnered Grain' Series (Zondervan Publishing, Grand Rapids, MI) ('To Carrie Judd Montgomery, whose devotion has been as a beacon of light; and whose fellowship is dearly cherished by Zelma Argue July 9, 1936')

Baker, H.A., *God in Ka Do Land*

Baxter, Mrs M., (Elizabeth), *The Living Word in the Gospel of John* (personal message 1884)

—*Thy Healer* (1885)

—*God's Prophets* (1886) (several copies and one with a personal letter to that says 'To my dearly loved Carrie F. Judd from your other English mother ... Baxter 1886')

—*Leaves from Genesis*

—*Trials and Teachings of Paul*

Blanchard, Charles A., *Getting things from God* (CJM's name on cover)

Boardman, W.E., *Faith Work Under Dr. Cullis* (Given to Carrie and signed by Cullis May 20, 1882)

—*The Lord that Healeth Thee* (presented to 'Carrie F. Judd, With much love from friend in England, October 25th, 1881, 1 Thess V:25')

Booth, Evangeline, *Love is All* (1925)

—*Toward a Better World* (1928) (Gift to CJM from Jamie Cashwood, S.A. Major? April 8, 1929)

William Booth: General of the Salvation Army

Bosworth, F.F., *Christ the Healer: Sermons on Divine Healing*

Carmichael, Amy, *Momosa, who was charmed* (1924)

—*Things as they are: Mission work in Southern India*

Carter, Kelso, *The Atonement for Sin and Sickness* (1884)

Clark, *The Offices of the Holy Spirit*

Clarke, Samuel, *A Collection of Scripture Promises* (given to George 1884)

Cullis, Charles, *Faith Cures* (1879) (Given to Carrie after her healing from her Aunt Carrie dated 1879)

Dempster, Joseph S., *From Romanism to Pentecost*

Dowie, John Alexander, A Reply by the Rev ... *Divine Healing Vindicated.*

Duff, Mildred and Noelle Hope, *Hezekiah the King* (Marshall publisher)

Dyer, Helen S., *Pandita Ramabai: The Story of Her Life*
—*Pandita Ramabai: A Great Life in Indian Missions*
Finney, C.G., *Revivals of Religion: Lectures by Charles Grandison Finney* with the Author's final additions and corrections. Edited by William Henry Harding (CJM's name written inside)
Frodsham, Stanley H., *Spirit Filled and Taught*
—*Rivers of Living Water*
Gordon, A.J., *Ecce Venit: Behold He Cometh* (1889) (Mrs O. K. Judd's book)
Griffin, Dora G., *Beulah or Two and a Half Years of Consecrated Life, showing that 'all things are possible to him that believeth'* (1888)
Hopkins, A.A., *Our Sabbath Evening*
Kenyon, E.W., *The Wonderful Name of Jesus*
Knapp, M.W., *The Double Cure*
Lawrence, B.F., *The Apostolic Faith Restored* (Said 'Please return to CJM ...')
Brother Lawrence, *The Practice of the Presence of God* (1892)
Mackintosh, C.H., *Notes on the Book of Deuteronomy*
Mahan, Asa, *Out of Darkness Into Light* (1876 by Cullis?)
Marsh, R.L., *'Faith Healing:' A Defense, or The Lord Thy Healer*
McPherson, Aimee Semple, *Sister Answers Dr. Harrison: WHY I am a Pentecostalist, I did Seek the Baptism, I Do Speak in Tongues* (Sept 13, 1936)
—*Foursquare Favorites*
Meyer, F.B., *A Cast Away*
Mills, A.M., *Life of Charles G. Finney* (1902 by Mrs M.W. Knapp) (CJM's handwritten name and address)
Murray, Andrew, *The School of Obedience* (1899?)
—*Abide in Christ*
—*The Cross of Christ*
—*The Ministry of Intercession*
—*Absolute Surrender*
Palmer, W.C., *Glimpses of Life in Soul Saving*
Pardington, George Palmer, *The Crooked Made Straight*
Pierson, A.T., *The Second Coming of Our Lord*
Prosser, Anna W., *From Death to Life* (1901)
Sankey, Allan, *Hallowed Hymns New and Old*
Simpson, A.B., *The Lord for the Body*
—*The Gospel of the Kingdom*
—*Wholly Sanctified*
Stanton, R.L., *Gospel Parallelisms*
Stevens, William C., *Mysteries of the Kingdom*
—Praying in the Holy Ghost: An Address Delivered at the Cazadero Camp Meeting
Stockmayer, Otto, *Church of God Awake!* (1904)
—*Triumph of Forbearing Love*

Taylor, J. Hudson, *Separation and Service*

Tomlinson, A.J., *The Great Vision of the Church of God: Being the Life and Vision of A.J. Tomlinson, General Overseer*

Von Bogatzky, C.H., *Golden Treasury for the Children of God* (Given to her by Mrs Whittemore)

Watson, *God's Eagles*

—*The Heavenly Life and Types of the Holy Spirit*

Wigglesworth, Smith, *Ever-Increasing Faith* (1924)

Yoakum, F.E., *Healing by the Lord* (1907) address at C&MA meeting (signed and given to her July 8, 1907)

Yeomans, Lilian B., *Healing from Heaven*

Zepp, Arthur C., *Demon Activity in the Latter Times*

Appendix 9

Flame of Love Exemplar?

The Flame of Love Project identifies people within the Pentecostal Movement who demonstrate godly love in attempts to understand what lies at the root of this quality. Heidi Baker currently is one of the chief 'Flame of Love exemplars' in the study.[1] In a recent letter including some of the Bakers' core values for Iris Ministries, they state that they

> try not to be controversial, and share with all Christian streams what no born-again believer can argue with: the glory of the basic Gospel, repentance and faith in Jesus, the simplicity and purity of devotion to Christ, avoiding anything that would empty the Cross of its power, knowing nothing but Christ and Him crucified when backed against a wall, seeking righteousness that comes from faith, transformation through adoption by our Heavenly Father, and understanding faith working through love as the only thing that counts (Gal. 5:6), with the hope of attaining to the resurrection from the dead (Phil 3:11). In the process we find that we cannot just be an orphanage, or a church, or a Bible school, or a humanitarian aid organization. We can't just hold bush conferences, plant farms and engineer micro-investment. We can't just specialize in education and technical assistance. We as a broadly-based international family must embrace all of the above, and more.

The above passage highlights a similar ethos in Carrie's ministry. A few more of the Bakers' core values are as follows: 'We understand that we can find God, and can experience intimacy, communication and companionship with Him in His Presence, if we share His love for righteousness ... We are totally dependent upon Him for everything, and we need and expect miracles of all kinds to sustain us and confirm the Gospel in our ministry'.[2] Throughout her own life, Carrie pursued increased intimacy

---

[1] 'The Flame of Love Project is a three-year collaborative effort by researchers at the University of Akron and The Institute for Research on Unlimited Love, funded by the John Templeton Foundation that will provide the scientific and theological foundation for a new interdisciplinary field of study: the science of Godly Love ... The Flame of Love project begins its investigation within the broadly-defined pentecostal tradition ... The project culminates in a national survey not limited to any specific religion. The primary goal is to use multiple methods to investigate the phenomena of Godly Love with the expressed purpose of fostering a wide-ranging interdisciplinary dialogue'. Sociologist Margaret M. Poloma is involved in this project. Information taken from <http://www3.uakron.edu/sociology/flameweb/about.html> on January 10, 2011.

[2] Heidi and Rolland Baker, 'Core Values at Iris: Simple, Controversial and not optional!, September 2010 taken from their Newsletter section on

with God in a similar way.[3] Influenced by Müller's example of living completely by faith, Carrie also consistently depended upon God to meet her needs.[4] And while not all of the Bakers' core values resonate exactly with Carrie's ministry, several of them show a remarkable likeness. Even though Carrie was more introverted than charismatic preacher Heidi Baker, their similar distinctives of praying for the sick, pursuing revival, preaching the Gospel, pursuing intimacy in God's presence, valuing unity in love, and responding to the needs of those around them would likely have made them good friends and co-workers if they lived at the same time.[5] Carrie probably would have even called her readers to financially support for Bakers' ministry to the poor in Africa as well as print her teachings in her periodical.[6]

In many ways, Carrie's mandate for unity in love resonates with chief 'Flame of love exemplar' Heidi Baker. If Carrie was alive today, she would also likely serve as a significant 'Flame of Love exemplar'. Carrie not only taught about love at great lengths but also attempted to live it through her actions as is evidenced through her orphanages and other extensive philanthropic work. In her teaching, Carrie regularly emphasized the fruits of the Spirit more than the gifts of the Spirit. She did this in relation to the gift of healing and the gift of tongues. With the first, she rarely spoke about it and with the latter, much of the time she did speak about it, she emphasized that love must always be present. Carrie's life provides an example of one who not only emphasized godly love in her teachings, but demonstrated it through her vast healing ministry, her extensive philanthropic endeavors, her ability to maintain unity in love with conflicting organizations, and her open arms to receive people regardless of racial, gender, or denominational barriers.

<www.irismin.org>. Accessed January 12, 2011. These values were articulated following a global Iris leaders meeting held in Pemba, Mozambique in 2010.

[3] See Chapter 6.

[4] See Chapter 2.

[5] Heidi Baker, Interview by Jennifer A. Miskov, February 26, 2011 at St. Aldates Church in Oxford, England. This interview includes a discussion of Heidi interacting and commenting on Carrie's ministry and her pursuit of the fullness of the Spirit.

[6] See Heidi and Rolland Baker's *Always Enough: God's Miraculous Provision among the Poorest Children on Earth* (Grand Rapids, MI: Chosen, a division of Baker Books, 2002); *Expecting Miracles: True Stories of God's Supernatural Power and How You Can Experience It* (Grand Rapids, MI: Chosen, a division of Baker Books, 2007); and Heidi Baker's *Compelled by Love: How to change the world through the simple power of love in action* (Lake Mary, FL: Charisma House, 2008).

BIBLIOGRAPHY AND SOURCES

PRIMARY SOURCES
A. By or in relation to Carrie Judd Montgomery
Triumphs of Faith 1881-1946

Judd, Carrie F., *Lilies from the Vale of Thought* (Buffalo, NY: H.H. Otis, 1878). Available<http://www.archive.org/details/liliesfromvalet00mongoog>.

—*Prayer of Faith* (Chicago and New York: Fleming H. Revell Company, 1880). Reprint in Donald W. Dayton (ed.), *The Life and Teachings of Carrie Judd Montgomery* (New York and London: Garland Publishing, Inc, 1985).

—*Zaida Eversey: or Live Two-Fold* (Buffalo, NY: H.H. Otis, 1881).

—'Address Monday to Wednesday: Address by Carrie F. Judd', in *Report of the Christian Convention at Old Orchard Beach, ME held July 31 to August 9, 1887* (New York, NY: Word, Work and World Publishing, 1887) accessed from CMA Archives <https://apas.box.net/shared/tvjm06q2vo>.

Montgomery, Carrie Judd. *Heart Whisperings* (Oakland: Office of Triumphs of Faith, 1897). Reprint (USA: Kessinger Publishing, no date).

—*Life of Praise* (Oakland, CA: Office of Triumphs of Faith, no date but possibly 1910?). This is a selection of articles from *TF* compiled by A.B. Simpson.

—*To My Beloved* (Oakland, CA: Office of Triumphs of Faith, 1912).

—*Secrets of Victory* (Oakland, CA: Triumphs of Faith, 1921).

—*Heart Melody* (Oakland, CA: Office of Triumphs of Faith, 1922). Reprint (USA: Kessinger Publisher, no date).

—*Under His Wings: The Story of My Life* (Los Angeles, CA: Stationers Corporation, 1936).

Personal Journals/Writings:

Montgomery, George S. *Pocketbook Personal Journal,* 1888 (Sept.-Dec.) [from the Berry family]

Judd, Carrie. Personal diary 1889 (only a few pages)

Montgomery, Carrie Judd. *Date Book for 1900: Handwritten Diary*, 1900.

Montgomery, Carrie Judd. *Date Book for 1909: Handwritten Diary,* 1909 [FPHC 27690]

Montgomery, Carrie Judd. Personal sketch book of poems (handwritten), 1911 [HOP]

Montgomery, Carrie Judd. Personal handwritten poems dated 1910-1911 [HOP]

Poem 'Sweet Clover' composed in 1910 at Nyack College for Mrs A. Kirk

Record of Christmas Cards Received 1925-1929 [HOP]

Her Records: [HOP]

Carrie Judd Montgomery, Handwritten Orphanage records (various dates: 1895-1897, 1899, 1901-08)

Finance Records Date books 1918-1920, 1925, 1926, 1933 (selected pages)

Guest Books: [HOP]

Guest Book for Home of Peace 1906-1910

Guest Book for Home of Peace 1911-1919

Guest Book for Home of Peace 1928-1938

Miscellaneous Letters: [FPHC 27691]

Feb 1838 Orvan and Electa Judd and Bakers?

March 13, 1880 Letter from Bielby to confirm Carrie's healing (in Albrecht's thesis)

Dec. 15, 1884 Letter from Bethshan to 'Brother' (Baxter/ Boardman?) saying to invite Carrie to conference

Dec. 19, 1884 Letter from W.E. Boardman to Carrie

March 19, 1885 Letter of invitation for Divine Healing and True Holiness conference from Boardman

Nov. 7, 1893 handwritten invite to dedication of The Home of Peace by CJM

1895 letter from George Montgomery to A.W. Dennett, deed of transfer of Lytton Springs and Cazadero.

No date: Excerpts of Montgomery and Break's prayer journal, prayer for Mexico, etc.

March 18, 1898: Letter to CJM from Emma Dougan? From Bible Work in Chicago

May 5, 1899 letter from Booth Tucker to CJM (Salvation Army)

Dec 16, 1900 postcard sent from Paris

Dec. 29,1900 letter from Louis Sanford

Jan 14, 1907: To Mother from CJM. Azusa Street, Mr Yoakum

April 22, 1911 Official letter to CJM from John G. Lake. Mention of Dowie and also of added power from Spirit Baptism.

July 12, 1911 Letter from Manoramabai (Pandita Ramabai's daughter) to Carrie

Nov. 18, 1915 and May 19, letter to George from W.R. Hatcher?

Nov. 24, 1917 to J.W. Welch from CJM

Nov. 30, 1917 To CJM from J.W. Welch, chairman of General Council of Assemblies of God

Oct. 18, 1918 letter to Montgomery's from H.R. Woauldorff?

Aug. 18, 1922 To E.N. Bell, chairman of General Council from CJM

Sept. 9, 1922 Questionnaire for Preachers that CJM filled out.

Oct. 16, 1922 Letter from Merrill Berry to George

Aug. 2, 1923 Letter to CJM from Paula and Frances

Aug 14, 1923 To Welch from CJM

1923 Questionnaire for Preachers

May 23, 1924 letter from George to Merrill in Mexico

July 15, 1924 from Mexico mines from Faith to Carrie.

Nov. 22, 1925 Letter from S.R. Break to George
Dec. 16, 1925 To George from Clara Miner in regards to payments
Dec. 7, 1926 To George from City of Berkeley (Granville E. Thomas)
April 1, 1927 Agreement about Cazadero camp grounds, sold part of it for $100
May 18, 1927 To George from Merrill Berry
July 14, 1947 To George from Sonoma County
Jan. 3, 1928 To George from Milton C. Lutz
Aug. 14, 1928 To George from City of Berkeley
Dec. 11, 1928 letter from George? To Thomas (City of Berkeley)
March 11, 1930 George to George Mattis (business)
March 14, 1929 Berkeley to Montgomery's about land in Cazadero
March 18, 1929 Thomas to Montgomery's about land
May 13, 1929 To George from Milton C. Lutz
June 17, 1929 To Lutz from George
March 4, 1930 To George from realtor
March 28, 1930 To Phillip Thayer from George in regards to land
May 29, 1930 from Merrill Berry
July 12, 1930 from Clara Etta Wilson-Berry to Lizzie and Beulah before Finley's death
Oct 23, 1934 To J.R. Evans, Secretary of AG from CJM
Oct 30, 1934 To CJM from J.R. Evans
Sept 17, 1938 To Stanley H. Frodsham from CJM
Sept 17, 1938 Questionnaire for Ordained Preachers
Aug 16, 1939 Questionnaire for Ordained Preachers
June 10, 1940 To J.R. Flower from CJM
July 17, 1940 To J. Roswell Flower, General Secretary from CJM
July 17, 1940 Questionnaire for Ordained Preachers
Oct 22, 1941 To Stanley Frodsham from CJM
Aug 30, 1941 Questionnaire for Ordained Preachers
June 24, 1942 Questionnaire for Ordained Preachers
July 4, 1942 To J. Russell Flower, General Secretary, ask for prayer for funds because Home of Peace may be shut down, also submitted article for Evangel.
July 15, 1942 To CJM from J.R. Flower acknowledging his prayers for her
June 28, 1943 Questionnaire for Ordained Preachers
Aug 29, 1944 Questionnaire for Ordained Preachers
June 20, 1945 Questionnaire for Ordained Preachers
July 10, 1946 Questionnaire for Ordained Preachers
Ordination Certificates for Assemblies of God 1914, 1917 for evangelist and missionary, records, Pastor-Evangelist, application for ordination

Tracts by CJM: [HOP].
Faith's Reckonings (taken from *TF* 1.1 [Jan 1881], pp. 1-4)
Faith Without Works (*TF* 1.10 [Oct 1881], pp. 145-46)
Our Position in Christ (*TF* 2.1 [Jan 1882], pp. 1-3)
How to Resist the Devil (*TF* 32.7 [July 1912], pp. 145-49)
Christmas Joy poem
Unwavering Faith (Evangel Tract No. 669, Springfield)

Shine on! (office of *TF*)

The Power of the Tongue (Elim Publishing House in Rochester, NY and also another one by Christian Union Publishers, MA and January 1915 by same)

'Come With Me' (*TF* Beulah Heights Oakland)

Praise At Midnight (*TF* Beulah Heights Oakland)

Sweet Love of Christ (*TF* Beulah Heights Oakland)

Other Tracts:

Mrs O.K. Judd, 'The Fount Revealed'

Sadie Cody- Miracle of Healing, intro by CJM (*TF* Beulah Heights Oakland) reprinted from *TF* (Aug 1911), pp. 185-89

B. Periodicals

The Apostolic Faith (Los Angeles, CA)

Bible Standard/Overcomer (Eugene, OR)

The Christian and Missionary Alliance Weekly (New York)

Confidence (Sunderland, UK)

The Latter Rain Evangel (Chicago, IL)

Pentecostal Evangel (Springfield, MO)

Triumphs of Faith (Buffalo, NY; Oakland, CA)

Word and Witness (Malvern, AR)

Word, Work, and World (New York)

C. Newspaper Articles

EAST COAST

The Brooklyn Eagle

'A Supposed Miracle Through Prayer', February 29, 1880, p. 2.

'Religious Notices', October 17, 1885, p. 5.

Buffalo Commercial Advertiser

'A Modern Miracle', October 20, 1879 (BECHS).

The Buffalo (Daily) Courier (same newspaper CJM approached editor).

Unless otherwise noted, accessed through <www.fultonhistory.com>.

'Miraculous Cures in Connecticut', *The Buffalo Daily Courier*, (Thursday) February 20, 1879 (found at Buffalo State University on microfilm).

'The Efficiency of Prayer', *The Buffalo Courier*, November 15, 1881.

'Alleged Miracle', *Buffalo Courier*, April 23, 1883.

The Buffalo Express

'Cures by Credulity ... A Visit to 'Faith Rest Cottage', October 26, 1885, p. 8.

'For and of Women', October 28, 1888.

No title, May 18, 1890.

'Wealthy Warriors: A Rich Salvationist and His Famous Wife ... Romance and Religion', *The Illustrated Buffalo Press*, May 8, 1892, p. 4. From New York State Library.

Courier and Republic, Evening Republic (Buffalo)
Judd, Carrie F., 'A Ghost', (Buffalo, NY), 1874.
'The Lincoln Birthday Association', (Buffalo, NY), March 30, 1876.

New York Times
'Christian Workers in Conference', September 11, 1884.
'The Christian Alliance', October 12, 1888.

The Oswego Palladium (New York)
'Faith Cure Closed', November 27, 1883.
'Among the Churches', *Oswego Daily Times*, July-October 1897. Accessed through
    <www.fultonhistory.com>.

The Sun (New York)
'Disease Cured by Prayer', October 29, 1885, p. 3. Accessed through <www.loc.
    gov/chronicalingamerica>.

Other New York
No title, article taken from *Troy Times* and reprinted in *The Daily Eagle* (NY), Au-
    gust 14, 1882.
'Faith Cure In Buffalo', *City and Vicinity*, November 27, 1882.
'The Salvation Army', *Daily Bulletin* (Auburn, NY), 1891.
'All For the Poor: Rich Salvationists to Work in the Slums of New York: Roman-
    tic Story of a Couple', *Middletown Daily Press,* April 12, 1892, p. 1.
'Long Range Cures: Mrs. Montgomery Rivals Schlatter', *The Sunday Herald* (Syra-
    cuse, NY), December 1, 1895, p. 14.
'Healing at Long Range: Mrs. Montgomery Performs Faith Cures by Corre-
    spondence', *The Brookfield Courier* (NY), January 15, 1896.
'Matter's Personal and Social', *The Binghamton Press*, (NY) July 9, 1910, p. 6.

Boston Daily Globe
'Will "Slumming" Go: Rich Californians Join the Salvation Army', Boston Daily
    Globe, April 12, 1892, p. 11.

The Washington Post
'Officers of the Christian Alliance', October 12, 1890, p. 9.

MISCELLANEOUS AMERICA
'Faith in Prayer', *The St. Paul Sunday Globe* (MN), February 5, 1882, p. 8.
    Accessed <www.loc.gov/chronicalingamerica>.
'Big Day for Salvationists', *The Salt Lake Herald* (Utah), November 4,
    1900, p. 7. Accessed <www.loc.gov/chronicalingamerica>.
'My Olive Branch', by Carrie Judd Montgomery in the *Christian Science
    Monitor*, December 6, 1913, p. 39.

Chicago (Daily) Tribune
'Trust the Lord', *Chicago Daily Tribune*, July 2, 1884, p. 8.
'Healed by Faith. Miss Carrie Judd, of Buffalo, Tells the Story of Her Cure', June 15, 1884, p. 11.
'The Ministers', September 30, 1884, p. 8.
'Faith Healers', December 2, 1885, p. 3.
'Announcements', December 7, 1887, p. 7.
'Miss Carrie F. Judd's Spine: It Was Out of Order but the Lord Healed It', December 6, 1888, p. 3.
'Nellie Vaughan's Cure', *Chicago Daily*, March 12, 1890, p. 1.
'Holds a Novel Tenet', *Chicago Daily*, May 31, 1895, p. 5.

The Daily Constitution (Atlanta, Georgia)
'Leaning on the Lord: Miss Judd's Decline and Rise', November 8, 1879, p. 1.
    This also includes letter from Mrs Mix and story told by Carrie of her healing.

WEST COAST
Los Angeles Times
'Brevities', January 15, 1890, p. 7.
'City Briefs', January 17, 1890, p. 8.
'Thanksgiving Services', November 29, 1893, p. 4.
'Southern California: Big Salvation Army Meeting', December 2, 1893, p. 11.
No title, December 3, 1893, p. 8.
'Christian Alliance', May 29, 1896, p. 8.
'City Briefs', May 30, 1896, p. 12.
'Church Record: Life's Mission', June 1, 1896, p. 8.
'Christian Alliance', June 2, 1896, p. 14.
'The Sixth Day', June 3, 1896, p. 9.
Article about Yoakum August 19, 1920 accessed on healingandrevival.com.
'Mass Meet Called to Pray for Rain', May 22, 1931, p. 1.

The Morning Call (San Francisco, CA) accessed through <www.loc.gov/chronicalingamerica>.
'At Beulah Park: Ministers and Laymen Preach the Word of Life to Great Audiences', July 13, 1892, p. 8.
'"Entire Consecration": The Subject Discussed at the Christian Convention', August 19, 1892, p. 7.
'Foreign Missions', January 11, 1894, p. 8.
April 27, 1894, p. 3. Talks about her slum work.
'Evils of Drink: Theme of the Temperance Congress', May 25, 1894, p. 3.
'Christian Outing. Pacific Coast Bible and Training School for Young Women', June 27, 1894, p. 3.
'To Better Their Sex: Christian Young Women Meet In Council', January 20, 1895, p. 5.
'Nothing Left. The Sterretts Made a Bad Bargain: Montgomery Got All', September 20, 1894, p. 12. (contains a drawing of CJM).
'Prayed Over It. How Montgomery Came to Purchase', October 18, 1894, p. 4.

Oakland Tribune
'Vast Fortune Given Away by Montgomery', Sept 9, 1930.
'Home of Peace', *The Oakland Tribune,* 26 July 1964 [IPHC].

The Record-Union (Sacramento, CA) accessed through <www.loc.gov/chronical-ingamerica>.
'Union Christian Convention', June 7, 1893, p. 4. Carrie gave devotional on 'Reception of the Spirit'.
'Millionaire Religionists Sued', September 20, 1894, p. 8.
'Bad Bargain by the Sterretts … Salvationist Montgomery Appears to Have Struck a Good Thing – The Sterretts are Broke', September 21, 1894.
'The Sterrett Mine Litigation: Carrie Judd Montgomery Relates Her Version', October 16, 1894, p. 6.

The San Francisco Call accessed through <www.loc.gov/chronicalingamerica>. (1895).
'Home for Little Ones: Opening of the Salvation Army Orphanage at Beulah To-Day', September 5, 1895, p. 11.
'Faith Cure Propaganda, Faith Home to be Used for Training Missionaries', September 8, 1895, p. 11.
'New From the Churches', September 8, 1895, p. 21.
'To Rescue Little Waifs', October 2, 1895, p. 10.
'Testing Faith Healing, Newly Arrived Minister Says It Is the Work of the Devil, Opposes Mrs. Montgomery', November 4, 1895, p. 9.
'A Girl's Life the Stake, The New Church of Christ Enters the Faith-Healing War', November 9, 1895, p. 13.
'Letters From the People: Healing By Faith: Mrs. Carrie Judd Montgomery Gives an Explanation of Her Belief', November 13, 1895, p. 6.
'Faith Cure Didn't Save', November 22, 1895, p. 11.
'A Noble Woman's Work', November 26, 1895, p. 11.
'History of a Day', November 27, 1895, p. 13.
'From Luxury to Labor', December 11, 1895, p. 11.
'Friends of Poor Children', December 22, 1895, p. 14.

(1896-1900)
'Helping the Fallen', January 7, 1896, p. 8.
'Miss Noble's Testimonial', February 17, 1896, p. 11.
'Faith-Doctors at Los Angeles', May 30, 1896, p. 5.
'Deserted Three Beautiful Babes', October 3, 1896, p. 11.
'Richest Salvation Junior in the Country', August 8, 1897, p. 15.
'Protected Aged and Infirm: New Home at Beulah Will Be Dedicated Next Sunday', August 21, 1897, p. 11.
'Dedication of A Bird's Nest', November 19, 1897, p. 9.
'A Third Healing Claimed: Experience of Mrs. Montgomery', June 13, 1898, p. 8.
'Church Notices', June 25, 1898, p. 12.

'Speaks of it as a Miracle: Mrs. Montgomery Tells of Her Healing', June 26, 1898, p. 15. This is recorded in Carrie's own words.

'He Heals By Prayer: Dr. Francis, Oakland's New Sensation', June 27, 1898, p. 7.

'Church Notices', June 28, 1898, p. 12.

James, Henry. 'With Entire Frankness', July 3, 1898, p. 6.

'Little Orth Raises a Row: Some Prominent People Called to Court', July 26, 1898, p. 9.

'Old Friends as Enemies: Mrs. Stocker Testifies for Mrs. Prescott', August 2, 1898, p. 9.

Bernard Shaw, Dr Kent, and Attorney D. Donohoe Jr. and Mrs Carrie Judd Montgomery. 'Was Christian Science Responsible for Harold Fredric's Death?', November 20, 1898, pp. 21, 26.

'Struggle Over a Girl', July 19, 1899, p. 9.

(1900-1910)

'Real Estate Transactions', November 21, 1901, p. 13.

'Four Women Want Little Doris', *The San Francisco Call*, January 3, 1902, p. 9.

'Montgomery's Testify in Way Case', May 15, 1902, p. 4.

'Transfer Valuable Lot to Salvation Army: George S. Montgomery and Wife Deed Property Upon Which Rescue Home is Situated', January 23, 1904, p. 6.

'Jerry McAuley Mission Inaugurated in City', March 4, 1904, p. 4.

'Says Rescue Home Made Her a Prisoner', February 11, 1905, p. 6.

'Christian Endeavors in County Convention: Young People Meet at Berkeley and Listen to Songs, Papers, and Addresses', March 26, 1905, p. 34.

'Earthquake and Fire: San Francisco in Ruins', April 19, 1906, p. 1.

'Missionary Society to Hold Convention', April 22, 1910, p. 8.

D. Interviews and Audio

Baker, Heidi. Interview by Jennifer A. Miskov, February 26, 2011 at St. Aldates Church in Oxford, England.

Berry, Faith (Montgomery). Interview by Wayne Warner, April 25, 1985. Recording at Home of Peace, Oakland, CA [FPHC].

Berry, Loren. Interview by Jennifer A. Miskov March 30-31, 2009. Recording at Cazadero family home, CA.

Frodsham, Stanley. 'Abiding Under God's Shadow', audio recording accessed November 8, 2010 at <http://brothermel.com/stanleyfrodshamrecordings.aspx>.

E. Random Papers [from the Berrys]

O.K. Judd Acrostic Poem

1874 finance sheet

Oct 22, 1879 wedding invite to Rose Bailey and Charles A. Judd's wedding

June 27, 1883 Death certificate of George's mother, Jane Montgomery

1884 poems by Mrs O.K. Judd

Aug 2, 1885 Check to Carrie from The Courier ($15)

Nov. 1, 1886 receipt for printing (2,200 Triumphs of Faith)

Sept. 21, 1887 wedding invite to Birdie A. Judd and Joseph Newton Cracker

1880s? Handwritten poem with picture by Carrie Judd/ a letter from St. John's Rectory

May 14, 1890 Marriage Certificate for CJM and George with A.B. Simpson's signature (Jer. 33.3)

Sept 21-23, 1892 program for Union Christian Conf. with Kelso Carter, CJM to speak at 3:00 pm

June 14, 1898 Home of Peace receipt for groceries and goods

Dec. 31, 1898 Tompkins v. George Montgomery (lady fell off carriage driven by employee of a hotel he owned in Cazadero and suing)

1914 Announcement of World-Wide Pentecostal Camp Meeting (July 8-Aug.9).

May 16, 1917 Marriage Certificate of Merrill Berry and Faith Judd Montgomery

Jan. 1920 checks from George to Clara Miner, Blairdill, Thomas, Cazadero store

Oct. 26, 1928 bill/receipt for CJM improvement of streets

Oct. 31, 1928 Deed in giving land to Glad Tidings Revival Assembly

Oct 13, 1931 George deceased and now distribution of his property to Carrie

Dec. 22, 1932 Quit Claim Deed and donation to Home for Aged and Infirm Colored People of California

Jan 1970 *TF* 89.1 About the Berrys

July-Sept. 1979 *TF* 98.3 Judd Finley Berry died/kitchen in Home of Peace dedicated to him

Orvan Berry's obituary/Montgomery Family Tree

Sept 2, 2004 Sonoma Community Profile on Don Berry

F. Book and Articles

Abrams, Minnie F. *The Baptism of the Holy Ghost and Fire* (Kedgaon: Pandita Ramabai Mukti Mission, 1906).

Bartleman, Frank. *Azusa Street: The Roots of Modern-day Pentecost* (April 1925, Los Angeles). Reprint (S. Plainfield, NJ: Bridge Publishing, Inc., 1980).

Boardman, W.E. *The Higher Christian Life* (1858). Reprint (USA: Kessinger Publishing, 2007).

—*Faith Work under Dr. Cullis in Boston* (Boston: Willard Tract Repository, 1873).

Booth, General William. *In Darkest England and the Way Out* (London: The Salvation Army, 1890) 1st edition accessed at <http://www.jesus.org.uk/vault/ library/booth_darkest_england.pdf>.

Bosworth, F.F. *Christ the Healer* (originally 1924). Reprint (Grand Rapids, MI: Chosen Books, 2008).

Buffalo City Directory (E.R. Jewett Publisher). [BECHS]

Cullis, Charles. *Faith Cures or Answers to Prayer in the Healing of the Sick* (Boston, MA: Willard Tract Repository, 1879).

Gordon, A.J. *The Ministry of Healing: Miracles of Cure in All Ages* (New York: Christian Alliance, 1882).

—*The Ministry of the Spirit. The Spirit in Missions* (1893).

Gortner, J. Narver. 'Carrie Judd Montgomery – A Tribute: address delivered at the funeral service of the late Carrie Judd Montgomery in the Christian and Missionary Alliance Tabernacle in Oakland, August 29, 1946'. [FPHC]

'Historic Buffalo: Erie Bicentennial Commission' (Buffalo, NY: Buffalo and Erie County Historical Society, 1974).

Johnston, J.B. *The Prayer-Meeting, and its History, as Identified with the Life and Power of Godliness, and the Revival of Religion* (Pittsburgh: United Presbyterian Board of Publication, 1870).

Johnson, James N (ed.), *The Poets and Poetry of Buffalo* (Buffalo, NY: James N. Johnston, 1904), pp. 319-25.

Mix, Mrs Edward. *The Life of Mrs. Edward Mix* (Torrington: Press of Register Printing Co, 1884, written by herself in 1880). Reprint (New York: Syracuse University Press, 2002).

—*Faith Cures, and Answers to Prayer* (Springfield: Press of Springfield Printing Co, 1882). Reprint, (New York: Syracuse University Press, 2002).

Palmer, Mrs Phoebe. *Faith and Its Effects* (New York: Published for the author, 1852).

—*The Way of Holiness, with Notes by the Way; being a Narrative Religious Experience Resulting from a Determination to be a Bible Christian* (New York: 200 Mulberry Street, Printed for the author, 1854) Accessed at Making of America Books <http://quod.lib.umich.edu/m/moa/>.

Simpson, A.B. *The Gospel of Healing* (New York, NY: Christian Alliance Publishing Co., 4th edn, 1890).

Smith, H. Perry (ed.), *History of the City of Buffalo and Erie County*. II. *The Churches* (Syracuse, NY: D. Mason & Co., Publishers, 1884).

Smith, Hannah Whitall. *The Christian's Secret of a Happy Life* (Chicago: F.H. Revell, 1883). Reprint (USA: Kessinger Publishing, no date).

Thomas' Buffalo City Directory (Thomas, Howard and Johnson Publishers). [BECHS]

Tomlinson, Homer A. *Miracles of Healing in the Ministry of Rev. Francisco Olazábal* (Queens Village, NY: Homer A. Tomlinson, 1939).

Torrey, R.A. *The Baptism with the Holy Spirit* (New York: Fleming H. Revell Company, 1897). Reprint in Donald W. Dayton, ed., *Late Nineteenth Century Revivalist Teachings on the Holy Spirit* (New York and London: Garland Publishing, Inc, 1985).

Wesley, Rev. John. *Sermons on Several Occasions* (London: John Mason, 1851).

White, Truman C. (ed.), *Our County and It's People: A Descriptive work on Erie County New York*. II. *Rt. Rev. Arthur Cleveland Coxe* (Boston, NY: The Boston History Company, 1898), pp. 37-39.

Willard, Frances E. and Mary A. Livermore (eds.), 'Montgomery, Mrs. Carrie Frances Judd', in *A Woman of the Century: Fourteen Hundred-Seventy Biographical Sketches Accompanied by Portraits of Leading American Women in All Walks of Life* (Buffalo, NY: Charles Wells Moulton, 1893), pp. 512-13.

SECONDARY SOURCES

Albrecht, Daniel E., 'The Life and Ministry of Carrie Judd Montgomery' (Master's thesis, Western Evangelical Seminary, 1984).

—'Carrie Judd Montgomery: Pioneering Contributor to Three Religious Movements', *Pneuma* 8.2 (Fall 1986), pp. 101-19.

Alexander, Kimberly Ervin. *Pentecostal Healing: Models in Theology and Practice* (JPTSup, 29; Blandford Forum: Deo Publishing, 2006).

Anderson, Allan. *An Introduction to Pentecostalism: Global Charismatic Christianity* (Cambridge: Cambridge University Press, 2004).

—*Spreading Fires: The Missionary Nature of Early Pentecostalism* (London: SCM Press, 2007).

Anderson, Robert Mapes. *Vision of the Disinherited: The Making of American Pentecostalism* (Oxford: Oxford University Press, 1979).

Archer, Kenneth. 'Pentecostal Hermeneutics: Retrospect and Prospect', *Journal of Pentecostal Theology* 8 (1996), pp. 63-81.

Arnold, Terry and Mike Claydon, 'The Foundation and History of the Pentecostal Movement', *Diakrisis Australia* 2.26 (Jan/Feb 2004), pp. 1-12.

Baer, Jonathan R. 'Redeemed Bodies: The Functions of Divine Healing in Incipient Pentecostalism', *Church History* 70.4 (Dec 2001), pp. 735-71.

Baker, Heidi. *Compelled by Love: How to change the world through the simple power of love in action* (Lake Mary, FL: Charisma House, 2008).

Baker, Heidi and Rolland. *Always Enough: God's Miraculous Provision among the Poorest Children on Earth* (Grand Rapids, MI: Chosen, a division of Baker Books, 2002).

—*Expecting Miracles: True Stories of God's Supernatural Power and How You Can Experience It* (Grand Rapids, MI: Chosen, a division of Baker Books, 2007).

— 'Core Values at Iris: Simple, Controversial and not optional!' September 2010 taken from their Newsletter on <www.irismin.org> accessed January 12, 2011.

Baumert, Norbert. '"Charism" and "Spirit Baptism": Presentation of an Analysis', *JPT* 12.2 (2004), pp. 147-79.

Bebbington, David W. *Evangelicalism in Modern Britain: A History from the 1730s to the 1980s* (Unwin Hyman Ltd, 1989). Reprint (London and New York: Routledge, 2002).

—*Holiness in the Nineteenth-Century England: The 1998 Didsbury Lectures* (Glasgow, Great Britain: Paternoster Press, 2000).

—*A History of Evangelicalism: People, Movements and Ideas in the English-Speaking World*. III. *The Dominance of Evangelicalism: The Age of Spurgeon and Moody* (Downers Grove, Illinois: Intervarsity Press, 2005).

Blumhofer, Edith L., *The Assemblies of God: A Popular History* (Springfield, MO: Radiant Books, 1985).

—'Carrie Judd Montgomery', in *'Pentecost In My Soul': Explorations in the Meaning of Pentecostal Experience in the Assemblies of God* (Springfield, MO: Gospel Publishing House, 1989), pp. 62-83.

—*Aimee Semple McPherson: Everybody's Sister* (Grand Rapids: William B. Eerdmans Publishing Company, 1993).

—*Restoring the Faith: The Assemblies of God, Pentecostalism, and American Culture* (Champaign: University of Illinois Press, 1993).

Blumhofer, Edith, Russell P. Spittler, and Grant A. Wacker eds. *Pentecostal Currents in American Protestantism* (Champaign: University of Illinois Press, 1999).

Bradley, James E. and Richard A. Muller. *Church History: An Introduction to Research, Reference Works, and Methods* (Grand Rapids: William B. Eermans Publishing Company, 1995).

Brand, Chad Owen. 'The Holy Spirit and Spirit Baptism in Today's Church', in Chad Owen Brand (ed.), *Perspectives on Spirit Baptism: Five Views* (Nashville: Broadman and Holman Publishers, 2004), pp. 1-14.

Brekus, Catherine A. *Strangers and Pilgrims: Female Preaching in America 1740-1845* in Linda K. Kerber and Nell Irvin Painter, (eds.), *Gender and American Culture* (Chapel Hill and London: The University of North Carolina Press, 1998).

Brooks, Abigail. 'Feminist Standpoint Epistemology', in Sharlene Nagy Hesse-Biber and Patricia Leavy, (eds.), *Feminist Research Practice: a Primer*, (Thousand Oaks: Sage Publications, 2007), pp. 53-82.

Burgess, S.M. and G.B. McGee. 'Signs and Wonders', in S. Burgess and E. Van Der Maas (eds.), *NIDPCM* (Grand Rapids: Zondervan, 2002), pp. 1066-67.

Bundy, David D. 'Keswick Higher Life Movement', in S. Burgess and E. Van Der Maas (eds.), *NIDPCM* (Grand Rapids: Zondervan, 2002), pp. 820-22.

—'Thomas Ball Barratt', in S. Burgess and E. Van Der Maas (eds.), *NIDPCM* (Grand Rapids, MI: Zondervan, 2002), p. 365.

Cartledge, Mark J. *Encountering the Spirit: The Charismatic Tradition* (London: Darton, Longman and Todd Ltd., 2006).

Cavaness, Barbara. 'Spiritual Chain Reactions: Women used by God', The Network for Women in Ministry, General Council of the Assemblies of God (Springfield, MO: Enrichment Journal Office, 2011) accessed February 11, 2011 at <http://womeninministry.ag.org/history/spiritu al_chain_reactions. cfm>.

Chapman, Diana. 'The Rise and Demise of Women's Ministry in the Origins and Early Years of Pentecostalism in Britain', *JPT* 2.2 (2004), pp. 217-46.

—'Carrie Judd Montgomery: Faith and Healing Homes', *in Searching the Source of the River: Forgotten Women of the Pentecostal Revival in Britain 1907-1914* (London: Push Publishing, 2007).

Chappell, Paul Gale. 'The Divine Healing Movement in America' (PhD dissertation, Drew University, 1983).

Cole, Ardra L., and J. Gary Knowles. *Lives in Context: The Art of Life History Research* (Walnut Creek: Alta Mira Press, a division of Rowman and Littlefield Publishers, Inc, 2001).

Cowardine, Richard J. *Evangelicals and Politics in Antebellum America* (New Haven and London: Yale University Press, 1993).

Cox, Harvey. *Fire from Heaven: The Rise of Pentecostal Spirituality and the Reshaping of Religion in the Twenty-first Century* (London: Cassell, 1996).

Cunningham, Raymond J. 'From Holiness to Healing: The Faith Cure in America 1872-1892', *Church History* 43.4 (December 1974), pp. 499-513.

Curtis, Heather D. 'Houses of Healing: Sacred Space, Spiritual Practice and the Transformation of Female Suffering in the Faith Cure Movement, 1870-1890', *Church History* (September 2006), pp. 598-611.

—*Faith in the Great Physician: Suffering and Divine Healing in American Culture, 1860-1900* (Baltimore: The John Hopkins University Press, 2007).

Donald D. Dayton, 'The American Holiness Movement: A Bibliographic Introduction', in Dayton, Donald W., David W. Faupel, and David D. Bundy, *The Higher Christian Life: A Biographical Overview* in Donald W. Dayton (ed.) (New York and London: Garland Publishing, 1985), pp. 1-56.

—*Theological Roots of Pentecostalism* (Metuchen: Scarecrow Press, 1987). Reprint (Peabody: Hendrickson Publishers, 2000).

Dieter, Melvin Easterday. *The Holiness Revival of the Nineteenth Century* (*Studies in Evangelicalism*, 1; Metuchen and London: The Scarecrow Press, Inc, 1980).

Dunn, James. *Baptism in the Holy Spirit: A Re-examination of the New Testament Teaching on the Gift of the Spirit in relation to Pentecostalism today* (London: SCM Press Ltd, 1970).

Dunning, H. Ray. 'A Wesleyan Perspective on Spirit Baptism' in Chad Owen Brand (ed.), *Perspectives on Spirit Baptism: Five Views* (Nashville: Broadman and Holman Publishers, 2004), pp. 181-229.

Durkheim, Emile. *The Elementary Forms of the Religious Life* (trans. Joseph Ward Sawin; London: George Allen & Unwin LTD, 1915, 5th edn, 1964).

Espinosa, Gastón. 'El Azteca: Francisco Olazábal and Latino Pentecostal Charisma, Power, and Faith Healing in the Borderlands', *Journal of the American Academy of Religion* 67.3 (1999), pp. 597-616.

—'LIBERATED and EMPOWERED: The Uphill History of Hispanic Assemblies of God Women in Ministry, 1915-1950', *AGH* 28 (2008), pp. 44-48.

Faupel, William. *The Everlasting Gospel: The Significance of Eschatology in the Development of Pentecostal Thought* (JPTSup, 10; Sheffield: Sheffield Academic Press, 1996).

Fee, Gordon D. 'The Disease of the Health and Wealth "Gospels"', reprinted in *SCP Newsletter* (Spring 1985), (Beverly, MA: Frontline Publishing, 1985), pp. 18-22.

Finke, Roger, and Rodney Stark. *The Churching of America 1776-1990: Winners and Losers in Our Religious Economy* (New Brunswick: Rutgers University Press, 1992).

Fonow, Mary Margaret and Judith A. Cook, 'Back to the Future: A Look at the Second Wave of Feminist Epistemology and Methodology' in Mary Margaret Fonow and Judith A. Cook (eds.), *Beyond Methodology: Feminist Scholarship as Lived Research* (Bloomington and Indianapolis: Indiana University Press, 1991).

Gladwell, Malcom. *The Tipping Point: How Little Things Can Make a Big Difference* (New York, Boston, London: Back Bay Books/ Little Brown and Company, 2000, 2002).

Goff, James and Grant Wacker. *Portraits of a Generation: Early Pentecostal Leaders* (Fayetteville: University of Arkansas Press, 2002).

Goff, James. 'The Faith that Claims', *Christianity Today* (February 19, 1990), pp. 18-21.

Gooden, Rosemary D. Introduction to *Faith Cures, and Answers To Prayer*, by Mrs Edward Mix (New York: Syracuse University Press, 2002).

Goodson, Ivor F. and Pat Sikes. *Life History Research in Educational Settings* (Buckingham and Philadelphia: Open University Press, 2001).

Goudy, Otis. 'The doctrine of Carrie Judd Montgomery on the initial evidence of the Baptism in the Holy Spirit', (Assemblies of God Theological Seminary research paper, 1990), [IHPC]

Grenz, Stanley James and Denise Muir Kjesbo. *Women in the church: a biblical theology of women in ministry* (Downers Grove, IL: InterVarsity Press, 1995).

Griffith, R. Marie. '"Joy Unspeakable and Full of Glory" The Vocabulary of Pious Emotion in the Narratives of American Pentecostal Women, 1910-1945', in Peter N. Stearns and Jan Lewis (eds.), *An Emotional History of the United States* (New York: Published by NYU Press, 1998), pp. 218-40.

—'Kathryn Johanna Kuhlman', in Susan Ware (ed.), *Notable American Women: a biographical dictionary completing the twentieth century* (Radcliffe Institute for Advanced Study; Cambridge, MA: Harvard University Press, 2004), pp. 354-56.

Griffith, R.M. and D. Roebuck. 'Role of Women' in S. Burgess and E. Van Der Maas (eds.), *NIDPCM* (Grand Rapids: Zondervan, 2002), pp. 1203-1209.

Gunther Brown, Candy. 'From Tent Meetings and Store-front Healing Rooms to Walmarts and the Internet: Healing Spaces in the United States, the Americas, and the World, 1906-2006', *Church History* (Sept 2006), pp. 631-47.

Hanegraaff, Hank. *Christianity in Crisis: 21st Century*, (Eugene, OR: Harvest House Publishers, 1993).

Hardesty, Nancy A. *Your Daughters Shall Prophesy: Revivalism and Feminism in the Age of Finney* in Jerald C. Brauer and Martin E. Marty, eds., *Chicago Studies in the History of American Religion* (Brooklyn: Carlson Publishing Inc, 1991).

—*Faith Cure: Divine Healing in the Holiness and Pentecostal Movements* (Peabody: Hendrickson Publishers, 2003).

Hart, Larry. 'Spirit Baptism: A Dimensional Charistmatic Perspective' in Chad Owen Brand (ed.), *Perspectives on Spirit Baptism: Five Views* (Nashville: Broadman and Holman Publishers, 2004), pp. 105-69.

Hocken, P.D. 'Cecil H. Polhill', in S. Burgess and E. Van Der Maas (eds.), *NIDPCM* (Grand Rapids, MI: Zondervan, 2002), pp. 991-92.

Hollenweger, Walter J. *The Pentecostals* (London: SCM Press, 1972).

—*Pentecostalism: Origins and Developments Worldwide* (Peabody: Hendrickson Publishers, 1997).

— 'Rethinking Spirit Baptism: The Natural and the Supernatural" in A. Anderson and W. Hollenweger, eds., *Pentecostals After a Century: Global Perspectives on a Movement in Transition* (Sheffield: Sheffield Academic Press, 1999), pp. 164-72.

The Holy Bible: New King James Version (Nashville: Thomas Nelson Inc., 1988).

Horton, Stanley M. Spirit Baptism: A Pentecostal Perspective', in Chad Owen Brand (ed.), *Perspectives on Spirit Baptism: Five Views* (Nashville: Broadman and Holman Publishers, 2004), pp. 47-94.

Howell, Martha and Walter Prevenier. *From Reliable Sources: An Introduction to Historical Methods* (London: Cornell University Press, 2001).

Hughes, Michael Gregory. 'Sacred Space and the Sanctification of Time with Reference to Orthodox Christian Communities in Birmingham' (Master's thesis, University of Birmingham, UK, 2003).

Jacobsen, Douglas G. *Thinking in the Spirit: Theologies of the Early Pentecostal Movement* (Bloomington: Indiana University Press, 2003).

Jones, C. E. 'Holiness Movement' in S. Burgess and E. Van Der Maas (eds.), *NIDPCM* (Grand Rapids: Zondervan, 2002), pp. 726-28.

Johnson, Bill. *When Heaven Invades Earth: A Practical Guide to a Life of Miracles*, (Shippensburg, PA: Destiny Image Publishers, Inc., 2005).

—*Strengthen Yourself in the Lord: How to Release the Hidden Power of God* (Shippensburg, PA: Destiny Image Publishers, Inc., 2007).

Johnson, Curtis D. *Redeeming America: Evangelicals and the Road to Civil War* in *The American Way Series* (Chicago, IL: Ivan R. Dee, 1993).

Kaiser Jr., Walter C. 'The Baptism in the Holy Spirit as the Promise of the Father: A Reformed Perspective', in Chad Owen Brand (ed.), *Perspectives on Spirit Baptism: Five Views* (Nashville: Broadman and Holman Publishers, 2004), pp. 15-37.

Kenyon, E.W. and Don Gossett *Words that Move Mountains*: Revised and Expanded version of *The Power of Spoken Faith* (New Kensington, PA: Whitaker House, 2003).

King, Paul L. *Genuine Gold: The Cautiously Charismatic Story of the Early Christian and Missionary Alliance* (Tulsa: Word & Spirit Press, 2006).

Knight III, Henry H. 'God's Faithfulness and God's Freedom: A Comparison of Contemporary Theologies of Healing', *JPT* 2 (1993), pp. 65-89.

Kydd, Ronald A.N. *Healing through the Centuries: Models for Understanding* (Peabody, Massachusetts: Hendrickson Publishers, 1998).

—'Healing in the Christian Church', in S. Burgess and E. Van Der Maas (eds.), *NIDPCM* (Grand Rapids: Zondervan, 2002), pp. 698-711.

Lake, John G. *John G. Lake on Healing* (New Kensington, PA: Whitaker House, 2009 by Roberts Liardon).

Land, Steven J. 'A Passion for the Kingdom: Revisioning Pentecostal Spirituality', *JPT* 1 (1992), pp. 19-46.

Long, Kathryn. 'The Power of Interpretation: The Revival of 1857-58 and the Historiography of Revivalism in America', *Religion and American Culture* 4.1 (University of California Press: Winter 1994), pp. 77-105.

—*The Revival of 1857-58: Interpreting an American Awakening* (New York: Oxford University Press, 1998).

Macchia, Frank D. 'Theology, Pentecostal', in S. Burgess and E. Van Der Maas (eds.), *NIDPCM* (Grand Rapids: Zondervan, 2002), pp. 1120-40.

—*Baptized in the Spirit* (Grand Rapids: Zondervan, 2006).

Marsden, George M. *Religion and American Culture* (New York: Harcourt Brace Jovanovich, 1990).

Martin, Walter. *The Kingdom of the Cults* (Minneapolis, MN: Bethany House Publishers, rev., expanded, and updated edn, 1997).

McGee, Gary B. 'Initial Evidence' in S. Burgess and E. Van Der Maas (eds.), *NIDPCM* (Grand Rapids, MI: Zondervan, 2002), pp. 784-91.

—'Baptism of the Holy Ghost and Fire! The Revival Legacy of Minnie F. Abrams', *The Enrichment Journal* (Springfield, MO: The General Council of the Assemblies of God, 2011).

McIntyre, Joe. *E.W. Kenyon and His Message of Faith: The True Story* (Lake Mary, FL: Charisma House, 1997).

McLoughlin Jr., William G. *Modern Revivalism: Charles Grandison Finney to Billy Graham* (New York: The Ronald Press Company, 1959).

Mendiola, Kelly Willis. 'The Hand of a Woman: Four Holiness-Pentecostal Evangelists and American Culture, 1840-1930' (PhD dissertation, University of Texas, 2002).

Mies, Maria. 'Women's Research or Feminist Research?' in Mary Margaret Fonow and Judith A. Cook (eds.), transl. Amy Spencer, *Beyond Methodology: Feminist Scholarship as Lived Research* (Bloomington and Indianapolis: Indiana University Press, 1991), pp. 60-84.

Miller, Donald E., and Tetsunao Yamamori. *Global Pentecostalism: The New Face of Social Engagement* (Berkeley and Los Angeles: University of California Press, 2007).

Miller, Robert L. *Researching Life Stories and Family Histories* (London: Sage Publications, 2000).

Miskov, Jennifer A. *Silver to Gold: A Journey of Young Revolutionaries* (Birmingham, UK: Silver to Gold, 2010)

—'Coloring Outside the Lines: Pentecostal Parallels with Expressionism. The Work of the Spirit in Place, Time, and Secular Society?', *JPT* 19 (2010), pp. 94–117.

—*Spirit Flood: Rebirth of Spirit Baptism for the 21*st *Century in light of the Azusa Street Revival and the Life of Carrie Judd Montgomery* (Birmingham, UK: Silver to Gold, 2010).

—'Kindred Spirits', *Alliance Life* (March 2011), accessible at <http://www.alliancelife.org/article.php?id=580>.

—'Missing Links: Phoebe Palmer, Carrie Judd Montgomery, and Holiness Roots within Pentecostalism', *PentecoStudies: An Interdisciplinary Journal for Research on the Pentecostal and Charismatic Movements* 10.1 (2011), pp. 8-28.

Mitchell, Robert Bryant. *The History of Open Bible Standard Churches*, (Des Moines, Iowa: Open Bible Publishers, 1982).

Mullen, John B. M.D., 'Acute Hyperesthesia After Spinal Trauma' in *Neurosurgery* (Congress of Neurological Surgeons, 1979), p. 432.

Murray, Iaian H. *Revival and Revivalism: The Making and Marring of American Evangelicalism 1750-1858* (Edinburgh: Banner of Truth Trust, 1994).

Niebuhr, H. Richard. *Christ and Culture* (New York: Harper Torchbooks of Harper & Row, 1951).

Nienkirchen, C. 'Albert Benjamin Simpson', in S. Burgess and E. Van Der Maas, eds., *NIDPCM* (Grand Rapids: Zondervan, 2002), 1069-70.

Noll, Mark A. *A History of Christianity in the United States and Canada* (Grand Rapids: William B. Eerdmans Publishing Company, 1992, 1998).

Owen, Linda. 'Story Behind The Song', *Today's Christian* 42.1 (March/April 2004), p. 14.

Parke, Catherine N. in Ron Gottesman (ed.), *Biography: Writing Lives*, (New York and London: Routledge, 2002).

Patton, Michael Quinn. *Qualitative Evaluation and Research Methods* (London: Sage Publications, 2nd edn, 1990).

Plummer, Ken. *Documents of Life: An Introduction to the Problems and Literature of a Humanistic Method* (*Contemporary Social Research Series*, 7; London: George Allen and Unwin, 1983).

Poloma, Margaret. 'Old Wine, New Wineskins: The Rise of Healing Rooms in Revival Pentecostalism', *Pneuma* 28.1 (Spring 2006), pp. 59-71.

Price, Lynne. *Theology Out of Place: A Theological Biography of Walter J. Hollenweger* (JPTSup, 23; London and New York: Sheffield Academic Press, 2002).

Reed, D.A. 'Oneness Pentecostalism' in S. Burgess and E. Van Der Maas (eds.), *NIDPCM* (Grand Rapids, MI: Zondervan, 2002), pp. 936-44.

Riss, Richard M. 'Faith Homes' in S. Burgess and E. Van Der Maas (eds.), *NIDPCM* (Grand Rapids: Zondervan, 2002), pp. 630-32.

Robeck, Cecil M., Jr. 'Aimee Semple McPherson', in S. Burgess and E. Van Der Maas (eds.), *NIDPCM* (Grand Rapids, MI: Zondervan, 2002), pp. 856-59.

—*The Azusa Street Mission and Revival: The Birthplace of the Pentecostal Movement* (Nashville: Thomas Nelson, Inc., 2006).

—'An Emerging Magisterium? The Case of the Assemblies of God' *Pneuma* 25.2 (Fall 2003), pp. 164-215.

Roberts, Brian. *Biographical Research* in Alan Bryman (ed.), *Understanding Social Research* (Philadelphia: Open University Press, 2002).

Ruelas, Abraham. *Women and the Landscape of American Higher Education: Wesleyan Holiness and Pentecostal Founders* (Eugene, OR: Wipf & Stock Publishers, 2010).

Scotland, Nigel. *Apostles of the Spirit and Fire: American Revivalists and Victorian Britain* (Milton Keynes, UK: Paternoster, 2009).

Shattuck, Gardiner H. 'Ambrose Jessup Tomlinson (1865-1943)', in Edward L. Queen, Stephen R. Prothero, and Gardiner H. Shattuck (eds.), *Encyclopaedia of American Religious History* (New York, NY: Facts on File, Inc., 3rd edn, 2009), p. 991.

Smail, Thomas, Andrew Walker, and Nigel Wright, '"Revelation Knowledge" and Knowledge of Revelation: The Faith Movement and the Question of Heresy', *JPT* 5 (1994), pp. 57-77.

Smith, Timothy L. *Revivalism & Social Reform: American Protestantism on the Eve of the Civil War* (Originally published in 1957 under the title: *Revivalism and Social Reform in mid-nineteenth-century America*, New York: Abingdon Press, 1957). Reprint (Baltimore and London: The John Hopkins University Press, 1980).

Smith-Rosenberg, Carroll. 'The Female World of Love and Ritual: Relations between Women in Nineteenth-Century America', in Linda K. Kerber and Jane Sherron De Hart (eds.), *Women's America* (New York: Oxford University Press, 3rd edn, 1991), pp. 189-90.

Stibbe, Mark. *Revival* in Clive Calver (ed.), *The Thinking Clear Series* (London: Monarch Books, 1998).

Stock, Jennifer. 'George S. Montgomery: Businessman for the Gospel, Part 1', *AGH* 9.1 (Spring 1989), pp. 4-5, 17-18.

—'George S. Montgomery: Businessman for the Gospel, Concluding Part', *AGH* 9.2 (Summer 1989), pp. 12-14, 20.

Storms, Jeannette. 'Carrie Judd Montgomery: The Little General', in James R. Goff, Jr. and Grant Wacker, (eds.), *Portraits of a Generation: Early Pentecostal Leaders* (Fayetteville: University of Arkansas Press, 2002), pp. 271-87.

Sumrall, Lester Frank. *Pioneers of Faith* (Tulsa: Harrison House, 1995).

Sutton, Matthew Avery. *Aimee Semple McPherson and the Resurrection of Christian America* (Cambridge, MA, London: Harvard University Press, 2007).

Synan, Vinson. *The Holiness-Pentecostal Movement in the United States* (Grand Rapids: William B. Eerdmans Publishing Company, 1971).

—*The Old-Time Power* (Franklin Springs: Advocate Press, 1973).

—*Aspects of Pentecostal-Charismatic Origins* (New Jersey: Logos International, 1975).

—'A Healer in the House? A Historical Perspective on Healing in the Pentecostal/Charismatic Tradition', *Asian Journal of Pentecostal Studies* 3.2 (2000), pp. 189-201.

—*The Century of the Holy Spirit: One Hundred Years of Pentecostal and Charismatic Renewal, 1901-2001* (Nashville: Thomas Nelson Publishers, 2001).

Thomas, John Christopher. *The Devil, Disease and Deliverance: Origins of Illness in New Testament Thought* (JPTSup, 13; Sheffield: Sheffield Academic Press, 1998).

Ware, Steven L. 'Restorationism in Classical Pentecostalism' in S. Burgess and E. Van Der Maas (eds.), *NIDPCM* (Grand Rapids, MI: Zondervan, 2002), pp. 1019-21.

Warner, Laceye C. *Saving Women: Retrieving Evangelistic Theology and Practice* (Waco: Baylor University Press, 2007).

Warner, Wayne E. 'Home of Peace Celebrates Centennial', *AGH* 13.3 (Fall 1993), pp. 18-19.

—'Carrie Judd Montgomery' in S. Burgess and E. Van Der Maas (eds.), *NIDPCM* (Grand Rapids: Zondervan, 2002), pp. 904-906.

—'Maria Beulah Woodworth-Etter' in S. Burgess and E. Van Der Maas (eds.), *NIDPCM* (Grand Rapids: Zondervan, 2002), pp. 1211-13.

—'Smith Wigglesworth', in S. Burgess and E. Van Der Maas (eds.), *NIDPCM* (Grand Rapids, MI: Zondervan, 2002), p. 1195.

—*Maria Woodworth-Etter: For Such a Time as This* (Gainesville: Bridge-Logos, 2004).

Waterman, Carla C. 'Carrie Judd Montgomery' in J.D. Douglas (ed.), *Twentieth Century Dictionary of Christian Biography* 1995 (Grand Rapids, MI: Baker Books, 1995), p. 258.

White, Charles Edward. 'Phoebe Palmer and the Development of Pentecostal Pneumatology' in Wesley Center for Applied Theology, 2000. Accessed April 28, 2008 <http://wesley.nnu.edu/wesleyan_ theology/theojrnl/21-25/23-13.htm>.

Williams, J.R. 'Baptism in the Holy Spirit' in S. Burgess and E. Van Der Maas (eds.), *NIDPCM* (Grand Rapids: Zondervan, 2002), pp. 354-63.

Wimber, John. *Kingdom Suffering: Facing Difficulty and Trial in the Christian Life*, Christian Essential Series (Ann Arbor, MI: Vine Books, imprint of Servant Publications, 1988).

Wimber, John and Kevin Springer. *Power Healing* (New York: Harper San Francisco, 1987).

Wolf, John. 'The Word of Faith Movement', Church Education Resource Ministries found at <www.cerm.info/bible_studies/Apologetics/WordofFaith.ht ml> assessed January 2, 2011.

Zeigler, J. R. 'John Graham Lake', in S. Burgess and E. Van Der Maas (eds.), (Grand Rapids: Zondervan, 2002), p. 828.

Websites Accessed/Research Engines:

Archive of some of Carrie's original works <http://www.archive.org/search.php?query=Carrie%20Judd>

Assemblies of God Minutes and Fundamental Truths <http://agchurches.org/> and <http://ifphc.org/>

Bill Johnson Ministries <www.bjm.org>

Biology Online <http://www.biology-online.org/dictionary/Hyperesthe sia>

Christian and Missionary Alliance official site <http://www.cmalliance. org/>

Encyclopaedia Britannica <http://www.britannica.com>

Flame of Love Project <http://www3.uakron.edu/sociology/flameweb/about.html>

Flower Pentecostal Heritage Center <http://ifphc.org/>

Healing and Revival Press <http://healingandrevival.com/>

Healing on the Streets (Mark Marx at Ireland Vineyard) <http://www. out-there. org>

Home of Peace's official site <http://homeofpeace.com>

Iris Ministries (Heidi Baker) <www.irismin.org>

Newspaper Research <http://www.loc.gov/chroniclingamerica> and <www.fultonhistory.com>

Salvation Army's official site <http://www.salvationarmyusa.org>

INDEX OF BIBLICAL REFERENCES

Index of Names

Made in the USA
San Bernardino, CA
10 April 2018